YOU WILL ALSO BE INTERESTED IN

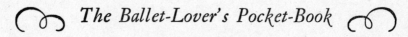 *The Ballet-Lover's Pocket-Book*

BY KAY AMBROSE

The reader will find here simple and compact explanations of the various steps, positions, and attitudes; the nature of performance and the role of the ballerina, the danseur, and the corps de ballet; the problems and methods of choreography; the costumes and their uses and traditions; the problems of lighting; and, finally, the way to a full appreciation of the spectacle as a whole. These explanations and definitions are presented not merely in words but in scores of little drawings as well.

"Contains an amazing amount of sound information about ballet art and ballet life . . . a sensible, accurate, and cordial book."

EDWIN DENBY
New York Herald Tribune

THIS IS A BORZOI BOOK

PUBLISHED IN NEW YORK BY ALFRED A. KNOPF

The Borzoi Book of Ballets

SWAN LAKE (Act III, *The Magic Swan*): Tamara Toumanova as Odile, André Eglevsky as Prince Siegfried)

THE
BORZOI BOOK
OF
BALLETS

BY

GRACE ROBERT

New York: ALFRED A. KNOPF 1947

THIS IS A BORZOI BOOK,
PUBLISHED BY ALFRED A. KNOPF, INC.

". . . here, in classical dancing, I see the triumph of studied conception over vagueness, of the rule over the arbitrary, of order over the haphazard. I am thus brought face to face with the eternal conflict in art between the Apollonian and the Dionysian principles. The latter assumes ecstasy to be the final goal—that is to say, the losing of oneself—whereas art demands above all the full consciousness of the artist. There can, therefore, be no doubt as to my choice between the two. And if I appreciate so highly the value of classical ballet, it is not simply a matter of taste on my part, but because I see exactly in it the perfect expression of the Apollonian principle."

STRAVINSKY: *An Autobiography*

✑ ACKNOWLEDGMENTS ✑

BECAUSE of the alphabetical arrangement of *The Borzoi Book of Ballets,* there are many repetitions. If the reader sometimes feels that this is where he came in, I trust that he will realize that a restatement of facts, appearing in accounts of several ballets by the same choreographer, or dating from a similar period, was unavoidable for the proper placing of a work against its historical or artistic background. In all cases, stage directions are given from the point of view of the audience—not the dancer. "Stage right" means the right side of the stage as seen from the auditorium.

For accounts of the historical past I have relied for basic facts on C. W. Beaumont's monumental *Complete Book of Ballets,* (Putnam, 1938). For more recent events in the world of ballet, I have used, in addition to the usual sources, my own collection of programs and other material. Chapter headings in italic type giving brief descriptions of the ballets are taken directly from programs, frequently those of first performances. I have tried to give casts and dates of first American performances, but in some instances have been forced to compromise on those of first productions in New York.

Research into the history of ballet is not made easier by the fact that ballet falls somewhere between the worlds of music and theater. The ballet material in the Music Division of the New York Public Library, where it is not the principal interest, would repay indexing and cataloguing. The Theatre Division's smaller collection is much more useful, not only because of the admirable system of cataloguing, but because of the co-operative spirit of the staff. Through the courtesy of Mrs. Gladys Y. Leslie and Miss Mary Sheldon Hopkins, I was given the freedom of the library at Bennington College, where I spent a week of intensive research, undisturbed by call slips.

Alpheus Koon not only collaborated in making the glossary but gave particular assistance in the technical aspects of *Billy the Kid, Princess Aurora, Giselle,* and *Les Sylphides.* A list of the dancers who have patiently answered questions would fill many pages. Special thanks must be given to Hugh Laing, Paul Petroff, Edward Caton, and Todd Bolender. John Leatham Walsh answered many questions pertaining to music. It must be clearly stated, however, that while I have endeavored to make the facts as accurate as possible, the opinions expressed are my own, arrived at during years of ballet going.

Dwight Godwin's photographs, some of them unusually fine action pictures, could only have been achieved by a dancer who knows the exact moment at which a pose or a movement may be seen at its best. Mr. Godwin, once a member of Ballet Theatre, received his dance training at the School of American Ballet and Sadler's Wells. His technical studies of Rosella Hightower, who gave up one of her rare free evenings during a New York season to pose for them, should prove helpful to readers who are interested in ballet technique. The five positions of the feet and the eight positions of the body, illustrated in Ian Campbell's charming sketches following page 352 are the basic material of which ballets are made—even those so apparently remote from the classic ideal as *Fancy Free*.

Thanks are due to Simon and Schuster for permission to quote from *Stravinsky: an Autobiography*, and to Cyril W. Beaumont for permission to quote from his *The Ballet Called Giselle*.

In conclusion, I must pay a debt of gratitude to Herbert Weinstock, without whose encouragement I should never have undertaken this work; to Ben Meiselman for invaluable help with the index; to John Jennings, who read the proofs; and to William Fry, my "first reader."

GRACE ROBERT

February 19, 1946

CONTENTS

Contents [xiii

ILLUSTRATIONS

[xv

The Borzoi Book of Ballets

INTRODUCTION

Ballet in the United States

SINCE 1933 interest in ballet has been growing in New York and America at large after a period during which ballet, save as an adjunct to opera or an interpolation in revue, had almost ceased to exist on a professional basis. Many who know of the American tours of Pavlova and the Diaghilev Ballet, fail to realize that ballet had a long and eventful history in this country, where it was an active element in the theatrical scene during a period that corresponded with the flowering of the romantic ballet in Europe. America, then as now, welcomed touring ballet companies from abroad, frequently absorbing them to the enrichment of the native theater.

As early as 1739, inhabitants of New York had an opportunity to attend a "new pantomime entertainment in grotesque characters" called *The Adventures of Harlequin and Scaramouch, or, The Spaniard Tricked*. Details of this entertainment have not survived, and it may have been a puppet play, but it does not require too much imagination to picture Harlequin performing the traditional dances of his species.

The Beggar's Opera was presented in New York at the Playhouse in Nassau Street in 1751, with "entertainments between the acts, viz., a Harlequin Dance, a Pierot Dance, and the Drunken Peasant, all by a gentleman lately fom London." For many years, Harlequin and his adventures were a staple of the New York theater. Singing, and dancing that was more or less related to the ballet dancing of the period were an essential part of these presentations, which, variations on a single theme, had many titles, all including the name of Harlequin. One of the more curious was an exposition of the Robinson Crusoe story called "a pantomimical romance," which employed, in addition to Robinson Crusoe and Friday, the full array of the characters of a harlequinade. This production, given in December 1791 at the John Street Theater, was distinguished by the presence in the cast, in the role of Friday, of John Durang, the first American (he was born in

Lancaster, Pennsylvania) who made theatrical dancing his profession.

The first mention of the word *ballet* in Ireland's *Records of the New York Stage*[1] is in an entry for February 3, 1792, which gives an account of the first appearance of the Placides. Alexandre Placide was a ropedancer and gymnast, Mme Placide a dancer and pantomime artist. They performed at the John Street Theater in tightrope feats and a ballet called *Two Philosophers* on the same bill as a play, *The Clandestine Marriage*. At M. Placide's benefit on February 8, in addition to ropedancing and balancing, the program concluded "with a Dancing Ballet, called the Return of the Labourers (with a Sabottiere Dance) by Mons. and Mad. Placide." With these two presentations, ballet in name if not in actuality may be said to have been launched in New York.[2]

Many dramatic pantomimes, first cousins of the *ballet d'action,* were seen in New York during the last decade of the eighteenth century. In 1794 Mme Gardie (who had a romantic history and a tragic end that would make excellent Sunday-supplement material) appeared in a "grand serious pantomime," *Sophia of Brabant,* with music by Pellesier. A curiosity of the same year was a pantomime called *Nootka Sound,* the dramatis personae of which included characters named Alknomook and Wampumpoo. Was this an early attempt at Eskimo atmosphere? These were offerings by the Old American Company, which, in addition to Mme Gardie, included John Durang, and had a repertoire of Harlequin plays, comic operas, and a ballet called *The Huntress, or, Tammany's Frolics.* There was also an operatic spectacle called *Tammany,* for which scenery was designed by Charles Ciceri, an Italian who returned to his native Italy after amassing a fortune, not in the theater, but as an importer. It would be a pleasant link with the romantic ballet if he were found to be related to Pierre Ciceri, who designed the original décor of *Giselle.*

In 1796 a troupe of French dancers came to New York. Their repertoire included *Pygmalion,* "a lyric scene of J. J. Rousseau," *Two*

[1] This work and Odell's *Annals of the New York Stage* are my chief authorities for this very brief account of ballet in New York.

[2] Alexandre Placide did not return to his native France. Leaving New York, he eventually became manager of the Charleston (South Carolina) Theater, which, to quote Ireland, "under his direction ranked with the first establishments of the country."

Huntsmen and the Milkmaid, "a grand comic pantomime dance" composed by M. Francisquy, and other *divertissements,* one of which was a Triple Allemande performed by Mmes Gardie and Val and M. Francisquy. There was also a production of a "national pantomime," with a cast of characters including President, Governor, Senator, America (Mme Gardie), Britannia, Goddess of Liberty, and an Old Woman (M. Francisquy).

Not all the imported dancers came from France. In 1797 Mr. and Mrs. Oscar Byrne arrived from London, where they had performed at Covent Garden. Ireland calls them "the most distinguished dancers yet seen in America," and rather smugly remarks: "beyond the character of the profession in which they were engaged, there was nothing in their course of life to distinguish them from the most respectable and worthy members of the community." It may be remarked in passing that Ireland's *Records* were published in 1866, when actors were barely tolerated and dancers were looked upon with automatic suspicion as frivolous, if not actually immoral. The respectable and worthy Byrnes were first seen at the New Theater, in the "grand pantomime ballet" *Dermot and Kathleen* on August 23, 1797. Later there was an ambitious presentation called *Columbus, or, A World Discovered* ("with entirely new scenery, machinery, and dresses"), for which the pageant and processions were arranged by Byrne. The playbill for this production has as many credits as a super-colossal Hollywood effort.

The Park Theater, which was to be New York's outstanding playhouse for fifty years, opened in 1798. During its first season little ballet was presented, though later ones made up for it. Mme Gardie and the Placides were seen from time to time, probably in *entr'acte divertissements,* without which an evening in the theater would not have been complete then or for many decades to come. In 1808 *Cinderella,* called a "ballet spectacle," was presented, and a year later came an Indian pantomime, *Harlequin Panattahah, or, The Genie of the Algonquins,* a title that evokes fascinating reflections as to just what result a combination of *commedia dell' arte* (however removed from its origins) and Indian atmosphere could produce.

A production closer to ballet as it was understood in nineteenth-century New York was *La Belle Peruvienne,* "grand ballet of action in three acts," presented on March 18, 1822, by MM. Tatin and Labasse. Of it Ireland says: "This must have been one of the best things of its kind witnessed in New York. However, it was not until the first years of the Bowery Theatre, 1826–1829, that New York saw anything like real ballet as understood by the French." *La Belle Peruvienne* boasted a grotto, a mirror dance, a temple of the sun, and anticipated *Le Corsaire* by introducing a shipwreck. The cast included the Durangs (Charlotte and Juliet), daughters of John Durang. The ballet was sufficiently successful to be revived several times, and a second production along similar lines, *The Siege of Tripoli,* found its way into the repertoire of the Park Theater.

On February 7, 1826 Mme Hutin, the most spectacular dancer to be seen up to this time in New York, made her debut at the Bowery Theater. Following a performance of *Much Ado about Nothing,* "a grand Pas Seul 'La Barege Coquette' was executed by Mme. Francisquy Hutin, her first appearance in America, and the first introduction of the modern French school of dancing to the American Stage. The house was crowded, and an anxious look of curiosity and expectation dwelt on every face; but when the graceful danseuse came bounding like a startled fawn upon the stage, her light and scanty drapery floating in air, and her symmetrical proportions liberally displayed by the force of a bewildering pirouette, the cheeks of the greater portion of the audience were crimsoned with shame, and every lady in the lower tier of boxes immediately left the house. But time works wondrous changes, and though for a while Turkish trousers were adopted by the lady, they were finally discarded, and the common ballet dresses, indecent though they be, were gradually endured, and are now looked upon as a matter of course. Madame Hutin was a skillful, graceful and daring dancer, and was greatly admired by the admirers of her peculiar school of art." One wonders what Mme Hutin's costume was like to have caused such a demonstration of moral indignation from the ladies "in the lower tier of boxes." And why only the lower tier? Were the upper tiers occupied by the more liberal-minded, with no pre-Victorian prudery to prevent their enjoyment of what appears to have been a virtuoso performance? Ireland, who wrote the above account of the episode, could not refrain from gloating over the fact that Mme Hutin ended her days as an indigent widow.

In the same year Mlle Celeste made her debut in a *pas seul* from the ballet *The Twelve Pages.* Celeste was an artist of international reputation who came to America heralded by much advance publicity. She was trained at the Paris Opéra, and specialized in dramatic pantomime, in which she sometimes appeared in male roles. She was a noted Fenella in *The Dumb Girl of Portici*. Of her Ireland remarks: "Her success in America has been equalled among women only by Fanny Kemble and Jenny Lind, and among the multitude she was undoubtedly the most popular of the trio."

In 1827 Labasse, one of the producers of the successful *La Belle Peruvienne,* arranged a ballet called *The Caliph of Bagdad* to music selected from Rossini's compositions. Both Celeste and Mme Hutin were included in the cast. This was succeeded by *Cleopatra,* in which the title role was performed by Mme Hutin, with Celeste as Julius Cæsar. Other troupes of French dancers tried their luck in New York, but it was not until M. and Mme Charles Ronzi Vestris arrived from the San Carlo in Naples that the ballet company at the Bowery had any real competition. Mme Vestris was considered by Ireland to have been equaled only by Fanny Elssler, whose American triumphs were still in the future.

One of the most famous of theatrical families, the Ravels, introduced to New York in 1832 their diversified offerings, which included ropedancing, herculean feats, and pantomime ballets. They began their long career in America with a two-week engagement at the Park Theater. More than fifty years later an article in *Music and Drama* said: "For years, the Ravel family—the distinctive name given to a troupe of about forty performers—has been before the American public. They have met with poor success, and had heavy losses by fire. They were, however, a long-lived combination. Hard work suited them, and hard luck had no daunting influence on their spirits. . . . They stuck to the venture till New York people found that the agile Frenchmen had a show worth seeing. They had such dancers as Yrka Matthias, Louise Lamoreux and a front and second line of coryphees who knew their business. Gabriel, Jerome, and François acted pantomime as though it were second nature to them; Leon Jovelli has never been surpassed as an acrobat. . . . They put all the spectacle possible into 'The Green Monster,' 'Asphodel,' 'Mazulm, or, The Night Owl,' and threw in the ballet while the tricks were in preparation."

La Sylphide, first of the romantic ballets, was originally produced in America at the Park Theater on April 15, 1835, with Celeste in the role made famous by Taglioni. As Celeste was more remarkable for "the force and intensity of her expressive pantomime than [for] the grace and elegance of her dancing," it is more than likely that the true ethereal atmosphere of the ballet was lacking.

A year later Augusta, high on the list of New York's favorite dancers for many years, made her American debut in a scene from *Les Naïades*. On December 3, 1836 she was seen as Zoloë in *La Bayadère*, a ballet that was perennial for a long time. A critic said of this production: "The dances and groupings of a full corps de ballet were especially arranged by Mlle. Augusta, whose delineation of character in the dancing heroine, threw Celeste (its original representative) entirely in the shade. Celeste's portraiture was a grand and spirited outline, but the filling up did not correspond with the beauty of the design; while for chasteness, delicacy of finish, softness of coloring, and harmonious mingling of light and shade, Augusta was altogether unapproached."

As *La Bayadère*, or, more properly, *Le Dieu et la bayadère*, has been performed in New York at least as often as *Swan Lake* or *Giselle*, it might be worth while to set down here some of the details of its production. It was originally produced as an opera-ballet at the Paris Opéra on October 13, 1830. The choreography was by Filippo Taglioni, and the score by Auber. The role of the dancing heroine, Zoloë, was created by Taglioni. *La Bayadère* was one of the last of the ballet-operas, of which there were many examples in the early French operatic repertoire. It is a form that must have appealed strongly to the New York public, as this particular example lasted longer than almost any other dancer's vehicle in local theatrical history.

The story,[3] based on a ballad by Goethe, is complicated, involving the rivalry of two bayaderes, one who dances (Zoloë) and one who sings (Ninka), for the love of an Unknown. The situation is further complicated by the evil passion of Olifour, the Chief Judge, for Zoloë, who after a series of tests and adventures is condemned to be burned alive. She is rescued by the Unknown, who, revealing himself to be the God Brahma, carries her to paradise. The plot offers endless opportunities for spectacular effects, pageantry, and processions.[4]

---

[3] Told in detail in Beaumont's *Complete Book of Ballets*.

[4] A strict ballet version, produced by Marius Petipa in 1875, may still hold its place in the repertoire of the Russian State Theaters. A movie short, called *Bayaderka*, with music by Minkus, has been seen in New York. It is notable for the spectacular

The cast of the Park Theater production of *La Bayadère* follows:

UNKNOWN	Mr. *Jones*	ZOLOË	Mlle *Augusta*
OLIFOUR	Mr. *Richings*	NINKA	Miss *Eveleen Cowan*
CHOPDAR	Mr. *Russell*	FATIMA	Miss *Kerr*
CAPTAIN OF THE GUARD	Mr. *Povey*	ZULMA	Mrs. *Archer*

◇◇◇◇◇◇◇◇◇◇◇◇◇◇◇◇◇

La Bayadère was performed by many dancers—Mme Lecomte, the Taglionis,[5] Mary Ann Lee, La Petite Augusta, Fanny Elssler ("who did not efface the impression made by Augusta"), Julia Turnbull, the Roussets, Annetta Galetti, the Ronzani troupe, and many others. Of this array of dancers, probably the most interesting to Americans is La Petite Augusta, who as Augusta Maywood had a successful career in Europe, appearing in leading roles in the most important lyric theaters after a debut at the Paris Opéra that was favorably reviewed by Théophile Gautier. Her popularity and standing with the European public are attested by a number of lithographs, as well as enthusiastic reviews in the contemporary press.

One of the innumerable revivals of *La Bayadère,* with Augusta, took place at the Park Theater on November 8, 1845. The *Spirit of the Times* reviewed it thus: "M'dlle Augusta appeared at the Park for the first time in some years: and was warmly welcomed back to the boards, where she won her laurels and her fame. . . . The ballet was the well known and favorite 'La Bayadere,' the music of which is far superior to that of any other ballet in existence. Augusta seems to have improved her style, since she was last here, without having lost any of her native graces: indeed, dancing which with others appears laborious and difficult, to her seems only a recreation and a pleasure; merely an emanation or display of her own joyous spirits." The more one reads accounts of Augusta written by her contemporaries, the more clearly she emerges as a true dancing artist who made no vulgar display of technical tricks or tours de force.

In 1837 Mme Lecomte made her American debut as Helena, the ghostly abbess in *Robert le Diable.* Complaints that she was too buxom did not prevent her from enjoying a career in the theater for some years, during which she appeared in roles ranging from Zoloë

dancing of Vachtang Chaboukiani, who displays a command of classical technique that has never been seen in a New York ballet performance.

[5] Paul Taglioni, brother of the famous Marie, and his wife, whose name was also Marie.

to Lise in *La Fille Mal Gardée,* in what was probably the first performance of that ballet in America, at the Park Theater on July 6, 1839.

In 1838 Paul and Marie Taglioni arrived in New York and danced in *La Bayadère* and *La Nayade* at the Park. Josephine Stephan (later known as Mme Victor Pettit) was seen at the National in a "grand heroic ballet," *Le Deliverance de les Grecs.* Certainly, the title of the production is a grand, heroic assault on the language of Voltaire. Later she danced in a ballet called *The Wild Girl,* in which the coryphées were said to have included "Mons. and Madame Hazard," a statement that M. Hazard might well have resented. In the same year Augusta danced in *La Somnambule* and *The Twelve Pages of the Duc de Vendome.*

When the Taglionis presented *La Sylphide* in May 1839, the *Corsaire,* a New York weekly, remarked: "We do not cotton much to male dancers, and cannot help looking on them as mere accessories to the complete development of the power and grace of the fair danseuse." The romantic age's prejudice against the male dancer was asserting itself in America. The Taglionis appeared off and on through the summer months at the Park Theater. *Nathalie,* a "fanciful and chaste little ballet," with Mme Giubilei in the title role, shared a bill with *Fidelio* at the Park in September, while the National offered *La Tarentule* with Mme Lecomte and M. Martin in November. Mary Ann Lee, an American dancer from Philadelphia, made her New York debut in 1839 in a *pas de deux* from *La Bayadère,* later sharing a program with Julia Turnbull, another native dancer, who was said by the critics to have "more youth and beauty than brilliance." Still more American dancers were cropping up: Master and Miss Wells made their debut at the New Chatham Theater in 1839—surely a banner year for ballet in New York.

The most important event in the dance world of 1840 was the arrival of Fanny Elssler, who made her American debut at the Park Theater on May 14. Her program included *La Cracovienne* (a *pas seul*), and a full-length ballet, *La Tarentule,* one of her most famous vehicles, created for her by Jean Coralli. There was vast enthusiasm for Elssler's dancing, but none at all for "her sordid and grasping disposition . . . her exorbitant claims were rarely relinquished until they had been satisfied to the uttermost farthing." Apparently the Divine Fanny, taking no chances on being cheated by the aborigines, was demanding payment in advance. She was seen in *La Sylphide,* distinctly not one of her European successes, on June 1. A critic remarked that "her recoveries from any tours de force or vigorous effort are instantaneous and her attitudes unstudied and easy."

Mme Lecomte challenged Elssler by appearing in *La Sylphide* on June 8, but the only comparisons were invidious ones. Meanwhile the Taglionis returned and were seen in *Nathalie* and *Undine.* The persistent Mme Lecomte offered *Marco Bomba* at the Bowery, and Celeste danced an excerpt from *L'Hirondelle.*

In January 1841 Mme Giubilei was at the Chatham with *Les Meuniers,* and something called *Lise et Colin,* which may have been *La Fille Mal Gardée.* There is nothing further of interest to ballet-lovers during this season until June, when Elssler, returning to the Park, for the first time danced *La Bayadère* in New York. Later she added her famous *Cachucha* to her repertoire. Julia Turnbull was a member of Elssler's supporting company during this season. Elssler was in and out of New York several times during 1841, her last new offering being *La Gypsy* in December.

Elssler again dominated the world of ballet in 1842, appearing at the Park in June. Her farewell performance took place on July 1, the program including *La Fille Mal Gardée, La Gypsy,* and *La Craco-vienne.*

During the summer the Ravels appeared at Niblo's Gardens, a theater that for many years was a pleasant feature of the summer season. The programs ranged widely through the diversified theatrical fare of the time, offering variety, drama, ballet, and spectacle. *Mazulm,* a forerunner of *The Black Crook,* was first produced by the Ravels during this season. It was still being performed well into the eighties. Julia Turnbull offered *Les Nayades* with C. T. Parsloe and Mme Victor Pettit. Later in the year Celeste was seen in *Don Juan,* a "pantomimic spectacle," in which she ambitiously played the title role.

The year 1843 offers little but repetitions of established favorites, but in 1844 Palmo's Opera House had a new ballerina, Pauline Desjardins, who was seen in *The Independence of Greece, or, The Woman Warriors.* Earlier in the summer she had appeared at Niblo's in *The Revolt of the Harem,* which was no doubt based on Filippo Taglioni's *La Révolte au Sérail,* originally produced at the Paris Opéra in 1833. Obviously the plot had comic possibilities, as it was

burlesqued in *Revolt in the Poorhouse,* which appeared at least once
on the same program as its more elegant prototype.

Little that was new was offered in 1845. An event of great interest
to modern ballet-lovers took place on February 2, 1846, when New
York saw its first *Giselle,* presented at the Park Theater with Augusta
in the title role. This was not the first performance of *Giselle* in
America: that honor belongs to Mary Ann Lee, whose performance
at the Howard Athenæum in Boston anticipated Augusta's by a
month. Mary Ann Lee was partnered in *Giselle* by George Washington Smith, the first American *danseur noble,* who had been a member of Elssler's supporting company during her American tour.

Giselle remained a feature of the theatrical scene for nearly thirty
consecutive years. The title role was performed by almost every
dancer who aspired to the dignity of *première danseuse,* and the roll
call may be found in the chapter devoted to *Giselle.*

In December 1846 *Les Danseuses Viennoises,* "forty-eight dear
little girls, wonderfully drilled by Mme. Josephine Weiss," won the
collective heart of New York theater-goers, then, as now, susceptible
to the charms of child prodigies, a species that at present is fortunately almost exclusively confined to the movies by the watchful care
of the Gerry Society, which protects children from theatrical exploita-
tion, and unsentimental adults from child performers. The darlings
from Vienna were the idols of the town, and in practically no time
were crowding the dramatic company at the Park Theater, the members of which were reduced to the status of fillers-in, more usually
the lot of dancers in the nineteenth-century theater. Their programs
appeared to consist of group numbers—*Pas de Fleurs, Pas Oriental,
Pas Hongroise,* etc.—probably resembling the less imaginative presentations at the Radio City Music Hall. *Les Danseuses Viennoises*
were frequently seen at the Park Theater, once at least sharing a
program with Edwin Forrest, whose vehicle on that occasion was
Spartacus—certainly a bill with a wide range of emotional intensities.

Two new ballet companies arrived to entertain New York during
1847: a French company featuring the Monplaisirs, who made their
debut in *L'Almée, or, an Oriental Vision,* and the Lehman family, a
group of ten dancers who were later absorbed by the Ravels. Adelaide
Lehman, the *première danseuse,* was burned to death three years
later when her costume caught fire from an unprotected gas jet—a
fate that overtook more than one dancer during the gaslit era in the

theater. Hermine Blangy, who had been a member of the Ravel company, began to make independent appearances, dancing in *Giselle, Le Lac des Fées, L'Illusion d'un Peintre, La Chatte,* and other ballets. In fact, 1847 had a very crowded dance calendar, the resident groups being augmented by several imported from Italy, notably Signora Ciocca and Signor Neri.

The year 1848 was marked by the production of *Le Diable Boiteux* and *La Vivandière* (with Hermine Blangy), *Le Diable à Quatre* and *Esmeralda* (with the Monplaisirs), and the usual revivals. The New Room at 332 Broadway announced the arrival of Herr Thiers' Opera and Ballet Company from Drury Lane, boasting the presence of Signorina Lohr from Paris, and M. Zavitowski from the Imperial Theater, Warsaw—an intimation of the wave of the future?

All through this period, dancers were a part of almost every theatrical program. If no "grand ballet" was featured, there was sure to be an *entr'acte divertissement* to liven up proceedings. One critic complained that the theater that depended too heavily on its ballet troupe was on the road to failure, but he did not dream of suggesting that dancing might be dispensed with altogether. An unadorned program in which a single play was presented would have been unthinkable to the theater-goer of the era. He expected and was given variety. It is just barely possible that he had a certain amount of justice on his side. I have seen any number of dull, talky plays presented by a small cast in a single drab setting that would have left a much brighter memory if the gloom had been mitigated by a well-executed *divertissement.* Any ballet-lover trapped into seeing (for example) *The Ryan Girl* would have welcomed the Bluebird *pas de deux.* This is not actually a plea for a disruption of such dramatic unities as have survived contemporary playwriting, but just a slight burst of ill temper at dullness in the theater.

In 1851 the Roussets (a family of five) made their first American appearance at Niblo's in *Catarina,* with Caroline Rousset in the title role. Adelaide Rousset danced male roles *en travestie,* helping to establish that very bad tradition, manifestations of which may still be seen at the Paris Opéra.

Late in 1851 Lola Montez began her tour of America at the Broadway Theater in *Betly, the Tyrolian.* She disappointed "public expectations" and was "graceful, but not brilliant." The public was no brighter than usual in expecting so intermittent a performer as Montez to be a fine dancer: her career in Europe had not allowed much time for the rigorous routine that lies behind the stage appearances of any serious dancer. Ireland indulges in a pious aside to the effect that Montez "died a repentant and humble Christian in 1861."

Louise Ducy-Barre and Yrca Matthias, the latter said to be from St. Petersburg and Moscow, made their respective bows to New York in 1853. A year later the performances of the Siegrist family at the Stadt-Theater in *Diana and Endymion* acquired an atmosphere of wholesome physical education by the interpolated "rotary exercises" by Herr Van Spingler.

A new influence was introduced into dance programs with the arrival of a Spanish ballet company of sixteen, which performed at Niblo's during the summer of 1854. There was little that was not revival or repetition during the next few seasons until the Ronzani Ballet Troupe came to the Broadway Theater in 1857. Among the members of this company was Cesare Cecchetti, accompanied by his small son Enrico—later to become one of the most honored names in ballet. Louise Lamoreaux, the *première danseuse,* was succeeded in a later season by Annetta Galletti, who gained a popular favor that was not extended to the rest of the company, although their presentations might have been more successful if their American tour had not coincided with a financial panic.

It is evident, however, that popular taste for ballet was running thin. A sign of the times (1861) was indicated by the advertisements of the Gaities—a place of dubious resort—offering "Handsome Ballet Girls and Waiter Girls" as attractions for stag parties. The management of this establishment waged an intermittent war with the municipal authorities, who finally succeeded in having it closed. This sort of thing did ballet no good in the eyes of the ordinary theatre-goer and brought ballet into general disrepute.

The Black Crook was first produced in 1866. Posters and photographs of legions of buxom dancers with legs of more than Degas amplitude may have a nostalgic charm for some, but look more like burlesque queens than ballet dancers. *Giselle* was performed for the last time in forty years in 1870, and thereafter ballet fled to the opera houses, sometimes receiving shabby treatment even there. The American Opera included *Sylvia* and *Coppélia* in their repertoire, and produced opera ballets with care and taste, but complaints about the Metropolitan ballet appearing in critiques early in the eighties might have been written yesterday. Apparently, they began the way they meant to go on.

The revival of ballet in New York may be said to have begun with the arrival in New York of Adeline Genée in 1908. Genée, in physique and personality a world away from the buxom beauties of *The Black Crook* (revived for the eighth time in 1903), left an impression of springlike charm, though she was handicapped by her vehicle—a musical comedy with the dreadful title *The Soul Kiss.*

In 1910 Pavlova and Mordkin were engaged by the Metropolitan and their first appearance in *Coppélia* entranced an audience into staying until the unprecedented hour of one in the morning. Later in the season they presented *The Legend of Azayiade, Giselle, Bacchanale,* and solo *divertissements*—*Le Cygne* and the *Arrow Dance.*

Gertrude Hoffman attempted with her *Saison Russe* to cash in on the interest created by Pavlova and Mordkin in New York and the Diaghilev company in Europe. She imported a company of European dancers, some of whom had been in the Diaghilev Ballet, and presented three ballets with an approximation of Fokine's choreography in settings that were approximations of the Bakst and Benois originals. The venture did not meet with much success, as it is likely that New York was not yet ready for ballet outside the opera house.

In 1911 Katerina Geltzer, following Pavlova at the Metropolitan, danced *Swan Lake* in a more or less complete version somewhat rearranged by Mordkin. She also danced in *Coppélia* and the usual *divertissements,* but did not succeed with audiences who had been carried away by Pavlova's slender elegance.

The third Metropolitan guest star was Adeline Genée, whose repertoire included *La Camargo,* the ballet from *Robert le Diable, Coppélia,* and *La Danse,* the last called "an authentic record of dancing and dancers between the years 1710 and 1845," the music for which included selections from Lully, Rameau, Corelli, Padre Martini, and Chopin.

The next high light in the progress of ballet toward popular acceptance in New York was provided by the arrival of the Diaghilev Ballet for an engagement that included seasons at the Century Theater and the Manhattan Opera House as well as the Metropolitan. Their glory was somewhat dimmed by the absence of the outstanding stars, Karsavina and Nijinsky. The latter was released from his internment in Hungary and arrived in New York three months later. Even without their most famous dancers, this group, with its superb ensemble, artistic décors, fine music, and high standard of execution, was dazzlingly unlike anything that had been seen in New York in any branch of the theater. Their repertoire included *Petrouchka, Prince Igor, L'Après-midi d'un Faune* (pounced on and bowdlerized by the Catholic Theatre Movement), *Cléopâtre, Les Sylphides,* and all the familiar ballets that have been given the status of classics, though there is little classical about them. A new ballet, *Tyl Eulenspiegel* to Strauss's tone poem, with choreography by Nijinsky and décor and costumes by Robert Edmond Jones, was presented at the Manhattan Opera House in 1916. Produced under circumstances of great confusion, some of which may have found its way into the choreography, it was nevertheless an artistic success. Surviving sketches and photographs show a mad architectural background inhabited by the creatures of a reasonably cheerful medieval nightmare. It is the one ballet performed by the Diaghilev company that America can claim as its own. Like the other Nijinsky ballets (always excepting that immortelle in the ballet garden, *L'Après-midi d'un Faune*) it presented difficulties impossible for a touring company to cope with. It was shelved after a few performances, leaving an unforgettable impression on those lucky enough to have seen it.

The 1916–17 seasons of the Diaghilev company (not repeated because inept management resulted in a financial fiasco) stimulated ballet in New York and in America, but not all who felt a desire to create in the new style had taste and technique enough to profit by what they had seen. It was easy to seize upon the superficial exoticism and ignore the technique that provided the underlying bony structure. Dancers with rudimentary training or merely an urge infested vaudeville, revue, and dance recital with exotic and Oriental dance dramas that were spineless and messy copies of the lusty originals. The Diaghilev Ballet and the tours of Pavlova made America dance-but not ballet-conscious. That was not to come until much later.

The Metropolitan, under this stimulus, produced a number of ballets: *Dance in the Place Congo* (1917), with choreography by Ottokar Bartik and a score by Henry F. Gilbert; *Le Coq d'Or* (1918), cherished memory to all who saw it as a ballet-opera; *Petrouchka* (1919), with Adolph Bolm in the title role; *Skyscrapers*

(1926) with a score by John Alden Carpenter that had been originally commissioned by Diaghilev. *Skyscrapers* anticipated *Fancy Free* by incorporating colloquial gesture and the steps of popular dances. The official *maître de ballet* had the assistance of Sammy Lee, arranger of line routines for Broadway musicals.

John Alden Carpenter also composed a score for Adolph Bolm's ballet *Krazy Kat,* with a book based on the surrealist antics of a comic-strip character. This was given at Town Hall in 1920, George Barrère's Little Symphony providing the accompaniment.

Michel Fokine came to New York, and was active in the theater from time to time. He arranged dances for at least one Hippodrome show, as well as a number of musicals—*Mecca* and *Aphrodite* come to mind. His finest work during this period, however, was for the Reinhardt production *The Miracle,* a wordless play that for colorful and gorgeous spectacle has never been surpassed in New York. Fokine had a flourishing ballet school and occasionally arranged programs to exhibit the talents of his pupils, sometimes himself appearing with his wife, Vera Fokina. Their Stadium ballet evenings were well attended, though not better attended than the dreary exhibitions staged by the Duncan Dancers. Occasional performances of ballets arranged by Fokine or other ballet masters living in New York, were isolated events—never seasons of ballet that might have created and held an audience. The pupils of the various schools who took part in them vanished into the commercial theater, no doubt making more money there than they could have commanded in the world of musical art, where ballet dancers are, financially speaking, the Cinderellas.

A superficial survey of the twenties might give one the idea that there was a great deal of ballet in New York. Actually there were a few isolated programs: the annual dance programs of the Neighborhood Playhouse, well up to the standards of a unique institution that united the informal atmosphere of the little theater with sound professional standards; the League of Composers, which, under the direction of Leopold Stokowski, produced outstanding ballet scores with suitable choreography—*Le Sacre du Printemps, L'Histoire d'un Soldat,* and *Les Noces*—and Adolph Bolm's Ballet Intime, which carried a contradiction in its very title. Ballet is not an intimate art, but a grand and spacious one, at its best on the stage of an opera house. There were also the movie palaces, which in pre-talkie days sometimes presented elaborate prologues. Some of them maintained troupes of ballet and precision dancers much as the Radio City Music Hall does today. Roxy's employed Léonide Massine as dancer and choreographer for two years, during which time he staged versions of familiar ballets—at least the titles were familiar, and the scores could sometimes be recognized after a slight effort, though the ballets themselves frequently suffered from elephantiasis to the point of being completely lost.

At the Metropolitan, where one might reasonably have expected to see good ballet, it was fast sinking back into the old apathy after the brief spurt of excitement. Oscar Wolfe, writing in *Dance* in 1929, said: "Mr. Gatti-Casazza, the director of the opera house, believes that the institution he manages should be devoted to opera only. That the composers of certain operas were weak-kneed enough to yield to the flippant tastes of their patrons and include ballets in their works, and that as a result of their lack of spiritual manliness ballets and ballet dancers became necessary to an opera troupe, is regrettable." It may be said in passing that though Gatti-Casazza has long since gone from the opera house, the same attitude may still be observed in those sacred precincts.

When in 1933 Colonel W. de Basil arrived in New York with his ballet, he was undeniably filling a long-felt want in the New York theatrical scene. The company was slow in establishing itself, probably because many people, among them myself, refused to believe that it was not just one more pupils' recital having a longer run than usual. If this skepticism seems unwarranted, consider the fact that incredibly dreary performances had been presented under the auspices of some of the greatest names in ballet. However, the charm and, as it seemed at the time to our yet unsophisticated eyes, the brilliant technique of the "baby ballerinas," backed by the artistry of Alexandra Danilova and Léonide Massine, now in his proper element, began to attract audiences who could not wait to tell anyone who would listen that at last there was authentic ballet in New York.

Their success, not overwhelming, but sufficient to keep them dancing, proved a vital stimulus, and though Colonel W. de Basil and the "baby ballerinas" have vanished from the scene, ballet is firmly established in New York and in America, to remain as long as its high standards are maintained. Hundreds of young American dancers have demonstrated that they are second to none, and are extending the scope of ballet, while preserving its great traditions. America is adding a new volume to the history of theatrical dance, and already several chapters have been written. All our young dancers require is an opportunity to dance and experiment with choreography, and managers and directors who will refrain from ruthlessly exploiting them. Let us look forward to the time when the United States will have an institution like London's Sadler's Wells, a company that is self-supporting and whose profits are used for new ballets rather than for the enrichment of booking agents.

THE AFTERNOON OF
A FAUN

THE *AFTERNOON OF A FAUN,* produced in 1912, has been the point of departure for many arguments and contradictory claims. The choreography by Vaslav Nijinsky to Debussy's *Prélude à l'Après-midi d'un faune* was, according to Igor Stravinsky, inspired in all its details by Léon Bakst and merely carried out under Nijinsky's direction. In the not too reliable biography of Nijinsky by his wife, she states that the ballet was an entirely original conception, and that Bakst and Diaghilev were admitted only to the final rehearsals. At this late date it is difficult to assess the claims and ascertain the real facts of the case.

There is no doubt at all about the furor caused by the first performance of *L'Après-midi d'un Faune,* which took place in Paris at the Théâtre du Chatelet on May 29, 1912. It was bitterly attacked on moral grounds by Gaston Calmette, editor of *Le Figaro,* and as hotly defended from an æsthetic point of view by Rodin. One might question the right of both editor and sculptor to define or defend the æsthetics of ballet, but there is no question of the value of the ensuing publicity, echoes of which have kept the ballet alive to this day.

The first American performance of *L'Après-midi d'un Faune* took place at the Century Theater on January 17, 1916, with a cast headed by Léonide Massine. The critic of the *New York Times* described it as "a vaguely-fascinating pastoral episode." The Catholic Theatre Movement, deciding that New York must be protected from the immoralities of a work that had shocked Paris, requested that the ending of the ballet be modified. This was done. The following is an excerpt from an item in the *Times* of January 26, 1916:

"In the two performances of the ballet given last week, the Faun, after he had frightened away the Grecian maidens who came to bathe near his cave, picked up a filmy garment one had cast off and placing it on the rock whereon he had been reclining, lay down upon it. Last night the Faun placed the drapery gently upon the rock and sat gazing at its silken folds. Then the curtain fell.

"When the audience had ceased applauding after the ushers had carried out huge armfuls of flowers,[1] sent to Leonide Massine with requests that they be delivered after his appearance as the Faun, M. de Diaghileff came smiling from his seat in the orchestra circle down the aisle to where Mr. Gatti-Casazza, John Brown and other heads of the Metropolitan were standing and said in French, 'America is saved!' "

It is unfortunate that America was not also saved from the many strange and inept adaptations of this ballet that were seen in the wake of the original performances by Sergei Diaghilev's Ballet Russe. It was not until many years later that a reasonably authentic revival was seen in this country. Described on the program as a "choreographic poem" with "choreography after Vaslav Nijinsky," it was performed by Colonel W. de Basil's Ballet Russe at the Metropolitan Opera House, New York, on November 1, 1936, with the following cast:

THE NYMPH   *Tamara Grigorieva* | THE FAUN   *David Lichine*
NYMPHS: *Mlles Abricossova, Chamie, Marra, Nelidova, Obidenna, Osato.*

◇◇◇◇◇◇◇◇◇◇◇◇◇◇◇◇◇◇

The simple story is unfolded before a backdrop set close to the footlights. To the left is a rock, on which reclines a Faun, who plays with a bunch of grapes. The Nymphs enter and one of them takes off a scarf, which she drops in terror when the Faun, wishing to join them, descends from his rock. The other Nymphs leave the scene. After a moment she follows them. The Nymphs advance and retreat in an ineffectual attempt to regain the scarf. The Faun, left alone, picks up the scarf, carries it to the top of the rock, and caresses it.

As presently performed, the movements of *The Afternoon of a Faun* have little or no relation to the Greek vase drawings by which they were purportedly inspired, still less to the rhythms and moods of Debussy's music. It is true that the evolutions of the Nymphs are performed in profile, but their heaviness in no way suggests the quality of Greek vase decorations, many of which have lightness and animation. The dreamy summer-afternoon feeling of the music is also conspicuously lacking.

At this distance it is difficult to imagine why a minor choreo-

---

[1] The custom of presenting flowers to male dancers has fallen out of fashion, except for a revival during Lifar's appearance with the Ballet Russe de Monte Carlo in 1938.

graphic effort aroused such a violent æsthetic controversy and so much moral indignation. This may be explained by the fact that the current audience sees only a pale approximation of the original. Or it may be that it was only a storm in a teacup in the first place. The real mystery is why *The Afternoon of a Faun* has held its place in the repertory for so long a time.

Within this ballet's circumscribed limits David Lichine gave an excellent performance. His admirable physique and clever make-up suggested a veritable classic god of the woods. Many other dancers have attempted this role in the last ten years, with nothing recognizable as success except by those members of the audience who, having read accounts of the ballet given in innumerable books, bring to the performance a determination to lose no part of their preconceived ideas about it.

It is possible that the real æsthetic purpose of *The Afternoon of a Faun* was to provide an antidote, very necessary in 1912, to the "Greek" dancing of Isadora Duncan's imitators.

THE AFTERNOON OF A FAUN (Igor Youskevitch)

ALEKO (Yura Skibine as Aleko, Alicia Markova as Zemphira, Hugh Laing as the Young Gypsy)

HOWARD ATHENÆUM

Director, Mr. W. F. Johnson------Stage Director, Mr. W. L. Ayling

NEW YEAR'S EVE!

LAST NIGHT BUT ONE OF

MISS MARY ANN LEE
AND
MR. GEORGE W. SMITH.

Two Entire Ballets on the same Evening,

LA BAYADERE & LA FLEUR DE CHAMP.

Price of Admission, - - - 50 Cents.

NOTICE. Time Altered. Doors open at 5 1-2 o'clock curtain will be raised at 6 1-2 o'clock.

☞ Ticket Office open from 10 A. M. till 2, and from 3 to 5, P. M. every day of Performance----when Seats will be secured for THAT NIGHT ONLY.

ON WEDNESDAY EVENING, DEC. 31 1845,

The Performance will commence with the Splendid Ballet Opera of

LA BAYADERE,
THE MAID OF CASHMERE,

With all the Original Music, by Auber.

UNKNOWN, - - - Mr. J. M. WHITE.
Olifour----Grand Judge of the City of Cashmere----Mr Whiting
Chopdar----Mr Parker
Ninka----Principal Singing Bayadere----Mrs MAEDER
Fatima----Mrs Hunt | Chloe----Mrs Howard

ZOLOE, - - - MISS MARY ANN LEE.

Singing Bayadres by Misses Smith, Deluce, Mace, Gould, &c.
Dancing Bayadres, Mesdames Jones, Stimson, Knight, and the Ladies and Gentlemen of the Company, who have kindly consented to lend their aid on this occasion.

SCENE I.—PRINCIPAL SQUARE OF THE CITY OF CASHMERE.
ENTRANCE TO THE PALACE OF THE GRAND JUDGE.
Citizens waiting. Chorus--"Slow wear the time," &c.
Solo----Olifour--"Happy am I; and I Judge Supreme."

Grand Entrance of Zoloe, Chloe, Fatima and the Bayaderes.
Chorus--"Music and mirth," &c. Solo--Unknown--"As strange, sir," &c.
"Yes, my heart is growing tender"--Olifour and Chorus. Recitative--Unknown--
"This bracelet, maiden." Chorus--Guards and Citizens--"Now must terror,"
&c. Solo--Ninka--"What gifts superb," and Chorus--"Hail, Queen of beauty,"
Trio--Ninka, Unknown and Olifour--"With a lover so tender," &c.

SCENE 1.—INTERIOR OF AN INDIAN THATCHED COTTAGE.
ACT II.
THE FUNERAL PILE.
Recitative--Unknown--"This, then, is your retreat." Cavatina--"Beats there
a heart," &c. Duet--Ninka and Unknown--"Happy Banks of Ganges."

GRAND TRIAL DANCE,
ZOLOE AND FATIMA.

Recitative--Unknown and Ninka--"The victory is yours." Solo--Unknown--
"I am oppressed with slumber."

SCENE LAST—THE INDIAN PARADISE.
GRAND ASCENT OF BRAMA AND ZOLOE

GRAND CHORUS, - - "GLORY! GLORY!"

To be followed by, 2d time, the amusing Farce of

MY SISTER KATE.

Charles Unit----Mr Howard | Servant----Mr Adams
Frank Morton----Mr Stark | Doctor's Boy----Mr Fox
Tom Chaff----Mr Whiting | Miss Pemberton----Mrs Hunt
Kate Morton----Mr Resor | First Fairy----Mrs C. W. Hunt
Emily Constant----Mrs Howard | (My Sister Kate)----Mrs W. H. Smith
| Mrs Scrubber----Miss Smith

The whole to conclude with the new and highly successful Fairy Ballet, for the 4th time, entitled

LA FLEUR DE CHAMP,
OR --- THE DAUGHTER OF THE DANUBE.

Fleur De Champ - - - Miss Mary Ann Lee.
RUDOLF - - - Mr G. W. SMITH.

Fairy King----Mr Binney | Second Imp.----Mr Davis
Baron----Mr Russell | Dame Jengarde----Miss Smith
Urick----Mr Resor | First Fairy----Mrs C. W. Hunt
Herald----Mr Adams | Second Fairy----Mrs Howard
First Imp.----Mr Taylor | Third Fairy----Mrs Jones

Imps and Fairies by the Ladies and Gentlemen of the Ballet.
In the course of the Piece, are the following CHORUSES and DANCES.--

OPENING CHORUS OF NYMPHS.

Pas de Flora by - - - Miss Lee and Mr Smith
Pas de Gallop by - - - Miss Lee and Mr Smith
Grand Pas de Tyrolean by - Mrs Hunt and Mrs Howard
Pas de Nayades by Miss Lee, assisted by Mrs Hunt and Mrs Howard
And the Ladies of the Corps de Ballet.

Is in rehearsal, and will shortly be produced, for the first time in this country, the brilliant and exciting Ballet, **GISELLE, OR LES WILIS.**

HOOTON'S PRESS--Haskins's Building, opposite the head of Hanover Street.

PLAYBILL (Boston, 1845) of *La Bayadère*, announcing first *Giselle* in the United States

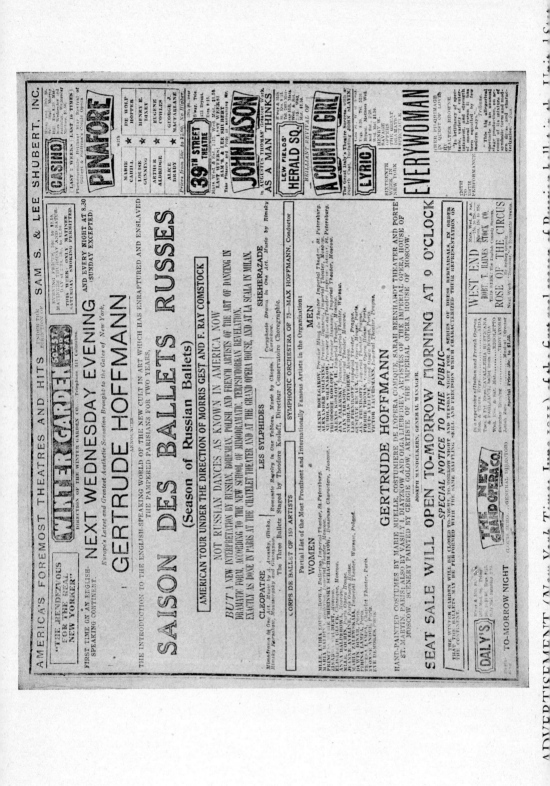

ALEKO

Ballet by Léonide Massine and Marc Chagall, inspired by Pushkin's poem "Gypsies"; music by Tchaikovsky, orchestrated by Erno Rapee; choreography by Léonide Massine; scenery and costumes by Marc Chagall; artistic collaboration by Henry Clifford.

ALEKO was performed for the first time by Ballet Theatre at the Palacio de Bellas Artes, Mexico City, during the fall season of 1942. The first New York performance took place at the Metropolitan Opera House on October 6, 1942, with the following cast:

ZEMPHIRA	*Alicia Markova*	ACROBAT	*Annabelle Lyon*
ALEKO	*Yura Skibine*	STREET DANCER	*Rosella Hightower*
YOUNG GYPSY	*Hugh Laing*	BATHERS	*Jean Hunt, Marie Karnilova*
ZEMPHIRA'S FATHER	*Antony Tudor*		*Nina Popova*
FORTUNE TELLER	*Lucia Chase*	BUTTERFLY	*Annabelle Lyon*
HORSE	*David Nillo*	PAN	*Ian Gibson*

GYPSIES: *Margaret Banks, Muriel Bentley, Jean Davidson, Barbara Fallis, Miriam Golden, Roszika Sabo, Hubert Bland, Charles Dickson, John Kriza, Jerome Robbins*
YOUNG BOYS: *Yura Lazovsky, Nicolas Orloff, Richard Reed*
Clown, Bondura Player, Bear, Peasants, Society Lady, Duke, Poet, His Beloved, Society Girls, Cat, Bat, Snake, and other creatures of Aleko's delirious fancy.

◆◆◆◆◆◆◆◆◆◆◆◆◆◆◆◆

Scene 1. The curtain rises on a gyspy camp. Zemphira and Aleko enter to the first strains of the music, cross the stage, and disappear—symbolic of their journey together from the city. The inhabitants of the camp lie in indolent attitudes around the fire. As they begin to stir, the boys incur the wrath of the Fortune Teller. Laughing at her scolding, they break into a wild dance. Zemphira's Father, sitting by himself away from the fire, has sensed the approach of Zemphira and Aleko, whose appearance is greeted warmly by the gypsies. The Father promises the young man that he will find happiness among the gypsies. A Young Gypsy comes in, accidentally brushing against Zemphira. They look at each other, but Zemphira joins Aleko, and the Young Gypsy is surrounded by the girls, who read his palm.

One makes the conventional promises of prosperity. Another is frightened by what she sees, foretelling that he will be stabbed to death by someone not far distant. The Young Gypsy is more amused than impressed, refusing to take the prophecy seriously. Zemphira and Aleko dance together. The gypsy boys return with a horse, leaping on and off its back exuberantly. All through these scenes there are many crossings of the stage by the gypsy band, symbolic of their various activities, as well as indicating the passage of time.

Scene 2. This is a scene of lively carnival. Aleko spreads a carpet for the Acrobat, who displays her skill. A Street Dancer performs. A Clown entertains the crowd with his antics. A Bear is led in. Musicians play. There is general gaiety, in which all join. Zemphira appears and dances.

Scene 3. Three girls who have been bathing are seen on the edge of a wheatfield in the bright sun of a summer afternoon. Three peasant boys join their play. By degrees the stage fills up with boys and girls dancing lustily. When they leave, Zemphira and the Young Gypsy enter. Zemphira has long since ceased to love Aleko and is finding happiness with her present companion. Aleko, reduced to a pitiable condition by the loss of Zemphira, follows her to implore her to return to him. She can scarcely spare him enough attention to say no to his pathetic plea. Heartbroken, he goes away. Zemphira and the Young Gypsy dance a triumphant mazurka. As the peasants begin to drift back, the lovers leave in opposite directions.

Scene 4. Aleko is discovered lying delirious on the ground. He is plagued by strange fantasies and nightmare creatures who weave endlessly in and out of his dreams. Dramas play themselves out before his eyes: a young poet obsessed with jealousy is killed in a duel; an aristocrat orders a policeman to lash a group of poverty-stricken wretches whose misery offends his sight. Aleko's mind whirls with delirious images, until he can scarcely distinguish the real from the visionary. When the gypsies enter, he is enraged by the sight of Zemphira and the Young Gypsy. Their happiness, contrasted with his own unhappiness, is too much for him, and he stabs Zemphira's lover. Zemphira, who does not wish to live without her lover, offers herself to Aleko's knife and joins the Young Gypsy in death. Zemphira's Father, scorning revenge, banishes Aleko from the company of the gypsies. Aleko drops senseless amid the mourning throng.

Aleko is a brilliant montage of a gypsy life that never existed out of the realm of poetry. When a realistic touch appears, it is only for the purpose of pointing up the fantasy. One must see this ballet many times before the wealth of detail may be absorbed. Fortunately, everything about it—décor, costumes, interpretation, and music—are of a quality that will hold the attention through repeated performances.

For those interested in modern painting, Marc Chagall's superb décor will be the first interest. Extraordinarily colorful and dramatic, they are among the most distinguished ballet settings since Diaghilev employed the finest easel painters of his period to work for his company. The backdrop for the last scene, with its white horse rearing in a nightmare sky that lowers over a red city, is a perfect setting for the strange creatures who whirl deliriously before it. It unites with Massine's groups to form a perfect whole. The costumes share the distinction of the settings, those for Zemphira being of especial beauty, with little of the conventional gypsy of the theater about them. The creatures of Aleko's delirium display considerable invention and a light touch. They do not attract the eye individually, but together produce a strange and dreamlike effect.

The great surprise of *Aleko* was the superb Zemphira of Alicia Markova that reminded those aware of her career before coming to America that not always had she dwelt on the remote heights of the *ballet blanc,* but had displayed her gaiety and wit in *Façade* and *Bar aux Folies-Bergère*. Her exquisite *Swan Lake* and matchless *Giselle* contained no hint of the fire and quite different sort of dramatic intensity of her gypsy. With sunburnt make-up, wild hair, and a vivid red costume, her very appearance was a shock, though a delightful one. Nothing was left of the familiar Markova but the thistledown lightness, and authoritative dancing style, now turned to the uses of *demi-caractère*. Hugh Laing, as the Young Gypsy, was strongly reminiscent of the Massine of a decade before. It made one wish to see him in other roles in the Massine ballets—the poet of *Symphonie Fantastique,* or the Hussar of *Le Beau Danube*. Yura Skibine performed Aleko with a restrained intensity that has not been seen in the role since his departure from the world of ballet. Lately Nora Kaye has given some fine performances of Zemphira. The ensemble, as in all Massine's symphonic ballets, are soloists. Recent substitutions have not always been for the better. Outstanding are John Kriza's gypsy boy, and Rozsika Sabo's peasant girl.

The music, Tchaikovsky's Trio in A minor, opus 50, bore up surprisingly well under orchestration, being essentially symphonic in its construction. The orchestration of the greater part of chamber music is a dangerous experiment, the quality of the work disappearing under the impact of instrumentation. The Trio, however, lost nothing, and its dramatic power, always evident, even gained somewhat. Erno Rapee approached his task with intelligence and skill. The result apparently did not offend the purists, though, indeed, these august persons rarely concern themselves with Tchaikovsky, regarding his music with no particular reverence.

Choreographically *Aleko* is in Massine's best symphonic manner. It joins classical with free plastic dancing in a manner that does violence to neither style. The wild dances of the gypsies in the first scene, the stylized Russian dances in the third, are exhilarating. The *pas de trois* is a strictly classical exposition of line, and when danced by Rosella Hightower and Alicia Alonso, takes on an extra dimension. When *Aleko* was first produced, there was a *pas de deux* (Butterfly and Pan) danced by Ian Gibson and Annabelle Lyon to the waltz section of the Trio. This has unfortunately since been cut, along with several sequences in the last scene. The spirited mazurka performed in the third scene by Zemphira and the Young Gypsy is an interesting elaboration of a folk-dance form for balletic purposes. The fourth scene is rich in plastic groupings—one in which girls wearing black gloves, with arms extended in the form of a Latin cross, are held high in the air to make a background for the drama is especially memorable.

Aleko is a worthy successor to Massine's best symphonic ballets. It is his last important work up to date.

APOLLON MUSAGÉTE

APOLLON MUSAGÈTE by Igor Stravinsky, which later, with choreography by George Balanchine, became part of the repertoire of the Diaghilev Ballet, was commissioned originally by Elizabeth Sprague Coolidge and presented at a performance of ballet on April 27, 1928 during a festival of chamber music held in the auditorium of the Library of Congress, in Washington. This was the first première of a ballet with a Stravinsky score to be performed in America. Stravinsky was allowed to choose his own subject, the only condition being that the score should not exceed a performance time of half an hour.

Stravinsky, who felt that the strings had been neglected in contemporary orchestral compositions, not excluding his own works, composed *Apollon Musagète* in the form of a suite for strings, visualizing the ballet in classical style, the various sections of his work (*Pas d'action, Pas de deux,* Variations, Coda) carrying out the idea.

The choreography of the American presentation was by Adolph Bolm. Whether it was a success or a failure is difficult to ascertain, various critics (all of the musical fraternity) having their own contradictory ideas. They do not agree even on the adequacy of the theatrical equipment, one claiming that the small auditorium, seating less than six hundred people, was a model of what a miniature musical theater should be; another stating flatly that "the tiny stage . . . is in no wise equipped for theatrical production . . . only four or five dancers . . . can move simultaneously, and even then with no room to spare."

A round-by-round description of the ballet, taken from the *Times* of May 6, 1928, reads as follows:

"Before the curtains a priest bears a huge glowing urn to the front of the platform. Three maidens in ballet skirts perform a brief symbolic worship before it and withdraw. Thus is Apollo born, in a manner less literal than the original scenario demanded. The curtains then open, and before us is a scene which suggests nothing so much as an 'elegant engraving' after Veronese. On our left is a huge pile of rocks and on our right a group of Corinthian columns in ruins. Between the two stands Apollo, clad in gold sandals, pink tights, and a gold tunic decorated with red festoons. Upon his long golden curls he wears a helmet from whose crest burst many fulsome plumes. In his hand is his lyre.

"To Apollo come Calliope, Polymnia, and Terpsichore, wearing the ballet costume of Taglioni, with a border of gold about their skirts, and fillets in their hair to show that they are Greek. To each of them he gives a particular mission. Calliope is presented with a tablet and pencil and is made the patroness of epic poetry: Polymnia receives the mystic veil and is charged with the care of sacred hymns: Terpsichore is given the Apollonian lyre itself and is made priestess of choral song and dance. This great business performed, the Leader of the Muses climbs up the slope of the rocks and is transfigured by a strong light. His three followers do obeisance to him and the curtains close.

"The composer in the present work turned to the melodious Bellini as his model, even renouncing his former aversion to strings and employing them exclusively because of their greater sweetness. Superficially, here was ballet music of the most conventional sort; but to the ear of the choreographer this pseudo-lyricism proved to be little more than a candy-coating for the most vicious contrary rhythms and the most persistent irregularities of time, which bore no more relation to the conventional ballet than to Bellini, under whose style they were so neatly tucked away. Yet the spirit of the music was undoubtedly of the early nineteenth century, and just as certainly the ballet of the early nineteenth century was strictly conventional.

"The ingenious fashion in which Mr. Bolm reconciled these two seemingly irreconcilable conditions furnished the chief delight of the performance. The obsolete elegances of the ballet of Taglioni's day, struggling against the underlying obstinacies of modernistic rhythms, mirrored the quality of the music exactly."

Other critics were less pleased with the score and the choreography. Lawrence Gilman referred rather bitterly to Apollo Smintheus [1] and thought the choreography "unimaginative and tepid."

The cast of *Apollon Musagète,* in addition to Adolph Bolm (Apollo), included Ruth Page (Terpsichore), Berenice Holmes (Polymnia), and Elise Reiman (Calliope). Hans Kindler conducted the orchestra. [2]

Stravinsky, in his autobiography, professes a lack of interest in Apollo's transatlantic apotheosis, but this did not mean that he was

[1] The Apollo of the Greeks presided over agriculture as well as the arts. One of his titles in that capacity was Apollo Smintheus—destroyer of mice.

[2] The program also included three additional ballets with choreography by Adolph Bolm: *Pavane pour une Infante Défunte* (Ravel); *Arlecchinata* (music by Jean Joseph Cassanea de Mondonville, drawn from his opera-ballet *Carnaval du Parnasse*); and *Alt-Wien* (Beethoven's *Elf Wiener Tänze*).

without ideas about how he wanted it produced. When Diaghilev expressed his wish to add the ballet to his new productions for the 1928 season, Stravinsky revised the orchestration of the score and worked closely with the choreographer, George Balanchine, who, he says, "had arranged the dances exactly as I had wished—that is to say, in accordance with the classical school. . . . It was the first attempt to revive academic dancing in a work actually composed for the purpose. . . . As for the dancers, they were beyond all praise. The graceful Nikitina with her purity of line alternating with the enchanting Danilova in the role of Terpsichore; Tchernicheva and Doubrovska, those custodians of the best classical traditions; finally Serge Lifar, then still quite young, conscientious, natural, spontaneous, and full of serious enthusiasm for his art—all these formed an unforgettable company."

Stravinsky was less enthusiastic about the décor. He had expressed a desire for the Muses to be costumed in the short white tutu of the classical ballet, and the action to take place in a conventionalized landscape. André Bauchant designed the décor and, as far as one can tell, seems to have followed Stravinsky's ideas. Photographs reveal the Muses in short tutus fitting rather closely over the hips, with camisole tops. The color is at least light, if not white. The décor is of great simplicity, with a rock at the rear of the stage. For the apotheosis, horses drawing a chariot amid clouds appear high above the stage. Possibly the *mise-en-scène* was rather more primitive than Stravinsky wished (André Bauchant is a painter whose easel work resembles that of Rousseau); otherwise it seems to follow his specifications rather closely.

The first performance of *Apollon Musagète* with Balanchine's choreography took place at the Théâtre Sarah-Bernhardt in Paris on June 12, 1928, with the composer conducting. It was well received by press and public. It was also performed during the London season, at His Majesty's Theatre, with the composer again conducting, this time at the première only.

The first revival of the Balanchine version of *Apollon Musagète* in America was presented by the American Ballet at the Metropolitan Opera House, New York, on April 27, 1937, with a cast that included Lew Christensen (Apollo), and Daphne Vane, Elise Reiman, and Holly Howard (the three Muses). For this performance seventy members of the New York Philharmonic played, conducted by Igor

Stravinsky. The program also included the first American performance of *Le Baiser de la Fée* and the world première of *The Card
Party*—in fact, it was a Stravinsky festival. This program (repeated
the following evening) was by far the best presented by the American Ballet during its entire existence. There was something for everyone—except the music critics, and even they had some fun running to earth the musical quotations in which the scores of *Baiser de
la Fée* and *Card Party* abounded. For the ballet audience there was
a choice between the mannered neo-classicism of *Apollon Musagète,*
the gaiety of *Card Party,* and the old-fashioned graces with a new-
fashioned turn, of the *ballet d'action* in *Baiser de la Fée.* For two
nights it seemed that there was really an American ballet at last, not
only on paper, but actually dancing on the stage of the Metropolitan
with every appearance of a desire to please its audience. Unfortunately, after these brilliant performances the American Ballet sank
back into apathetic appearances at the opera, for audiences that
failed to appreciate even their better efforts.

This production of *Apollon Musagète* rejoiced in a décor and costumes by Stuart Chaney that were several degrees removed from
Stravinsky's notions of what they should be. The Muses were clad in
conventional Greek tunics. The setting, a naturalistic landscape, was
cluttered with an assortment of objects: broken columns, urns, a
colossal head, capitals, and a rock for the apotheosis, the whole over-
hung with a great set of draperies, complete with fringes and tassels.

Choreographically, *Apollon Musagète* had its brilliant as well as
its bewildering moments. The birth of the god was achieved in the
following manner: the nymph Leto is seen on the rock; suddenly
the figure of Apollo appears, bound with hieratic swathings, like a
mummy; two nymphs propel him forward; they hold opposite ends
of the confining band, while Apollo frees himself with a pirouette.
From then on, his principal task was to pilot the Muses through a
pas de quatre, which exploited every acrobatic predicament and con-
volution that the ingenuity of the choreographer could devise. At
least one of the critics was amused by the portentous solemnity of the
action, remarking in his review: "There was something to tempt the
risibles . . . in the sight of one of the muses sitting down momentarily on the recumbent Apollo's knee, her back to the audience, and
then flitting away as if some important bit of allegory has been visualized." Of the cast, only Holly Howard gained critical praise. Lew

Christensen received no credit for a fine performance, though his
admirable physique, classic dignity, and controlled technique were
perfect for the role of Apollo. Several years later, when Ballet Theatre revived the ballet, André Eglevsky, whose performance did not
in any way measure up to Christensen's, received the acclaim of the
critics, who by that time had been more or less beaten into an acceptance of Balanchine's advanced style.

Apollon Musagète made several appearances during the 1937–8
opera season, usually as a curtain-raiser to performances of *Salome*,
forming a pleasant variation from the customary *Cavalleria Rusticana* or *Pagliacci*. It would be idle to pretend that the opera audience
appreciated the ballet. They have never accepted operas that have
any breath of musical controversy about them until a lapse of at least
twenty years. It follows that ballet also to gain favor among operagoers, must beguile these conservatives with the balletic equivalents
of Verdi and Puccini.

The programs for these presentations offered more information
than appeared on the program for the première. One dated February 16, 1938 lists the following cast:

APOLLO, Leader of the Muses
                   Lew Christensen
CALLIOPE   *Daphne Vane*
POLYMNIA   *Holly Howard*
TERPSICHORE   *Elise Reiman*

TWO NYMPHS
     Kyra Blanc, Heidi Vosseler
LETO, Mother of Apollo
               Lillian Reilly

Scene 1. The Birth of Apollo. (Leto, two Nymphs, Apollo)
Scene 2. Olympus.
    Variation of Apollo. *Pas d'action* (Apollo and the Muses). Variation of
    Calliope (L'Alexandrine). Variation of Polymnia. Variation of Terpsichore.
    Variation of Apollo. *Pas de deux* (Apollo and Terpsichore). Coda—Apoth-
    eosis (Apollo and the Muses).

◇◇◇◇◇◇◇◇◇◇◇◇◇◇◇◇◇

Ballet Theatre revived *Apollon Musagète,* now called *Apollo,* and
performed it several times during the 1943 spring season, with
Stravinsky conducting. The cast consisted of the following dancers:
André Eglevsky (Apollo), Vera Zorina (Terpsichore), Nora Kaye
(Polymnia), Rosella Hightower (Calliope), Miriam Golden and
Shirley Eckl (two Nymphs), and June Morris (Leto). The Muses
were clad in white tunics of conventional design, and the décor, from
the E. B. Dunkel Studios, was nondescript.

The critics greeted this revival as an artistic achievement, having at last caught up with Balanchine's neo-classic masterpiece, which had been in existence for fifteen years. No doubt they were influenced by the superior stagecraft of Ballet Theatre's cast and the superior dancing of the Muses, at least two of whom excelled the American Ballet entries. Eglevsky made an earthy Apollo, who traveled on a less Olympian plane than Lew Christensen.

When Vera Zorina's engagement as guest artist with Ballet Theatre came to an end, *Apollo* was temporarily dropped from the repertoire. Ballet Theatre has recently revived it, with André Eglevsky in the title role, and with Alicia Alonso, Nora Kaye, and Barbara Fallis as the Nymphs. Igor Youskevitch is slated for the title role during Ballet Theatre's 1946 season at the Broadway Theater in New York.

BACCHANALE—LABYRINTH—
MAD TRISTAN

Bacchanale (Venusberg): first "paranoic"[1] performance; scenario and scenery by Salvador Dali, based on the Bacchanalia of Tannhäuser; music by Richard Wagner; choreography by Léonide Massine; costumes executed by Mme Karinska, based on suggestions by Salvador Dali.

B*ACCHANALE* was performed for the first time by the Ballet Russe de Monte Carlo at the Metropolitan Opera House, New York, on November 9, 1939, with the following cast:

Louis II	*Casimir Kokitch*	The Nymph	*Nathalie Krassovska*
Venus	*Nini Theilade*	The Faun	*André Eglevsky*
Her Companions		Two Cupids	
	Mlles Rklitzka, Williams		*Mlles Pourmel, Etheridge*
The Three Graces	*Mlles Rostova,*	Two Bacchantes	
	Kelepovska, Geleznova		*Mlles Lvova, Rosson*
Lola Montez	*Milada Mladova*	The Satyrs	
Knight of Death	*Chris Volkoff*	MM. *Armour, Katcharoff, Godkin*	
His Suite	MM. *Milton, Steele*	Sacher Masoch	*Marc Platoff*
		His Wife	*Jeannette Lauret*

Nymphs: *Mlles Franca, Grantzeva, Marra, Roudenko, Scarpova, Lelanova, Korjinska, Vallon, Chamie, Hightower, Flotat, Lacca.*
Fauns: MM. *Beresoff, Irwin, Starbuck, Dickson, Gibson, Bocchino, Goudo, vitch, Belsky.*

◇◇◇◇◇◇◇◇◇◇◇◇◇◇

The curtain rises on a setting that is described in Dali's program notes as "Mount Venus (the Venusberg, near Eisenach), the background showing Salvador Dali's birthplace, the Emporda Valley, in the centre of which rises the temple as seen in 'The Betrothal of the Virgin' by Raphael." Dali forgot to mention that the most prominent

[1] This was no more paranoiac than subsequent performances, though possibly more hysterical, as it began after what may well have been the longest intermission in the history of the Metropolitan. The grapevine telegraph had it that the dancers were completely bewildered by the costumes, which had not been finished in time for a dress rehearsal.

feature of the décor was a gigantic swan with outspread wings. There was a large jagged hole in the swan's breast through which a skull-shaped opening was visible. When the curtain rose, Lola Montez was standing in this recess. Her costume, a daft combination of harem trousers and hoop-skirt, was decorated with a double row of teeth, which completed the skull illusion. As the ballet proceeded on its way, many very odd characters indeed appeared: a woman with a rose-colored fish head; faceless Graces with strange protuberances; Venus in a pale pink union suit and a magnificent blond wig; nymphs clad in schizophrenic costumes, one half frilly organdy party frocks, one half men's underwear; satyrs with horns and branches growing out of their heads; fauns that were Tarzans with lobsters decorating their loincloths. The Knight of Death was a large, black, perambulating umbrella whose handle was decorated with a skull, his suite two men who were wrapped in opposite ends of a winding sheet. Sacher Masoch and His Wife,[2] in spite of their case-book antics, were positively restful in their realism after this welter of nightmares. A satyr, with his miniature counterpart seated in a downstage corner, knitted a red sock through such proceedings as did not offend his sense of propriety. However, when nymphs and fauns rolled amorously on the floor, he packed up his knitting and departed, snorting indignantly, his small friend clinging to his leg as he walked off. A good many of the audience were in perfect accord with his sentiments.

After the orgy a couple of weary celebrants were propped up on either side of the stage by the Cupids (quite the busiest members of a very busy cast), who used a variety of crutches for this purpose. Leda, high above the stage, performed a dizzy *pas de deux,* with the swan as a sort of static partner. Ludwig's death brought the ballet to a close. As he fell carefully in the center of a royal robe spread on the floor for him by the nymphs, his descent set off a mechanical device that caused four large black umbrellas, planted at the corners of the robe, to open with stately dignity.

That portion of the audience who had read a little Freud had an interesting time discussing Dali's deviations from the standard clichés of symbolism. These were few enough, for in this period, as

[2] If *Bacchanale* had ever been given at the City Center of Music and Drama (New York), this delightful pair would have given Commissioner Moss something serious to worry about.

far as ballet was concerned, Dali was inclined to follow the text books rather than invent personal symbols.

The only section of the audience that was seriously upset by *Bacchanale* were the devoted adherents of Wagner.[3] The ballet enjoyed a *succès de scandale* as long as it was a novelty. When the organdy frills grew limp, the slightly obscene costumes of the three Graces receded behind modest veils, and the umbrellas began to miss their cues, *Bacchanale* faded from the repertoire, to be succeeded by *Labyrinth*.

Labyrinth had a libretto by Dali, based on the classic myth of Theseus and Ariadne, and choreography by Massine. The music was the great C major Symphony of Franz Schubert. The first performance, by the Ballet Russe de Monte Carlo, took place at the Metropolitan Opera House, New York, on October 8, 1941. Bogged down in a mass of mythology and "props," it was remarkable chiefly for the silly misuse of the magnificent music, by the same choreographer who had given *Chorearteum* to the world. André Eglevsky (Theseus) did his best with unpromising material. Tamara Toumanova (Ariadne), dressed in a costume resembling those worn by the nymphs in *Bacchanale* (it was singularly unbecoming), went virtually unnoticed. She was required to do little more than lie around and watch the others perform. In the second tableau, which touched with Daliesque vagueness on the Minotaur legend, Toumanova, perched high on the scenery, impersonated something that appeared to be a spool of thread, slowly turning to unwind the clue that led to the lair of the monster. After one or two performances she gave up even this slight activity, and this part of Ariadne's role was relegated to another dancer. At various times, Igor Youskevitch and Frederic Franklin assumed the role of Theseus. Of the three interpreters of the part, Youskevitch was the finest. Apparently oblivious of the nonsense going on around him, his dignified simplicity was rather touching and worthier of a better cause.

In the third tableau two dancers (Nicolas Beresoff and Alexis Kosloff) dressed as roosters pantomimed a cockfight. The ingenious costumes, designed to be worn backward, took advantage of the natural bend of the human knee to lend realism to the roosters'

---

[3] This group included the ushers at the Metropolitan—a very conservative body, inclined to look down on ballet unless in a strictly classical vein.

leg movements, as well as allowing the arms to function more plausibly as wings.

The fourth tableau contained the choreographic high light of *Labyrinth*: a *pas de deux,* classic in feeling, performed by George Zoritch (Castor) and Chris Volkoff (Pollux). There was also one of Massine's most brilliant groups for the corps de ballet, who in this scene, costumed in blue-green union suits with headdresses strongly suggesting those worn by Sisters of Charity, impersonated nothing less than the sea. Gathered in a clump, with headdresses massed to form a white crest, they became a great wave on which Theseus appeared to be tossed. For this tableau, from every point of view the most interesting in the ballet, there was a superb backdrop in which Dali demonstrated what a fine painter he can sometimes be.

In a long ballet these few episodes, lasting but a short time each, were not enough to leaven the dull mass. If anything could have kept *Labyrinth* alive, it was the music, one of the greatest of all symphonies. Ballet audiences as a rule are not particularly interested in music for its own sake and do not clamor for ballets on the basis of music alone.[4] *Labyrinth* in its turn has now vanished and its place remains happily vacant in the repertoire of the Monte Carlo Ballet.

Still another collaboration by Dali and Massine, *Mad Tristan,* was performed by Ballet International for the first time on December 15, 1944, at the International Theater, New York. This was called on the program "The First Paranoic Ballet Based on the Eternal Myth of Love in Death." The cast included Francisco Moncion (Tristan), Toni Worth (Isolde), and Lisa Maslova (Chimera of Isolde). Moncion's performance might have been a fine and moving one, in spite of the general delirium, if he had not been forced to wear an idiotic costume almost identical with those worn by the gigantic burlesque Brünnhildes in the "Aryans under the Skin" number from *This Is the Army.* Even Youskevitch could not have risen above such a handicap. The woman who impersonated Isolde behaved like a refugee from Broadway, and was quite devoid of a dancing technique or the authority and stage presence necessary for even a surrealist Isolde. There was one amusing episode in which the Flute Player (whose operatic prototype has bored generations of operagoers) got his comeuppance at last.

[4] This is probably just as well, the standards of performance by ballet orchestras being notoriously low.

The symbolism employed in *Mad Tristan* has become obscure, and is less related to the textbooks of abnormal psychology than in the two former ballets. Dali seemed to have become obsessed with wheelbarrows, which were pushed about the scene by a group of dancers realistically pantomiming the tics of spastic paralysis. There were several female dancers dressed in what looked like white tulle evening dresses, their heads concealed by globe-shaped arrangements of flowers or dandelion seeds. In this third collaboration of Dali and Massine the tricks are less amusing, the element of surprise having vanished. The music from *Tristan und Isolde,* arranged by a brave man named Ivan Boutnikoff, sounds very thin as played by a small orchestra.

It is possible that the lode is running out, and that surrealism in ballet may take a new turn or even revert to the more balletic manner of *Jeux d'Enfants*. Ballet really cannot survive without dancing.

LE BAISER DE LA FÉE

IN 1927 Ida Rubinstein commissioned Igor Stravinsky to compose a ballet for her company. It was to be in the spirit of the Tchaikovsky-Petipa ballets. Stravinsky, free to choose his subject, selected Hans Christian Andersen's story *The Ice Maiden,* which seemed to Stravinsky to have an allegorical significance. Drawing a parallel to the Ice Maiden's magic kiss, which bewitches the boy in the story from birth, he says: "This subject seemed to me to be particularly appropriate as an allegory, the muse having similarly branded Tchaikovsky with her fatal kiss, and the magic imprint has made itself felt in all the musical creations of this great artist."

As usual, Stravinsky had a number of ideas as to how he wished the ballet to be produced: "I pictured all the fantastic roles as danced in white ballet skirts, and the rustic scenes as taking place in a Swiss landscape, with some of the performers dressed in the manner of early tourists and mingling with the friendly villagers in good old theatrical tradition."

The choreography, by Bronislava Nijinska, failed to meet with Stravinsky's approval, but it was too late for changes to be made, even if she had been willing, when Stravinsky arrived in Paris to conduct the first performance at the Opéra on November 27, 1928. After five performances the ballet was dropped from the repertoire of the Rubinstein Ballet. In 1932 Nijinska revived *Le Baiser de la Fée* at the Teatro Colón, in Buenos Aires.

Stravinsky made an orchestral suite from the score of *Le Baiser de la Fée* which occasionally appears on concert programs.

In 1935 *Le Baiser de la Fée* was produced with new choreography by Frederick Ashton and décor by Sophie Fedorovitch. It was first performed by the Sadler's Wells Ballet at the Sadler's Wells Theatre, London, in November 1935. The cast included Margot Fonteyn (Bride), Pearl Argyle (Fairy), and Harold Turner (Young Man). This production would have been at least partially approved by the composer, as photographs of the scene in the mill show the feminine members of the cast clad in the short classical tutu.

Le Baiser de la Fée was performed for the first time in America by the American Ballet on April 27, 1937 at the Metropolitan Opera House, New York. There was new choreography by George Balanchine, and the décor and costumes were by Alice Halicka. The cast included the following:

THE GIRL	*Giselle Caccialanza*	THE FAIRY	*Kathryn Mullowney*
HER FIANCÉ	*William Dollar*	THE MOTHER	*Annabelle Lyon*

◇◇◇◇◇◇◇◇◇◇◇◇◇◇◇◇

The curtain rose on a snowy landscape in which a mother, clasping her baby in her arms, is overtaken by a snowstorm. As she lies dying of cold and exposure, the Ice Maiden bends over her. Taking the baby in her arms, she kisses him. She vanishes at the approach of a rescue party from a near-by village. The baby is carried to safety by the men.

Twenty years have elapsed. The baby whom the Ice Maiden kissed, grown to manhood, is celebrating his betrothal to a girl of the village, the daughter of the miller. A fete is in progress, the merriment being accompanied by the music of a brass band. A mysterious woman, unknown to the villagers, appears. She reads the palms of several by-standers, including that of the young man, who is strangely attracted to her. He is puzzled, acting as though he were trying to remember something that eludes him.

The scene changes to the interior of the mill, where the miller's daughter, surrounded by her friends, is dressing for her wedding. As her Fiancé approaches, the bridesmaids lead her out of the room. While the young man waits alone for her coming, a veiled figure appears. He advances eagerly, lifts the veil, and discovers to his amazement that it is the strange woman to whom he was drawn at the village fete. She is now transformed into a radiant figure, glittering with icy jewels. It is the Ice Maiden, come to claim the boy she had made her own with a kiss twenty years before. Forgetting his bride, he follows her, the walls of the mill opening to allow their passage.

The young man struggles to climb a dizzy height, at the summit of which he sees the shining apparition of the Ice Maiden.

Balanchine's choreography for this revival of *Le Baiser de la Fée,* was a tribute to the ballets of the classic period. The opening scene,

with its snowflake ballet patterned after the one in *The Nutcracker;*
the gay village fete; the scene in the mill, with its corps de ballet of
bridesmaids; and the spectacular ending would not have been inappropriate (with the scale enlarged) for a ballet performed at the
Marinsky Theater in the 1890's. The beautifully arranged ensembles,
the several *pas de deux* and solos, with only a slight spicing of contemporary complexities, testified to Balanchine's love for and profound knowledge of the classical style.[1] There was a particularly
charming *pas de deux* in the first scene, for the Ice Maiden and her
attendant shadow, dressed in identical costumes, one icily glittering
white, the other somber black.

Kathryn Mullowney was outstanding in the role of the Fairy. Her
young elegance of line and flair for the dramatic aspects of the role
were memorable. Other members of the cast displayed a poise and
competence that previous performances had scarcely promised.

It is difficult to understand why *Le Baiser de la Fée* was not performed during the opera season. It would have made a far more
acceptable curtain-raiser for the two Strauss operas in the repertoire
of the 1937-8 Metropolitan season than *Gianni Schicchi* (sung in an
inept English translation) or that dreary duo *Cavalleria Rusticana*
and *Pagliacci*. It would have made many more friends for ballet
among opera subscribers than the difficult *Apollon Musagète*. This
omission is probably due to managerial unwillingness to pay for the
orchestra rehearsals necessary to learn two new Stravinsky scores.

The score of *Le Baiser de la Fée,* as befits a tribute to Tchaikovsky,
draws heavily on his work for inspiration. A barcarolle, a nocturne,
and a humoresque (all piano pieces) were detected by one critic. The
finale was an arrangement of "None but the Lonely Heart." The first
scene, though no one pointed it out, sounded uncommonly like a
Stravinsky-eye view of the Snowflake Ballet from *The Nutcracker*.
It is more than likely that the general public enjoyed the score more
than the critics.

The American Ballet gave two performances of this charming
work, and that seemed to be the end of it until it was revived by the
Ballet Russe de Monte Carlo. The first performance of this revival

[1] Owing to the passage of time, choreographic details emerge only hazily. At one
point one of the ballerinas (was it the Bride?) crossed the stage in a series of
brisés. A lovely moment in a *pas de deux* occurred when the girl executing a *pas de
bourée* was slowly lifted in a diagonal, still continuing the *bourées*. It gave an
exquisite floating effect.

took place at the Metropolitan Opera House, New York, on April 10, 1940, with the following cast:

THE FAIRY	*Mia Slavenska*	HER FRIEND	*Nathalie Krassovska*
HER SHADOW	*Milada Mladova*	THE BRIDEGROOM	*André Eglevsky*
THE BRIDE	*Alexandra Danilova*	HIS MOTHER	*Nini Theilade*

❖❖❖❖❖❖❖❖❖❖❖❖❖❖❖

The program for this production was considerably more informative than the one given out at the première in 1937. *Le Baiser de la Fée* was designated a "ballet-allegory in four scenes, by Igor Stravinsky, inspired by the music of Tchaikovsky, based on the tale *The Virgin of the Lake*, by Hans Christian Andersen."[2]

This production used Alice Halicka's charming décor and costumes, originally designed for the American Ballet. They may or may not have pleased Stravinsky, but undoubtedly delighted the audience. The female soloists were costumed in an adaptation of the romantic tutu *à la* Taglioni, the corps de ballet in stylized peasant costumes. The settings had a theatrical reference to the Swiss locale of the story. The final setting, something between storm-tossed waves seen from an airplane and a mountain in a high wind, was later simplified, possibly to prevent the performer of the Bridegroom's role from succumbing to premature old age. The slow striving upward on the waving net was undeniably effective, but unnecessarily hard on the dancer who had to do the climbing. A ramp and suitable dramatic pantomime were substituted shortly after the first performance.

Alexandra Danilova made an exquisite Bride. Those who had seen the American Ballet's Kathryn Mullowney found Mia Slavenska a heavy and overdramatic Fairy. Nathalie Krassovska lacked the technique for the vertiginous turns performed so brilliantly by Leda Anchutina (unnamed on the American Ballet program). André Eglevsky and Frederic Franklin, performing at various times as the Bridegroom, gave fine interpretations of a role demanding both dramatic and technical ability.

Le Baiser de la Fée, after 1942 absent from the New York stage, was revived there in the spring of 1946 by the Monte Carlo Ballet.

[2] Stravinsky calls this story *The Ice Maiden.*

BALLET IMPERIAL
DANSES CONCERTANTES
WALTZ ACADEMY
(*Balanchine*)

BALLET has gone through many stages since Fokine's assault on the rigid classical formula opened the way to the new romanticism. In the hands of choreographers deficient in taste this freedom frequently oscillated between an overripe lushness and triviality. Ballet became subject to new influences, with the trend toward psychological drama. Conservative ballet-lovers often felt that the art of dancing was beginning to disappear in the shuffle and watched with dismay while outstanding dancers and choreographers turned their talents to the presentation of wordless plays. Fortunately, a revival of interest in the classics has arisen and with it a new type of neo-classic ballet, requiring a high standard of execution from dancers. The demise of dancing, announced by die-hard critics every time a new tendency is observed, appears to be averted for the time being. The prophet of the new dispensation is George Balanchine, who began his career in the Imperial School of Ballet in St. Petersburg in 1914. His stay in the school was interrupted by the stormy period of the Revolution, which, though it resulted in a tremendous social upheaval, had little or no effect on the ideology of the school, where the strict pre-Fokine approach to ballet was the rule. After Balanchine's graduation he attempted to stage ballets in a free style, using a group of young dancers who shared his desire for wider horizons. He succeeded in arranging a single performance, but the advanced tendencies that his choreography displayed frightened his conservative seniors in the hierarchy of the State Theater, and he was prevented from making further experiments. A few years later, together with Alexandra Danilova and Tamara Gevergeva,[1] he left Russia. After various adventures the little company joined the Diaghilev Ballet.

[1] Better known as Tamara Geva—member of the *Chauve-Souris* company, and later star of *On Your Toes,* a musical for which Balanchine arranged the dance routines.

Balanchine followed Nijinska as choreographer for the Diaghilev company, arranging a number of ballets, only one of which has reached America—*Apollon Musagète,* originally produced by Balanchine in 1928, revived in 1937 for the American Ballet, and later in 1943 for Ballet Theatre. After the death of Diaghilev, in 1929, the company scattered, and for a period of several years there seemed to be an end of ballet except as an adjunct to opera. However, in England [2] and on the Continent love of ballet as Diaghilev had presented it was too strongly rooted to die away, and in 1932, when René Blum and Colonel W. de Basil organized a ballet company, Balanchine produced two ballets, *Cotillon* and *La Concurrence,* both exploiting the personality and individual technique of the young Toumanova. Later Balanchine seceded from this group to form a new company, Les Ballets 1933. Of the repertoire of this company, *Errante, Songes,* and *Mozartiana* were revived by the choreographer for the American Ballet, founded by Lincoln Kirstein and Edward Warburg and directed by Balanchine, who had been invited to the United States to guide the new venture.

Balanchine's choreography passed through many stages before it achieved the ideal of austere classicism that is its latest and most interesting manifestation. Intimations of the new approach were to be found in *Serenade,* produced in 1934. This, performed to Tchaikovsky's Serenade for String Orchestra, opus 48, is as abstract as any ballet danced to such moody and expressive music could be. Its real quality was not immediately evident; the coltish charm of the young company being better adapted to the gay romping of *Alma Mater* (1934) and *The Bat* (1936). Later, when *Serenade* was revived for the Monte Carlo Ballet, although the lines of their corps de ballet may not have been so precise as those of the young company, the performance of Alexandra Danilova was a revelation. Still later, when the role passed to an inferior dancer, *Serenade* again lost its luster.

Meanwhile Balanchine had reverted to the tangled complexities of

[2] England made a modest beginning toward a national ballet in 1931. In spite of seasons in London by the more glamorous Russian companies, the Sadler's Wells Ballet has become a permanent feature of the theatrical scene, triumphantly surviving blitz, buzz bomb, and the loss of male dancers to the armed forces. It offers a repertoire of ballets by English choreographers, and classic revivals. One of its outstanding assets is a training school from which it can draw a constant supply of young dancers.

Apollon Musagète in the opera-pantomime *Orpheus* (1936), classical
only in its imposition of a highly personal style on music about
which most of the audience had preconceived equally personal and
quite different ideas. This production, received with blank incom-
prehension by most of those who saw it, did nothing to help Balanchine to win the battle against the fusty tradition of bad ballet prevailing at the Metropolitan, whose directors in one of their periodical
spasms of bad conscience had engaged the American Ballet as the
official opera-ballet.

After the dissolution of the American Ballet, whose memorable
Stravinsky festival in 1937 was the climax of its career, Balanchine
arranged dance routines for the movies and the commercial theater.
In 1941 he returned to the ballet field with the controversial *Balus-
trade,* arranged for the Original Ballet Russe to Stravinsky's Violin
Concerto. The audience was distracted from the choreography by
the freakish costumes designed by Pavel Tchelitchew.[3] Not even the
presence of Stravinsky as guest conductor prevented a hostile demonstration from a section of the spectators. Whether this was caused by
eccentricities of choreography or costume it is difficult to say. Certainly, only members of the *avant-garde* were pleased by the production. The last presentation, on January 26, 1941, was followed by the
liveliest exhibition of disapproval to greet a theatrical performance
in a decade. Those members of the audience who disliked the ballet
but felt that the dancers were not to blame for what they were called
upon to do or wear started a counter demonstration. The rise of the
curtain on *Aurora's Wedding* finally calmed the minor war. At that
moment it would have taken a very perspicacious prophet indeed to
foresee in Balanchine the savior of the art of the dance.

When Lincoln Kirstein organized a new American Ballet in 1941,
to tour South America as one of the many ambassadors of North
American culture to the neighboring continent, Balanchine arranged
for the repertoire two ballets, *Concerto Barocco* and *Ballet Imperial,*
both of which have been revived with great success by the Monte
Carlo company.

The first of these is danced to the Concerto for two violins and
orchestra by Bach. The original décor and costumes by Eugène

---

[3] Irving Kolodin, reviewing the performance in the *Sun,* said: "The dancers
appear in costumes that look vaguely like what a bat might wear if dressed by
Hattie Carnegie."

Berman were not available for the revival by the Monte Carlo Ballet on September 9, 1945 at the City Center of Music and Drama. It is idle to say that they were not missed, but the elegance and clarity of the choreographic line triumphed over the austerity of the plain backdrop and black practice costumes of the dancers. The admirable cast was headed by Marie-Jeanne (in the role that she created in 1941), Patricia Wilde, and Nicolas Magallanes. The exquisite precision of the corps de ballet was reminiscent of the early days of Ballet Theatre. *Concerto Barocco* achieves an abstract musicality that exactly parallels the line of the concerto. There is no story or situation, overt or implied, the ballet being quite simply the music made visible.

Ballet Imperial, with costumes and scenery by Mstislav Doboujinsky, danced to Tchaikovsky's Second Piano Concerto in G major, was originally designed to replace *Swan Lake* and *Aurora's Wedding* in the repertoire of the American Ballet. By no means a slavish imitation of a Tchaikovsky-Petipa work, it evokes the atmosphere of the great period of the classic ballet, much as *Les Sylphides* was a tribute to the romanticism of *La Sylphide* and *Giselle*. Without an actual plot, there is a love story suggested by the pantomime of the prima ballerina and her cavalier. At least two styles of classical dancing are employed: the brilliance and bravura of the prima ballerina, whose archetypes were the Auroras and Odiles of the nineteenth-century ballets, and the soft lyricism of the second ballerina, echoing the Lilac Fairy. Both of these roles demand a high degree of technical achievement from their executants. *Ballet Imperial* was one of the most successful presentations on the South American tour, audiences everywhere hailing its neo-classicism with delight. It also served the admirable purpose of reminding music-lovers that there was a piano concerto by Tchaikovsky that had not yet been cheapened by the juke-box.

Ballet Imperial was revived by the New Opera Company at the Broadway Theater in 1942, with Mary Ellen Moylan as the prima ballerina, and William Dollar in his original role. This production, in spite of Dollar's spectacular performance, had an amateurish air, the corps de ballet being not only feeble in execution but lacking in style.

On February 20, 1945 *Ballet Imperial* was revived by the Monte Carlo Ballet with Mary Ellen Moylan, Maria Tallchief, and Nicolas

Magallanes. Mary Ellen Moylan had gained in authority and stage presence, and Maria Tallchief was wholly admirable in the secondary role. The corps de ballet performed with expertness their complicated patterns, displaying a sense of the period that revealed new charms in this delightful reminiscence of the vanished grandeur of the true golden age of ballet. Only Magallanes, a competent enough dancer technically, lacked the personality and stature of the *danseur noble*. One longed for Youskevitch in the role. Since Mary Ellen Moylan has left the Monte Carlo Ballet, Nathalie Krassovska has replaced her—a substitution disastrous to the ballet, the dancer being hopelessly lacking in the style and technique necessary for a bravura performance. *Ballet Imperial* is much too fine to be allowed to suffer from miscasting in a company that has so many young dancers of ability.

The most recent of the Balanchine ballets to glorify the art of dancing is the enchanting *Danses Concertantes,* created for the Monte Carlo Ballet to an original score by Stravinsky, with décor and costumes by Eugène Berman. It is an admirable display piece, exploiting Alexandra Danilova's delicious sparkle and Frederic Franklin's extrovert charm. They are supported by an ensemble of soloists, a phrase that may seem to carry a contradiction, but is actually the only accurate description of corps de ballet that includes the foremost dancers of the company. The group makes its entrance by threes in front of an inner curtain, followed by Franklin, then Danilova, whose gay flirtation set the mood of the ballet. As the inner curtain rises, the ensemble is seen arranged symmetrically, their colorful costumes taking on an added brilliance against the charcoal backdrop. The ballet is a series of *pas de trois,* varied by the shifting patterns of the groups, solo variations, and a *pas de deux* for the principals. The ballet ends when the entire company runs forward and bows to the audience as the curtain falls behind them. The mood and some of the movements of the ballet carry an intimation of the *commedia dell' arte,* but it is only a faint flavor, the choreographic pattern following the Stravinsky rhythms with admirable fidelity. One of the critics, with a notable lack of perception, complained that *Danses Concertantes* had an aura of 1925 about it. In view of the fact that ballet was noticeably absent from the New York scene in 1925, and such local manifestations of the dance as were visible were extremely fancy and full of plot, one wonders just what he was driving at.

Balanchine's neo-classic ballets can be performed only by dancers with a finished technique. Sloppy execution of steps, ragged lines, and an obtuse approach to style cannot exist in the face of the demands made on the dancers. As long as ballets like *Concerto Barocco, Ballet Imperial,* and *Danses Concertantes* remain in the repertoire of a company, they will be a source of inspiration and a challenge to serious and talented dancers, and a means of screening out the incompetent performers who would probably be happier in the commercial theater.

Balanchine has also created a ballet for Ballet Theatre: *Waltz Academy,* first seen in New York at the Metropolitan Opera House on October 11, 1944. This was termed on the program "a series of waltz variations by George Balanchine to an original composition by Vittorio Rieti." The scenery was designed by Oliver Smith, and the costumes by Alvin Colt.

Waltz Academy is an amiable trifle that gives a highly picturesque and romantic view of a ballet class. It has a charm that occasionally borders perilously on the cute, though that undesirable quality is not present in the choreographic patterns, but in the byplay that interrupts them. The action of the ballet begins when the curtain rises revealing a setting that recalls the much photographed domed rehearsal room at the Paris Opéra. The dancers drift in and take their places at the *barre,* the inevitable late comer rushing in at the last moment. They go through the *pliés;* then a series of dances begin: a *pas de six,* a *pas de quatre,* two *pas de trois,* a *pas de deux,* and a final ensemble. Of these numbers, the most interesting are the two *pas de trois*: the first, for two girls and a boy (Miriam Golden, Diana Adams, and John Kriza), includes an amusing burlesque of the arm weavings that characterized Balanchine's tangled period; the second (Nora Kaye, John Taras, and Rex Cooper) contains some brilliant lifts and a bravura solo for the girl. The *pas de deux* has many supported poses (most of them taken with a *plié*) and several daring lifts, which Nana Gollner and Paul Petroff performed with such relaxed ease that their difficulties never became apparent. *Waltz Academy* had a certain charm, but was handicapped by the music, whose hollow and tinny rhythms did not bear repeated hearings.

Balanchine's work for Ballet Theatre has been less happy than for the Monte Carlo Ballet. The production of the hopelessly dated *Errante* in 1943 was a reminder of a period of striving and yearning to music over which a veil of kindly oblivion should be drawn. *Apollon Musagète,* slated for revival in 1945, is a much finer work, but its *terre-à-terre* entanglements do not have the charm of the two revivals and the original creation for the Monte Carlo Ballet.

Balanchine has a following among aspiring choreographers, who, fortunately, have been influenced by his most recent trend. Todd Bolender's charming, though pretentiously named *Commedia Balletica* (called more suitably by the choreographer *Musical Chairs*) was produced by the Monte Carlo Ballet on September 22, 1945. The music was a portion of Stravinsky's *Pulcinella* suite, and the décor and costumes were by Robert Davison. John Martin's review called it "a kind of youthful echo of 'Danses Concertantes.' But in spite of this obvious debt . . . the choreography has its own skill, its own humor and strong evidence of its own latent style. Toward the end . . . it breaks away considerably from influences and speaks with an authentic voice."

An adequate appraisal of the Balanchine ballets can only be made in terms of musical analysis for which no one but a more than competent musician is qualified; it is the subject for a work that many admirers of Balanchine hope will be written while the ballets are still in active performance, fresh from the choreographer's hand.

LE BEAU DANUBE

Le Beau Danube (The Beautiful Danube): character-ballet; music by Johann Strauss, arranged and orchestrated by Roger Desormière; book and choreography by Léonide Massine; scenery by Vladimir Polunin, after Constantin Guys; costumes by Count Etienne de Beaumont.

L*E BEAU DANUBE,* a ballet in two acts, was presented during a season organized in Paris in the spring of 1924 by Count Etienne de Beaumont. A revised one-act version was produced for Colonel W. de Basil's Ballet Russe, the first performance taking place in Monte Carlo at the Théâtre de Monte Carlo on April 5, 1933. The opening program of this company at the St. James Theater, New York, on December 22, 1933, included *Le Beau Danube* along with *Les Présages* and *La Concurrence.* Alexandra Danilova and Nina Tarakhanova alternated as the Street Dancer and Tatiana Riabouchinska and Tamara Toumanova as the Daughter. The following cast[1] is taken from a program dated October 20, 1935:

THE STREET DANCER	THE ATHLETE *Edouard Borovansky*
Alexandra Danilova	THE MANAGER *Jean Hoyer*
THE DAUGHTER	THE MOTHER *Anna Adrianova*
Tatiana Riabouchinska	THE FATHER *Boris Belsky*
THE FIRST HAND *Irina Baronova*	THE ARTIST *Alexis Kosloff*
THE HUSSAR *Léonide Massine*	THE GARDENER *Jean Hoyer*
THE KING OF THE DANDIES	
David Lichine	

Modistes, Needlewomen, Ladies of the Town, Salesmen, Dandies

❖❖❖❖❖❖❖❖❖❖❖❖❖❖❖

The curtain rises on a corner of a public garden in Vienna. The Gardener is sweeping the paths, making everything tidy against the coming of the holiday throng. Impatiently he drives an Artist out of his way, forcing the youth to take his easel elsewhere. People begin to gather: a bourgeois family (Father, Mother, and two Daughters), girls skipping rope, seamstresses, young men in attendance. The

---

[1] This with one exception was the ideal cast for *Le Beau Danube.* David Lichine was not equal to Yurek Shabelevsky as the King of the Dandies.

First Hand, pert and pretty, attracts the attention of the Artist, who has returned to the scene, this time with a sketching pad instead of the easel. He asks her permission to draw her portrait, which she allows him to do, though not without a great deal of advice and many suggestions. This project is brought to an abrupt conclusion by the arrival of the King of the Dandies. The First Hand finds this dashing fellow more to her taste than the Artist, whom she promptly abandons for the newcomer.

The Hussar enters with a military stride. He joins the family group, paying special attention to the elder of the two daughters. They dance together and afterwards stroll out of sight.

The Manager of a trio of street entertainers comes in, distributing handbills. With a flourish he introduces the Dancer, who performs for the delighted crowd. At first she dances alone. As a climax to her turn she is joined by the Athlete, who combines weight-lifting with adagio, and the Manager, who can dance as well as "bark."

The Hussar and the Daughter return from their walk. The Dancer recognizes the Hussar as an old flame. She stages a jealous scene. The Daughter, unused to this sort of thing, faints. She is tenderly cared for and taken away by her indignant family. The Dancer, not to be outdone, also collapses into a handy chair. The Manager tries to revive her by blowing on her. The bystanders, who have shown much interest in this little drama, begin to leave, making scornful gestures at the Hussar, who stands still and disdains to answer them. The Hussar and the Dancer are left alone. He feels a stirring of his former interest in her and holds out his arms. She goes to him and they dance together, at first slowly and then with mounting excitement and speed. Suddenly the Daughter, having eluded her family, comes back to claim her lover. She faces the Dancer, braving her abuse. The Hussar, touched by the young girl's courage and devotion, repudiates the Dancer, who, knowing that she has lost, leaves with a gesture which plainly indicates that there are better fish in the sea. The girl's family enters looking for her. The Daughter and the Hussar ask for the Father's approval of their engagement. He refuses, but weakens when the younger sister intercedes.

The ballet ends with the return of the crowd, who celebrate the fortunate termination of the incident. Even the Dancer, forgetting her displeasure, enters into the gaiety.

Le Beau Danube is the very essence of youth, gaiety, and the glamour of a romantic uniform. It evokes nostalgia for a Vienna that never existed except in some exile's dream. It is one of the most enchanting ballets in the repertoire.

A frequently heard criticism of contemporary ballet is that it lacks dancing. No one can ever level this censure at *Le Beau Danube*. There are very few moments in it when there is no dancing. The Gardener dances as he sweeps; the children dance as they skip; the holiday crowd dances as it flirts. The dancing is briefly interrupted for two short dramatic scenes. The curtain descends as the dancers whirl madly, sending the audience home (*Le Beau Danube* should always conclude any program on which it appears) with uplifted hearts and the firm conviction that dancing is the easiest accomplishment in the world to acquire.

Le Beau Danube, abounding in joyous dance patterns, possesses in addition a logical and uncluttered plot. The Street Dancer with her beautifully stylized vulgarity, the dashing Hussar, the *jeune fille,* the First Hand, and the King of the Dandies are all recognizable human beings and dance in characteristic and individual styles.

Ballet-lovers fortunate enough to have seen *Le Beau Danube* with the cast given above have a rare theatrical memory to cherish. The enchanting Street Dancer of Danilova is still to be seen, but how much more brightly it shone in a setting worthy of it! Irina Baronova in the small role of the First Hand contributed a charming bit of pantomime in her scene with the Artist. In the finale she executed a dazzling series of *fouettés en tournant* which seemed a spontaneous expression of gaiety rather than a technical tour de force. Tatiana Riabouchinska was the personification of young girlhood. Her two dances with Massine might have been the choreographic high lights of the ballet if the equally thrilling and stylistically different *pas de deux* of Massine and Danilova could be forgotten. In the Hussar, Massine had one of those characteristic roles that are the despair of dancers who have to follow him in them. Shabelevsky's crisp elegance was admirable in the King of the Dandies.

The score, an arrangement of Strauss melodies drawn from many sources, made a sparing and effective use of the waltz, the *Blue Danube* being used for the *pas de deux* by the Street Dancer and the Hussar. Waltz time becomes monotonous if used to excess. Roger

Desormière avoided this by varying his waltzes with lively polkas and marches.

The décor of *Le Beau Danube* was delightful. The colors ranged from creamy white through beige to brown, the men's green coats, the girls' petunia petticoats, and the Street Dancer's wine-colored costume providing the perfect contrast. When, as a result of litigation arising from dissension in the company, the settings and costumes became the property of Colonel W. de Basil and the choreography that of Massine,[2] subsequent performances lost their luster. The new costumes were graceless and the colors unpleasant. The division in the company sent the dancers into different camps. Only Danilova and Massine retained their roles, the substitutes for Riabouchinska, Baronova, and Shabelevsky being far inferior to their predecessors. It is possible that newcomers to ballet who have not seen the original cast perform in the original setting may find current performances of *Le Beau Danube* exhilarating. Danilova is still unrivaled as the Street Dancer. Older members of the audience find this enchanting performance a jewel in an inferior setting.

It is said that Massine composed *Le Beau Danube* as a relaxation after his strenuous labors with *Le Sacre du Printemps*. It has outlasted the titanic Stravinsky work by many years.

[2] This decision matched the more famous one by King Solomon.

BILLY THE KID

Character-ballet in one act; music by Aaron Copland; choreography by Eugene Loring; scenery and costumes by Jared French.

BILLY THE KID was first performed by the Ballet Caravan in October 1938 in Chicago. As far as may be ascertained, the first presentation of *Billy the Kid* in New York took place at the Martin Beck Theater on May 24, 1939, in a short season in which Ballet Caravan and the American Lyric Theatre joined forces to present opera and ballet. The cast was as follows:

BILLY THE KID	*Eugene Loring*	ALIAS	*Todd Bolender*
HIS MOTHER	*Marie-Jeanne*	DANCE-HALL GIRLS	*Anne Campbell,*
PAT GARRETT, his friend			*Mary Heater, Lorna London*
	Lew Christensen		

Billy the Kid was included in the repertoire of Ballet Caravan during its appearance in a Holiday Dance Festival at the St. James Theater, New York, during Christmas week of 1939. There were two changes in cast: Michael Kidd (Billy) and Alicia Alonso (Mother). In neither Ballet Caravan program was the fact made clear that the dancer who impersonated Billy's Mother also appeared as the Mexican Sweetheart.

Ballet Theatre revived *Billy the Kid,* performing it for the first time in New York at the Majestic Theater on February 13, 1941, with Eugene Loring and Alicia Alonso. The other soloists were Richard Reed (Pat Garrett), David Nillo (Alias), and Miriam Golden, Mimi Gomber, and Maria Karnilova (Dance-Hall Girls). The Copland score, played in a two-piano version by Ballet Caravan, was orchestrated by the composer for Ballet Theatre. The program also indicated that Alicia Alonso was performing a dual role.

As the curtain ascends on *Billy the Kid,* Pat Garrett is seen advancing into the level rays of the setting sun. He leads the "March" of the pioneers. A throng of frontiersmen and their women are seen. Their movements are indicative of the laboriousness of the push to the West and the alertness and driving urge of the pioneers.

They pass and the lights gradually come up on the "Street Scene." There is a motley throng—cowboys, prospectors, Indians, ranch women and dance-hall girls. A rodeo takes place, the riding and roping being vigorously pantomimed. As the rodeo concludes, the cowboys become conscious of the dance-hall girls. Billy and his Mother enter just as a quarrel breaks out among the cowboys. To the consternation of all, a shot goes wild and kills Billy's Mother. Pat Garrett carries her away, returning in time to see Billy stab Alias, the killer, in the back. This method of getting an enemy is in contravention of Western frontier ethics. Pat, expostulating with Billy sympathetically enough, is rudely shoved aside as Billy runs from the scene. The sobered people walk in the evening, discussing the violent occurrence. The hush is briefly disturbed by the passage of the Cowboy in Red, who rides by on some mysterious errand and then retraces his path in the direction from which he entered. One by one the people leave the scene.

Without a pause, the scene drifts into "Billy's Soliloquy." Alone, he is practicing his card-shuffling technique. Alias (as a land agent) enters and Billy invites him to a game. He distracts Alias's attention by throwing a card into the air. For a second, Alias's glance follows the flight of the card. Turning back to the game, he discovers Billy cheating. He challenges Billy's methods and is shot.

A campfire lights the "Card Game on the Desert," in which Pat Garrett, Billy, and the Cowboy in Red are engaged. Two girls ride up and join the game. Pat accuses Billy of cheating. After some high words Pat rides away into the darkness. As light begins to appear in the sky, the sound of an approaching posse is heard. Billy and his gang, becoming uneasy, start shooting, and the "Gun Battle" begins. In a short time Billy and his gang are surrounded. The gang is killed and Billy is taken prisoner, but not before he has killed Alias (as a sheriff). Billy is taken off to jail, the corpses are removed from sight, and the "Macabre Dance" begins. At the conclusion of the dance Billy's Mexican Sweetheart enters, looking for him. She calls him. Receiving no answer, she asks the cowboys where he may be found. Scornfully they ignore her.

In the "Jail Scene" Billy escapes by a trick, killing Alias (as jailer).

Billy finds his way to the hide-out of his Mexican Sweetheart in the "Desert" with the aid of Alias (as an Indian guide). A posse searching for him rides quickly by, failing to see him in the darkness. Billy, shedding some encumbering garments, disposes himself to rest. While he sleeps, the Mexican Sweetheart appears. For a while she holds his interest. Billy's preoccupation with the danger of his situation brings out his coldness and egotism. He has no thought to spare for anyone but himself. Rebuffed, the girl goes away. Billy sleeps again. The Indian Guide returns bringing Pat Garrett to Billy's hiding-place. Disturbed, Billy moves quietly to investigate. He calls: *"Quién es?"* ("Who is it?") into the silence. Receiving no answer, he shrugs his fear away and lights a cigarette. Pat Garrett fires and "Billy's Death" occurs.

Now the scene changes to the "Pietà." Groups of mourning Mexican women pass by in procession.

The ballet ends with the "Closing March" of the pioneers led by Pat Garrett.

The story of *Billy the Kid* is based on the life of William Bonney, one of the more vivid desperadoes of the American frontier. His character was not unlike that of a movie gangster of the George Raft type—not devoid of personal charm and social grace, but utterly cold and cruel. Lincoln Kirstein is said to be responsible for the plot of the ballet, although he is credited only as producer on Ballet Theatre's program and not mentioned at all on Ballet Caravan's. He explains the treatment of the story in his *Blast at Ballet*: "Instead of taking a picturesque cowboy legend and making it the tragedy of an individualistic, romantic desperado, *à la* early 'Western' serial movies . . . which would have been the obvious thing to do, we saw the Kid's life as only a fragmentary, if symbolic, incident in the expansion of our vast frontier." It is possible that *Billy the Kid* might have been kept down to earth without resorting to the corny tricks of the Western serial. There are times when the effort to make the ballet symbolic also renders it meaningless, unless the plot has been carefully explained in advance. Symbolism in ballet should be self-explanatory. Any idea stated in terms of gesture and music should be clear enough to be understood in those terms. *Billy the Kid,* seen for the first time, appears to be a string of episodes in which one character kills another with various changes of costume and lighting, the general effect being a sort of slow whirl on a merry-go-round. This may be symbolism, but it is also rather silly, as unions of the realistic and the symbolic generally prove to be. If one can stop trying to make sense out of the plot, the ballet becomes a series of fascinating vignettes of frontier life.

Choreographically *Billy the Kid* has many subtleties. When Pat Garrett opens the "March" at the beginning of the ballet, his theme is a stylized version of work movements—driving a wagon, breaking a path through the wilderness. His extended hand is a friendly gesture to the Indians. His alert pose, with pistol cocked, shows readiness in the face of hostility or danger. The chain of steps that he performs is taken up by each male dancer as he enters, in the manner of polyphonic music. The procession ends with all the men performing a series of steps (pirouette, *soutenu* turn, and double *tours en l'air*) in unison, as all the musical voices come together to proclaim the original theme of a fugue.

The "Street Scene" is a montage of the activities of a frontier community, steps and movements again suggesting occupations. Prospecting, riding, and roping may be recognized. The riding and roping pantomime has been a godsend to Broadway musicals and ballets based on Western life and has been used without any acknowledgment to Eugene Loring. Does this indicate that the sequence has attained the status of a classic to be quoted freely as one quotes Hamlet? The slow, subtly self-advertising walk of the dance-hall girls has also been used effectively by other choreographers, any admission of source being conspicuously lacking. After the catastrophe in this episode, the dancers walk about the scene, each in his own pattern, the whole having the deceptive simplicity of a Mozart symphony.[1]

"Billy's Soliloquy" is in an ingenious adaptation of classical steps to the purposes of a modern dance drama. It includes double pirouettes which lead directly into double *tours en l'air*. The technical high light is a series of *chaîné* turns, executed with a deep *plié*, simultaneously with flashing hand movements that suggest a riffle of cards. This concludes with a series of single turns performed in place. After the murder of Alias, Billy does a large *jeté* to one side, which closes the scene. The whole variation with its tautness of execution suggests the callous and cruel personality of the bandit.

The card game is indicated in the simplest possible manner. A

---

[1] My technical adviser, a veteran of many performances of *Billy the Kid,* says that the crowd scene in *Petrouchka* is child's play to this episode.

baby spot in the footlights for the campfire and slightly stylized gestures evoke the scene with admirable economy. The activities of the posse have a fugal pattern, which comes together at the conclusion of the fight when the dancers form a double diagonal line. Here the movements are an almost literal translation into dance of the act of firing a gun. The "Macabre Dance" which follows is a stylistic treatment of authentic square-dance steps—the dos-à-dos and others may be recognized.

The role of the Mexican Sweetheart is almost purely classical, with an occasional distant reference to Mexican dance steps. The *pas de deux* owes a little to Balanchine's influence. This *pas de deux* has a strange dreamlike quality. It is never made quite clear whether the girl's entrance in this scene is an actual occurrence or is merely a fantasy. The ineffectual conclusion—almost a fade-out—does lend itself to the idea that it is a dream and not a reality.

From the time that the Indian Guide makes his second exit until the shot is fired the action is unaccompanied by music. The stalking of Pat and Billy and the lighting of the cigarette take place in a profound silence broken only by Billy's call into the night (one of the very few effective uses of the human voice in ballet). The orchestra crashes thrillingly just as Pat fires his gun. The whole scene achieves a high degree of dramatic intensity. The closing march brings the ballet back to its point of departure.

There have been a number of fine interpretations of Billy's role, by Eugene Loring, Michael Kidd, Charles Dickson, and Ian Gibson. Of these, Ian Gibson's had a tautness and crispness of delineation, as well as a technical excellence that cleared up much that had been obscure or merely sketched by the others. It may be argued that Eugene Loring gave the best interpretation of a role of which he was not only the creator but the choreographer. Let it be said, however, that composers are not always the best conductors of their own works.

The Mexican Sweetheart has been danced by Marie-Jeanne, Alicia Alonso, Annabelle Lyon, and Janet Reed. This is not a very rewarding role for the ballerina, as it is completely overshadowed by the male members of the cast. Lew Christensen's Pat Garrett was the perfect cowboy sheriff, his admirable physique and relaxed movement making him ideal in the part. Richard Reed made the most of this part, which he performed for Ballet Theatre's production of

Billy the Kid, although it was far removed from his more usual romantic roles.

The most recent revival of *Billy the Kid* under Eugene Loring's direction was given by Dance Players at the National Theater, New York, on April 21, 1942. The cast included Eugene Loring (Billy), Lew Christensen (Pat Garrett), and Bobbie Howell (Mother and Sweetheart). Bobbie Howell was miscast, her technical equipment being completely unequal to the choreographic demands of the role.

Billy the Kid, in spite of certain mannered weaknesses, is undeniably the finest ballet up to date on an American theme. Jared French's simple setting evokes the spaciousness and grandeur of the West. Aaron Copland's superb score is not only an oustanding contribution to American music, but extraordinarily fine theater music. Eugene Loring in subsequent works has been marking time and repeating himself. *Billy the Kid* was infinitely more than promising, it was a mature work of art. Possibly if Loring is given further opportunities to create under conditions similar to those which resulted in this work, something fine may be presented for the admiration of the ballet public. In the meantime this large group would gladly settle for the privilege of welcoming *Billy the Kid* back to the repertoire.

BLUEBEARD

Ballet in two prologues, four acts, and three interludes, by Michel Fokine, after the opéra bouffe by Meilhac and Halévy; music by Jacques Offenbach, arranged by Antal Dorati; choreography by Michel Fokine; scenery and costumes by Marcel Vertès.

BLUEBEARD was first produced by Ballet Theatre at the Palacio de Bellas Artes, Mexico City, on October 27, 1941. The United States première took place at the Forty-fourth Street Theater, New York, on November 12, 1941. The cast was as follows:

KING BOBICHE	*Antony Tudor*	The Queen's Lovers:		
COUNT OSCAR	*Borislav Runanine*	ALVAREZ	)(	*Dimitri Romanoff*
BARON BLUEBEARD	*Anton Dolin*	ARMANDO	)(	*Donald Saddler*
ALCHEMIST POPOLONI		ANGELO, a page	)(	*Annabelle Lyon*
	Simon Semenoff	ALFONSO	)(	*Jerome Robbins*
Wives of Bluebeard:		ORLANDO	)(	*Hugh Laing*
HELOISE	) (*Miriam Golden*	QUEEN CLEMENTINE		*Lucia Chase*
ELEANORE	) (*Jeannette Lauret*	FLORETTA (Princess Hermilia)		
ROSALINDE	) (*Nora Kaye*			*Alicia Markova*
BLANCHE	) (*Rosella Hightower*	PRINCE SAPPHIRE		*Ian Gibson*
ISAURE	) (*Maria Karnilova*	BOULOTTE, sixth wife of Bluebeard		
				Irina Baronova

Ladies of the Court, Gentlemen of the Court, Soldiers of the King, Bluebeard's retainers, Pages, Peasant Girls, Peasant Boys, Shepherds, Shepherdesses.

❖❖❖❖❖❖❖❖❖❖❖❖❖❖❖❖❖❖

The plot of *Bluebeard* seems fantastically complicated. Actually, two distinct stories reach a climax simultaneously, solving their common difficulties.

Prologue 1. King Bobiche, followed by his chancellor, Count Oscar, creeps stealthily to the river bank. He wishes to dispose of his unwanted new-born daughter, Princess Hermilia. The King removes a diadem from her head and hangs a pendant around her neck. Count Oscar places her in a basket, which he starts on its way down the river.

Prologue 2. Bluebeard, with the aid of the alchemist Popoloni, disposes of five wives in swift succession.

Act I. Eighteen years later. Queen Clementine has a rendezvous with her lover Alvarez. Count Oscar spies on them and calls the King. Horrified, the King summons his guards, who remove Alvarez to be hanged. Armando meets a similar fate. The Queen mourns her lonely state until the page, Angelo, runs in. Angelo dances to cheer her. Just as he is about to be rewarded with a kiss, King Bobiche rises from behind the bench on which the Queen is reclining. Again the guards are called. Count Oscar places a rope around Angelo's neck. He is led off, blowing kisses to the Queen. The King is becoming annoyed and drags the Queen into the castle. Alfonso and Orlando, two Spanish gentlemen, arrive with guitars to serenade the Queen. Just as they are about to fight a duel to settle who shall have the privilege of remaining, the Queen reappears and manages by an impartial distribution of kisses to make them both happy. They dance a gay *pas de trois* until the busybody Count Oscar sees them and again calls the King. "Two this time," he pantomimes. The familiar routine of guards and halters is repeated. The Queen retreats into the castle.

The unhappy King weeps, mopping his tears with the edge of his ermine cape. Count Oscar reminds him of the castaway Princess. Maybe she can be found and the King enjoy a peaceful family life. The King agrees. Producing the small diadem he had removed from his daughter's head before abandoning her, he gives it to Oscar and bids him begin the quest.

The Queen returns. Having lost all her lovers, she wishes to make peace. The King is furious and raises his hand to strike her—a gesture he is forced to arrest in mid-air when the Ladies and Gentlemen of the Court enter with their pages. Bowing profoundly, they bid King and Queen good-night in a stately ceremonial.

First Interlude. Count Oscar meets the procession of doomed lovers on their way to be hanged and releases Alvarez, first in line. Offered a bribe, he bridles coyly, but takes it. The rest of the lovers have no difficulty at all in persuading him to accept their contributions. Indeed, Angelo, a penniless page, is almost handed back to the hangmen. The lovers dance off joyously in one direction, Count Oscar, juggling purses, in the other.

Act II. Peasant girls and boys, shepherds and shepherdesses, are dancing a lively tarantella. Conspicuous among them is Floretta. Her beauty and grace have attracted the attention of Prince Sapphire. He gives his plumed hat and sword to his page, who provides him with a shepherd's coat and hat to hide his princely garb. Thus disguised, he partners Floretta and detains her when the others leave. While he is telling her his love, they are interrupted by Boulotte, who tries to win him away. They retreat from her importunities.

Popoloni arrives and calls the village maidens. He instructs them as to their behavior in the presence of Bluebeard, who is expected at any moment. Seated in a fantastic carriage, attended by guards, Bluebeard comes to choose a new wife. He inspects the girls, remaining unimpressed until Boulotte makes a belated entrance. She is pleased with the Baron's blue beard and strokes it affectionately. He is enchanted and asks her to be his bride. She accepts and promenades proudly, accepting the homage of the villagers. She leaps into the carriage. Followed by the crowd, they drive away, leaving Popoloni behind.

Count Oscar, searching for the lost Princess, wanders in. He consults Popoloni as to her whereabouts. Popoloni is dubious until Floretta and Prince Sapphire stroll by, absorbed in each other. He points her out to Count Oscar. As Oscar advances, Sapphire hastily retreats, not wishing to be recognized. In proof of her claim to be the Princess Hermilia, Floretta displays the pendant on the blue ribbon around her neck. In some miraculous way the pendant seems to have kept pace with the owner's growth, as it is now of the exact size to be most becoming to a young lady of eighteen. Count Oscar gives Hermilia the diadem entrusted to him by the King. He calls guards, who bring an equipage to take the Princess back to her father. As he moves to join her, she waves him away, calling Prince Sapphire to escort her.

Second Interlude. The carriages of Princess Hermilia and Bluebeard meet. When Bluebeard sees the Princess, his fickle heart is won from his bride. He gracefully yields the right of way. (This Interlude is often omitted.)

Act III. Popoloni is pursuing his alchemistical studies in a dark and dismal crypt. In the rear are six graves, one yawning ominously. Bluebeard enters and tells Popoloni to prepare a poisoned draught for Boulotte. At this moment she comes in, looking around her curiously. She sees the graves and points in horror at the open one. Bluebeard bows politely. "It's all yours, madame," he seems to say. Boulotte, frantic with fear, implores pity. Bluebeard casts her off and departs, leaving Popoloni to make final arrangements. Popoloni gives Boulotte two cups of poison, telling her to drink. She exchanges them for another potion on Popoloni's table. All are apparently lethal. She falls unconscious. Popoloni arranges her dress in a seemly fashion and calls Bluebeard to witness that the murder has been done. Bluebeard pantomimes a decent grief, but unable to restrain a burst of gaiety at the thought of being free, leaps from the scene.

When Popoloni is quite sure that Bluebeard has gone, he takes a feather and, muttering a spell, tickles Boulotte's nose. She sneezes herself back to consciousness. Bewildered, she runs to the open grave looking around questioningly. Popoloni explains that her predecessors are also alive, preserved from death by his magic arts. He calls them. To a lively air, they trip in, one by one. All engage in a *pas de sept,* with Popoloni in the place of honor.

Third Interlude. Bluebeard is haunted by the spectral presence of his six wives. Draped in filmy white, they circle around him, with ghostly despairing gestures. (Now often omitted.)

Act IV. There is a formal assembly of all King Bobiche's court. Count Oscar announces the arrival of Princess Hermilia. He escorts her, dressed in a manner suitable to her rank, to meet her father. The King is delighted with her. Vainly he tries to convince the courtiers that she resembles him. He leads her to Queen Clementine, who greets her tenderly. This pretty scene is brought to an abrupt close when the King shows his daughter two betrothal rings. She is furious, throws them to the floor, and rushes about smashing vases. The courtiers eye one another knowingly. The King is crushed, seeing his dreams of domestic peace fade. Prince Sapphire enters, no longer incognito. When Hermilia sees him, she stops in the middle of a destructive gesture and embraces him. A frantic search for the scorned rings ensues. When they are found, a solemn betrothal takes place.

The rejoicings over this pleasant event have scarcely begun when Bluebeard arrives. He pays his respects to the King, then demands the Princess for his seventh bride. On being refused, he calls his retainers, a burly lot armed with halberds. Amid the general confusion Sapphire is the only one brave enough to challenge Bluebeard. They fight, but by an unfair trick Bluebeard wins. Pages sadly carry the

Prince away. Hermilia, weeping bitterly into a large handkerchief, is married to Bluebeard.

Led by a strange figure in red, a group of gypsies comes to entertain the court. They are masked and sinister. Something familiar about the gypsy girls disturbs Bluebeard. Suddenly they unmask. They are his wives. Terrified, he runs from them. During the disturbance Sapphire slips back and sits beside Hermilia in the place vacated by Bluebeard. Taking advantage of Bluebeard's unusual discomfiture, King Bobiche pronounces wholesale divorces. The Queen's lovers and Bluebeard's wives are then paired off to everyone's satisfaction, including Bluebeard's. After his experience with a weeping fury he is not averse to beginning his marriage to Boulotte all over again. His resentment against Popoloni, who had led the band of gypsies, flares up. Boulotte persuades him to make peace.

The story comes to an end in a blaze of general gaiety.

Bluebeard got off to a slightly confused start. Even at the first performance, however, its quality was evident. It is a visual *opéra bouffe*—an improvement over the singing variety, the audience being spared the inadequate vocalism, dreary humor, and topical allusions often found in modern revivals of this form of entertainment. After a few performances, when certain *longueurs* in the first act had been cut and delays due to the awkwardness of stage hands removed, *Bluebeard* emerged as a perfect comedy ballet. The arrival of Yura Skibine to assume the role that had been created for him added the last necessary touch.

The enchanting Offenbach score, tailored largely from that of *Barbe-Bleu,* and containing excerpts from *La Grande Duchesse de Gerolstein,* vied for the audience's approval with the delightful décor by Marcel Vertès. Vertès is associated in the public mind with perfume advertisements, textile designs, and screens. In his settings for *Bluebeard* he demonstrated a striking flair for theatrical design. There is a central scheme that features whites, grays, and pastel shades in a manner that achieves a vigor hard to attain with such a limited palette but admirably in keeping with the lusty humor of the ballet.

The dance patterns of *Bluebeard* abound in choreographic gems. The title role, visualized in staccato movement, in which even the eyes play their part, established Anton Dolin as the first comedy dancer on the American [1] stage. As he grew into the role, he added new touches, always within the choreographic limits. This is the prerogative of the dancer in a comedy ballet, but the privilege is safe only in the hands of a first-rate artist. There are steps specially devised for the court ritual, including something that can only be called a charleston, irresistibly funny to any member of the audience who remembers when this antic step was in its heyday.

In Act I there is a solo for Angelo that is a balletic equivalent of *"Non so più cosa son."* This was originally danced by Annabelle Lyon, a figurine in pink and gold. Her several successors have been adequate, but Miss Lyon's personal magic is altogether lacking from their technically excellent performances.

Boulotte as danced by Irina Baronova had a down-to-earth lustiness amazing to an audience that recalled her exquisite legato in *Les Sylphides* and her sculptured Aurora. There is an appropriate use of *fouettés* in the village scene, in which Boulotte pursues Sapphire in a series of traveling turns that exactly indicate the vigor and force of the character. These were performed with a skill equal to Baronova's by her successors, Karen Conrad and Maria Karnilova. However, they failed to achieve the same effect in Miss Conrad's case because she was more interested in the performance of steps than in the creation of character, while Miss Karnilova's aristocratic loveliness automatically disqualified her from being a convincing peasant in spite of her excellent technique.

Princess Hermilia is couched in strangely shrewish terms for the heroine of a medieval love story. Alicia Markova was shrewish, proud, and vixenish by turns, dancing like an angel all the while. Later performers of this role have made it a sweet, conventional figure, thereby depriving the steps of their point. Lately Alicia Alonso seems to be recapturing some of its original flavor.

Prince Sapphire is a very conventional ballet hero. The part was first performed by Yura Skibine, whose personal radiance occasionally lifted the ballet to levels of romance it was never intended to reach. Later André Eglevsky, John Kriza, and Richard Reed have assumed it. All of these young men dance it well, though a new costume should be designed for them, as the ability to wear the original becomingly was Skibine's alone.

---

[1] Accounts of Robert Helpmann's performance as Mr. O'Reilly in *The Prospect before Us* (London, 1940) set the geographical limit to this statement.

There are two interesting character parts—Popoloni and Count Oscar, created by Simon Semenoff and Borislav Runanine. They are now performed more than adequately by John Taras and Alpheus Koon, two promising young character dancers.

Bluebeard is still an active part of the repertoire of Ballet Theatre. It has survived changes of cast, careless and unrehearsed performances—in fact, all the evils of a ballet that has been in the repertoire for more than two seasons—because of its sound basic structure. *Bluebeard,* the last work of Michel Fokine, is unmistakably the work of a master choreographer.

LA BOUTIQUE FANTASQUE

La Boutique Fantasque (The Fantastic Toy-Shop): ballet in one act; music by Rossini, orchestrated by Respighi; choreography by Léonide Massine; curtain, scenery, and costumes by André Derain.

L*A BOUTIQUE FANTASQUE* was first produced by Diaghilev's Ballet Russe at the Alhambra Theatre, London, on June 5, 1919. The cast included Enrico Cecchetti (Shopkeeper), Serge Grigoriev (Russian Merchant), Lydia Sokolova and Leon Woizikovsky (Tarantella Dancers), Lydia Lopokova and Léonide Massine (Cancan Dancers), Stanislas Idzikowsky (Snob), Lubov Tchernicheva (Queen of Clubs), and Vera Nemchinova (Queen of Hearts).

During the period when the Neighborhood Playhouse was attracting uptown New Yorkers to Grand Street, its Junior Players borrowed the score and plot of *La Boutique Fantasque* for a ballet. Just how much this production owed to Massine's choreography is a matter for conjecture. *La Boutique Fantasque* reached New York in its original form on March 20, 1935, at the Majestic Theater. A program dated October 13, 1935 gives the following cast:

THE SHOPKEEPER *Marian Ladre*	THE KING OF DIAMONDS
HIS ASSISTANT *Vania Psota*	*Roland Guerard*
AN AMERICAN *Marc Platoff*	THE SNOB *Yurek Shabelevsky*
A RUSSIAN MERCHANT	THE MELON HAWKER *Jean Hoyer*
Serge Grigoriev	THE COSSACK CHIEF *David Lichine*
TARANTELLA DANCERS	THE COSSACK GIRL
Olga Morosova, Roman Jasinsky	*Eugenia Delarova*
THE QUEEN OF CLUBS	DANCING POODLES
Tamara Grigorieva	*Vera Nelidova, Serge Lipatoff*
THE QUEEN OF HEARTS	CANCAN DANCERS
Nina Verchinina	*Alexandra Danilova, Léonide Massine*
THE KING OF SPADES *Serge Bousloff*	

The curtain rises on a toy-shop where the business day has not yet begun. The Shopkeeper and his Assistant enter. They pull back the curtains from the broad windows, letting in the morning sunshine and revealing a view of a Mediterranean harbor. A thief takes advantage of the open door. Sneaking in, he looks about for loot. He is thwarted by the Assistant, who chases him out with a great display of energy. The thief collides with two elderly ladies, the first customers of the day. Their shaken nerves are not calmed by the antics of the zealous Assistant, eager to make a sale. The arrival of the American family causes the Shopkeeper to intervene. The American children prance gaily around the shop admiring the mechanical dolls. When they have been persuaded to sit down, two porters wheel in a stand on which the Tarantella Dancers are posed. They are assisted to descend. To a lively air they perform a tarentella. The customers are pleased, but not enthusiastic. Removing the Tarantella Dancers, the porters lead on four dolls dressed as court cards who move through the measures of a stately mazurka.

More customers are arriving—a Russian Merchant and his family, who, quite overcome by the heat, are glad to take refuge in the airy shop. After the confusion of their entrance has subsided, two mechanical toys are introduced: the Snob—a terrific dandy—and the Melon Hawker. As they perform their respective routines, something goes wrong. The toys collide and the Snob, losing not a particle of his aplomb, is knocked down. The porters quickly set them to rights. The performance concludes with the Snob slightly off balance. They are followed by a troup of Cossack dolls, six soldiers and a girl who exhibit a characteristic Russian dance. The Merchant, much pleased, kisses the Cossack girl with nostalgic affection, much to the annoyance of his wife. Their exit makes way for a pair of Dancing Poodles. The children are delighted, the parents less so when one of the dogs misbehaves. The affectionate pose of the Poodles at the end of their act horrifies the American parents, who shield the eyes of their children from this horrid sight. They rise and prepare to leave. The Shopkeeper implores them to remain, promising to show them his rarest treasures. He orders the porters to open two large brightly decorated boxes: and Cancan Dancers are revealed. To the gayest possible music they perform a brisk cancan with much fluttering of the girl's lacy petticoats and antic gestures by the man. At last the customers are really impressed. The children surround the dolls, fingering their costumes and capering in delighted imitation of the dance. The parents need little persuasion to buy, and it is arranged that each family will purchase one of the pair. The dolls are replaced in their boxes, ready to be delivered the following day. After payment has been made, the customers leave. The Shopkeeper and his Assistant close up for the night, but not until there has been a little altercation, in which the Assistant endeavors to retain some of the money he has received from a customer, but is bested by his employer.

In the quiet darkness life begins to stir. The dolls awaken to their own secret existence, which begins only when everyday folk have gone away. A group of dancing dolls drifts in. They are joined by the Cossacks. The Snob appears and performs an acrobatic variation, turning somersaults on horizontal bars formed by the Cossacks' batons. All the dolls appear except the Cancan Dancers, who must be released by their friends from the confining boxes. The girl dances a solo in which she delicately indicates her despair at being separated from her companion. Suddenly the dolls are frightened and run off. After a pause they reappear. The male Cancan Dancer enters carrying his sweetheart. They dance together and the Cossacks lift her high in the air on their crossed batons and carry her away. Again the shop is empty, but not for long. The mood changes. All the dolls join in a boisterous romp that brings the midnight revels to a close.

Morning has come again. The Shopkeeper and his sleepy Assistant begin their day's work. Scarcely have they drawn the curtains and put things in order when yesterday's customers appear, crossly demanding to know why their purchases have not been delivered. The Shopkeeper reassures them, but when he and his Assistant open the boxes, they are horrified to find them empty. The customers' fury is quickly subdued by the appearance of the entire troupe of dolls, who have banded together to protect the Cancan Dancers. Pursued by the Cossacks and the Poodles, the customers are glad to leave the shop. They do not even stop to demand the return of their money. The dolls surround the Shopkeeper, who recovers his good humor, glad to be able to keep his favorite Cancan Dancers. The baffled customers peer in the windows at the rejoicing company.

There have been many ballets in which toys come to life. Indeed this is a favorite subject for choreographers and is not unknown to the opera librettist. The idea is very appealing to adults and children. Who has not dreamed of a cherished toy having a life of its own? *La Boutique Fantasque* is pre-eminent in this group because of its wholly enchanting musical score, assembled from unpublished manuscripts of piano pieces by Rossini and orchestrated by Ottorino Respighi. These "musical jests and fancies" bear such whimsical titles as *Hors d'Œuvres, Almonds, Asthmatic Study, Ugh, Peas! Castor Oil* and *Capriccio Offenbachesque* (the cancan music). The only familiar air is *La Danza* (the music for the tarantella).

The usual critical complaints that attend any arrangement of music on behalf of ballet were neatly disposed of by Francis Toye in his biography of Rossini. He says:

"Owing to the passing of the convention to which his operas conform, the supersession of his idiom and an entire change of conditions in the musical theater, we can never recapture wholly the thrill of delight and surprise felt by Rossini's contemporaries. But there remains behind the idiom and the conventions something that can still give us unique pleasure, as indeed was proved by the success of *La Boutique Fantasque,* which, despite its modern trappings, possessed the merit of preserving the genuine flavor of the original Rossinian ingredients. . . . Rossini purists seem to unite in a chorus of disapproval of what they presumably consider Respighi's sacrilege. I should like to indulge in a dissentient solo. It seems to me that Respighi performed a great service to the old master whom he notoriously loves so well. If he had performed his task with less sense of style, there might be cause for complaint, but, thanks to his technical skill and fine scholarship, he has succeeded in preserving admirably the basic flavor of Rossini's music, thus making for the composer many new friends to whom he would otherwise have been known only as the composer of *The Barber of Seville."*

After the heavily exotic atmosphere that characterized much of the repertoire of the early Diaghilev period, the artful simplicity of *La Boutique Fantasque* must have seemed like a fresh morning breeze. Its unaffected gaiety and extrovert humor hark back to the ballets of a less sophisticated age. It shares with them a timeless quality, surviving many changes of cast in a manner few ballets since the classic period can boast.

La Boutique Fantasque is a *ballet d'action,* but it reverses the usual pattern. Ordinarily the plot is disposed of first and a *divertissement* forms the climax. Massine places the *divertissement* at the beginning and later uses these dances as patterns for group and individual movements as the plot and the characters develop. The Cancan Dancers exhibit a fairly literal version [1] of this antic music-hall turn.

[1] One critic deplored "the fact that a great part of it was but a reproduction of the grosser cabaret dances of Paris," including "the last atrocious pose of the can-can

Later the steps of the cancan are transmuted into material for one of Massine's most beautiful and moving *pas de deux,* a truly balletic use of what would appear to be unpromising material. This same development may be observed in the dances of the other characters of this little drama. The steps that they perform mechanically as dolls assume freedom and fluidity when the dolls take on human personalities.

The two elderly ladies with their elegant carriage and prim gestures have had their echoes in other ballets, notably *La Concurrence* and *Pillar of Fire.* The latter reference may seem a little far-fetched, but at least one member of the audience was irresistibly reminded of them when the two friends of the Eldest Sister made their stately passages across the stage in the Tudor ballet.

Many ballerinas have appeared as the Cancan Dancer: Lydia Lopokova, Tamara Karsavina, Vera Nemchinova, and Vera Zorina. In America Alexandra Danilova has made it her own. With the Glove-seller (*Gaité Parisienne*) and the Street Dancer (*Le Beau Danube*), it forms a triptych of that magical gaiety of which she alone possesses the secret. It is difficult to believe that other dancers, however celebrated, have rivaled Danilova in these roles.

At least two members of the first cast have appeared in the United States in their original parts: Serge Grigoriev (the Russian Merchant) and Léonide Massine (Cancan Dancer). David Lichine has on occasion assumed the latter role, but it is one of those characterizations which Massine has so marked with his individuality that others are heavily handicapped when undertaking them. The Snob, danced first by Stanislas Idzikowsky, later by Leon Woizikowsky, is now associated with Yurek Shabelevsky, whose crisp and slightly raffish elegance in the part is unforgettable. André Eglevsky replaced David Lichine as the Cossack Chief, and his superb *tours en l'air* and pirouettes made the audience realize what the choreographer really intended.

La Boutique Fantasque has formed part of the repertoires of Colonel W. de Basil's Ballet Russe and the Ballet Russe de Monte Carlo. In 1943 it was revived by Ballet Theatre. Massine in his original role, Eglevsky as the Cossack Chief, and Jean Hunt as one of the

itself"—known to vaudeville as the flying split. Let us hope that this delicate æsthete did not see *Gaité Parisienne,* which features an all-out version of the cancan, not a balletic one executed *sur les pointes.*

Poodles gave excellent performances. Karen Conrad, heavily conscientious as the Cancan Dancer, was badly miscast. The ballet was dropped after a few performances. With the ineptitudes of the 1945 season of Ballet Theatre freshly in mind, a return engagement of *La Boutique Fantasque* properly cast[2] and rehearsed would be doubly welcome.

[2] It would be a pleasure to see Rosella Hightower or Alicia Alonso as the Cancan Dancer. Better still, they might alternate.

CHOREARTEUM

Choreographic symphony; music, Brahms's Fourth Symphony; choreography by Léonide Massine; scenery and costumes by Constantin Terechkovitch and Eugene Lourie; curtain by Georges Annenkoff.

CHOREARTEUM was first presented by Colonel W. de Basil's Ballet Russe at the Alhambra Theatre, London, on October 4, 1933. The first New York performance took place at the Metropolitan Opera House on October 16, 1935, with a cast that included the following dancers:

Tamara Toumanova, David Lichine, Vera Zorina, Paul Petroff, Anna Adrianova, Nina Verchinina, Tatiana Riabouchinska,Yura Lazovsky, Alexandra Danilova, Roman Jasinsky.

These dancers, whose names are arranged in the order of their first entrances, were the high lights of the cast. *Chorearteum* employed a large company, none of whom could be called corps de ballet, the nature of the work requiring that all be soloists.

Chorearteum, in which the choreographic patterns follow or parallel the progress of Brahms's great Symphony in E Minor, has nothing that even faintly resembles a plot. Arnold Haskell calls it "forty minutes of individual and group movement, always beautiful, logical and yet surprising, with every member of the huge cast an individual and at the same time a part of a fresco."

In an abstract ballet of this duration it would be impossible not to find sequences that are more absorbing than others. Massine's invention is likely to flag when the composer becomes involved in passage work. This is seldom enough for *Chorearteum* to leave a vital and enduring memory.

The first movement is a swiftly moving frieze of epic nobility. Adrian Stokes (*Russian Ballets*) says: "We are not shown Apollo standing in the chariot of the sun or Neptune riding the seas drawn by spuming horses: there is not one idyllic or heroic reference. . . . Yet Apollo . . . and Neptune ride as they never rode before, though there is no Apollo and no Neptune and no horses. These figures belong to our impression because the equine freedom, the nobility of poise, so dear to the Greek imagination, are added to the rich and gloomy splendours of the Brahms symphony." He calls it the summit of balletic art up to date and, remembering, one is almost inclined to agree. The first movement concludes with an episode of stunning grandeur. Following an instant when the stage is empty, a great wave of dancers flashes past heralding a group that holds a figure aloft posed *en arabesque*. It is as though one had witnessed the passage of a god.

The second movement was danced by a long line of women in dark red draperies. They formed a mourning frieze before which Nina Verchinina's solo was a wordless threnody. Here Massine borrowed heavily from the central-European school of dancing. Fokine referred to it somewhat bitterly as "Wigman *sur les pointes*." This protest came rather oddly from one whose revolutionary ideas paved the way for modern dance movements. Ballet is a living art able to absorb the innovations of rebels and experimenters.

The third movement is the least successful of the four. It would appear to be a village frolic complete with clowns, but the costumes relate to nothing definable and the merriment seems a little forced.

The fourth movement with its stately chords opens with a group of male dancers who, arranged in a diagonal line, successively perform *tours en l'air*. The style reverts to the living fresco of the first movement and, performed by dancers in black and blue-gray costumes, is suggestive of a wintry sky. It concludes with one of the most effective groups in all ballet: a mighty swirl that rises to the principal figures held high in the air.[1]

During its first season in the United States Colonel W. de Basil's Ballet Russe had included *Les Présages* in an early program. This had been an outstanding success of the London season, but New York, long out of touch with ballet, failed to appreciate it, and John Martin remarked in a review that "its early demise makes practically certain the fact that *Chorearteum* will not see the light of day in New York." Ballet management was probably less subservient to newspaper criticism at that time than it later became, because *Choreateum* did see, if not the light of day, at least the lights of the

[1] At one point in this movement a dancer executes a series of *fouettés*. This unfortunately gave those members of the audience who were interested in circus feats an opportunity to annoy those who were interested in symphonic ballet by bursting into loud applause.

Metropolitan Opera House. Though not greeted with any critical acclaim, it was well received by audiences and remained a valuable part of the repertoire until the de Basil company ceased to visit this continent in 1938. It was successfully revived by the Original Ballet Russe during its season at the Fifty-first Street Theater in 1940–1.

Chorearteum had weathered previous critical diatribes. London audiences were delighted with it, London music critics were not. Bitter complaints arose about the wickedness of dancing to symphonic music quite as if it had never happened before. The use of symphonic suites such as *Scheherazade,* the tone poems *Prélude à l'Après-midi d'un faune* and *Thamar,* and the absolute music of Schumann, Scarlatti, and Chopin had been pointing the way for years. The employment of the Tchaikovsky (*Les Présages*) and Brahms symphonies was merely another step forward. Audiences continued to applaud *Chorearteum* and the critics to deplore it until 1936, when Ernest Newman, the music critic of the London *Sunday Times,* rose to defend the validity of Massine's right to use symphonic music for balletic purposes. In five articles published in successive issues of the *Sunday Times* he made a case for the symphonic ballet which few lesser critics had the hardihood to challenge. Answering the charge that Massine was attempting to interpret the symphony, he says: "There is no question whatever . . . of a claim on Massine's part . . . that he is 'interpreting' the symphony, for a symphony is purely and simply its own interpretation: there is no need, therefore, for 'sensitive musicians' to feel outraged. 'Les Présages' and 'Chorearteum' are not attempts at 'translations' of the untranslatable, but purely choreographic creations that run parallel throughout their design with that of the symphony, and at the same time set before us, in logical cohesion and sequence, a train of poetic associations that have been set up in Massine by the music." The symphonic ballet could not be defined and described more simply or more clearly.

Leopold Stokowski, ever ready to welcome innovations, placed his seal of approval on *Chorearteum* by conducting the Brahms Fourth at ballet performances given at the Academy of Music in Philadelphia on November 12 and 15, 1935. For those lucky enough to be present it was an unforgettable experience.

In an ensemble of artists it is an invidious task to single out one or another. Memories of Tamara Toumanova and David Lichine, however, are inseparable from the first and fourth movements of *Chorearteum*. Nina Verchinina led the chain of mourning figures in the second movement with a noble grandeur. Actually this ballet produced its results from the cumulative effect of absolute fidelity to tempo and rhythm and precise timing in the entrances and exits. It offered no scope for personal display or virtuosity. At its best it seemed to grow spontaneously from the music.

Nothing but a cherished memory now, *Chorearteum* has not been seen in New York since 1941.

CINDERELLA

Cinderella (Cendrillon): ballet in three parts after Perrault's fairy tale; music by Frederic d'Erlanger; scenes and dances by Michel Fokine; scenery and costumes by Nathalie Gontcharova.

CINDERELLA was first produced at the Royal Opera House, Covent Garden, London, in 1938. The first New York performance, by the Original Ballet Russe, took place at the Fifty-first Street Theater on the afternoon of November 16, 1940, with the following cast:

CINDERELLA *Tatiana Riabouchinska*	THE LORD OF THE MOUNTAIN
THE TWO UGLY SISTERS	*Yura Lazovsky*
H. Algeranoff, M. Ladre	THE LORD OF THE VALE *Boris Belsky*
THE GOOD FAIRY *Tamara Grigorieva*	THE CHAMBERLAIN *Dimitri Rostoff*
THE CAT *Kira Bounina*	A FAIR PEASANT GIRL *Anna Volkova*
THE PRINCE *Paul Petroff*	A DARK PEASANT GIRL *Sono Osato*

Heralds, Retinue of the Fairy, Denizens of Fairyland, Lords and Ladies of the Court, Peasants

The action of the ballet follows the age-old story of Cinderella, the only variations being introduced for balletic purposes.

❖❖❖❖❖❖❖❖❖❖❖❖❖❖❖

Scene 1. There is confusion in Cinderella's kitchen. Her Ugly Sisters, who have been invited to a court ball, are unable to dress without her help. They are not at all grateful for her assistance, taunting her because she has not been invited. When they have gone, Cinderella sadly sits by the table, under which the Cat has been hiding from the turmoil. The Cat emerges and comforts Cinderella. There is a mutter of thunder. A storm breaks out. Terrified, Cinderella and the Cat huddle together. There is a knock at the door. Cinderella opens it to find an aged crone cowering from the rain on the threshold. Cinderella invites her in to the fireside. The storm dies away. The old woman throws off her cloak, revealing herself to be a beautiful Fairy in a glittering dress. Cinderella, frightened, is assured that the Fairy is her godmother, come to restore her to her proper place in society. The room is filled with the Fairy's retinue.

Gently they remove Cinderella's gray rags, dress her in a filmy gown, and place satin slippers on her pretty feet, hidden until now in shapeless felt shoes. She is ready for the court ball. The scene is transformed to a beautiful landscape where a magnificent coach is waiting, suitably attended by youths and maidens. The faithful Cat is not left behind; as the curtain falls, an attendant carries her to the carriage.

Entr'acte. A curtain is seen picturing the flight of the coach through clouds, drawn by winged horses.

Scene 2. Courtiers dance while awaiting the arrival of the Prince, in whose honor the ball is being given. The Ugly Sisters are conspicuous for their silly behavior and air of affected elegance. Heralds announce the Prince's approach. Curtains are drawn aside and he is seen standing on a magnificent staircase. After a formal greeting, the ball is continued, all the court ladies competing for the honor of being the Prince's partner. Suddenly the lights dim and the scene is transformed. Outside a colonnade Cinderella's coach with its elegant suite is seen. Awe-stricken, the court awaits her entrance. The Prince, enchanted with her loveliness, goes to meet her. The scene resumes its former brilliance, the ball goes on, but now the Prince will dance only with Cinderella. They are wholly absorbed in each other, until abruptly Cinderella becomes conscious of the passage of time. At midnight her hour of splendor will come to an end and already the clock is striking. While she stands gazing at the Prince, unable to tear herself away, the Cat unties her slipper. Cinderella and the Cat run away. The Prince, attempting to follow her, is stopped by the Cat, who returns carrying Cinderella's slipper in her mouth. The Prince takes it from her and presses it to his heart.

Scene 3. The Prince, despairing of finding his mysterious love, tries a last expedient. He issues a proclamation that he will marry the lady whose foot will fit the lost slipper. Prince, court, and people assemble to watch the trials. A number of ladies, including the Ugly Sisters, whose efforts to don the slipper amuse everybody, submit to the trial, carried out by the grave and dignified Chamberlain. All fail. Cinderella, in the crowd of peasants, watches with heartsick anxiety. Unable to bear it any longer, she makes her way through the guards and implores the Chamberlain to allow her to try on the slipper. The Prince brushes his refusal aside and carries out the test himself. To his delight and amazement, the slipper fits and Cinderella is proclaimed the Prince's bride. She is invested with royal robes and a diadem. Now the Fairy Godmother appears to give the young lovers her blessing.

The Ugly Sisters are filled with hate and envy, but the people rejoice.

You may be sure that the Cat shares Cinderella's happiness.

Cinderella was advertised in the words of the old bromide: *"Cinderella* is the ideal holiday treat for children aged six to sixty." For once this was quite true. A beautifully enacted fairy tale could not fail to attract any child reasonably uncorrupted by Hollywood, and adults were delighted with a story sensitively and wittily told in terms of dance. Unfortunately only the matinee audience ever had a chance to see it. For some unknown reason, it was never given an evening performance. Possibly the management was apologetic for the simplicity of *Cinderella,* though it had more to recommend it than many another ballet in the repertoire.

Cinderella was beautifully mounted, with sets and costumes by Nathalie Gontcharova, in a manner that recalled pages from an illuminated manuscript. The entr'acte curtains were particularly charming.

The musical score of *Cinderella* by Baron d'Erlanger was perhaps the weakest feature of the ballet, though it had the merit of being specially composed. It was in the style made familiar by his music for *The Hundred Kisses.* Both of these scores seem to a casual hearer to have been inspired by the more superficial aspects of César Franck's *Psyché.*

Tatiana Riabouchinska gave a touching performance of Cinderella —the very embodiment of Perrault's and the world's heroine. The role stressed characterization rather than virtuoso dancing. It would be difficult to forget Riabouchinska's gentle patience with the demanding Ugly Sisters, or her lovely attitude of humility when her elevation to royal rank is acclaimed by the crowd.

The Ugly Sisters, in accordance with a ballet tradition shared by pantomime, were played by male dancers. They supplied an earthy humor that was an interesting contrast to the prevailing mood of the ballet.

The Cat was introduced, not for her feline charm, but to enable the plot to reach a conclusion. It is practically impossible for a female dancer to lose a ballet shoe,[1] and as Cinderella without a lost slipper is unthinkable, the Cat was provided for the purpose of untying the ribbons of Cinderella's shoe that it might plausibly be lost. The role of the Cat proved an excellent vehicle for Kira Bounina, who as Jean Hunt (her real name) was a valued member of Ballet Theatre for several seasons.

Choreographically *Cinderella* introduced no innovations, but was marked by a witty use of well-known steps and poses. The most memorable feature was the fitting of the slipper, which became the basis for a charming *pas de deux* in which Cinderella's leg extensions matched the Prince's arm movements and led to the triumphant conclusion that the slipper was indeed a perfect fit.

Cinderella should be revived for the delight of matinee audiences, which are bound, sooner or later, to become bored with *Peter and the Wolf*.

[1] There was a performance when Paul Petroff, dancing the role of the Prince, lost his shoe—a much easier matter for a male dancer. The audience was very hilarious at this assumption of Cinderella's prerogative.

CONCERTO IN E MINOR

Music by Frédéric Chopin; choreography by Bronislava Nijinska; décors and costumes by W. Borowski.

CONCERTO IN E MINOR was presented for the first time in America on June 6, 1939 at the Hall of Music, World's Fair Grounds, New York. The principal roles were performed by Olga Slawska, Nina Juszkiewicz, and Zbigniew Kilinski. There was a corps de ballet of sixteen women and ten men.

The choreography of *Concerto in E Minor,* abstract in form, followed the rhythms and prevailing spirit of the music in a manner made familiar by *Chorearteum,* though in a much less imaginative fashion. The soloists danced well, Olga Slawska revealing herself to be an artist with admirable line and beautiful, fluid movements. The décor was a colorless backdrop on which the play of light indicated changes of mood. The costumes were simple adaptations of the dress of the romantic period.

Concerto in E Minor did not register any particular success with audience or critics, though unfavorable circumstances—an overlarge auditorium, a stage with footlights high enough to hide the dancers' feet, as well as other disadvantages [1]—might have had their effect.

On October 12, 1942, *Concerto in E Minor,* revised by Nijinska and rechristened *Chopin Concerto,* was performed by the Ballet Russe de Monte Carlo at the Metropolitan Opera House, with a cast headed by Alexandra Danilova and Igor Youskevitch. Nathalie Krassovska, Frederic Franklin, and Roland Guerard were among the supporting artists.

Apparently the critics, at least, had changed their minds in the interval separating them from the original production. Mr. Martin hailed its "crystalline beauty" and claimed that it "projected its underlying romanticism with fine musicianship, as well as with a magnificent sense of visual theatre" (*New York Times,* October 20, 1942).

It is possible that *Chopin Concerto* in its second incarnation had

[1] The delights offered by the Polish Ballet at the World's Fair were "barked" over a loud speaker in a manner that would have been slightly vulgar for a strip-tease.

the benefit of more stagecraft on the part of its cast and a background more conducive to appreciation. It has not exactly replaced *Les Sylphides* in the repertoire, though it holds its position. Recently it has been again revised to allow a corps de ballet of eighteen women and six men.

Chopin Concerto shares with *The Hundred Kisses* the position of being the last valid work of that very uneven choreographic artist, Bronislava Nijinska, whose zenith was *Les Noces* and whose nadir is *Brahms Variations*.

CONSTANTIA

A classic ballet in one act; music by Frédéric Chopin (First Piano Concerto), orchestrated by Adolf Schmid; choreography by William Dollar; scenery by Horace Armistead; costumes by Grace Houston.

CONSTANTIA was first performed by Ballet International at the International Theater, New York, on October 31, 1944. William Dollar, Marie-Jeanne, and Yvonne Patterson were the principal dancers.

Constantia was a revision of a work by William Dollar that had been presented at the Metropolitan Opera House by the American Ballet during its ill-starred career as the official opera ballet. Ballet at the Metropolitan has always enjoyed the status of an idiot child in a brilliant family. The American Ballet's efforts to fit into the organization fared worse than they deserved, although their dependence on a single choreographer of advanced tendencies did them no service. The Metropolitan audiences, practically innocent of any taste for ballet, might have been gently led up the garden path of appreciation if they had been offered well-staged presentations of standard classics. Instead they were given several variations of Balanchine's "reeling, writhing, and fainting in coils" school of choreography, which they were quite incapable of absorbing, because they had no background of experience of ballet in any form, except fragmentary ballets in operas that bear the same relation to true ballet as movie accompaniments do to the great body of music. Let me hasten to say that there have been a number of fine scores for movies, just as there are certain opera ballets that are not unworthy. The number of the latter, however, is few, and as performed at the Metropolitan, even they are not distinguished. The American Ballet, without a sound backlog in the shape of a traditional and classical repertoire, had an uphill task, and succeeded in annoying almost everyone.

In the general confusion, William Dollar's first essay at choreography, *Classic Ballet* (the original title of *Constantia*), passed unnoticed, although it was danced by a fine cast, and even succeeded in achieving a performance in the regular subscription season, appearing on a program paired with *The Clandestine Marriage* of Cimarosa on February 25, 1937. The music critic of the *Times* did not so much as mention the ballet in his review. The only dance critic then working for a New York daily newspaper apparently had other commitments, for he did not give either this or any other performance of *Classic Ballet* a criticism.

Classic Ballet was apparently not considered important enough by the opera organization to rate a décor or proper costumes. It was performed by a cast in practice clothes, before the black curtains that are still casting a blight over any ballets that may find their lonely way into a Sunday concert program at the Metropolitan.

Classic Ballet was a joint composition, William Dollar being responsible for the Maestoso and Allegro Vivace movements of the concerto, and George Balanchine for the Larghetto. The cast included Giselle Caccialanza, Yvonne Patterson, Annabelle Lyon, Holly Howard, Leda Anchutina, William Dollar, Charles Laskey, and Lew Christensen. There was no such cast available for the revival of *Classic Ballet,* when William Dollar revised it for Ballet International, under the title of *Constantia.*

Constantia, when it reached the stage of the International Theater, was to all intents and purposes a new ballet. *Classic Ballet* was a charming, slightly immature production that had an inevitable lack of balance due to Balanchine's more experienced second movement. Although he had made a sincere effort to keep within the framework of the ballet, this could not fail to stand out as the work of a finished choreographer. In *Constantia,* Dollar had enlarged his original conception without losing any of its charm or innate musicality. The Larghetto (called Andante on the Ballet International program) was entirely new. The approach to the music was more or less abstract, a conflict being implied rather than overtly expressed.

Constantia was cursed by a backdrop that appeared to have been borrowed from a third-rate vaudeville house of the twenties. Only the frame of advertisements for local merchants was missing to complete the illusion. The pastel costumes were sweetly sentimental in a manner totally unworthy of music or choreography.

Constantia is scheduled for revival by the Original Ballet Russe in 1946. Advance publicity unfortunately indicates that no change is contemplated in scenery or costumes.

COPPÉLIA

ARTISTICALLY, *Coppélia* represents the halfway point between the misty poetry of *La Sylphide* and *Giselle* and the classic splendors of the Tchaikovsky-Petipa collaborations, *Swan Lake* and *Sleeping Beauty*. French ballet, fast becoming a rigid formula, was briefly rescued from desuetude by the delightful scores of Léo Délibes, who had received some of his musical training from Adolphe Adam, composer of *Giselle* and other ballet scores. Délibes was already well established as a composer of music for the theater when he made his debut in the ballet world by collaborating with Ludwig Minkus [1] in the score of *La Source* in 1866. The following year he was asked to compose a *"Pas de Fleur"* to be interpolated in a revival of *Le Corsaire*.[2] *Coppélia,* his first independent ballet score, was completed in the same year. The libretto of *Coppélia,* based on a story by E. T. A. Hoffmann, was arranged by C. Nuitter and A. Saint-Léon, and the choreography by Louis Mérante, who was later responsible for Delibes's third ballet, *Sylvia*.

Difficulties in casting delayed the production of *Coppélia*. Beaumont in his account of *Coppélia* (*Complete Book of Ballets*) relates how the producers of the ballet selected Léontine Beaugrand for the role of Swanilda, but their choice was overruled by the directors in favor of Adele Grantsova, one of the earliest of the Russian ballerinas to seek fame in western Europe. Grantsova was forced to return to Russia before *Coppélia* was ready for the stage, and Beaugrand was passed over a second time and the role given to Giuseppina Bozacchi. The première of *Coppélia* finally took place on May 25, 1870, at the Paris Opéra, having been in rehearsal for three years.

Bozacchi, prototype of de Basil's "baby ballerinas" (she was fifteen

[1] Ludwig Minkus and Cesare Pugni share an unenviable reputation as composers of the glib melodies and hackneyed rhythms that passed for ballet music during the nineteenth century.

[2] *Le Corsaire,* with an elaborate plot based on Byron's poem and a score by Adolphe Adam, was a popular ballet that long survived in the repertoire of the Russian theaters. Karsavina, in her enchanting *Theatre Street,* gives an account of her experiences in the role of Medora. The ballet concluded with a spectacular shipwreck scene.

years old), was outstandingly successful as Swanilda, but her career was brought to an untimely close during the siege of Paris, when she died of fever. Later, when *Coppélia* was revived, Beaugrand at last achieved the role that she had twice missed. Her interpretation received the accolade of Théophile Gautier, who found in her a successor to Carlotta Grisi.

Coppélia, reaching New York in 1887, was performed at the Metropolitan Opera House on March 11 of that year. It shared a double bill with *The Marriage of Jeannette,* a one-act opera by Victor Massé. This was not part of the regular Metropolitan season, but one of a series of performances by the American Opera, whose guiding spirit was Theodore Thomas. The American Opera, founded by Mrs. Jeannette Thurber in 1885, had as its ideal the presentation of opera in English by American singers. Their attempts to induce New York to accept opera in English appear to have been no more successful than those of subsequent organizations. Unlike the Metropolitan, they appear to have taken ballet seriously, and made an honest attempt to revive ballet as an art form in a period when it had sadly degenerated.

The *Spirit of the Times,* a weekly devoted in unequal proportions to the horse and the arts (about ninety-nine per cent to the former), announced: "Friday night will be ballet night, and Coppelia, a grand ballet d'action, in three acts will be produced for the first time in New York. . . . We have not had a grand ballet for many years: it will be a novelty to our public and those theatre-goers who think that ballet means a dance in The Black Crook will be surprised to see the sort of entertainment which their grandsires and granddames admired, and which is still fashionable in the European capitals." [3]

The cast of this production, staged by Mamert Bibeyran, was as follows:

SWANILDA	*Marie Giuri*	LORD OF THE MANOR)	
FRANTZ	*Felicita Carozzi*	BURGOMASTER)	*M. Romeo*
COPPELIUS	*Mamert Bibeyran*	HIS ASSISTANT	*M. Spinaponti*
BELL-RINGER	*M. Cammarano*	COPPÉLIA	*Mlle Paporello*
LANDLADY OF THE TAVERN			
	Catarina Coralli		

[3] Quoted from a column called "The Spirit of the Theatre," a weekly feature of the *Spirit of the Times,* compiled from reports of scattered, and anonymous, correspondents. Not all of the items dealt with the New York theater, and styles of writing vary considerably.

It will be seen that the French custom of assigning the role of Frantz to a *danseuse en travestie* was adhered to in this production—an eccentricity of casting not unknown in contemporary performances of *Coppélia* at the Paris Opéra.

So many versions of *Coppélia* have been seen in New York that the following detailed account of the plot as set forth in the American Opera's libretto (called, heaven knows why, *Ye Book of Ye Words*) probably bears the closest resemblance to the original production:

Act I. The action takes place in a Galician village, in a square surrounded by houses—those of Swanilda and Coppelius, among others. Swanilda comes out of her house and sees Coppélia sitting reading at an upper window in the house of Coppelius. Swanilda greets Coppélia, who takes no notice of her. Frantz, Swanilda's betrothed, approaches, and as Swanilda has been suspicious of his interest in the mysterious figure in the window, she hides to see what he will do. She is annoyed to find that Coppélia returns Frantz's greeting, but fails to see that Coppélia's bow is the result of manipulations by Coppelius, who has also noticed the young man's attentions. Coppelius draws the curtains at the window and the young man is forced to look elsewhere for amusement.

Swanilda runs into view, chasing a butterfly. Frantz catches it and pins it to his blouse. His unthinking cruelty offends Swanilda. Her expostulations are interrupted by the entrance of the villagers, who dance a polka (actually a mazurka.).

The Burgomaster announces that there will be a fete on the following day in honor of a new bell that the Lord of the Manor has presented to the village. While he is speaking, sounds are heard in the workshop of Coppelius, whose strange activities are regarded with superstitious awe by the villagers. This interruption past, they listen with great enthusiasm while the Burgomaster tells them that the Lord of the Manor means also to award dowries to several young couples. He asks Swanilda if she means to take advantage of this opportunity to marry Frantz. In answer, Swanilda takes a straw and, holding it to her ear, listens. She asks Frantz to listen as well. Frantz claims that he can hear nothing. Swanilda calls a bystander, who pretends to hear what the straw says. Thereupon Swanilda breaks the straw, telling Frantz that their engagement is at an end. (This somewhat mysterious performance apparently means that the straw, if listened to carefully, can tell whether a lover is true or not.

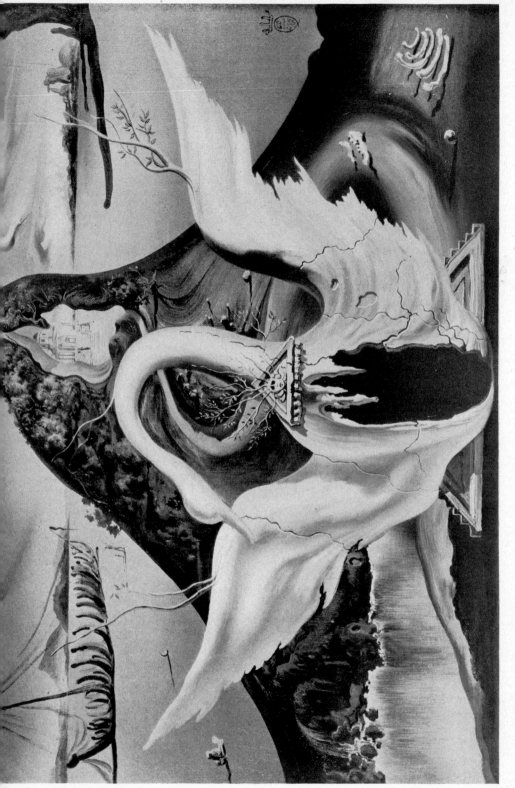

BACCHANALE (backdrop by Salvador Dali)

COPPELIA. Phyllis Bedells as Swanilda. Ronald ...

DANSES CONCERTANTES (Alexandra Danilova and Frederic Franklin)

DARK ELEGIES
(Miriam Golden and
Antony Tudor)

DIM LUSTRE
(Nora Kaye)

In Monte Carlo Ballet performances the straw is an ear of wheat.)

Frantz leaves the scene. Swanilda dances with her friends. As night falls, the village boys and girls dance the czardas, drifting away at its conclusion.

Coppelius, a dark-cloaked figure, leaves his house. He is surrounded by the young men of the village, who have been waiting for him hidden in the shadows. He is subjected to some rough horseplay and hustled from the scene. In the confusion he drops his house key, which is picked up by Swanilda, returning with her friends. This is a heaven-sent opportunity to explore the mysterious house and make the acquaintance of the enigmatic figure who sits so quietly at the window. The girls are frightened, but their curiosity overcomes their terror and, led by Swanilda, they enter the house of Coppelius.

Frantz enters, carrying a ladder, which he places against the window where Coppélia usually sits. As Coppelius returns in a fever of anxiety, looking for his key, Frantz hastily leaves, taking the ladder with him. When Coppelius sees the door of his house open, his worst fears are confirmed. He rushes in to see who has dared to intrude upon his mysteries.

Act II. 1st Tableau. The scene is Coppelius's workshop, dark, shadowy, and inhabited by a group of silent, immobile figures. The girls gather timorously at the threshold, advancing and retreating many times before they can summon enough courage to enter. Swanilda sees Coppélia in a curtained alcove. Braver than the rest, she pushes forward, determined to see her rival. Receiving no answer to a polite bow, she goes close enough to see that Coppélia is a doll. She is at once amused and relieved. One of the girls, stepping back with a sudden movement, sets the mechanism of an automaton in motion, and the whole mystery of Coppelius's workshop is revealed.

Coppelius now enters, infuriated at this invasion. The girls run away, abandoning Swanilda, who has hidden in the curtained alcove where Coppélia sits apart from the other dolls, and is unable to escape. Frantz climbs in through a window. Thinking that he is alone, he looks around curiously, until he is seized by Coppelius, who asks him why he has entered so surreptitiously. Frantz confesses his love for Coppélia, but is forced to plead poverty when the old man inquires into his ability to support a wife. Coppelius offers Frantz a drink, plying the young man with drugged wine until he passes into a stupor. Coppelius brings out a large, ominous book and finds the magic spell by which he hopes to transfer Frantz's vital forces to his masterpiece, Coppélia, the most beautiful and lifelike product of his workshop.

Coppelius goes to the alcove and draws out a platform on which Coppélia, holding a book, is rigidly posed. As the old man works his magic, Coppélia begins to move, at first stiffly, then with a growing fluidity and grace, until at length she breathes and becomes a living woman. She is curious and full of caprices. Coppelius is just in time to prevent her drinking the remains of the drugged wine. She turns the pages of his precious book with her toe, then examines the automatons. She pays particular attention to Frantz, whom Coppelius claims as one of his creatures. She finds a sword and threatens Coppelius with it, chasing him around the room. With difficulty he succeeds in disarming her, then drapes a cloak around her. She dances a bolero, and when she discovers a Scottish scarfpin in the cloak, dances a jig. With energy still unabated, she goes on a rampage. In the confusion Frantz revives. Coppelius forces his unruly doll back on her platform, which he wheels away. Returning, he shoves Frantz toward the window by which he entered. Swanilda runs out of the alcove, setting the automatons in motion as she escapes. Coppelius is left with his favorite doll, whose clothes are unaccountably missing. Slowly he realizes that he has been tricked by Swanilda's impersonation.

Act II. 2nd Tableau. The blessing of the bell takes place in a meadow outside the village. The young couples who are to receive the dowries are presented to the Lord of the Manor. Swanilda and Frantz, their differences reconciled, are among them. The joyful scene is interrupted by the entrance of Coppelius, who lodges a complaint against Swanilda and Frantz, accusing them of destroying his masterpiece. Swanilda is ready to give him her dowry as compensation, but the Lord of the Manor intervenes. He gives a bag of gold to Coppelius and dismisses him. Disillusioned, the old man sadly leaves.

Act. III. (This is quoted directly from the libretto.)

"The Bell-ringer alights first from the car.

"He summons the Morning Hours.

"They appear, quickly followed by Wild Flowers.

"The bell rings! It is the Hour of Prayer. Aurora vanishes, chased by the Hours of Day.

"These are the working hours, and the young girls and reapers begin their work.

"The bell rings again! It announces a wedding, and Hymen appears accompanied by a little Cupid.

"All at once the air is rent with discord and sounds. It is War, it is Discord. Arms are raised, and flames of fire illumine the darkened sky. But soon all is calm again. The bell which a few moments before was calling to arms, makes the glad sound for the return of peace. Discord is dispelled and with the evening hours and night, begin pleasures and joys."

The *Spirit of the Times* approved highly of this production of *Coppélia* and reviewed it in the issue of March 19, 1887: "This little story delighted a large audience for two hours. The most prudish could find no fault with the charming but decorous costumes and the chaste but picturesque evolutions. The characters acted as well as they danced and there was an intelligent meaning in every waltz, polka, jig and czardas. . . . To see a grand ballet as beautifully costumed and exquisitely danced, one would have to travel to Paris or Vienna. Even London has not seen anything like it in modern times, excepting occasionally at the Alhambra." The various dancers were individually commended, and the interesting fact that Swanilda was supported in the Act III *adage* by the Bell-ringer (a character unknown in the contemporary local productions of *Coppélia*) is made clear. This review ended with a plea for more serious ballet.

Apparently the critic of the *Spirit of the Times* had only recently become ballet-conscious, as he speaks of *Coppélia* as the first "grand" ballet (as opposed to *The Black Crook* and the offerings at Niblo's) seen for generations in New York. Actually, a production of *Sylvia,* with Theodora de Gillert, billed as "principal dancer from the Imperial Theatre, Moscow," in the title role, had formed part of the American Opera's repertoire in 1886. This presentation, to quote advance publicity, featured a "Dancing Ballet of 75. In the tableaux and marches the entire Chorus of the American Opera will appear in order to give additional effect to the scenes in the last act." One hopes that the members of the American Opera's chorus were more svelte as well as more co-operative than members of the Metropolitian Opera chorus, who never overlook an opportunity to interpose their solid persons between the audience and the ballet, with effects that are less than impressive.

Coppélia was revived at theMetropolitan Opera House during the season of 1903–4. Details are unavailable, and the programs are missing from the bound files of Metropolitan Opera programs at the New York Public Library. This production was probably one of the Metropolitan's sporadic efforts, recurring through the years, to indicate awareness of the fact that ballet has a place in every first-class opera house and, by throwing out an occasional carelessly produced classic, to demonstrate to the subscribers that they are really not missing anything.

There was a brief period, however, when the Metropolitan made an effort to liven up the corpse of ballet by applying outside stimulus. The 1909–10 season was distinguished by the engagement of Pavlova and Mordkin, which Irving Kolodin in *The Metropolitan Opera* calls "an evidence of the directors' intention to establish the Metropolitan on a well-rounded plan." The debut of these outstanding artists took place on February 28, 1910, and their vehicle was *Coppélia*. This was presented on a double bill, preceded by Massenet's *Werther*. As the curtain did not rise on the ballet until after eleven o'clock, the performance did not end until the unconscionable hour of one. A review in the *Boston Transcript* (March 1, 1910) said:

> "So lost is the art of tiptoe dancing that a wonderful thing was seen at its importation last night into the land of America, which has sent the oriental St. Denis, the Grecian Duncan and Allan, the fiery Fuller and all the brood of unschooled natural grace, and unsoled flatfoot interpretation to stir the senses of a jaded old world. . . . The Golden Horseshoe was filled until the amazing hour of nearly one o'clock this morning. . . . The ovation was such as no singing prima donna has had at a Metropolitan debut in many seasons."

Coppélia as presented by Pavlova and Mordkin had a Russian flavor in spite of the fact that they used the permanent ballet of the opera in supporting roles. A tragic element was introduced by changing the plot so that Coppelius, instead of being paid for his losses by the Lord of the Manor, dies of the shock of disillusionment. This may have been the manner of presentation at the Imperial Theater in Moscow, where Mordkin received his training, but it introduces a heavily dramatic note for which there is little sanction in the light-hearted score. Pavlova's Swanilda was a revelation to audiences who had learned, at the Metropolitan at least, to look upon ballet as a dreary interlude to be endured while waiting for the reappearance of the singing stars. Pavlova and Mordkin were engaged for the following season, their performances usually sharing a bill with a short opera. On one occasion they danced a *pas de deux* from *Coppélia,* "in the midst of which was interpolated the air of Tschaikowsky to which Mordkin does his arrow dance," according to an unidentified critic. Was it to provide a breathing-spell?

The Metropolitan for two subsequent seasons continued to give serious ballet a place in its repertoire, engaging Katerina Geltzer in 1912, and Adeline Genée in 1913. Alexander Volinine partnered both of these eminent dancers in performances of *Coppélia.* It is more than likely that Genée, with her fine sense of comedy allied with an effortless virtuosity, gave Pavlova serious competition in the role of Swanilda, which Genée had introduced to London in 1906 at the Empire Theatre.

It was not until October 1938 that the Metropolitan stage again saw a full-dress performance of *Coppélia.* This production had "choreography by Petipa and Cecchetti, reconstructed by Nicolas Sergueff from his notes on the original choreography." There were also two dances (the Automatons' Dance in Act II, and the Betrothal Dance in Act III) by Léonide Massine. The scenery and costumes by Pierre Roy suggested the Hungarian locale of the story, the villagers' costumes being particularly effective. The incomparable Swanilda was Alexandra Danilova, and Michel Panaieff was a more capable Frantz than his performances in other roles had led audiences to expect. The mazurka and czardas, led by Eugenie Delarova and Frederic Franklin, were as lively and spirited as they should be. Tatiana Grantseva was admirable in the Dawn variation, and Nini Theilade brought her peculiar other-worldly quality to the companion Prayer. On the whole this production of *Coppélia,* well cast and beautifully danced, was worthy of its position as a classic of the dance theater.

Above all, this presentation was distinguished by the superb performance of Swanilda, the dancing equivalent of a coloratura role in opera, by Danilova. Her authoritative style, exquisite sparkle, and inimitable pantomime were for once brought to bear on a role worthy of her art. It is true that the difficult *penché arabesques* in the Act III *pas de deux* were probably sustained with more rocklike steadiness (a quality more desirable in the living pictures of the *ante* Norman Bel Geddes circus than in ballerinas) by Mia Slavenska, who was also seen in the role. From all other angles Danilova's interpretation was, and fortunately remains, a standard of balletic elegance. In later seasons Toumanova was also seen as Swanilda, but this dancer, though impressive in the heavily dramatic roles of ballet, lacks the musicality and light touch that this role demands.

The Monte Carlo Ballet's production of *Coppélia,* unlike many other fine ballets (a list may be had on application), remains in the repertoire, though it has been shorn of its third act and relegated to matinees. Along with the vagaries of casting, the selection of ballets considered suitable only for matinee audiences (usually composed of harassed elders accompanied by badly behaved children who had rather be at the movies) is one of the mysteries of the managerial mind. Probably because *Coppélia* has a plot involving dolls it is considered suitable for children. As an adult who finds nothing engaging in the antics of rude children and is not amused by the unanswerable questions reiterated throughout the performance by the little angels, may I register a protest, and ask that at least one *Coppélia* (as grown-up entertainment as *The Red Poppy*) be performed on an evening program?

Ballet Theatre revived *Coppélia* in October 1942, in a condensed version, with choreography by Simon Semenoff, "after Mérante," which did not differ materially from that of the Monte Carlo production, although the latter was attributed to other sources. The scenery and costumes were by Roberto Montenegro. Irina Baronova (Swanilda) and Anton Dolin (Frantz) led the cast. This production was a creditable effort, but the unaccountable omission of the czardas, one of the most effective uses of a folk dance in the entire range of ballet, was difficult to forgive. There were also certain strange overtones in the décor and costumes, no doubt due to the fact that Montenegro saw the original Hungarian locale of the ballet through Mexican eyes. The results appeared to belong to no particular time or place except possibly some mythical kingdom remarkable for its unattractive architecture and ugly costumes.

Baronova made a charming and capable Swanilda, substituting a soubrettish quality for the inimitable Danilova sparkle. Dolin was miscast as Frantz, but that was remedied when André Eglevsky took over the role. The Coppelius of Simon Semenoff was a distinguished example of the art of pantomime and the most authoritative interpretation of the part seen in New York during the current revival of ballet.

When Baronova left Ballet Theatre, *Coppélia,* shelved for a time, was revived for Rosella Hightower, the first important role assigned to this young artist. She did not disappoint her many admirers (a group that includes most of the discerning ballet-lovers who attend performances at the Metropolitan). Her purity of line and the true coloratura quality of her dancing revealed a Danilova in the making, wanting only the authority of stage experience to be an artist of the first rank. Unfortunately, *Coppélia* has now been withdrawn from the active list, no doubt to make room for such triumphs of ineptitude as *Moonlight Sonata*. With a new décor and the czardas restored, it would do much to give interest to a repertoire that is becoming duller every season.

No doubt the choreography of *Coppélia* has changed with the generations. Productions seen in America during the twentieth century are based on those given in the Imperial Theaters, probably arranged by Lev Ivanov, rather than the original Paris Opéra version by Mérante. Swanilda holds the stage during the better part of Acts I and II, and with Frantz performs a *pas de deux* of appalling technical difficulty in Act III. Her dance with her friends in Act I is the balletic equivalent of an operatic *scena* in which the coloratura holds forth supported by a chorus. There are many passages, echoed by the group, that are true danced cadenzas. Act II is largely pantomime, interrupted by Swanilda's delicious Spanish and Scottish variations. The manner of introducing these has changed over the years. The 1887 libretto informs us that Coppelius wraps Swanilda in a cloak secured by a Scottish scarfpin (a cairngorm?). Currently Coppelius, to distract Swanilda from her efforts to awaken Frantz, pins a mantilla to her hair and gives her a fan. At the conclusion of the Spanish dance he removes these ornaments, substituting a scarf, which he arranges over her shoulder in the manner of a plaid. The pantomime in this scene is never for a moment dull or lacking in interest and is at all times admirably supported by the music. Act III has changed considerably: in the Monte Carlo version, it opens with a Dance of the Hours performed by twelve members of the corps de ballet, followed by the Dawn and Prayer variations, a betrothal dance, a *pas de deux* for the principals, and a number of dances for the ensemble; Ballet Theatre omitted practically all of this, retaining only the *pas de deux* and a finale. Hymen and Cupid, as well as the alarms and excursions, have disappeared from both versions.

The czardas in Act I is said by Beaumont (*Complete Book of Ballets*) to have been originally danced by Swanilda and her friends.

This seems rather doubtful, as the czardas, except in a highly stylized form, would scarcely lend itself to performance by dancers in ballet shoes. Currently, it is a reasonably authentic form of the folk dance. Anyone who saw it performed by the Monte Carlo corps de ballet in their delightful Hungarian costumes, led by Delarova and Franklin, can testify that it was rarely exhilarating. Its slow opening rhythms changing to a frenetic whirl were an unfailing delight. Why Ballet Theatre retained the relatively commonplace mazurka and omitted the czardas is one of those balletic mysteries to which there is no sensible answer. The introduction of the czardas into *Coppélia* is said to have been its first appearance in serious ballet.

The score of *Coppélia* is not the least of its charms. It is one of the few nineteenth-century ballet scores to achieve the dignity of being arranged for concert performance. Carl Van Vechten, obviously suffering from an overdose of the atonality, modality, and just plain unmelodiousness of modern music, wrote a delightful article on Délibes in the *Musical Quarterly* (October 1922). In it he calls the score of *Coppélia* "a model of conciseness, witty music, and spirited and refined melody." Speaking of the ballet music generally, he says: "Délibes's ballet music is piquant and picturesque, nervous and brilliant, shot with color and curious harmonic effects, subtle in rhythm, and, above all, his melody has a highly distinguished line. . . . It has even occurred to me to wonder if any composer really gifted with the power of creating melody has ever found it necessary to try to create anything else."

Those elfin creatures who arrange program copy for the printers have had considerable difficulty over the years with the name of one of the librettists—Charles Louis Etienne Nuitter. The American Opera program presented him correctly, then chaos set in. He appears as Neweter (Pavlova-Mordkin), Newetter (Geltzer-Volinine), and Nutter (Monte Carlo Ballet). Simple justice to the coauthor of a charming ballet plot requires that his name be correctly recorded, although often enough the librettist is the forgotten man of ballet.

Coppélia, after a career of seventy-five years in the dance theater, retains a freshness and charm that is not surpassed by any other ballet. It has been called "the last flowering of the Second Empire" and "the only work of art produced by that system during the decade of the seventies."

LE COQ D'OR

LE COQ D'OR began its controversial career in the musical theater as an opera by Nikolai Rimsky-Korsakov, with a libretto by V. I. Byelsky based on a poem by Pushkin. As originally conceived, it is a satire on conditions in Czarist Russia. In 1905 Rimsky-Korsakov had been dismissed from his professorship at the St. Petersburg Conservatory for his expressed sympathy with the revolutionary ideas of a group of students. Bureaucracy punished him again by forbidding the production of his latest opera, *Le Coq d'or,* unless he consented to a number of cuts. As he refused to compromise with the censors, the opera was not performed during his lifetime. More than a year after Rimsky-Korsakov's death *Le Coq d'or* was performed for the first time at Zimin's Private Opera House in Moscow on September 24, 1909. A production took place in St. Petersburg in 1910.

In 1914 Diaghilev had the brilliant idea of presenting *Le Coq d'Or* as an opera-pantomime with a double cast of singers and dancers. This production was bitterly protested by the Rimsky-Korsakov family, who were already cherishing a grievance over the disregard for the composer's program in the action of the ballet *Scheherazade.* They should have been grateful for the Fokine-Diaghilev treatment of *Le Coq d'Or.* New York has seen both choreographic and "straight" presentations of the opera and there can be little doubt of the superiority of the former. There are few coloratura sopranos capable of doing justice to the singing and dancing requirements of the role of the Queen of Shemakha. None of these prodigies has been visible in New York, although Gabrielle Ritter-Ciampi, of the Paris Opéra, is reported to have given a more than acceptable performance in this difficult role.

The opera-pantomime version of *Le Coq d'Or* was first produced at the Paris Opéra on May 21, 1914, with the following dual cast:

	Dancers	Singers
QUEEN OF SHEMAKHA	*Mme Karsavina*	*Mme Dobrovolska*
AMELFA	*Mme Jezierska*	*Mme Petrenko*
KING	*M. Bulgakov*	*M. Petrov*
ASTROLOGER	*M. Cecchetti*	*M. Altchevsky*
GENERAL	*M. Kovalsky*	*M. Belianin*
GUIDONE	*M. Grigoriev*	*M. Frohman*

This production was an immediate success with the audience, who for once in their opera-going lives saw an approximation of both composer's and librettist's intentions. Mmes Karsavina and Dobrovolska by their joint efforts solved all the problems of the Queen of Shemakha—one of the most difficult roles in opera. Pedantic musicologists raised protests that disturbed no one's enjoyment of an enchanting spectacle.

Le Coq d'Or in this novel form reached the Metropolitan Opera House, New York, on March 6, 1918. It was produced by Adolph Bolm, and the brilliant and imaginative décor was by Willy Pogany. The double cast was as follows:

	Dancers	Singers
QUEEN OF SHEMAKHA	*Rosina Galli*	*Maria Barrientos*
AMELFA	*Regina Smith*	*Sophie Braslau*
KING	*Adolph Bolm*	*Adamo Didur*
THE GENERAL	*Ottokar Bartik*	*Basil Ruysdael*
ASTROLOGER	*Giuseppe Bonfiglio*	*Rafaelo Diaz*
PRINCE	*Hall*	*Pietro Audisio*

Once more operatic history was made. Public and critics had a thoroughly good time, and the faint wails drifting in from critical sidelines were disregarded. *Le Coq d'Or,* in this form, held its place in the repertoire for many seasons, and achieved the respectable total of forty-two performances. At various times Mabel Garrison, Amelita Galli-Curci, Thalia Sabanieeva, and Marian Talley sang the role of the Queen. Prima donnas with more than usually exhibitionistic tendencies did not care much for the part, the method of production requiring them to wear a costume uniform with the rest of the singing cast and sit side by side with lowly members of the ensemble in bleachers that were set on either side of the stage at oblique angles to the footlights.

On the afternoon of February 4, 1937 *Le Coq d'Or* was revived in strict operatic form at the Metropolitan Opera House, with Lily Pons (Queen of Shemakha) and Ezio Pinza (King Dodon) heading the cast. Miss Pons's ladylike ambling, suggestive of a society amateur at a charity entertainment, was the complete answer to critical complaints about the dual cast. Truth compels one to admit, however, that Ezio Pinza's King is the best that has yet been seen on the Metropolitan stage in either opera or ballet versions, but artists of his vocal and plastic gifts are as rare as the phœnix.

In the same year *Le Coq d'Or* was presented as a ballet, in a completely new version by its original choreographer, Michel Fokine. The settings and costumes were by Nathalie Gontcharova. It was first performed in New York at the Metropolitan Opera House on October 23, 1937, with the following cast:

THE GOLDEN COCKEREL	GENERAL POLKAN
Tatiana Riabouchinska	*Edouard Borovansky*
QUEEN OF SHEMAKHA *Irina Baronova*	THE ASTROLOGER
KING DODON *Marc Platoff*	*Harcourt Algeranoff*
King Dodon's Sons:	VISIONS: *Roman Jasinsky, Paul Pet-*
PRINCE GUIDON) (*Yura Lazovsky*	*roff, Tamara Grigorieva, Olga Mo-*
PRINCE APHRON) (*Serge Ismailoff*	*rosova, Sono Osato, Lubov Rostova*
AMELPHA *Tatiana Chamie*	

Boyars, Russian Dancers, Cooks, Messengers, Youths, Warriors, Oriental Dancers.

❖❖❖❖❖❖❖❖❖❖❖❖❖❖❖

As this version of this protean work of art is best known to the ballet audience, there follows a detailed account of the plot.

Prologue. The Astrologer, dressed in a dark cloak decorated with stars and crescent moons, gazes at the sky through a telescope. He sees the Queen of Shemakha, the daughter of the air. Deciding that she must be his, he considers how best to gain possession of her. With mystic passes, he evokes the Golden Cockerel whose radiant plumage glows like the sun. Hiding the bird beneath his cloak, he begins his journey to the court of King Dodon.

Act I. The Court of King Dodon. The King, stupid and enormously fat, is holding a council with his boyars. He strives to impress them with his heavy duties and responsibilities. He asks their assistance and advice. No one speaks until Prince Guidon rises and extols the arts of peace and the pleasures of dancing and music. Prince Aphron brushes him aside and praises military glory and the rugged joys of war. King and boyars debate these viewpoints, with much impassioned oratory on both sides, with the busybody General Polkan well to the fore. Civil war seems about to break out in the court, when there is an interruption. It is the Astrologer, who has brought the Golden Cockerel as a gift to King Dodon. This is a magic bird that will warn King Dodon of the approach of enemies. He and his kingdom may enjoy security with the possession of the Golden Cockerel. The General is dubious about accepting the gift, but he is over-

ruled by the King, who is delighted with the new toy. He offers the
Astrologer a coffer of jewels as a return gift. The Astrologer refuses
payment for the moment, but extracts a promise from the King that
some time in the future he will be repaid in accordance with his
wishes, at present unexpressed.

King Dodon forgets his cares, dismisses his court, and calls for his
Nurse. She comes, surrounded by girls who spread a feast for the
King, feed him, and dance for his amusement. Now he is drowsy.
The Nurse orders his bed to be prepared. With the aid of the girls,
she settles him amid piles of luxurious pillows. He dreams of a
lovely Queen who hovers just out of his reach. The vision fades when
the Golden Cockerel flashes by, sounding a warning. Reluctantly
the King awakens, summons his sons, whom he dispatches with part
of the army to look for the enemy. The King goes back to sleep, resuming his dream where he left off. Again the Golden Cockerel
crows, heralding disaster. For the second time, the King is forced to
rouse himself. He curses the Golden Cockerel, realizing that this
time he will have to take charge of things himself. He sends for his
horse, which obviously he has not mounted for years. The combined
efforts of Nurse, General, and soldiers get him aboard the animal.
He makes a determined attempt to assume a martial demeanor and,
calling his troops to follow him, sets out for the wars.

Act II. The Battlefield. A dismal scene of carnage is revealed. It is
the cold hour before dawn when unwilling birds are beginning to
wake up. The King, the General, and the army arrive. They are
quite deflated, all ideas of military glory quenched. The King discovers the bodies of his sons. Their posture plainly indicates that they
have quarreled and killed each other. There are no signs of enemies,
dead or alive. There is mourning, until the General orders the bodies
to be removed.

In the distance there is a steadily expanding glow of light, and a
tent is seen rising from the ground. The alarmed King orders the
artillery brought up. With much bumbling inefficiency this is done.
While the gun is being aimed, there is a black-out. Completely de-
moralized, King and army retreat.

When the eclipse has passed, it is seen that this is no hostile army,
but the lovely Queen of Shemakha and her court. They are arrayed
in shimmering colors, as becomes children of the air. The King and

the General cautiously return. As nothing untoward happens to them, the army creeps back, too.

The Queen, ordering her women to bring wine, drinks with the King. Then she dances. The King is overcome. Never has he seen such beautiful women, such divine dancing. The Queen suggests that he in his turn entertain her. The King shows a justifiable reluctance. He has not the figure for dancing, and he is unwilling to make a zany of himself in front of his entourage. However, he is unable to resist the Queen's persuasion. He takes off his crown and lays aside his scepter. Quickly she ties a scarf around his head, *babushka* fashion, and gives him a fan. Ordering his followers to turn their backs, he attempts to imitate the dance pattern set by the Queen, until, caught by the spirit of the thing, he dances until he falls from exhaustion.

In spite of being placed in this humiliating position, the King has enjoyed himself very much indeed. Over the General's protests, he asks the Queen to accompany him back to his kingdom as his bride. There is a great triumph, in which the followers of both King and Queen participate.

Act III. King Dodon's Kingdom. King Dodon's subjects are in a state of great anxiety. They gather to await news of the King's expedition. A Messenger runs in. Breathlessly he announces the deaths of the King's sons. While he is still telling his tale, a second Messenger arrives, proclaiming the imminent approach of the King with his bride, the Queen of Shemakha. With popping eyes he describes the wonders they are about to see.

A burst of music, and the procession comes into view. It is wonderful to behold: giants, dwarfs, fabulous animals, slaves carrying trays of jewels, the Queen's attendants, her army of Amazons, and finally a magnificent equipage in which the King and the Queen are seated. With stately ceremonial they descend amid the plaudits of their subjects.

The Astrologer enters. The King greets him warmly and invites him to look upon the happy consequences of the gift of the Golden Cockerel. The King's cordiality cools when the Astrologer tells him that he has come to collect his debt. In exchange for the Golden Cockerel, the Astrologer wishes the King to give him possession of the Queen of Shemakha. The King offers him jewels, even a part of his kingdom. When the Astrologer proves obdurate, the King flies into a fury and kills him with a blow of his scepter.

There is an ominous pause, broken by a laugh from the Queen. Suddenly the Golden Cockerel flashes into view. With a triumphant crow, he pecks the King's head. The King falls lifeless. Darkness covers the scene. Again the Queen is heard laughing. When light returns, it is seen that the Queen and all her strange cavalcade have disappeared. The people, mourning King Dodon, set up a great wail.

Epilogue. The Astrologer appears. He warns all onlookers to behave honestly or a fate similar to King Dodon's will overtake them.

Le Coq d'Or once more demonstrated its vitality and universal appeal by winning both critical and public praise in this new version. It was impossible not to miss the vocal portion of the score—which had been made into a compact orchestral suite by Nikolai Tcherepnin. This was marked by much less repetition than may be found in the original. It was an unalloyed delight to see Fokine's choreography fresh from the master's hands. Previous versions seen in New York had been staged by Adolph Bolm. A quick survey of Mr. Bolm's own ballets would not be reassuring as to the quality of his own contributions or additions to Fokine's original ideas.

Once more there were the routine complaints from musicologists—this time about the vandalism of reducing an opera to an orchestral suite, quite as though it were the first event of its kind in the history of music. On this occasion Olin Downes came to the rescue and in a long article in the *New York Times* (November 21, 1937) pointed out that the composer himself had given permission to Maximilian Steinberg and Alexander Glazunov to make an orchestral suite from the score of *Le Coq d'or*. Downes also quoted Fokine's answer to the critics who had quibbled about his changing the libretto for ballet purposes, which was to the effect that V. Byelsky, the librettist, had changed Pushkin's poem for operatic purposes. The public, not interested in this minor warfare, went to see *Le Coq d'Or* in droves, necessitating extra performances.

Le Coq d'Or was distinguished by simple, direct choreography, magnificent settings, and superb performances by principals and ensemble. Heading the cast was Irina Baronova as the Queen of Shemakha. She ran the range of queenly grandeur, coquetry, and plain mischief, in a manner that astonished even her admirers. Her opening solo was performed with a deceptive ease and simplicity that made light of its formidable technical difficulties. There was also a supported adagio with two partners, in which she displayed a nice appreciation of the Oriental style in which it was designed. This was not the arm-wriggles and *danse du ventre* commonly associated with the East, nor yet a photographic reproduction of the authentic Hindu dancing made familiar by Uday Shankar. It was rather a series of plastic pictures capturing the essence of Hindu sculpture. One had to see another dancer in the role to realize how much depended on Baronova's kinetic memory and feeling for style. In the scenes of King Dodon's seduction she was all coquetry and guile, performing without losing a jot of her queenly dignity, something that might be described as "trucking" *sur les pointes*.

Tatiana Riabouchinska as the Golden Cockerel had an unusual opportunity to exhibit her superb elevation. In a wonderful costume—gold tights with sleeves made to represent wings and a feathered headdress—she glittered like a creature of mythology. Her unbelievable *grands jetés* were the subject of many action photographs. It is common knowledge that a dancer's elevation can be considerably improved by camera angles. In this case the photographers captured what the audiences thought they saw, and so were true to the spirit of what they photographed—usually the prerogative of artists in a less mechanical medium.

The smaller roles in *Le Coq d'Or* were beautifully performed. The group composing the Queen's attendants was especially noteworthy. Wonderfully costumed, they formed a colorful background for the Queen's movements and brought the correct note of fantasy to the ensemble scenes.

When internal strife split Colonel W. de Basil's Ballet Russe into two companies, *Le Coq d'Or* remained in the possession of Colonel de Basil. The Ballet Russe de Monte Carlo, finding it difficult to replace this fascinating spectacle for their American audiences, pulled a long and highly involved opus, *Bogatyri,* out of a hat. It was termed a choreographic legend, and a more wildly confused plot never found its way to the Metropolitan stage. Comparatively speaking, *The Magic Flute* and *Oberon* are miracles of clarity. Thus handicapped, gorgeous settings by Nathalie Gontcharova, music by Borodin, and a charming performance by Danilova were not enough to interest the audience, and *Bogatyri* was quickly shelved.

Le Coq d'Or had its most recent revival as a ballet in New York at the opening performance by the Original Ballet Russe at the Fifty-first Street Theater on November 6, 1940.[1] The cast was substantially the same as in 1937, with Baronova and Riabouchinska in the roles they had created. Although the production suffered from being given on a small stage, it was cordially welcomed by an audience that had been waiting for three years to see if it was really as good as they remembered it to be.

There are many books describing the overwhelming impact of the Russian Ballet on western Europe during its golden age—roughly 1909 to 1914. Readers of these books go to current ballet performances expecting to experience something similar. Confronted with a dusty *Scheherazade* and a tired *Prince Igor* (they choose these ballets because they have read about them), they are apt to wonder what all the uproar was about. Any member of this section of the ballet audience who was lucky enough to encounter *Le Coq d'Or* on his first visit to the ballet was not disappointed. Its combination of gorgeous spectacle, exotic atmosphere, and virtuoso dancing could not fail to thrill. It cannot be claimed that its effect on the practiced ballet audience would be so immediate. Modern ballet-lovers have learned to look for something more subtle. To the historically minded newcomer to ballet, however, *Le Coq d'Or* was an invariable delight and presented the synthesis of the picturesque, ornate style, exotic music, and manner of performance he had been led by reading to expect.

---

[1] In 1945 there was another Metropolitan revival of *Le Coq d'Or* in its operatic form, this time in English. Having heard it only on the radio, I hope that the cast were first-rate dancers and actors, the singing being dreadful beyond belief.

DARK ELEGIES

Ballet in one act by Antony Tudor; music by Gustav Mahler; décor by Raymond Sovey, after sketches by Nadia Benois; designed by Raymond Sovey; choreography by Antony Tudor.

DARK ELEGIES was first performed by the Rambert Ballet, at the Duchess Theatre, London, on February 19, 1937. The American première, presented by Ballet Theatre, took place at the Center Theater, New York, on January 24, 1941.

The music for this ballet was the *Kindertotenlieder* (*Songs on the Death of Children*), by Gustav Mahler. The following dancers performed:

I. *Nun will, die Sonn' so hell aufgehen.* Nina Stroganova, with Chorus
II. *Nun seh' ich wohl, warum so dunkel Flammen.* Miriam Golden and Antony Tudor.
III. *Wenn dein Mütterlein.* Hugh Laing, with Chorus
IV. *Oft denk' ich, sie sind nur ausgegangen.* Lucia Chase
V. *In diesem Wetter.* Dimitri Romanoff, with Chorus
CHORUS: *Audrey Castello, Maria Karniloff, Nora Koreff-Kay, Tania Dokoudovska, Kirsten Valbor, Hubert Bland*

❖❖❖❖❖❖❖❖❖❖❖❖❖❖

The *Kindertotenlieder* is a cycle of five songs, the lyrics of which were selected by Mahler from a series of poems by Friedrich Rückert, a German lyric poet of the early nineteenth century. These poems were a personal expression of Rückert's sorrow for the death of his two children, who were carried off suddenly in a cholera epidemic. The poems that Mahler set for his song cycle are chosen to voice the curve of bitter grief into a resigned acceptance of the tragedy. In the first song the father looks with astonishment at the bright sunny day. He cannot believe that the whole face of the sun is not darkened by his sorrow. In the second he recalls the bright eyes of his children, wondering if their lambent flame was not a portent of untimely death. In the third he sees the mother entering the room. Unconsciously his eyes seek the lower level beside her where the children would appear. With a new shock he realizes that never again will he see them. In the fourth, noticing the quiet of the house, he thinks that the children have gone out for a short time and will return. Then he remembers that they are not coming back. In the fifth he becomes aware of a storm. He is worried about the children, whom he would never have allowed out in such weather. After a pause, he accepts the fact that they are safe, not only from this storm, but from all the storms of life. At length he is resigned to his bitter loss.

Dark Elegies might have been a literal conveyance of the incidents and resulting reflections expressed by these lyrics. Antony Tudor, however, does not see them in that light. For the sorrows of a middle-class poet, sincere and bitter though expressed in romantic formulas, he substitutes the group emotions of a community of what would appear to be peasants. There can be no quarrel with Tudor's choice of music. That war, begun by Isadora Duncan, was won more than a generation later by Léonide Massine. One may take exception, however, to the distortion of the music. The *Kindertotenlieder* are simple and moving. When taken too slowly as a ballet accompaniment, they become lugubrious. Mahler's time indications are quite clear. For the first song in the cycle, his wishes are expressed in the words: *"Langsam und schwermutig, nicht schleppend"* ("Slow and heavy-spirited, not dragging"); for the second: *"Ruhig, nicht schleppend"* ("Calm, not dragging"); for the third: *"Schwer, dumpf"* ("Heavy, dull"); for the fourth: *"Ruhig bewegt, ohne zu eilen"* ("Calmly moving, without hurrying"); for the fifth: *"Mit ruhelos schmerzvollen Ausdruck"* ("With restless, painful expression"). Now, these directions make it amply clear that Mahler does not wish the singer to retard the pace of the songs. Twice he specifically prohibits dragging. One may express heaviness and dullness without seeming also to stand still. The prohibition of hurrying does not mean prohibition of any movement whatever. Compare the admirable recording of the *Kindertotenlieder* by Heinrich Rehkemper with the performance that accompanies the ballet, and the variation in the tempo from that set in the ballet is striking.

Choreographically, *Dark Elegies* makes little use of the vocabulary of the classical dance. The brilliance of beats and multiple turns would be incongruous in the expressions of such grim emotions. The women rise occasionally to their points. Otherwise there is nothing to distinguish this ballet from a work proceeding out of a modern dance studio. A highly stylized version of folk-dance steps appears at one point. Several of the solos are performed within a circle of seated or kneeling figures. A feeling of Spartan control over personal sorrow is communicated by the rigid movements. Now and again a single dancer seems to give way to a normal expression of mourning to revert quickly to an unbending attitude. The man's solo performance to the first half of the fifth song is characterized by strange leaps straight into the air, with one arm held high, the other clutched tightly to his body. The ballet ends with a simple processional during the second section of the fifth song, the dancers leaving the stage in double file.

Dark Elegies is taken very seriously by the dancers performing it. Consequently one never sees an obviously unrehearsed or careless performance, every member of the cast uniting to convey the utmost in disciplined emotion. Miriam Golden's expressive interpretation of the adagio performed to the second song was memorable. Dimitri Romanoff is at his best in the difficult solo in the first section of the fifth song. However, this is not a ballet in which personal expression or virtuosity is appropriate, and individual members of a cast of serious artists should not be singled out for commendation which all earn at every performance.

The settings and costumes by Raymond Sovey follow those of the original London production by Nadia Benois. A spare, cold landscape is inhabited by figures clad in costumes that suggest the working clothes worn by northern peasants. The men wear jumpers and slacks, the women the simplest form of female attire in dull blues and grays, with an occasional purple and dark red. Their hair is tightly drawn back and partly concealed by headcloths. *Dark Elegies* has quite the starkest décor and simplest costumes seen in ballet since *Les Noces*.

It is not my intention to challenge Antony Tudor's choice of music for this ballet of undeniable power, although I feel that he might have resisted the temptation to use the ready-made emotions of the lyrics of the *Kindertotenlieder*, and found music more expressive of peasant grief. Rückert's poems are the intimate utterance of personal tragedy. A German poet of a romantic period (he lived from 1788 to 1866), he saw things in a romantic way that seems incompatible with the group emotions of workers as we see them in the ballet. It is impossible not to be distracted by the cross-purposes in the atmosphere of the lyrics and the milieu of the ballet.

DEVIL'S HOLIDAY

Devil's Holiday (Le Diable S'Amuse): ballet in a prologue and three scenes by Vincenzo Tommasini; music by Tommasini on themes by Paganini; choreography by Frederick Ashton; scenery and costumes by Eugène Berman.

D EVIL'S HOLIDAY was given its first performance by the Ballet Russe de Monte Carlo on October 26, 1939 at the Metropolitan Opera House, New York, with the following cast:

THE OLD LORD	*Simon Semenoff*	THE OLD WOMAN	*Tatiana Chamie*
HIS DAUGHTER	*Alexandra Danilova*	THE BEGGAR	*Robert Irwin*
THE YOUNG LOVER	*Frederic Franklin*	THE HAT-SELLER	
THE FIANCÉ	*George Zoritch*		*Alexander Goudovitch*
THE DEVIL	*Marc Platoff*		
THE GYPSY GIRL	*Nathalie Krassovska*	Bailiffs, hunters, guests	

Prologue. The plot of the ballet concerns itself with the Devil's efforts to amuse himself by taking a hand in human affairs. Disguised as a mortal, he wanders in Venice until attracted, along with a collection of street merchants and a beggar or two, by a commotion at the gate of a shabby, but once palatial dwelling. The Old Lord and his Daughter are trying to stave off a group of importunate creditors. The Devil pays them what they ask and with careless generosity includes the bystanders in his largess. They rush away, pleased with their good fortune. One of the beggars, a handsome young man, is more interested in the Daughter than in gold, and lingers. The Old Lord invites the generous stranger to his Daughter's betrothal ball. The Devil seeing an opportunity for mischief, invites the Beggar to accompany him.

Scene 1. The Ball. Surrounded by guests, the Daughter dances somewhat apathetically with her Fiancé. When the Devil enters with the Beggar, now richly dressed, she shows great interest. They dance alone, and are discovered in an embrace by the Devil, who calls the

Old Lord, the Fiancé, and the guests. The Daughter sinks beneath their scorn, and the Devil drags the Fiancé away.

Entr'acte. The Beggar and the Daughter meet in a dream of love's frustration.

Scene 2. The Forest. A party of hunters enters. They dance triumphantly around a fox they have killed. Suddenly they are put to flight. It is not a dead fox, but a live Devil. He chases them from the scene and dances a gay and sardonic solo. The Beggar enters in despair, lamenting his lost love. The Devil conjures up a Gypsy Girl, whose wild dancing causes the Beggar to forget his sorrow. The Daughter wanders in, and devilish arts fail in the presence of true love. The Beggar, abandoning the Gypsy Girl, drives the Devil from the scene with the aid of the returning hunters.

Entr'acte. The Devil dresses for the carnival. Two servants help him to don his cloak and mask.

Scene 3. The Carnival. Carnival revelers in fantastic disguises enter. The Devil's presence casts constraint on their festive mood. They tear his sinister mask away and shrink back appalled by his true identity. They are terror-stricken, but deliverance is at hand. The clock strikes twelve, the Devil vanishes, and maskers and the characters of the drama whirl in carnival gaiety.

Frederick Ashton's ballets form an important part of the repertoire of the Sadler's Wells Ballet, the national ballet of England. He is known to New York chiefly as the choreographer of the Gertrude Stein and Virgil Thomson opera, *Four Saints in Three Acts. Devil's Holiday* is his first ballet to reach the United States. It is a delightful example of modern adaptation of the *ballet d'action* dear to nineteenth-century ballet audiences. Complicated on paper, the story is admirably clear in the theater, and moves on to its end dancing all the way. Its only weakness lies in the third scene, traditionally given to *divertissements.* With one or two exceptions these lack interest. Up to that point *Devil's Holiday* need not give place to any contemporary work in a similar genre. The use of the corps de ballet in the ballroom scene, the tender *pas de deux* of the dreaming lovers, and the solos devised for Devil and the Beggar are marked with distinction.

Alexandra Danilova gave a delightful account of the Daughter. Alicia Markova occasionally performed this role. Perfect technically, her interpretation lacked the exquisite emotion of Danilova's. Frederic Franklin had in the Beggar a role that for suitability and charm were not equaled in his repertoire until the advent of *Rodeo*. His forest-scene solo, expressive of the Beggar's frustration and longing, is one of the high points of contemporary ballet. Igor Youskevitch also appeared in this part, but did not develop its dramatic opportunities.

The settings and costumes by Eugène Berman were delightful forerunners of his superb work for *Romeo and Juliet* and other ballets. The music arranged by Vincenzo Tommasini, and based largely on the twenty-four *Caprices* of Nicolò Paganini, admirably supported the actual movements of the dance and underlined their dramatic implications.

It is a pity that this ballet was ever dropped from the active repertoire. No doubt the ballet management lent too sensitive an ear to the critics. One of this august group was clumsily patronizing; another scored it for many of the episodes that gave it distinction. An early revival would be welcome to the ballet public.

DIM LUSTRE

Ballet by Antony Tudor; music by Richard Strauss; costumes and scenery by Motley.

Dim LUSTRE was presented by Ballet Theatre for the first time on October 20, 1943 at the Metropolitan Opera House, New York, with the following cast:

THE WALTZING LADIES AND THEIR PARTNERS: *Barbara Fallis* and *Harold Lang; June Morris* and *Kenneth Davis; Rozsika Sabo* and *Fernando Alonso; Mimi Gomber* and *John Taras; Mary Heater* and *Alpheus Koon.*

THE LADY WITH HIM	*Nora Kaye*		(*Janet Reed*
THE GENTLEMAN WITH HER		WHO WAS SHE?	(*Albia Kavan*
	Hugh Laing		(*Virginia Wilcox*
A REFLECTION	*Muriel Bentley*	SHE WORE A PERFUME	
ANOTHER REFLECTION	*Michael Kidd*		*Rosella Hightower*
IT WAS SPRING	*John Kriza*	HE WORE A WHITE TIE	
			Antony Tudor

A magnificent ballroom lit by many crystal chandeliers gradually fills with dancing couples. In the course of the dance, little incidents or accidents recall to the minds of one of the couples several episodes out of the past.

Hugh [1] kisses Nora on the shoulder. Instantly there comes to her mind the memory of a boy who once kissed her on a day in spring, when she was very young. The thought comes quickly and vanishes like a flash.

A waltzing lady and her partner pause for a moment beside Hugh and Nora. A touch on Hugh's shoulder by the partner causes him to relive an incident on a summer afternoon when he encountered three charming young girls. They elude and confuse him, his attempt to kiss one of them being prevented by the others.

Nora drops her handkerchief. As Hugh restores it to her, its perfume reminds him of quite a different moment in the past. A vision

[1] The characters of the ballet have no names. For purposes of identification, I shall borrow the names of the dancers who created the roles.

of a lady, sophisticated and charmingly capricious, arises in his thoughts, his glamorous moment with her vivid in his memory.

Something about the shape of Hugh's tie recalls to Nora another episode in which, as a young girl, she encountered the experienced love-making of a man of the world.

As the dance comes to an end, Hugh and Nora look at each other with new eyes. Regretfully they realize that the feeling they had for each other cannot survive the impact of memory.

The lights of the chandeliers fade. The waltzing couples leave the dark ballroom.

Dim Lustre employs a movie technique, if not for the first time in ballet, at least in the most effective manner up to date. Each of the evocations of the past is announced by the appearance on the darkening stage of the dancer's double seen as a mirror image. As the mirror images vanish, the memories appear in a half-light. At the conclusion of each episode the ballroom scene is resumed at the exact instant at which it was arrested. Much of the effectiveness of the ballet depends on split-second timing of lights and entrances.[2]

Choreographically, *Dim Lustre* uses the characteristic Tudor adaptation of classical technique. The "waltzing ladies and their partners" waltz only on the program, their movements being an approximation to ballroom dancing, or a glorification of it, the girls performing *sur les pointes*. The variation called "It Was Spring" is marked by *grands jetés* and pirouettes performed at lightning speed. The "Who Was She?" *pas de quatre,* the least distinguished of the episodes, conveys an atmosphere of a summer afternoon, the girls' filmy scarves and sashes contributing their own movement to the scene. "She Wore a Perfume" is the high point of the ballet from a choreographic point of view, as well as a brilliant characterization expressed by means of movement. A thousand words could scarcely tell the story of this passing episode in the life of a sophisticated mondaine more clearly than the light steps and elusive gestures. She *bourrées* into view with her back to the audience. The little turn of her head as she drops her handkerchief and catches sight of the young man calls up an era when flirtation was an art to be practiced

[2] In theaters where the lighting technician is something less than an expert, *Dim Lustre* can be reduced to complete confusion in spite of every effort on the part of the performers.

with all the finesse of a polished technique. "He Wore a White Tie" has a dreamlike quality in spite of its swiftness. The girl, posed *en arabesque,* is seized and whirled through a stylized waltz, ending in an embrace.

Dim Lustre, sophisticated and mannered, has the flavor of a chapter of *Swann's Way.* The slight circumstances that set up the trains of thought that lead to the remembered episodes have the irrelevance of similar accidents in real life, or in Proust. The mood of the ballet is half wry, half bitter-sweet. There is nothing quite like it in the whole range of the dance drama.

The performances in *Dim Lustre* are on a very high level. Nora Kaye, America's outstanding dramatic ballerina, adds a new portrait to her distinguished gallery of impersonations. Typed by *Pillar of Fire* as an interpreter of grimly intense roles, she displays in *Dim Lustre* an ability to reveal the character of a woman in a milieu that could not be further removed from that of the troubled Hagar. True, the woman in *Dim Lustre* is not without emotional difficulties, but they belong to an entirely different world—the Edwardian world of crystal chandeliers, *chypre,* and shoulder-length gloves. Her emotions are light and variable. The current flirtation has been marred by inconvenient memories, but there will be another, equally delightful, tomorrow. This is no mean feat of character-building in view of the rapid tempo at which the ballet proceeds. Technically, Hugh Laing and Nora Kaye perform the difficult steps with ease and a certain sense of period elegance that accentuates the Edwardian atmosphere.

John Kriza, in the first dream sequence, is called upon to perform brilliant technical steps at a breath-taking tempo. This variation must be quite the most swiftly paced thirty seconds of dancing in the entire range of ballet. Only Riabouchinska's delirious solo in *Paganini* can compare with it. Rosella Hightower, as an *élégante* who might be one of the younger duchesses, demonstrates her ability as a character dancer in a role that is in marked contrast with her classic Swan Queen and Princess Florine (Bluebird *pas de deux*). Due tribute must be paid to the ensemble of soloists who impersonate the "waltzing ladies and their partners" whose superb timing adds greatly to the effectiveness of the ballet.

The music for *Dim Lustre* is Richard Strauss's *Burleske* for piano and orchestra. The drum-rolls, recurring at intervals, serve to intro-

112]   *The Borzoi Book of Ballets*

duce the memory episodes and provide natural divisions for the ballet. Its febrile mood is wonderfully in keeping with the atmosphere of this haunted ballroom.

The setting by Motley, with its crystal chandeliers retreating in perspective, is a perfect background for the dancers. The women's costumes, ranging in color from deep wine-red to pale rose beige are stylizations of Edwardian ball dresses, the coiffeurs and long gloves adding their own period charm. The men's costumes are less successful. Similar in color range to the women's dresses, in form they are unfortunately reminiscent of bellboys' uniforms in a chic hotel. Something really ought to be done with them. The costumes of Nora Kaye and Hugh Laing, similar in design to the others, are carried out in an intense and startling white. The dancers in the memory sequences are dressed in grays and greens in muted variations, beautifully appropriate to the dream world in which they live. Rosella Hightower's costume with its high feathered headdress is especially memorable.

Though *Dim Lustre* may not be the most intensely dramatic work in the list of Tudor ballets, it is undoubtedly one of the most charming.

DON JUAN

Choreographic tragi-comedy after G. Angiolini; new version by Eric Allatini and Michel Fokine; music by Gluck; staging and choreography by Michel Fokine; curtain, scenery, and costumes by Mariano Andreù.

DON JUAN was performed for the first time by René Blum's Ballets de Monte Carlo on June 25, 1936 at the Alhambra Theatre, London. The first American presentation was given by the Ballet Russe de Monte Carlo at the Metropolitan Opera House, New York, on October 27, 1938, with the following cast:

DON JUAN	*Michel Panaieff*	THE CHIEF FURY	*Lubov Roudenko*
DONNA ELVIRA	*Jeannette Lauret*	THE CHIEF JESTER	*Roland Guerard*
THE COMMANDER	*Jean Yazvinsky*	THE DUENNA	*Ludmilla Rklitzka*
SGANARELLE	*Simon Semenoff*	THE SERVANT	*Robert Irwin*
THE GYPSY	*Nathalie Krassovska*	TAMBOURINE DANCER	*Nini Theilade*

Jesters, Guests, Musicians, Pages, Lackeys, Mourners, Furies, Demons

❖❖❖❖❖❖❖❖❖❖❖❖❖❖❖❖❖❖❖❖

The action of *Don Juan* takes place on two levels. When the curtain rises, two baroque doorways with heavy broken pediments topped by classic busts are seen. They are set at oblique angles to the footlights at opposite corners of the stage. Four broad steps elevate the inner stage, before which hang blue-gray curtains with formal designs in dark colors. These curtains are drawn aside to reveal the action on the inner stage.

A group of musicians are seen seated on the steps. Four lackeys carrying lanterns enter between the curtains and draw them back, disclosing the house of the Commander. Sganarelle, Don Juan's servant, waves the musicians forward. As they begin their serenade, Donna Elvira, the Commander's daughter appears at an upper window. Don Juan, wrapped in a dark cloak, enters and knocks at the door of the house. Hiding in the darkness, he slips past the Duenna when she comes in answer to the summons. While he is paying court to Donna Elvira, the Commander arrives home. He is ordering the musicians away as Don Juan and Donna Elvira emerge from the house. Angrily, he commands his daughter to return into the house and challenges her impudent suitor to a duel. The old man is easily overcome by the practiced swordsmanship of Don Juan. The arrival of the Commander's soldiers fails to prevent the escape of Don Juan and his servants. When Donna Elvira and the Duenna come out of the house again, they find the Commander dying on the ground.

The curtains are closed by a group of cowled figures dressed in mourning black.

A richly dressed couple followed by a group of dancing torch-bearers cross the stage. Behind them comes the Jester, who dances a gay solo.

The torchbearers draw back the curtains, and a throng of merry-makers is revealed. Don Juan, surrounded by his mistresses and guests, is watching a formal dance performed by several ladies. They are joined by a group of men, then by Don Juan himself, who dances a slow and stately variation. When this is concluded, a table is brought in, and the guests seat themselves for a banquet. The feast is interrupted by a portentous knocking. The Commander, pale and unearthly, appears. Don Juan frivolously invites the ghost to drink wine with him. When the Commander disappears, Don Juan calms the fears of his guests and orders the entertainment to continue. In succession, the jesters, three girls with tambourines, and a Gypsy dance. A veiled woman is brought in by Sganarelle and a group of lackeys. When the veil is removed, the woman is seen to be Donna Elvira in deep mourning for her murdered father. Obviously, she has been brought there against her will. When Don Juan insolently presents her to his company of mistresses, she is deeply humiliated. He forces her to join the guests at the table. The Commander makes a momentary reappearance, vanishing quickly. Don Juan, by his seeming unconcern, composes the disquiet of his friends. The knocking is heard once more. The servants, terrified, rush in, and Don Juan himself, candlestick in hand, goes to answer the summons. He remains cool when for the third time he sees the Commander. His offer of wine is brushed aside by the Commander, who extends a counter-invitation for Don Juan to visit him in his tomb. As Donna Elvira falls senseless and the guests recoil in horror, Don Juan, accompanied by Sganarelle, prepares to follow the Commander.

The curtains are closed by the musicians, and after an interlude the torchbearers open them again.

The scene is the cemetery. To the right is a receding row of cypresses silhouetted against an angry sky; to the left is the tomb of the Commander, surmounted by a large equestrian statue. Don Juan, entering with the reluctant Sganarelle, formally greets the statue, which bows its head in return. Sganarelle rushes fearfully away, but Don Juan remains imperturbable. The Commander conjures up the apparitions of Don Juan's dead mistresses. The libertine, unimpressed by this mournful company, laughs at them mockingly. Venturing within reach of the statue, he is seized in its stony grip. Furies appear, surging around the statue, and wrest Don Juan from its grasp. Flung from one group to another, he disappears like a wounded animal worried by a wolf pack. Retribution has overtaken the transgressor.

The score of *Don Juan,* by Christophe Willibald von Gluck, was written for a ballet with a plot based on Molière's play, *Don Juan, ou le Festin de pierre.* This was produced at the Burgtheater in Vienna in 1761, with choreography by Gaspare Angiolini. *Don Juan* was a *ballet d'action,* and the specially composed music was written in the manner of a modern ballet score, with a view to emphasizing the theatrical values of the plot. As music for the theater it was well in advance of its time, comparing favorably for dramatic atmosphere and style with any modern ballet score. Gluck even emphasized the Spanish locale of the story by employing Spanish thematic material. The Dance of the Furies, which concludes the ballet, was later expanded by the composer for his opera *Orfeo ed Eurydice,* composed a year later.

The score of the ballet had to be assembled from several sources for the modern production of *Don Juan,* which was suggested to René Blum by Roger Desormière. Eric Allatini undertook to locate the score, a task that took him to the libraries of several European opera houses.

Michel Fokine staged the ballet, basing the action, as in the original ballet, on Molière's drama. *Don Juan* emerges as a dramatic pantomime interspersed with dancing. Some of the dances, notably Don Juan's solo, are based on eighteenth-century dancing technique. Fokine's choreography, however, is by no means an archæological reconstruction of a period piece, the pantomime being expressed in general and universally applicable terms. There are certain weaknesses, both dramatic and choreographic: the gypsy's solo, and the tambourine dance are dull numbers, out of place in the period, and with no particular distinction of their own to make them acceptable; the three entrances of the Commander in the banquet scene would be more effective if reduced to one as in Mozart's opera.

When René Blum's Ballets de Monte Carlo was absorbed by the Ballet Russe de Monte Carlo, *Don Juan* and *L'Épreuve d'Amour* became part of the latter company's repertoire. Something like the same fate overtook them both. Originally produced with taste and suitably cast, they were later neglected and the roles assigned to dancers whose names were obviously pulled out of a hat, as they lacked any qualifications for their roles. Don Juan, created by that great classical dancer and mime Anatole Vilzak, was given to Michel Panaieff, who had not a trace of the grand manner, nor even the physique to wear the costume. The role of the Jester, designed for André Eglevsky, was danced by Roland Guerard, an excellent dancer in his own fashion, but lacking the personality to take over a typically Eglevsky part. Jeannette Lauret in her original characterization of Donna Elvira gave an authoritative performance, as did Jean Yazvinsky as the Commander. These two artists were unable to impart their sense of period style to an inferior cast. The ensemble scenes were ragged and under rehearsed. As in the case of *L'Épreuve d'Amour,* a beautiful ballet with a fine musical score was ruined by stupidity and negligence.

The settings by Mariano Andreù are architectural in character, forming an admirable and diversified background for the action. The use of the curtains, opened and closed with appropriate pantomime by various groups, added comment to the drama. The costumes were less interesting. Miscellaneous in character, they ranged through several periods, those of the principal dancers conforming to the accepted date of the plot.

Some of the money spent producing dull novelties (a fine selection might be made from the repertoires of all companies) might well serve to revive *Don Juan*. With some slight revisions, if properly cast, and rehearsed with the same attention that is accorded to other ballets, it would form a valuable addition to the number of dance dramas that are important musically as well as balletically.

L'ÉPREUVE D'AMOUR

L'Épreuve d'Amour, or Chung-Yang and the Mandarin: ballet in one act; book by André Derain and Michel Fokine; music by Mozart; scenery and costumes by André Derain.

L'*ÉPREUVE D'AMOUR* was originally presented by René Blum's Ballets de Monte Carlo, at the Théâtre de Monte Carlo, Monte Carlo, on April 4, 1936. Brought to New York by the Ballet Russe de Monte Carlo, its American première took place on October 14, 1938 at the Metropolitan Opera House, with the following cast:

CHUNG-YANG	*Nathalie Krassovska*	HIS TWO FRIENDS	*Robert Irwin*
THE LOVER	*Michel Panaieff*		*Yura Skibine*
MANDARIN	*Jean Yazvinsky*	THE BUTTERFLY	*Lubov Roudenko*
THE AMBASSADOR	*Roland Guerard*		

Friends of Chung-Yang, Monkeys, Soldiers, Friends of the Lover, Servants

◆◆◆◆◆◆◆◆◆◆◆◆◆◆◆◆◆◆

The plot is as follows:

A Mandarin is seen seated on the ground meditating. His reflections are interrupted by a plague of monkeys who dance around him mockingly. He drives them away, but they are succeeded by a persistent Butterfly, who gives him no peace until it is driven away by the approach of Chung-Yang, his daughter, and her Lover. By this time the Mandarin is in a vicious temper and he takes it out on the Lover, who is good and kind but unfortunately poor and therefore ineligible to be the husband of a mandarin's daughter.

An Ambassador from the Western World, accompanied by his friends and a train of servants, arrives. Impressed by his appearance of wealth, the Mandarin offers the Ambassador his daughter in marriage. As Chung-Yang is gentle and lovely, the Ambassador is not averse to this idea.

A huge Dragon appears, surrounded by a band of brigands in ferocious masks. Mandarin, Ambassador, friends, and servants flee in terror, abandoning the Ambassador's baggage, which includes

several boxes of treasure. The brigands seize the treasure and disappear with the Dragon.

The Mandarin and the Ambassador return to the scene. When the
Mandarin finds that the treasure has gone, he withdraws from his
former idea of giving Chung-Yang to the Ambassador.

Now the inner story of the robbery comes out. The Lover and his
friends approach. Explaining that he was the Dragon and his friends
the brigands, he returns the treasure to its owner. At once the
Mandarin veers back to his original position, but this time the Ambassador will have none of it. He sees beyond doubt that it was only
his wealth that made him desirable.

With the help of the Ambassador, Chung-Yang persuades her
father to give her to her Lover. Reluctantly he consents. There is a
lively wedding procession. The bride and bridegroom are carried
off in a palanquin amid rejoicing on the part of everyone but the
Mandarin, who returns to his reflections, now more bitter than ever.
The monkeys, finding him alone, resume their mocking game. When
the Butterfly reappears he furiously flings a stick at it.

The scenery and costumes by André Derain were the outstanding
feature of the production of L'Épreuve d'Amour. Of extraordinary
beauty, they formed a link with Diaghilev's second period, Derain
having been responsible for the décors of La Boutique Fantasque
(1919) and Jack in the Box (1926). They exactly paralleled the
delicate eighteenth-century chinoiserie of the music, which is said to
be a recently discovered work by Mozart. There is no reference to
this score in Alfred Einstein's Mozart (1945), nor is it listed in the
Köchel Catalogue. It is very charming, however, with moods and
rhythms that set off the dance patterns admirably.

The choreography was worthy of the best traditions of Michel
Fokine, expressing with lyric elegance the playful fantasy of the
story, as well as a charming sense of the period.

In everything but its cast L'Épreuve d'Amour had the elements of
success. The part of Chung-Yang, created by Vera Nemchinova
and later danced by the exquisite Alicia Markova, was given in New
York to Nathalie Krassovska, whose prettiness and theatrical presence are by no means backed by anything resembling an adequate
dancing technique. In a role (the Lover) designed for André
Eglevsky, Michel Panaieff could scarcely hope to excel. The in-

eptitude of this bit of miscasting was equaled only by the appearance of Lubov Roudenko as the Butterfly. To call upon this young dancer, who was admirable as the leader of the cancan in *Gaité Parisienne* and later a more than adequate substitute for Agnes De Mille in *Rodeo,* to be a Butterfly was like asking Mae West to play Ariel. Only Jean Yazvinsky and Roland Guerard were worthy of the little masterpiece in which they appeared.

This managerial stupidity and the effects of an ill-natured and ill-informed review by a music critic turned dance critic for the evening combined to remove *L'Épreuve d'Amour* from the active repertoire. Restudied and properly cast, it would prove a delight to current audiences.

THE FAIR AT SOROCHINSK

Ballet in four scenes by David Lichine, based on stories by N. Gogol; music by Modest Mussorgsky, adapted by Antal Dorati; scenery and costumes by Nicolas Remisoff.

THE first performance of *The Fair at Sorochinsk* took place on October 14, 1943 at the Metropolitan Opera House, New York, with the following cast:

KHIVRIA	*Lucia Chase*	SEXTON	*Simon Semenoff*
RED COAT	*Anton Dolin*	DRUNKARD	*Alpheus Koon*
PARASSIA, Khivria's Stepdaughter		PEDDLER	*Michael Kidd*
	Margaret Banks	CANDY GIRL	*Janet Reed*
GRITZKO	*André Eglevsky*	THREE GYPSIES	*Jerome Robbins,*
FATHER	*Rex Cooper*		*Richard Reed, John Kriza*
FRIEND	*John Taras*	HOPAK LEADER	*Nicolas Orloff*
MAYOR OF SOROCHINSK		THE CAT	*Janet Reed*
	Dimitri Romanoff	WHITE WITCH	*Rosella Hightower*

People of Sorochinsk, Peasant Women, Witches and Devils

❖❖❖❖❖❖❖❖❖❖❖❖❖❖❖❖

Both musically and dramatically this ballet bows in the general direction of Mussorgsky's unfinished *The Fair at Sorochinsk*. The plot is largely based on Ukrainian folk tales.

Prologue. A blind storyteller slowly crosses the stage, led by a little boy.

Scene 1. Khivria's Inn. The witch Khivria arrives at her inn by way of the chimney, just in time to receive a group of peasants on their way to the fair at Sorochinsk. Crossing themselves, they greet her with low bows. The holy sign makes the witch faint. Parassia, her stepdaughter, revives her. Gritzko is attracted by Parassia's beauty, and displays his dancing ability for her benefit. When she shyly responds to his advances, the witch is infuriated by the sight of innocent young love and conjures up a horrid swarm of monsters, who frighten the villagers out of the inn. Gritzko takes Parassia with him.

The Mayor of Sorochinsk arrives and, inspired by vodka, makes

rude love to Khivria. The approach of another visitor causes Khivria
to bundle him into a sack in the chimney corner. This time it is the
Sexton, aged and sanctimonious, who flirts with the witch. A burst of
wild music tells Khivria that Red Coat is on his way. She hastily
shoves the Sexton into the sack in which the Mayor is hiding. She
preens and arranges her costume, for Red Coat is her demon lover.
He arrives with a rush down the chimney. He calls for food and
drink. When replete, he belches politely—this devil has an Oriental
turn to his manners. After a loving passage or two, witch and devil
depart for the fair on a broomstick, Red Coat carrying the sack in
which Mayor and Sexton have been concealed.

Entr'acte. Procession of peasants on their way to the fair, followed
after an interval by Khivria and Red Coat.

Scene 2. Fair at Sorochinsk. The fair is in full swing. Young and
old in festal attire mill about in gay abandon. Parassia and Gritzko
are conspicuous among them. A Peddler of cheap jewelry is mobbed
by the young girls, who buy all his merchandise. His elation at this
quick turnover annoys Three Gypsies, who chase him away. Khivria
and Red Coat, carrying the sack, arrive. He flings it down, and the
curious peasants form a circle. Red Coat, flourishing a wreath of
garlic, makes them sneeze. The sack flies open; Mayor and Sexton
fall out, amazed and sheepish at finding themselves in such a public
predicament. A Drunkard who has been weaving aimlessly through
the crowd attracts Red Coat's attention. With his devilish arts, Red
Coat turns him, very appropriately, into a goose. One of the villagers
notices something suspicious about Red Coat and investigates—it is
a tail. The indignant crowd chase him away. He eludes them and,
coming back, finds the scene deserted save for Khivria and the
Drunkard, restored to his proper form. Swearing the Drunkard to
silence with threats, Khivria helps Red Coat to hide. The villagers
give up and trickle back to the fair. The Drunkard is unable to
keep silence and indicates Red Coat's hiding-place. Gritzko prods
him out of it with a pitchfork, and he escapes in a mad dash with
Khivria.

Now the strains of a hopak sound and some of the crowd begin to
dance. One of the village bucks turns a somersault and lands performing a wild *prisiadka* without a break in his rhythm. He and
Gritzko engage in a sort of competition which neither can win because they are equally matched. The frenzy mounts and exhausts

itself. It is evening, and time for the old to go home and the young to go courting.

A crescent moon rises. Parassia and Gritzko come in just in time to meet Khivria and Red Coat and their friends, the Mayor and the Sexton. Khivria roughly drags Parassia away. Gritzko, with a contemptuous gesture, walks off, but not far. Parassia eludes her stepmother and rejoins Gritzko. Now the boys and girls stroll together in the moonlight. Quietly they depart in pairs, leaving the scene deserted.

A hand holding a bottle appears over the edge of a barrel in the rear of the stage. It is the Drunkard, who has been having a quiet nap. Khivria and Red Coat have been looking for him. His betrayal of Red Coat's hiding-place must be punished. He hastily retreats into his barrel, but they turn it on its side and roll it away. Red Coat comes back; he has forgotten something. The coming witches' Sabbath may not take place under the moon. He climbs high, steals the moon, and gives it to Khivria, who covers its light with her shawl.

Scene 3. Night at Bald Mountain. In a mountain glen, gruesome with hanging moss, a wild orgy led by Khivria and Red Coat takes place. All the characters of the drama appear. The Mayor and the Sexton tangle weirdly with the White Witch and the Cat. The Drunkard dances a wavering *pas de deux* with his barrel. Gritzko and Parassia are dragged in. Their love and courage sustain them through all violence. At last the blessed day dawns. Devils and witches melt away; a church is seen on the hillside. The young lovers kneel and cross themselves.

The blind storyteller, led by his small guide, slowly recrosses the scene. His story has been told.

Fair at Sorochinsk has been given a bright and colorful production by Ballet Theatre. The setting for the fair scene, with its suggestion of fields stretching off into space, is very effective. The costumes are a theatrical version of Ukrainian dress.

The musical score is based on Mussorgsky's opera *The Fair at Sorochinsk,* selections from *Pictures at an Exhibition,* and *A Night on Bald Mountain.*

Choreographically, *The Fair at Sorochinsk* has several interesting features. The outstanding role is that of Red Coat, created for Anton Dolin, whose ability to dance on point was demonstrated early in his career, in Bronislava Nijinska's ballet *Les Fâcheux,* originally produced in 1924. There are few artistic reasons for male dancing *sur les pointes,* one being that it is a traditional dance form among the Cossacks. Red Coat being a Russian devil, this use of male point work is appropriate on both national and psychological grounds. Dolin performed the role brilliantly, and when it was taken over by a less accomplished dancer its effectiveness was greatly diminished.

Even without this startling tour de force, there remains the scene at the fair, which may well be compared with a similar scene in *Petrouchka.* Every movement of the crowd is carefully planned, and the result is a realistic scene in which incidents happen naturally and the confusion makes an interesting pattern. The hopak, taken up by small groups until everyone on the stage is involved, is certainly the most exciting mass movement seen on the ballet stage in years. It invariably stops the show, and it is a pity that the ballet does not end with it. Although the dance of the young people in the moonlight provides an interesting contrast, the confusion (real, not planned) of the witches' Sabbath is a depressant. The sentimental ending—a throwback to Disney's *Fantasia*—seems more like cinema than ballet.

If *The Fair at Sorochinsk* is to survive, it should be revised and its really excellent features allied to a plot that would allow the climax of the ballet to come where it properly belongs—at the end.

FANCY FREE

Ballet in one act concerning three sailors on shore leave; music by Leonard Bernstein; choreography by Jerome Robbins; scenery designed by Oliver Smith; costumes designed by Kermit Love.

FANCY FREE was performed for the first time by Ballet Theatre on April 18, 1944 at the Metropolitan Opera House, New York, with the following cast:

BARTENDER	*Rex Cooper*	PASSERS-BY	*Muriel Bentley,*
SAILORS	*Jerome Robbins,*		*Janet Reed, Shirley Eckl*
	Harold Lang, John Kriza		

Time: The present, a hot summer night. *Place*: New York City, a side street.

◇◇◇◇◇◇◇◇◇◇◇◇◇◇◇◇◇◇◇◇

The action of the ballet is heralded by the sultry voice of a blues-singer emerging from a record slightly hoarse with age. The curtain rises to reveal on the left a typical bar of the lower kind. At the right the street outside may be seen, the whole backed by the topless towers of Manhattan. The weary, unshaven bartender is just stopping the record-player before relapsing into a between-customers coma. As the first lively crashes from the orchestra sound, three sailors burst around the corner of the street outside the bar at a terrific clip. Obviously, their shore leave has just begun, and the first exuberance has not yet subsided. They come to a stop, pausing to discuss plans that first and foremost include girls. After a bit of friendly horse-play they become aware of the bar. Two of them are inside ordering beers before the third catches the idea. He joins them in time to participate in the drinking ritual and gang up on the quietest member of the trio, cheating him into paying for the beers.

They leave the bar and stand aimlessly outside. One of them passes gum around, and they chew it ruminatively, while trying to think of something to do. The problem is partly solved by the entry of a passer-by—a dark girl with a red purse. Immediately she is surrounded by all three sailors, each of whom outdoes himself in the effort to attract her exclusive attention. The situation develops into a boisterous scramble, in which the red purse is grabbed and handed around. The girl, however, is a firm young person, well able to take care of herself. She regains possession of her purse and stalks off with much dignity, hotly pursued by two of the sailors. The third sailor, who couldn't win anyway, is left alone. As he stands glumly contemplating this fact, a girl pauses under the lamppost to read her tabloid. She is pretty and a redhead. In record-breaking time the sailor has established contact and is piloting her into the bar.

(A blackout indicates a lapse of time.)

Girl and sailor have been sitting at the bar for quite a while. He is handing her a persuasive line, which must be running a trifle thin, as she shows signs of restiveness. To detain her, he asks her to dance with him. When the music comes to an end, they walk back to the bar. He makes a tentative pass in her direction, but thinks better of it.

Just as they are settling down for more conversation, there is a disturbance outside. His two friends have come back, having established friendly relations with the owner of the red purse. They run in while the third sailor endeavors to make a quick get-away with his prize, whom he has no idea of sharing with the others. The girls, however, have other notions. They are friends, and as they have not met for at least a week, they greet each other with shrill squeals of delight and a gush of conversation. This puts an end to any idea of flight, and the sailors debate the insoluble problem of how to divide two girls between three cavaliers. It can't be done, and they resort to rough measures, winding up by all five going into the bar. There is another rough-and-tumble skirmish inside, until they decide that, instead of fighting it out, they will dance it out. After some argument, the order of the performance is settled, and sailors and girls seat themselves at a table to watch.

The first sailor is a very happy character indeed. He performs a mad series of turns and tumbles out of sheer joy of living. He concludes his entry with a good deal of satisfaction in his own performance, glad that his audience likes it too, but not really worried about it.

The second sailor has an unexpected touch of poetry. His solo has a softness and an appeal about it. He is dancing not for himself, but to please the girls. He concludes gazing wistfully at them until reminded that his turn is over.

The third sailor is a complex creature. Apparently quite cocksure, he gives himself away by sneaking a look at his audience every now and again to see if they really approve. He has probably made several South American ports on his last trip, for his solo has a distinct Latin-American turn.

The end of the three dances leaves the situation exactly where it was in the first place. This time the fight that breaks out is a real slug-fest that frightens the girls out of the bar, the sailors being so absorbed in their three-cornered battle that they fail to notice that the causes of the feud are gone.

Cold reason sets in, and the sailors decide that the whole thing has been completely nonsensical. They make peace with a ritual beer, for which the quietest one is again gypped into paying. Back in the moonlit street, they chew more gum and swear off girls. Just as they have agreed on this noble resolution, a luscious blonde comes into view. She is something pretty special, but, after all, women lead to trouble and the breaking of friendships. The blonde is obviously completely nonplused: three sailors and not even an appreciative whistle. As she disappears around the corner of the saloon, one of the sailors (the one who was most vehement against women) takes after her with a feverish burst of speed, closely followed by the others.

Fancy Free is the first choreographic work by Jerome Robbins, who began his career in Ballet Theatre in the corps de ballet, whence his outstanding ability, both comic and dramatic, soon removed him. His range of characterization extends from Petrouchka to his own sailor with the Latin-American overtones, his first notable role being the youth in the mad crimson costume in *Three Virgins and a Devil*. There is nothing of the tentativeness or lack of dramatic balance that might reasonably be expected in the first work of a young choreographer in *Fancy Free*—a perfect American character ballet.

Choreographically *Fancy Free* is a mixture of colloquial gesture, everyday incidents, acrobatics, ballroom (Savoy) dancing, and plain vaudeville routine, all held together by a basically balletic treatment that harks right back to the Marinsky and Petipa. Even the repetitions are in the soundest classical ballet tradition, by which almost every tour de force is performed twice.

The *pas de deux,* a tender and grave interlude in the uproar, employs jitterbug lifts, slowing the giddy antics to the tempo of *adage.*

The three variations for the sailors are revelations of the individual characters as well as displays of virtuosity. The first of these, performed by Harold Lang, follows a dramatic pause in the orchestra. To a sustained drum-roll he executes a double *tour en l'air,* followed immediately, without any transitional step, by an *écartement* (known to vaudeville as the splits). After several *grandes battements à la seconde* he does a complete somersault, coming up into a very cocky pose with a gay wave of his arm. He proceeds to the bar in *chaînés,* jumping to the top of it, where he performs a stylized *adage,* marked by big extensions and a *penché arabesque* (see *Les Sylphides*). He returns to the floor, starts a series of *chaînés,* and pauses for the drink that the bartender hands him, continuing to mark the rhythm of the *chaînés* with his hand until the drink is downed. He picks up the rhythm, does a series of turns (distantly related to *coupés jetés*) ending in a *grande pirouette à la seconde,* and concludes with more *chaînés* and a pose with hands clasped over his head and leg in *à la seconde* position. The whole thing can be set down in the terms of the *danse d'école.* It is actually a completely cuckoo burlesque of the important male variation in a Tchaikovsky-Petipa ballet, and all the more amusing because of it.

The second variation, performed by John Kriza, is lyrical, a danced love song in three parts, with a flavor of jazz. It begins with a step *en balançoire* and a *fouetté* performed slowly. This beguiling combination is repeated several times and then the solo continues in a dreamy vein until the music quickens. He does slides to right and left, followed by an antic combination of swing, shag, Harlem lindy, and bumps.[1] He goes to the bar and jumps over the three stools, performing a double *tour en l'air* between jumps. The music reverts to the original slow tempo and the opening *enchaînement* is repeated. The variation ends with the dancer lying on the floor, supporting chin on hand, gazing sentimentally at the girls. This variation has great charm and one weakness: it is difficult to imagine who could possibly perform it acceptably except the dancer whose individuality it was designed to exploit.

The third variation borrows heavily from Latin-American dance forms, combining them with pirouettes and *sautés à la seconde.* There is an amusing introduction of a rumba-like walk, several times repeated. The climax of the variation (coming at the end) is a suc-

[1] Not the first appearance of bumps in ballet. See *Rouge et Noir.*

cession of varied rhythmic beats, first on the bar stool, then on the bar, to the top of which the dancer jumps, continuing the beats on his chest, bringing the solo to an end by leaping to the floor into a kneeling pose, arms clasped overhead. This variation is less balletic in content than the others, although the material is organized in a balletic manner.

All three variations together form the high light of the choreography. They are artfully designed to reveal the personalities of the characters, as well as the virtuosity of the dancers, all of whom gave superb performances. The three girls were less favored by the choreographer, being called upon to display the minimum of virtuosity, though much in the way of character projection was required of them.

The performances of the entire cast were quite simply perfect— from Rex Cooper's slightly surly and detached bartender to Shirley Eckl as the blonde postcript. The three sailors were quite the most ingratiating and vivid characters seen in a ballet in many seasons: Harold Lang, a kobold with charm, John Kriza, a Third Avenue troubadour, Jerome Robbins an up-to-date Hermes minus some of that character's self-assurance. The girls were less differentiated, but might have been a couple from the gang that goes for cokes to the corner candy store.

The première of *Fancy Free* was greeted with a thunderous ovation from the Metropolitan audience. Politely attentive at the beginning of the ballet, the house was waked up with a bang by Harold Lang's variation with its opening tour de force, the applause lasting all through the solo and continuing for some minutes after its conclusion. The other variations, though less sensational, were well received. From then on, everyone on both sides of the footlights was aware that a success was being born—a most exhilarating experience in the theater. The critics were equally enthusiastic. John Martin, writing about a performance of the ballet given in the following season was even more enthusiastic than in his initial review:

"*Fancy Free* enters its second season with its original brilliance undimmed. It remains, indeed, a rare little genre masterpiece—young, human, tender and funny, and impeccably formal withal under its frolicsome exterior. The original cast plays it now with perhaps even a trifle more authority, and there ought to be a law of some kind to insure that it will never be recast. Mr. Robbins himself, John Kriza, Harold Lang, Janet

Reed (who is a darling), Muriel Bentley, Shirley Eckl and Rex Cooper are just as nearly perfect as anybody has a right to ask, and they dance the work as if it really belonged to them."

The score by Leonard Bernstein was especially commissioned for the ballet. Supporting the mood and the action expertly at all times, it occasionally sounds a bit like nights with the great composers: Bernstein has borrowed freely and in all directions, ranging from Dohnányi, to Mussorgsky, but the whole is undeniably effective theater music.

Oliver Smith's setting is a stylization of skyscraper architecture seen by night, suggesting a view of the city, not from a side street as the stage directions state, but from one of the peripheral streets of lower Manhattan, probably South Street, a perfectly natural locale for the action of the ballet. The foreground, with both interior and exterior of the bar visible, with lights changing as the sailors and their girls surge back and forth, is really a masterly piece of stage design. A good deal of its effectiveness depends on the timing of the lights changes, although these seem to trouble electricians on tour less than the complexities of *Dim Lustre*.

Fancy Free continues in the active repertoire of Ballet Theatre. The girls of the cast still remain unchanged, although substitutions have occurred among the sailors, distinctly not for the better. It would be kinder to remove *Fancy Free* from the performance list than have it meet the blight that has fallen on *Rodeo*.

LA FILLE MAL GARDÉE

LA FILLE MAL GARDÉE is the oldest ballet in the active repertoire. It is the sole surviving work of Jean Dauberval (1742–1806), pupil of Jean Georges Noverre, great choreographer and innovator, whose *Lettres sur la danse* are a classic of dance æsthetics. What relation the current productions of *La Fille Mal Gardée* bear to the original is a matter for conjecture. The romantic revival, with its enormously developed technique and freedom from the restrictions imposed by eighteenth-century costumes and conventions, intervenes. Ballet is an art in which traditions and roles are handed from one dancer to another through succeeding generations. However modified and changed, something of the primary intention remains. It is safe to say that the nameless dancer who created the role of Lise in Bordeaux in 1786 would recognize her modern counterpart though she would be amazed at the short tutu and steps executed *sur les pointes.*

The music for *La Fille Mal Gardée,* sometimes called traditional on programs, is often attributed to Hertel,[1] no initials being given. This composer is probably Peter Ludwig Hertel (1817–99), who may have arranged the traditional music or even composed a new score for a later production.

La Fille Mal Gardée under the title of *Vain Precautions* was part of the repertoire of the Russian Imperial Ballet and has been revived by the Soviet State Ballet. Anna Pavlova was seen in a version by Auguste Bournonville. Lydia Kyasht and Adeline Genée have danced it in London.

La Fille Mal Gardée was first performed in New York on July 6, 1839 at the Park Theater. The leading role was performed by Mme Lecomte (this was a period when first names never appeared on programs). Mme Lecomte was one of the many French dancers who came to try their luck in the New World. She was criticized for being too buxom, but probably like many present-day dancers she did not read the reviews unless they were favorable. Undaunted,

---

[1] On a program of a Pavlova performance this was spelled Gertel—a little Russian confusion between G and H?

she pursued her career. She had a way of following another dancer's success by bobbing up at another theater with a version of her own. She followed Augusta's performance in *Giselle,* and even had the hardihood to challenge Fanny Elssler by appearing in *La Sylphide* a week after Fanny had won the town by her interpretation of the leading role. Mme Lecomte was a lady with a brand of optimistic persistence that might have carried her far if she had possessed talent to match.

Mme Giubelei appeared in a ballet called *Lise and Colin* in January 1841. This was probably an adaptation of *La Fille Mal Gardée,* those being the names of the principal characters.

Fanny Elssler, whose appearances in New York caused a furor in the early 1840's, included *La Fille Mal Gardée* in her repertoire and was seen in it on her farewell performance in New York, on July 1, 1842. After that presentation no more is heard of the ballet in New York until it was revived by Mikhail Mordkin at the Alvin Theater in 1938. Mordkin himself assumed the role of Mother Simone, traditionally given to a male dancer. The cast included Lucia Chase (Lise) and Dimitri Romanoff (Colin). Later this production was taken over by Ballet Theatre, Bronislava Nijinska being called in to revise the choreography, which is substantially the same as that seen in Russian theaters. It was performed for the first time on January 19, 1940 at the Center Theater, New York, with the following cast:

MOTHER SIMONE	*Edward Caton*	THOMAS	*Charles Ewing*
LISETTE (Lise)	*Patricia Bowman*	ALAIN	*Alexis Kosloff*
COLIN	*Yurek Shabelevski*		

Village Notary, Neighbors, Friends of Lisette, Villagers, Gypsies

◇◇◇◇◇◇◇◇◇◇◇◇◇◇◇◇◇◇

Act 1. Scene 1. Exterior of Mother Simone's house. It is harvest time and the day's work is just beginning. Lisette watches the harvesters on their way to the fields for a sight of her lover, Colin. She is obliged to see him surreptitiously as her mother, a wealthy widow, does not approve of his suit. Lisette, called away before Colin arrives, leaves a ribbon for him as a token. He enters, finds the ribbon, and ties it to a staff that he is carrying. He tries to call Lisette. Instead he rouses Mother Simone, who tells him to be off, while Lisette hovers anxiously in the background. More harvesters leave for the fields. Lisette, attempting to join them, is ordered by her mother to stay home and attend to the churning. With much fuss and scolding Mother Simone follows the harvesters, whereupon Colin returns. He teases Lisette with the ribbon-bedecked stick, and a gay romp ensues. This is brought to an abrupt close when Mother Simone comes back. She is cross with Lisette for neglecting her work, and orders her into the house.

Thomas, a rich vinegrower, arrives with his son Alain and some friends. He wishes to betroth his son to Lisette, thus uniting two prosperous households. Mother Simone is delighted. This is her idea of the perfect match for her daughter. Alain is completely indifferent to the whole project. In fact, he is indifferent to anything except his hobby, which is catching butterflies. All the while the interview is taking place he leaps about, brandishing his butterfly net. When the conversation is concluded, Mother Simone invites the group to picnic with the harvesters in the fields, even Lisette being included in honor of the auspicious occasion.

Interlude. Lisette, Mother Simone, Thomas and his friends, with Alain still pursuing butterflies, pass by on their way to the fields.

Scene 2. In the fields. A harvest festival is in progress. The field hands dance. Various members of the party entertain. A band of gypsies appears and moves through the fast and furious measures of a dance.[2] Suddenly storm clouds darken the sky and rain scatters the crowd. Colin, who has been lurking in the sidelines, seizes the opportunity to run off with Lisette. Alain and Mother Simone become entangled in their efforts to escape the rain. The scene ends in confusion.

Act 2. Interior of Mother Simone's house. Mother Simone and Lisette, home from the picnic, settle down for a quiet evening of spinning, Mother Simone first taking the precaution of locking the door. The hum of the spinning-wheel makes her drowsy. When she nods Lisette tries vainly to gain possession of the key. Every time she approaches Mother Simone, the old lady wakes up. In order to keep alert, Mother Simone suggests that Lisette dance to amuse her. To the rhythm of a tambourine played by her mother, Lisette performs, conscious that Colin is watching from a convenient window. When

---

[2] This episode is not part of the plot as related by Beaumont. Mme Nijinska borrowed the choreography for the gypsy dance from her ballet *Danses Slaves et Tsiganes,* first produced by Colonel W. de Basil's Ballet Russe at the Metropolitan Opera House, New York, on April 17, 1936.

Mother Simone again falls asleep, she tries to speak to him, but a lusty thump on the tambourine starts her dancing again.

A group of harvesters carrying sheaves comes to the door. Mother Simone admits them, and when they have stacked the sheaves in a corner of the kitchen she invites them into another room for a drink, first making certain that Lisette is locked in. Suddenly the pile of sheaves falls apart and Colin emerges. Lise, who is really a very nice girl, is quite upset at being alone with her lover and begins to cry. Colin takes off his scarf to dry her tears. Lisette consoled puts the scarf around her neck, giving Colin her neckerchief in exchange. Hearing Mother Simone's footsteps, Lisette hastily bundles Colin into her room, which opens to one side. Mother Simone's suspicions are aroused by the strange scarf around Lisette's neck, but fortunately for her daughter, Thomas and Alain, accompanied by the village notary, arrive at this moment to sign the marriage contract. Mother Simone locks Lisette in her room before discussing business. Details being disposed of, Mother Simone gives the lackadaisical Alain the key to Lisette's room. When after some urging Alain unlocks the door, the company is astounded to see Lisette and Colin, with straws in their hair, standing in the doorway. Obviously the wedding arrangements are at an end. Mother Simone is wild with rage, but is persuaded to calm herself and make the best of a bad situation by consenting to Lisette's engagement to Colin. The young couple kneel before her to receive her blessing.

Scene 2. The village. A festival takes place to celebrate the wedding of Lisette and Colin. Alain, very glad to be allowed to get on with his butterfly-catching, is as happy as any guest present.

Ballet Theatre's several attempts during its first season to revive classics did not meet with any conspicuous success. It had a superb corps de ballet (the best that has ever been seen in New York), but was lacking in ballerinas with the authority to do justice to *Swan Lake, Les Sylphides,* and *Giselle. La Fille Mal Gardée* was a pleasant exception. In Lisette Patricia Bowman found a role that displayed all her childlike charm and sure technique. If Yurek Shabelevski was none too happy as Colin, that was quickly remedied when in subsequent performances he was replaced by Dimitri Romanoff, who gave a convincing interpretation of a part that requires acting as well as dancing ability. Yurek Shabelevski, an impressive Polovtsian Warrior, was somewhat remote as a rustic lover.

In 1941 *La Fille Mal Gardée,* renamed *The Wayward Daughter,* was revived by Ballet Theatre with a really outstanding cast:

MOTHER SIMONE	*Simon Semenoff*	THOMAS	*Nicolas Orloff*
LISETTE	*Irina Baronova*	ALAIN	*Ian Gibson*
COLIN	*Dimitri Romanoff*		

❖❖❖❖❖❖❖❖❖❖❖❖❖❖❖

This cast was a distinct improvement over the previous one. Irina Baronova as Lisette was at her delightful best. Simon Semenoff, one of the foremost character actors of the dance theater, allowed no facet of Mother Simone's character to escape him. Ian Gibson's Alain was a revelation. His controlled technique and surpassing elevation had to be seen to be believed. Alain was his first leading role and he made the most of it. There was a moment in the storm scene when any member of the audience who had read of Nijinsky's ability to pause in mid-air suddenly realized what that phrase really meant.

When Ballet Theatre gave its first season at the Metropolitan Opera House in the spring of 1942, *La Fille Mal Gardée* again formed part of the repertoire. For some unfathomable reason the management had seen fit to give it a third name. It turned up with the same outstanding cast under the title of *Naughty Lisette.* Whatever it was called, it was still one of the most charming ballets given that or any other season, though only matinee audiences had an opportunity to see it.

With the departure of Irina Baronova from Ballet Theatre, *La Fille Mal Gardée* has been relegated to the inactive list. A revival with really good scenery and costumes (the current scenery and costumes are cheap and tawdry) would be a valuable item in a repertoire that becomes duller every season. When Ballet Theatre had two such brilliant classical dancers as Alicia Alonso and Rosella Hightower, why such an obvious opportunity to exploit their gifts was overlooked is difficult to explain. Possibly the company policy of ignoring its own talented group in favor of Hollywooden guest stars and Broadway dancers seeking to acquire prestige is the answer. The same brilliant minds who conceived calendar art (*Moonlight Sonata*) and fifth-rate vaudeville (*Rendezvous*) as worthy additions to the repertoire of an artistic enterprise have discarded *Coppélia* and *La Fille Mal Gardée.*

DEVIL'S HOLIDAY (Alexandra Danilova)

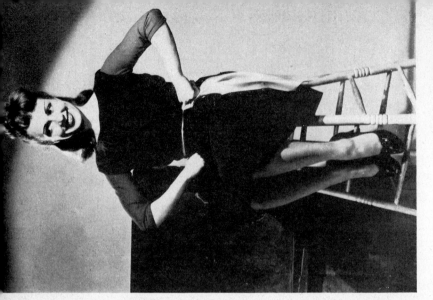

Janet Reed

Harold Lang

Muriel Bentley

FANCY FREE

Miriam Golden as the Italian Ballerina and Antony Tudor as her Cavalier

GALA PERFORMANCE

Mimi Gomber, Shirley Eckel, Rozsika Sabo, and Muriel Bentley as coryphées

Alicia Markova as Giselle

Alicia Markova as Giselle and Anton Dolin as Albrecht

GISELLE

FILLING STATION

Ballet document in one act; music by Virgil Thomson; costumes by Paul Cadmus; choreography by Lew Christensen.

FILLING STATION was first performed by Ballet Caravan, in Hartford, Connecticut, in November 1937. A program for a performance given at the Martin Beck Theater, New York, on May 18, 1939, gives the following cast:

Mac, the filling-station attendant		The Motorist	*Harold Christensen*
	Lew Christensen	His Wife	*Anne Campbell*
The truck-drivers		The Rich Boy	*Fred Danieli*
Ray)	(*Eugene Loring*	The Rich Girl	*Gisella Caccialanza*
Roy)	(*Erick Hawkins*	The Gangster	*Dwight Godwin*
The State Trooper	*Ray Weamer*		

◆◇◆◇◆◇◆◇◆◇◆◇◆◇◆◇◆

Mac, the filling-station attendant, is for a few brief moments enjoying an unaccustomed solitude. He is a tall, good-looking young man, with an air of being quite capable of coping with any emergency. The quiet is broken by the arrival of Roy and Ray, the truck-drivers, in the throes of one more brush with their natural enemy, the State Trooper. They are amiable young toughs dressed in greasy work clothes. Roy has a sprig of lilac stuck in his cap. Their exuberance is toned down a little when the State Trooper catches up with them and tells them what he thinks about their disregard for speed laws. A family party, Husband, Wife, and Child, stop for gas, a visit to the washroom, and a look at the road map. This group is singularly lacking in charm—the Husband, smoking a long cigar, is dressed in plus-fours, Hollywood plaid sports jacket, and a straw hat; his Wife's emphatic bulges are not minimized by beach pajamas, nor her personality enhanced for the better by brass-blond hair and a green eyeshade; the Child, a truly appalling brat, who "wants to go" and is not shy about indicating the fact. Mac deals with this group with calm efficiency. The next customers are more attractive but none the less difficult. The Rich Boy and Girl are alcoholic refugees from the country-club dance. They feel the urge to perform a rumba, and their drunken revolvings leave Mac quite calm. The rest of the group join in the dancing, but the fun is rudely interrupted by the entrance of the Gangster, who has a nervous trigger finger. Mac takes care of him and with the aid of the truck-drivers and the State Trooper thwarts his attempt at a holdup. Unfortunately the Rich Girl has managed to get in the line of fire, and when order is restored she is discovered lying dead on the floor. Her limp body is carried away. The customers, thoroughly shaken, go on their way. Mac, alone once more, settles down to wait for the next arrivals with his radio and a tabloid.

Filling Station is one of the most soundly constructed works in the repertoire of Ballet Caravan. It is a dramatization of an item in the newspaper, and there is nothing in the least arty or symbolic about its approach to an everyday scene. The definite and well-rounded characters have their prototypes in every state from Maine to California. Even the family party, exaggerated to a point that is rather larger than life, is only a little more dreadful than similar groups to be encountered everywhere on the road. All of these types, however, are seen in terms that are balletic. Mac's opening solo is a brilliant and appropriate adaptation of a classical variation. The rough-and-tumble performance of Roy and Ray is good character dancing borrowed from vaudeville and presented with balletic over-tones. The solo for the Child, straight from the June recital of a third-rate ballet school, could not be more expressive of a horrid little show-off. The *pas de deux* for the Rich Boy and Girl is based on a ballroom rumba. The succeeding ensemble is a simplified ver-sion of the big apple—one that could not have been performed, how-ever, by the ordinary big-apple group unless it had been well grounded in ballet technique.

One of the most interesting choreographic features of *Filling Sta-tion* is the pursuit of the Gangster. On a completely darkened stage several figures carrying flashlights cover the stage in *grands jetés*. The dark leaping forms and the patterns made by the beams of light pro-duce an effect dramatic out of all proportion to the simplicity of the means employed.

Lew Christensen in the role of Mac is the perfect embodiment of what one would like to think is the ideal young American. His strong technique and excellent stage presence dominate the scene. Gisella Caccialanza made a very ingratiating figure of the Rich Girl. Her performance in the alcoholic *pas de deux,* in which even her eyes rolled drunkenly, managed to be at once charming and irresistibly funny.

The décor for *Filling Station,* by Paul Cadmus, was slight but effective, and the costumes decorative adaptations of contemporary dress. Those of the truck-drivers are especially memorable, with greasy hand prints applied in appropriate spots.

Ballet Caravan, which originally presented *Filling Station,* was, to quote the booklet of the School of American Ballet, "a company of American born dancers and choreographers, whose members are graduates of the School." This group had an interesting and varied repertoire of small-scale ballets, the most notable of which were *Air and Variations* (choreography by William Dollar, music by Bach), and *Billy the Kid* (choreography by Eugene Loring, music by Aaron Copland). The latter was expanded for performance by a larger company. Ballet Caravan seasons in New York were limited, often conflicted with performances by other companies in more accessible theaters, and were insufficiently publicized. These factors combined to deprive all but the most determined ballet-lovers of an opportunity to see their programs. Probably more people in Rio de Janeiro have seen *Filling Station* than in New York, as it was a popular item of the repertoire of the American Ballet [1] on its South American tour in 1941.

All that currently survives of *Filling Station* is the score by Virgil Thomson. This is bright, full of charm, and admirably suited to its purpose, never descending to Tin-Pan Alley clichés to make its points. One does, of course, hear an occasional strain of *We Won't Get Home until Morning* and *Hail, Hail, the Gang's All Here*—fair enough in the circumstances. A suite arranged from the ballet score gets an occasional hearing in concert or on the air.

[1] This was not the company originally known as the American Ballet, but a group of dancers assembled by Lincoln Kirstein specially for the South American tour.

FRANCESCA DA RIMINI

Ballet in two scenes by David Lichine and Henry Clifford, partly from Dante; music by P. Tchaikovsky; choreography by David Lichine; scenery and costumes by Oliver Messel.

FRANCESCA DA RIMINI was first produced by Colonel W. de Basil's Ballet Russe at the Royal Opera House, Covent Garden, London, on July 15, 1937. The first New York performance took place at the Metropolitan Opera House on October 24, 1937, with the following cast:

FRANCESCA	*Lubov Tchernicheva*	Domenico	*Yura Lazovsky*
GIANCIOTTO MALATESTA	*Marc Platoff*	ANGELIC APPARITION	
PAOLO MALATESTA	*Paul Petroff*		*Tatiana Riabouchinska*
CHIARA	*Vera Nelidova*	GUINEVERE	*Alexandra Danilova*
GIROLAMO	*Edouard Borovansky*	LANCELOT	*Roman Jasinsky*

Signors of Rimini, Dwarfs, Francesca's Ladies, Chorus, Musicians, Soldiers, Servants, Townspeople

◆◆◆◆◆◆◆◆◆◆◆◆◆◆◆◆◆◆

Scene 1. Throne room in Malatesta's Castle. Surrounded by a throng of followers, Gianciotto awaits the arrival of Francesca, the bride whom he has married by proxy. This marriage is important to the peace of Rimini, which has been at war with Ravenna for many years. Francesca's marriage to Malatesta, heir to the lordship of Rimini, is to be the seal of peace. Malatesta, ugly and deformed, has been persuaded to send his younger brother, Paolo, a gentle youth, as his ambassador and proxy. Doubts have arisen as to the wisdom of this proceeding and an altercation breaks out among Malatesta's followers. At the height of the argument Francesca and Chiara her nurse arrive, escorted by Paolo and Girolamo, Malatesta's spy. Girolamo manages to whisper his suspicions that Francesca has fallen in love with Paolo. Malatesta's rising anger is appeased by the submissiveness of Francesca, who kneels before him. Prepared to be dutiful, she shrinks from the sinister figure of her husband, whom she is seeing for the first time. Malatesta seizes her roughly and carries her away. Chiara, attempting to protect her, is struck to the ground by Girolamo. Paolo is a helpless witness of this brutal scene. When Francesca returns, he tries to aid her to escape, but his efforts are thwarted by the spy, while the dwarfs caper with malicious delight.

Scene 2. Francesca's Apartment. Paolo and Francesca are reading the story of Lancelot and Guinevere. The air is filled with music, and angelic apparitions surround them. Lancelot and Guinevere enact a scene that depicts their tragic love. Paolo and Francesca turn their attention from the book to each other. They kiss. Suddenly there is a sound of trumpets heralding the arrival of Malatesta. Francesca, terrified, insists that Paolo hide. Great doors fly open, revealing Malatesta standing with drawn sword accompanied by his dwarfs. These horrible creatures scurry about, searching for Paolo. His hiding-place is discovered. A violent sword fight ensues in which the gentle Paolo, no match for his brother, is killed. The people of Rimini, petrified with fear, watch as Francesca bares her bosom to her husband's sword.

Francesca da Rimini can scarcely be called a ballet. It is a tautly dramatic pantomime played at a headlong tempo. The action parallels the intensely dramatic music (Tchaikovsky's orchestral fantasy) although ignoring Tchaikovsky's program and making only a distant bow to Dante.

Lichine's version of this tragic story is not its first appearance as a ballet. On November 28, 1915 Michel Fokine produced a ballet to the Tchaikovsky music at the Marinsky Theater, Petrograd, in which Lubov Egorova and Pierre Vladimiroff were the doomed lovers. This work followed the program of the music more or less faithfully and employed a movie technique in which the various episodes of the drama appeared in flashbacks. This ballet was given at a charity matinee and was not a part of the regular repertoire of the Marinsky Theater.

Lichine's ballet made a splendid vehicle for the superb mimetic gifts of Lubov Tchernicheva, who had long been a member of the Diaghilev Ballet, having appeared with that company on its American tour in 1916–17. This artist, who will be remembered for her more recent performances in Colonel W. de Basil's Ballet Russe in *Scheherazade* (Zobeide) and *Le Tricorne* (Miller's Wife), brought an authority to her roles that is probably the last manifestation of the truly grand balletic manner which America is likely to see. Since her retirement the part of Francesca has been performed by Tamara Grigorieva.

With one exception the other roles in *Francesca da Rimini* were shadowy in comparison with the title part. The terrific pace with which the plot progressed scarcely allowed for fine shades or development of character. However, the sinister figure of Malatesta stood forth, the very embodiment of a Renaissance tyrant. Marc Platoff (now to be seen only in movies and musicals) emerged from the corps de ballet to give a fine and telling account of it.

The vivid violence with which *Francesca da Rimini* progressed left the audience dazed. One felt a sense of shock as though it were a personal experience through which one had somehow passed physically uninjured but mentally numb. It is likely that its very vehemence defeated it, for this ballet did not appear to make much of an impression on the audience, which was probably too stunned to applaud. This state of affairs might have been remedied if the episode of the lovers' meeting had had time to register with the audience. There were some charming elements—the pictures made by the Botticelli angels, led by Tatiana Riabouchinska, were memorable; but attention was distracted from them by the moody *pas de deux* performed by Lancelot and Guinevere, handicapped by the only unsuccessful costumes in the production. The general effect was one of a dreamlike confusion where quite a different note was wanted to contrast with the hurly-burly of the first and last scenes.

The costumes by Oliver Messel with the exceptions previously mentioned were handsome theatrical adaptations of those seen in early Renaissance paintings, Malatesta's, patterned after a drawing by Leonardo, being particularly impressive. The settings, especially the second scene, were a powerful aid to dramatic action. When the great doors flew open and the figure of Malatesta was seen looming high over the unfortunate lovers the tensely dramatic effect was more than a little due to the scenic designer.

Francesca da Rimini was revived by the Original Ballet Russe at the Fifty-first Street Theater, New York, in 1941, Dimitri Rostoff replacing Marc Platoff as Malatesta, and again, at the Metropolitan Opera House on October 3, 1946, with Roman Jasinsky (Paolo) and Lubov Tchernicheva (Francesca).

GAITÉ PARISIENNE

Ballet in one act; music by Jacques Offenbach, orchestrated by Manuel Rosenthal in collaboration with Jacques Brindejonc-Offenbach; choreography by Léonide Massine; décor and theme by Count Etienne de Beaumont.

GAITÉ PARISIENNE was first performed by the Ballet Russe de Monte Carlo at the Théâtre de Monte Carlo on April 5, 1938. The American première took place at the Metropolitan Opera House, New York, on October 12, 1938, with the following cast:

GLOVE-SELLER	Alexandra Danilova	THE DUKE	Casimir Kokitch
FLOWER GIRL	Eugénie Delarova	TORTONI)	Robert Irwin
LA LIONNE	Lubov Rostova	DANCE MASTER)	
THE PERUVIAN	Léonide Massine	LEADER OF THE CANCAN GIRLS	
THE BARON	Frederic Franklin		Katia Geleznova
THE OFFICER	Igor Youskevitch		

Girl Attendants, Café Waiters, *Cocodettes*, Billiard-players, Soldiers, Dandies, Cancan Girls

◆◆◆◆◆◆◆◆◆◆◆◆◆◆◆◆◆◆

A slender thread of plot holds the action together.

The curtain rises on a luxurious café in Paris of the Second Empire. It is shortly before opening time, and the waiters are busy with last-minute preparations. Cleaning women are scrubbing and dusting, but not too busy to join the waiters in a gay dance. The Flower Girl bustles in. She is evidently popular with the waiters, who help her water the flowers and display them on a stand. The Glove-seller arrives with her stock of gloves in a basket. When they are arranged, she tosses the basket to a waiter.

Now the café is ready for the evening. Students in floppy berets appear, accompanied by several *cocodettes*. Their frolic is interrupted by the boisterous entrance of the Peruvian, carrying two bags that he carefully guards from the curiosity of the *cocodettes*. He is enthralled by the beauty of the Glove-seller, who puts a pair of gloves on his hands—a difficult feat as he is palpitating from head to foot with delight. The *cocodettes* seize this opportunity to run off with his bags. The arrival of the Baron causes the Glove-seller's attention to wander, and the Peruvian rushes away to regain his property.

The Glove-seller and the Baron have obviously fallen in love at first sight. Their raptures are interrupted by the music of a march. Soldiers file in, led by a dashing Officer. The *cocodettes,* responsive to the lure of a uniform, flirt with the soldiers, who strut for their benefit in an ultramilitary manner. La Lionne, gorgeously dressed in red and escorted by the Duke, makes an impressive entrance. The Officer is lured from his dalliance with the Glove-seller by La Lionne —a lady who obviously likes two strings to her bow. The Flower Girl, after making sporadic efforts to attract a friend for the evening, tries her wiles on the Baron—a wasted effort.

The Peruvian has not forgotten the Glove-seller. He tries to make an engagement with her to meet after the café closes. She appears to consent, but her heart is with the Baron. The Peruvian, elated, rushes away, leaving a fine trail of confusion in his wake. Everyone becomes involved in a fight except the Baron and the Glove-seller, who quietly disappear. The waiters drive the patrons out. When they are about to relax, the Peruvian is discovered hiding under a small table; with flicks of their napkins they whip him out, leaving the café empty.

The Baron and the Glove-seller return and dance together in the deserted café.

There is a burst of clamorous music, and the Dance Master enters leading the Cancan girls. The patrons come back to see the performance. Carried away by the ebullience of the cancan, everyone joins the dance. The Glove-seller's version is restrained and elegant, the Flower Girl's rowdy. Even La Lionne condescends, pulling up her crinoline to display daring red stockings and gold garters. The leader of the Cancan girls spins frenetically around the stage, urged on by the Peruvian.

Reaction sets in. To soft music, all pair off and leave the scene with a gliding step reminiscent of a gondola's passage through quiet waters. The Flower Girl finds a friend at last and departs on the arm of the Duke. No one is left but the Glove-seller and the Baron, who are having a romantic interlude on the terrace. The Peruvian arrives to claim the Glove-seller's promise. The lovers laugh, waving an ironic farewell. The Peruvian drops his bags, falls into a limp pose, and the curtain comes down.

The Glove-seller's role is an ideal vehicle for the less serious side of Alexandra Danilova's art. Her steps are as light and glittering as the diamonds in her ears. Other dancers perform this role, but the spirit of the ballet suffers. There are no substitutes for Danilova.[1]

Frederic Franklin made his American debut as the Baron, immediately establishing himself with the ballet audience. The Peruvian was one of Massine's most successful and characteristic roles. Igor Youskevitch soon surrendered the part of the Officer to Marc Platoff, to whom it was more appropriate. Other parts have also changed hands, not always for the better.

Though by no means pedantically accurate, the settings and costumes suggest the spirit of the Second Empire. They are gay and colorful, the most robust notes being supplied by La Lionne's red dress and the soldiers' uniforms.

The Offenbach score is skillfully tailored from several of his operettas with delightful effect. The temptation to include the hackneyed "Barcarolle" from *The Tales of Hoffmann* was not resisted, but ingenious use of it is made by the choreographer, who moves his characters off the stage in the finale to its quiet strains.

Gaité Parisienne has given pleasure to uncounted numbers of the ballet audience—particularly the more unsophisticated members of it, who go to the ballet in a simple search for entertainment. Designed to be a companion piece to *Le Beau Danube* in the repertoire, *Gaité Parisienne* is light, frothy, and at times not devoid of a touch of slapstick. However, the art of Danilova and the personality of Franklin keep this ballet from sinking below the artistic Plimsoll line. Only when these two dancers are out of the cast does one see that the *pas de deux* is not too glorified ballroom dancing, that the cancan has been lifted straight from a Paris *boîte de nuit*,[2] and that there are at least three climaxes. *Gaité Parisienne* is a lively closing number, but

[1] When a movie short was made of *Gaité Parisienne* with true Hollywood ineptitude a sweetly pretty dancer was cast in this role. No doubt she was photogenic, but lovers of ballet deplored the lost opportunity to perpetuate Danilova's art, even in such an unimportant role.

[2] Contrast the use of the cancan in *Gaité Parisienne* with that seen in *La Boutique Fantasque,* where it receives truly balletic treatment.

it is scarcely ballet in a higher sense of the word, any more than a Broadway adaptation of a Viennese musical is opera.

Gaité Parisienne, under the proper circumstances, can offer gay and spirited entertainment. On these occasions one cannot but conclude that Second Empire café society was infinitely more amusing and more decorative than the current variety.

GALA PERFORMANCE

Ballet by Antony Tudor; music by Serge Prokofiev, specially orchestrated for Ballet Theatre by Paul Baron; décor and costumes by Nicolas de Molas.

GALA PERFORMANCE was originally performed by the London Ballet at the Toynbee Hall Theatre, London, on December 5, 1938, with a cast that included Maud Lloyd, Peggy van Praagh, Gerd Larson, Hugh Laing, and Antony Tudor. The American première, presented by Ballet Theatre, took place at the Majestic Theater, New York, on February 11, 1941, with the following cast:

La Reine de la Danse (from Moscow)	*Nora Kaye*	Cavalier to the French Ballerina	*Hugh Laing*
La Déese de la Danse (from Milan)	*Nana Gollner*	Cavalier to the Italian Ballerina	*Antony Tudor*
La Fille de Terpsichore (from Paris)	*Karen Conrad*		

Attendant Cavaliers: *Dwight Godwin, John Kriza, Richard Reed, Jerome Robbins*

Resident Coryphées: *Alicia Alonso, Muriel Bentley, Jean Davidson, Maria Karnilova, Marjorie Moore, Olga Suarez, Rozsika Sabo, Kirsten Valbor, Virginia Wilcox, Betty Yeager*

Maître de Ballet	*Edward Caton*	Conductor	*Robert Wolff*
A Dresser	*Tania Dokoudovska*		

Scene: The stage of the Theatre Royal, where three world-famous ballerinas are gathered together for the first time in their careers.
Time: Toward the turn of the century.

◆◆◆◆◆◆◆◆◆◆◆◆◆◆

Part 1. Before the performance. As the curtain rises, a view of the stage never seen by the audience is disclosed. It is set for the performance about to take place, and the unpainted sides of the flats are visible. Illumination is provided by a single light, and the general effect is gloomy. One lone coryphée is seen warming up. Clinging to a bit of scenery, she is practicing *frappées*. By degrees the stage is filled up with girls. One of them good-naturedly fastens another's costume.

When a second one presents herself to be hooked up, the good-natured one haughtily stalks away, leaving any further assistance to the Dresser, who now puts in an appearance. The boys drift in. Little clumps stand about gossiping, no doubt about the latest *scandale*. The warming up also proceeds, some of the girls trying supported pirouettes with the aid of the boys. The Maître de Ballet comes in with last-minute directions. The more or less friendly bustle is brought to an abrupt halt by the arrival of the Russian ballerina. There is a great deal of hand-kissing by the boys and curtsies from the girls, one of whom is singled out for special attention by the guest artist. This unfortunate coryphée has seen fit to wear a necklace (no doubt a tribute from an admirer), which she is ordered to remove at once. As she departs in tears to obey this command, La Reine de la Danse smugly arranges her own elaborate jewels. She now rehearses her curtain calls, rushing up to the center of the stage with all-enveloping gestures. She repeats this performance several times, to the delight of the resident company, who have been watching her, fascinated by these antics. Becoming aware of their amused scrutiny, she angrily tells them to resume their warming up.

At this point the French ballerina, followed by her partner, bustles in. She has on new toe shoes which she is breaking in, taking quick little steps on point. She runs past the Russian to the opposite side of the stage. As courtesy demands, she and her colleague for the evening are introduced, but the greetings are scarcely effusive. The French ballerina is quickly surrounded by the boys of the company, with whom she talks, oozing charm at every pore. The Conductor, baton and score in hand, now appears, to be seized at once by the Russian ballerina, who instructs him how she thinks the music ought to be played. As he is trying feebly to argue with her highly personal ideas of the correct beat, La Fille de Terpsichore, becoming aware that in all probability she is going to be overlooked in the battle of the tempi, hurls herself into the fray. As the Russian Ballerina leaves the stage dragging the harassed maestro after her, her fellow artist, popping with fury which her partner vainly attempts to subdue, hurries after them.

As befits her exalted position, La Déese de la Danse makes her appearance last. Her ominous dignity, set off by an imposing black costume and a towering headdress, causes the resident company to freeze in motionless silence. The Maître de Ballet recovers his wits first. After all, guest artists and their vagaries are probably an old story to him. With a peremptory gesture he waves the boys forward for the ceremonial salutation. Warily they advance to kiss the hand that the "goddess" extends at arm's length, retreating as quickly as they can. The Dresser is requisitioned to hold a mirror that she may give her make-up a final inspection. Distracted by a detail of a passing costume, the Dresser moves the mirror a trifle off-center and receives a hearty box on the ear to remind her where her attention belongs. Having surveyed her kingdom and established her authority, the Italian ballerina stalks haughtily away.

Left to themselves, the resident company seriously get on with their preliminaries. The boys jump high, executing *changements;* the girls line up in front of the curtain under the direction of the Maître de Ballet and perform *glissades* and arabesques over and over. The principal coryphée, who will be called on to lead the others and perform a small solo, has an attack of stage fright. The Maître de Ballet comes to her assistance, and her particular friend encourages her. She bends to touch the floor of the stage (an old theatrical good-luck charm) and crosses herself fervently. The lights come up, the orchestra is heard in a crescendo. With frantic confusion, the girls dash to find their places. The performance is about to begin.

Part 2. "Gala Performance." The lights come up, revealing the coryphées grouped before a setting of more than baroque splendor. Every cliché of the scenic designer's art—palatial columns seen in long perspectives, balconies, huge draperies, and frozen fountains— is revealed in all its grandeur. The coryphées, including the victim of stage fright, go through their routine with perfect self-assurance, not too absorbed to count the house and look for their particular friends out front. The Russian ballerina enters for her solo. She is all personality, projection, and pirouettes. She loves her audience and is completely certain that her audience loves her. She maneuvers as close to the footlights as she can without actually tripping over the prompter's box. At the conclusion of her variation she can scarcely bear to leave the stage, rushing back for the expected ovation. Overcome by her emotions, she clings to the scenery and has to be removed practically by force to make way for the Italian ballerina.

In profound silence this awe-inspiring personage makes her solitary entrance from the upper right. With lofty dignity she slowly advances to the center, walks downstage, rises *sur les pointes,* secures her pose, and nods to the conductor to begin. Her specialty is balance. She can hold a pose longer than any other living dancer, and she does, with and without the aid of her partner, who has made an unobtrusive appearance from the side. Framed by static groups of coryphées and cavaliers, she coldly exhibits her command of *adage,* making no concessions to the audience. From them she exacts only reverence and homage, and would scorn to woo them as the Russian ballerina does. At the conclusion of her *adage* she leaves the stage in a *grand jeté,* supported by one of the cavaliers and followed by her partner. She has probably seen a performance of *Swan Lake* and, not to be outdone, will have two *porteurs* to enhance her consequence, though there is no choreographic reason for more than one.

Her curtain calls she grants as favors to the audience. With queenly grandeur she walks to the center of the empty stage, where she makes a low *révérence*. Her second call is delayed until the resident company and her partner form a tableau, before which she again bows. This group hastily dissolves at a glare from the star and leaves the stage, her partner, in accordance with ballet etiquette, remaining to share the next call. With an imperious gesture she orders him, quite deflated, into the wings. After a third *révérence* she retraces her path of entrance and leaves the stage. The apotheosis of the goddess has come to an end.

The French ballerina, with her partner, now takes the stage. Bubbling with charm, she bounds at a terrific pace in a series of *grands jetés*. Obviously this is her strong point, and the whole variation is made up of this step, which she and her partner perform with airy elegance, finally disappearing into the wings. She runs on for her curtain calls, hotly pursued by her partner, who, when he does catch up with her, is pushed into the wings for his pains. Her charm plainly does not extend to him.

The three main events are over. Now comes the coda. A coryphée cautiously peering out of the wings for the conductor's signal, leads the corps de ballet out on the stage. By now their morale has been a trifle shaken and their lines are even more ragged than they were at first. The three ballerinas enter together, proceeding to the footlights with little steps *sur les pointes*. Each maneuvers for the central position, but neither the Russian nor the French entries have the slightest chance against the superb egotism of the Italian. In a succession of entrances each performs her tour de force: the French ballerina does a series of pirouettes, ending on one knee; the Russian ballerina performs *fouettés en tournant,* single and double, as well as *gargouillades;* the Italian ballerina executes *demi-fouettés* in alternating directions. This last is dutifully echoed by the corps de ballet until their endurance gives out, to be furiously ordered to continue by the "goddess." The French ballerina and her partner cross and recross the stage, performing *pas de papillon.* This brilliant confusion is brought to a grand finale when the entire company poses picturesquely around the guest stars.

A shower of bouquets testifies to the enthusiasm of the audience. A sudden raising of the curtain reveals a little dispute among the rivals for their possession, with the Italian ballerina winning the skirmish. The Russian ballerina manages to be left on the audience side of the curtain at its second descent. Losing no time, she frantically blows kisses right and left. When the curtain rises again, she looks triumphantly at her temporary colleagues, who, livid with rage, are trying to scowl at her and smile at the audience simultaneously.

Gala Performance began as a satire on the exaggerated technical tricks and over-accentuated mannerisms of those dancers who live in a rose-pink haze of self-delusion. They not only were indigenous to gala performances at the turn of the century, but, unfortunately, may be found in the ballet world in every period of the history of the dance. The three baroque specimens in *Gala Performance* have their easily recognizable prototypes in the contemporary scene.

The French ballerina may be more or less ignored. She is the perpetual soubrette, possibly making an expedition from revue or musical comedy into the world of art in search of prestige. She is usually charming enough, and does no permanent harm to ballet because she does not linger long enough in this, to her rarefied, milieu.

The Russian ballerina must be taken more seriously. Her counterpart in real life need not necessarily be Russian, although she is usually a veteran of a Russian company, in which she may have alternated with other dancers in classical roles and certainly was subjected to actual discipline as well as that imposed by competition. Her status is generally that of permanent guest artist, turning up for seasons in the larger cities, where her alleged box-office appeal enables her to take roles away from other and better dancers. Subject to no discipline or criticism, and surrounded by a cooing circle of relatives and friends, she makes her triumphant appearances, with every assistance that the publicity department can provide. She invariably has a repertoire of tricks: multiple *fouettés,* flashy pirouettes, the ability to hold a pose on point for what seems an indefinite length of time. This last she pushes to the edge of absurdity on every possible occasion, while the music leaves her far behind, forcing her to change the choreography in order to achieve anything that even the musically obtuse in the audience can recognize as a tempo. These tours de force enchant ballet-goers who should have gone to the circus in the first place, and revolt the unfortunates who value musicality, a fine legato, and correct phrasing as valuable and indispensable in ballet, as in any other form of musical art. If ballet is visible music, then this ballerina is the equivalent of a brass band. People who like brass bands seldom go to the opera house to hear them. The assault on the classics made by this not too hypothetical character keeps the real ballet-lover at home.

The calm contempt for the audience that is the Italian ballerina's most striking idiosyncrasy characterizes quite a different type of dancer from the subject of the above tirade. Far from seeking the approval of the audience, this artist looks upon herself and a few selected colleagues as ministers of a cult so precious and remote from the common uses of humanity that she performs the sacred rites in a sort of holy vacuum. Human nature being contradictory, she would, of course, like to display her scorn to large enthusiastic audiences. This complex flourishes luxuriantly among American dancers who began their careers in native companies untainted by any admission of Russian influences, although, strangely enough, they were trained by Russian teachers. In their efforts to avoid sugar-coating and glamour, they forgot that ballet is still an art of the theater and cannot flourish without the co-operation of audiences who go to the theater in the expectation of receiving something in the way of a communication. It is possible that if these companies had survived long enough to outgrow their narrow ideals, something fine might have emerged to make the public take legitimate pride in American ballets performed by an American company or group. Many of their dancers have come down to earth and are giving warm and glowing performances that must shock the more parochial-minded survivors who seem unable to make themselves at home on the stage and who give their best performances in the classroom. Native art is not produced in chauvinistic strait-jackets to the screaming of eagles.

The antics of the three ballerinas have provided the text for a sermon undoubtedly not contemplated by the choreographer, who would probably be quite surprised to read it. *Gala Performance* has long since ceased to be a satire and has become a hilarious burlesque. Although it has lost subtlety, its comedy value remains unimpaired. Nora Kaye's Russian ballerina continues to demonstrate that this remarkable young artist has a comic side to her intensely dramatic projection. Nana Gollner's Italian ballerina, technically remarkable, lacks the imposing grandeur of the interpretation by Miriam Golden, whose slow fury seemed capable of blasting the theater flat. There have been several charming performers of the French ballerina: Karen Conrad whose impressive *grands jetés* will be remembered, Annabelle Lyon, Janet Reed, and Albia Kavan. Antony Tudor and Hugh Laing as the Cavaliers contribute amusing portraits indicative of the low estate to which the male dancer had descended fifty years ago.

The décor and costumes by Nicolas de Molas are delightful evocations of the naïve grandeur of the past. The girls' tutus with their slight suggestion of bustle are especially amusing. Of the soloists' costumes, that of the Italian ballerina is the most impressive, as indeed it should be. A very dark green with tinsel high lights, it looks black when worn on the stage, the tall feathers and ornate necklace adding to the effect of somber magnificence.

It is possible that more suitable music might have been found for *Gala Performance* than Prokofiev's Classical Symphony. Something by Minkus or Pugni, official composers who reeled out ballet rhythms by the yard without a trace of originality or inspiration, would have been the obvious choice. The Classical Symphony, however, with its buoyant elegance seems to add a comment to the satirical proceedings on the stage and is certainly easier on the ears than the arid banalities of the ballet music of the period of the work. The first movement of the Piano Concerto is a stroke of genius as an accompaniment to Part 1. The slow building of an atmosphere of tension rising to a crescendo is highly appropriate to the action on the stage.

Choreographically the role of the Italian ballerina is the most interesting feature of *Gala Performance*. Based on Cecchetti technique, it features the roundness and perfectly balanced *port de bras* characterizing that method. The forward-bending pose in which the goddess of the dance displays her balance was inspired by a painting by G. A. Turner of Fanny Cerito in an exactly similar pose from the famous *Pas de l'Ombre* from Jules Perrot's *Ondine, ou la Naïade,* a ballet first performed in 1843. The use of this essentially romantic pose in a ballet danced for display fifty years later (the period of *Gala Performance*) has its own reference to the static state of the classical formula in the generation preceding Fokine. The episodes involving the other ballerinas are satires or burlesques of styles in temperament rather than technique.

The opening scene of the ballet, except for the warming-up steps, entirely in mime, is a delightful depiction of the goings-on on stage (frequently quite as interesting as the performance) before the curtain goes up. Audiences often catch fascinating glimpses of feet in action below the curtain prior to a performance. This episode in *Gala Performance* conveys more or less what the owners of the feet may be up to. It should be quickly explained, however, that personal violence has gone out of fashion. Ballerinas, however lofty their status, do not slap their dressers in this decade of the twentieth century. Hand-kissing and curtsies are not unknown, particularly in European companies, and the universal traits of exaggerated self-importance, jealousy, and superstition still have their manifestations backstage as everywhere else.

Gala Performance annoyed one or two of the more partisan-minded critics who suspected, not without reason, that one of their sacred cows was being put on a highly conspicuous spot. The audience has always greeted the ballet joyously, and it remains one of the most popular items in the repertoire of Ballet Theatre.

GHOST TOWN

An American folk ballet, in one scene, prologue, and epilogue; libretto by Richard Rodgers; historical research by Gerald Murphy; music by Richard Rodgers, orchestrated by Hans Spialek; choreography by Marc Platoff; settings and costumes by Raoul Pène duBois.

GHOST TOWN was first performed by the Ballet Russe de Monte Carlo at the Metropolitan Opera House on November 12, 1939, with the following cast:

EILLEY ORUM	*Mia Slavenska*	BOY HIKER	*Charles Dickson*
ORSON HYDE, MORMON APOSTLE		GIRL HIKER	*Milada Miladova*
	Roland Guerard	OLD PROSPECTOR	*Simon Semenoff*
HIS FIVE WIVES		ASSAY OFFICER	*Paul Godkin*
Rosella Hightower, Katia Gelez-		"BENICIA BOY" HEENAN	
nova, Virginia Rosson, Mugi Novi-			*Robert Steele*
kova, Nesta Williams		ALGERNON C. SWINBURN	
RALSTON	*Frederic Franklin*		*James Starbuck*
JENNY LIND	*Nini Theilade*	"THE MENKEN"	*Marina Franca*
BONANZA KING COMSTOCK			
	Casimir Kokitch		

Housewives, Lady Shoppers, Bonanza Kings, Town Boys, "Bright Star" Miners, Firemen, Town Girls, Comstock Miners, Vigilantes, Dance-hall Girls

❖❖❖❖❖❖❖❖❖❖❖❖❖❖

Prologue. Two young hikers happen on the ruins of a mining settlement, a typical ghost town of the Sierras. While they are exploring, an aged Prospector appears and tells them the story of

The Town. A crowded picture is evoked by the old man's tale— children, housewives, dance-hall girls, rival gangs of miners throng the street. An incident in which Ralston becomes involved with a thief attracts the attention of Eilley Orum, who is escorted by Bonanza King Comstock. A brawl breaks out between the Bright Star miners and the Comstock faction. The fire department restores peace. A Mormon and his five flirtatious wives add to the confusion.

Comstock sells Ralston a mine. Ralston in his excitement drops the claim papers, which are picked up by Comstock. Eilley distracts Comstock and manages to get the papers into her own possession.

The stagecoach arrives, bringing the actress Adah Menken, Jenny Lind, Algernon Swinburn, and "Benicia Boy" Heenen, a boxer, who are going to participate in the opening of a new opera house.

Ralston finds gold on his newly purchased claim. He celebrates his wealth by buying a red coat with large gold buttons.

Comstock accuses Ralston of claim-jumping. As the young man is unable to produce the papers that prove possession, the Vigilantes take a hand. Eilley intervenes and saves him.

Jenny Lind sings *The Last Rose of Summer* to entertain the crowd.

Word comes from the Assay Office that the yield of gold has reached the vanishing-point. There is a panic. Inhabitants and visitors prepare to abandon the town. Ralston, believing that the town has a future, tries to persuade Eilley to remain. Unconvinced, she leaves with Comstock.

Epilogue. The colorful scene vanishes. The story has been told. As the hikers leave, they notice the large gold buttons on the old man's faded coat.

Ghost Town was one of several attempts on the part of the management of the Ballet Russe de Monte Carlo to satisfy the clamor of the critics (who had apparently changed their minds since the production of *Union Pacific*) for a ballet with an American background. Other ballets in this category were *The New Yorker* and *Saratoga*, not noticeably successful with critics or ballet public, who do not care for dull ballets, American or Russian.

Ghost Town was by far the most ingratiating of these ballets. The first work of Marc Platoff (now Mark Platt), it had many of the faults of youth, principally an overcrowded canvas. With judicious pruning it might have held a place in the repertoire for many seasons.

There were several good moments and one excellent character — the Mormon Apostle. It is difficult to forget his stately strut followed by his covey of demure wives. His sanctimonious expression was belied by the twinkling *entrechats six* into which he broke as though by compulsion. Roland Guerard was never seen to better advantage. Rosella Hightower as one of the wives demonstrated that she possessed no mean gift for comedy. Nini Theilade, in a characterization not in the least like the historical Jenny Lind, danced and mimed a charming solo to *The Last Rose of Summer,* making a very effective picture.

Frederic Franklin, in Ralston, had a role that was a sort of preliminary sketch for the Champion Roper in *Rodeo*. If he failed to make the most of its opportunities, he must not be blamed too severely. He was required to partner Mia Slavenska, whose appearance as Eilley Orum was a triumph of miscasting.

The score by Richard Rodgers was undistinguished and gave no hint of *Oklahoma!* to come. It might have been fair musical-comedy music, but struck quite the wrong note at the Metropolitan Opera House.

The settings and costumes by Raoul Pène duBois were pure delight. It is unfortunate that they have disappeared into the oblivion that swallows unperformed ballets.

GISELLE

OF all the ballets in the contemporary dance theater, there is only one that, when presented at the Metropolitan Opera House, causes the passer-by to wonder if an out-of-season performance of one of the more popular operas is being given. A long line of prospective standees reaching around the corner to Thirty-ninth Street and down to Seventh Avenue is a sight often seen during the opera season, which for the most part consists of subscription performances and during which ordinary music-lovers must either get in line or do without opera. For this to occur before a ballet performance, when all tickets are available at the box office, can mean one thing only: Markova is going to dance *Giselle*. Now this great artist has many roles in which she excels, and *Giselle* has been danced in New York within the last decade by several ballerinas, but only the combination can bring out such eager throngs.

Giselle is the oldest ballet in the active repertoire to boast a continuous history of performance. Originally produced in 1841, it is the archetype of the ballets of the romantic age, an era that saw one of those recurring periods of artistic flowering in the history of the dance. Fortunately, it was a period that was well documented (it boasted some fine and articulate critics), and it has been preserved for the admiration of future generations by delightful lithographs and prints by artists not yet frightened away from ballet as a subject by the overpowering shadow of Degas.

Giselle, with its visions of moonlit spirits, was not an isolated phenomenon. In 1831 Meyerbeer's opera *Robert le Diable* was given at the Paris Opéra. One of the most successful features of a successful production was the third-act ballet, which had for its subject an evocation from their tombs in a ruined abbey of a company of ghostly nuns, whose costumes prefigured those later to be associated with the romantic ballet. The Abbess of this spectral throng was Marie Taglioni, whose effortless floating style of dancing seemed to have been developed for the express purpose of portraying just such a character. Inspired by the unusual atmosphere of this ballet, Adolphe Nourrit (that wonder of the musical world, an intellectual tenor), who created the role of Robert in the opera, wrote a libretto for a ballet adapted from a romantic fantasy by Charles Nodier called *Trilby ou Le Lutin d'Argaïl,* and submitted it to the director of the Opéra. With this as a basis, *La Sylphide,* the first full-fledged romantic ballet, was created.

La Sylphide, with choreography by Filippo Taglioni and a musical score by Jean Schneitzhoeffer, was produced with all the scenic resources of the Opéra. It was not only an immediate success with the public, but a turning-point in the progress of ballet. The story, a tale of a sylph in love with a peasant; the locale, the Scottish Highlands, popularized as the very home of romance by the widely read narrative poems and novels of Sir Walter Scott; the choreography, which used *pointes* extensively for the first time—all these factors combined to give ballet a new direction. The majestic eighteenth-century spectacles masquerading as ballets met their final defeat in a wave of romanticism. Sylphides, nymphs, Nereids, and naiads replaced the mythological goddesses; princes and princesses gave way to peasants and fishermen as suitable protagonists in dance drama. The male dancer began to lose his importance before the wonder inspired by feminine dancing *sur les pointes.* It is true that danseuses had been on the verge of accomplishing this miracle since early in the nineteenth century, as contemporary prints testify. Now Taglioni rose from the earth clad in the cloud of misty tulle that bears her name to this day, and new ideals and new techniques superseded the old.

La Sylphide swept the civilized world. Styles were created and named in its and Taglioni's honor; poems were written; prints, lithographs, and paintings memorialized it. Taglioni toured Europe, and of all her repertoire, *La Sylphide* was greeted with the loudest acclaim. Almost every dancer of the period at one time or another assumed the title role, and though none eclipsed Taglioni, her exquisite lightness and surpassing elevation became an inspiration to other dancers.

La Sylphide was first performed in New York on April 15, 1835, probably at the Bowery Theater, by that very versatile artist Celeste. As a child Celeste had studied at the Paris Opéra. She was a feature of the American theatrical scene for many years, appearing occasionally in ballet, though her talents were more often exercised in the field of dramatic pantomime, Fenella in *La Muette de Portici* being one of her favorite roles. When Paul Taglioni (brother of Marie) and his wife made their debut at the Park Theater (New York), on May 21, 1839, *La Sylphide* was their vehicle. A contemporary critic wrote that Mme Taglioni's "feathery, floating lightness, and the spirituelle school in which both she and her husband had studied, gave them a decided superiority over all who had preceded them." "La Petite Augusta," a "baby ballerina" (not necessarily a contemporary manifestation, though the phrase was not to be coined for a hundred years), made her last American appearance in *La Sylphide* before departing to pursue her studies in Paris. This she did with such good results that she remains to this day the only native American dancer who ever achieved the status of *première danseuse* in a European opera house of the first rank, and that in an era when ballet equaled, and at times excelled, opera in popularity. Mme Augusta, a dancer greatly esteemed in New York at this time, also assumed the role of the Sylphide, but an artist was on her way whose interpretation was to be hailed as the finest yet. This was Fanny Elssler, who followed her American debut at the Park Theater, on May 14, 1840, with a performance on June 1 of *La Sylphide*. New Yorkers were not aware that Elssler's Sylphide had been considered an error by European critics, and probably would not have cared if they had known it, so carried away were they by her charming personality. She was supported in the ballet by M. Sylvain, whose dancing the local critics compared unfavorably with Paul Taglioni's, hinting darkly that his real name was O'Sullivan, as though that were the deciding factor. Mme Lecomte, a somewhat buxom dancer who had been on the New York scene for several years and had, indeed, appeared as the Abbess in *Robert le Diable* in 1837, challenged the European star by performing *La Sylphide* a week later at the National Theater, "just as if Fanny Elssler had not been here," as one critic rather bitterly remarked. *La Sylphide,* as a ballet and at times as a ballet-opera, held a place in the repertoire of American theaters for many years and was not superseded even by the arrival of *Giselle.*[1]

Meanwhile in Paris and London new ballets were produced glorifying peasant maids and the creatures of the new mythology:

[1] *La Sylphide* was part of the repertoire of the Royal Ballet in Denmark long after it had faded from memory in other musical theaters. Paul Petroff, as a child, saw it in Copenhagen, where it was performed with flying dancers on wires, and the stage machinery the romantic theater knew so well how to use. He claims that it could be revived quite as successfully as *Giselle.*

Nathalie, ou La Laitière Suisse, La Fille du Danube, L'Ombre, La Gitana, and many others, most of which were carried across the Atlantic without much delay. A rival for the public favor accorded so overwhelmingly to Taglioni had arisen in Elssler, whose bravura, warmth, and voluptuousness probably saved ballet from dissolving into a cloud of moonlit muslin, although, as has been seen, she had the hardihood to challenge Taglioni on her own ground and in her greatest role, by appearing in *La Sylphide*—an ill-advised venture.

A whole decade elapsed before the true successor to *La Sylphide* appeared: *Giselle,* the perfect romantic ballet, a pure distillation of the romantic age. Like the best of the Diaghilev ballets, it was the result of close collaboration among men of ability: Vernoy de Saint-Georges, the librettist, Adolphe Adam, the composer, and Jean Coralli and Jules Perrot, the choreographers. The Diaghilev of the group was Théophile Gautier, who had read the legend of the Wilis in a book by Heinrich Heine, published in French as *De l'Allemagne* and in German as *Zur Geschichte der neueren schönen Literatur in Deutschland.* Attracted by the balletic possibilities of the dancing spirits, Gautier, after sketching several tentative plots, passed on the idea to Saint-Georges, who wrote the libretto. Enchanted with the story, the collaborators worked quickly, and in little more than a week the ballet was in rehearsal.

The première of *Giselle* took place at the Paris Opéra on June 28, 1841. The settings were by Pierre Ciceri, the costumes by Paul Lormier. The cast was as follows:

ALBRECHT	*Lucien Petipa*	BERTHE	*Mlle Roland*
WILFRID	*Eugene Coralli*	GISELLE	*Carlotta Grisi*
HILARION	*M. Simon*	MYRTHA	*Adèle Dumilâtre*
BATHILDE	*Mlle Forster*		

❖❖❖❖❖❖❖❖❖❖❖❖❖❖❖❖❖❖

In that amazing labor of love by C. W. Beaumont, *The Ballet Called Giselle* (to which this account is deeply indebted), there is considerable discussion of the exact measure of the contributions made by the two choreographers, Coralli and Perrot. The latter, having no official standing at the Opéra, received no acknowledgment on the program, but it was a matter of general knowledge that he had arranged the role of Giselle, whose creator was Carlotta Grisi, his wife. From internal evidence and a vast knowledge of the period as well as of the individual styles of the two men, Beaumont has made an analysis of the choreography:

"Can the respective contributions of Perrot and Coralli be assigned with any degree of exactitude? I think not: at best we can but speculate. It is not unreasonable, however, to accept the contemporary statement that Perrot 'arranged all his wife's *pas* and scenes.' It is very possible that he was also responsible for the episode in which Hilarion is trapped by the Wilis. As to the balance, I think we may fairly assign to Coralli all the mimed scenes in the first act associated with Hilarion, Albrecht, Wilfrid, and Berthe; and in the second act, the entrance of the huntsmen,[2] Hilarion's scene, the dance of Myrtha and the Wilis, the scene (now omitted) between the peasants and the Wilis. Coralli's major contribution is certainly his dances for Myrtha and the Wilis, which reveal much imagination and thought. It is possible that the March of the Vinegatherers—long since omitted—was also the work of Coralli, but it is well to remember that Perrot, too, had a flair for processions, as witness the famous Procession of Fools in his ballet *Esmeralda*."[3]

Giselle was as immediate a success as *La Sylphide* and was attended by similar evidences of popular favor. Carlotta Grisi became the idol of the hour, with Gautier as her chief publicist. She was hailed as another Taglioni, probably with more truth than any other dancer until the debut of the ill-fated Emma Livry.

Giselle began its career in the lyric theaters of Europe at once, and the outstanding dancers of the time were seen in the title role.

"A melodramatic ballet" called *Giselle or the Doomed Bride* was presented at the Olympic Theater, New York, on November 1, 1841, with a cast that included Mr. and Mrs. Wells, Mrs. Watts, and Mrs. Baldock. It was on a program with a farce called *Bob Short*. Just what relation this production may have borne to the original ballet it is impossible to conjecture, and I have not found any contemporary announcements or reviews that might furnish clues. Even the *Spirit of the Times,* a periodical with a great deal to say about the theater in general, merely remarks in the November 6 issue: "Mitchell [4] has produced a new extravaganza and a new ballet. Both good in their way, and both drawing money to his snug little box," without specifying any details. This production may have been an attempt to cap-

---

[2] Omitted in most American productions, unless the group of figures playing dice seen for a while in Ballet Theatre's *Giselle* may be a reference to it.

[3] Beaumont: *The Ballet Called Giselle,* Chapter ii.

[4] Manager of the Olympic Theater.

italize on the success of *Giselle,* accounts of which must have crossed the Atlantic shortly after its première.[5]

We hear no more of *Giselle* in New York until January 24, 1846, when "Things Theatrical," a column in the *Spirit of the Times* devoted to the drama, announced: "Augusta is engaged, and 'La Giselle' is in preparation to be brought out with great splendor." A week later further details appeared in the same column: "On Monday evening, Mdlle. Augusta opens in the Ballet of 'Giselle.' A well selected *corps* will support her, headed by the talented and interesting Miss Ince. The scenery, costumes, and decorations are all entirely new, and have been prepared with the usual liberality which characterises this establishment" (the Park Theater).[6] This advance notice has a feature seldom encountered in the modern variety—it actually wishes the enterprise well.

On February 2, 1846 *Giselle or the Willies* was presented at the Park Theater, New York, with the following cast:

GISELLE	*Augusta*	BERTHA	*Mrs. Dyott*
MYRTHA	*Emma Ince*	ALBERICH [as spelled in Odell]	
OLLA	*Miss St. Clair*		*Mons. Frederic*
ARISSA	*Miss Jessalyne*	HILARION	*C. T. Parsloe*
PRINCESS BATHILDE	*Fanny Gordon*	GRAND DUKE	*Mr. Anderson*

◇◇◇◇◇◇◇◇◇◇◇◇◇◇◇◇◇◇◇

Of this production the *Annals of the New York Stage* says rather unkindly: "I do not venture to guess what the director of the ballet of the Paris opera of those days or of today would have thought of that host of supernumeraries. The fantastic toe may not have been very light." The critic of the *Spirit of the Times,* however, no doubt hardened to the producers' habit of filling the background of ballets with an untrained corps capable of little more than marching, wrote an enthusiastic review for the February 7 issue:

"Augusta opened at the Park, on Monday evening in the pantomime Ballet of 'Giselle; or the Willies,' to a very good house. The greeting with which she was received was most cordial, and the feeling of delight seemed

[5] Even so diligent a researcher as Lillian Moore, an authority on the romantic ballet in America, has not located any contemporary reference to this production. It is listed, however, in Ireland's *Records of the New York Stage* and Odell's monumental *Annals of the New York Stage,* my authorities for the account of *Giselle* in nineteenth-century New York.

[6] "Boxes $1—Pit, 50cts—Gallery 25cts. Doors open at 6½ o'clock, and curtain will rise precisely at 7."

reciprocal, for we never saw the lady more enchantingly perfect than upon this occasion. The ballet is in two acts, and of course, boasts only sufficient plot whereon to base the incident, but is charming and beautiful in the enactment. The scene of the first act is laid upon the Rhine, that of the second in the *monde des Fées*. Giselle, (Augusta) a blithe and sprightly peasant girl is beloved by Count Albrecht, (Fredericks) and Hilarion, the latter a gentleman of loose moral principles and no very visible means of subsistence. The former of the two *amans,* disguises himself as a vine-dresser, and secures the love of the dancing peasant girl. Hilarion, jealous of his rival's better fortune, reveals the fact of his being a nobleman, a piece of information which he has obtained by crawling in at the window of the pretended peasant's hut, and discovering there, his sword, spear, etc., which with an eye to caution, he ought to have left at home. Giselle, overcome with chagrin and sorrow, falls upon the sword and dies.

"The second act opens with a dance of fairies. From the grave of Giselle a shadowy form arises, and, in fulfilment of the prophecy of the anxious mother, is admitted to the fairy band, whose constant business is—

> *'To dance all night, till broad daylight*
> *And fade away in the morning.'*

Hilarion, whose business, being of a very mysterious nature, leads him that way, is fascinated by the Willie dance, and is obliged to join in it, 'Willy, nilly;' the result of which course of conduct is, that the bold, bad man finds a watery grave in the Fairies' Lake: that being the punishment inflicted upon all mortals enticed within the magic circle, and unable to dance as long and vehemently as the Willies.

"The Count Albrecht, too, happens that way, but Giselle, knowing the sad fate of all neophytes in dancing, when engaged with these adepts, warns him of his danger, and entreats him to seek shelter under the cross reared to mark her grave—Alas! not her resting place. This he does, but enchanted by her dancing, which the laws of fairyland render imperious upon her, he forgets himself, joins in the figure, and is on the point of sinking, exhausted, like his immediate predecessor, when day breaks and the Willies separate to their hiding places. Giselle falls upon the earth and vanishes from the sight of the disconsolate Albrecht, to whom nothing is left but her memory and a rose which he plucks from her grave.

"The scenery of the piece, though slight, is beautiful, and the costumes [7] and machinery are very well. The corps de ballet is not large nor were the members as perfect on the first representation as we trust they will become. As for Augusta, to quote the words of a contemporary, 'not even in her favorite part of the Bayadere is she more fascinating. With all her accustomed grace in action, in attitude, in everything she does, she displays in this charming character, all the higher qualities of the artiste. Her face,

[7] Augusta's costume was described by another critic as "after the style adopted by the great Taglioni. The skirts fell below the knee in fleecy, classic folds, and the shoulders rose out of a cloud of lace which completely hid her bust."

so expressive—her form, so perfect and symmetrical,—her poses, so statuesque and her movements so graceful and poetical, she finds in "La Giselle" exactly the vehicle for her best and most beautiful ideas. We have never seen anything in the choreographic art more perfect than Augusta's first bounds, at the commencement of her portion in the second act, when, touched by the magic wand, she finds herself possessed of wings, and soars away upon the buoyancy, as if she were indeed the transformed creature she seems.' "

In spite of a very bad pun and a premature bow to the cult of unintelligibility, it is obvious that the critic and the contemporary whom he quotes knew what they liked. Both Augusta and *Giselle* met with their enthusiastic approval. Augusta, who had been one of New York's favorite artists for several years, came to this country from Munich, by way of the Paris Opéra, where she is said to have received her training. She made her local debut in a scene from *Les Naiades,* appearing later in the year (1836) as Zoloë in *La Bayadère,* a vehicle that served to exhibit the talents of almost every dancer who appeared in New York for more than two decades, from "La Petite Augusta" to Fanny Elssler. Augusta varied her American appearances with tours to Cuba, Mexico, and South America. Retiring from the stage in 1853, she survived until 1901. She is the subject of a number of lithographs that attest to her popularity with her contemporaries.

Mary Ann Lee, an American dancer who had studied in Paris, was the next Giselle to be seen in New York, appearing at the Park Theater on April 13, 1846, with a supporting cast that included Mrs. C. W. Hunt (Myrtha) and George Washington Smith (Albrecht). Mary Ann Lee not only was the first American dancer to appear as Giselle, but actually introduced the ballet to America, her performance at the Howard Athenæum in Boston on January 1, 1846 having antedated Augusta's by a month.

After their New York appearances Lee and Smith returned to Boston for an engagement at the National Theater. A playbill in the Theater Collection of the New York Public Library may give modern audiences some idea of the miscellaneous programs that ballet-lovers, until well into the nineteenth century, were forced to endure for a glimpse of their favorite ballets. The program began with a comedy, *Forty and Fifty.* Act I of *Giselle* followed. Then came another farce (short, let us hope), *Dunn Brown, or My Friend the Captain,* and the performance concluded with *Fleur de Champs, or*

The Daughter of the Danube (one of Taglioni's most famous vehicles). This last might well have been a circus from the description
on the playbill, the anonymous author of which could have given
pointers to the Hollywood geniuses who compose the dithyrambs
used to arouse interest in the "coming attractions" at a neighborhood
movie. The audience was not left in any doubt as to what they
might expect to see in Act I of *Giselle,* the program containing a
round-by-round description.[8]

Giselle remained for many years one of the standard presentations
in New York theaters. Rivals to Augusta and Mary Ann Lee arose,
though none of them appears to have equaled the former in popularity. Hermine Blangy was seen as Giselle in August 1846 at Niblo's,
a summer theater that was one of New York's institutions for several
decades. A critic remarked; "The town seems really charmed at the
exquisite acting and refined dancing of Mlle. Blangy, in the character of Gizelle. It entirely outstrips her former popular performances
and the critics . . . are all, without exception loud in her praise." It
seems that there was a certain amount of rivalry between Augusta
and Blangy, and both had their partisans—an infallible method,
then as now, of keeping dancers at the top of their form.

A new Giselle, Henrietta Vallée, was seen at the Chatham Theater

[8] Here it is, complete with period spelling:

"Scene First—Gathering of grapes from the vineyards. Hilarion appears and re-
gards the abode of Giselle with Love and that of Loys (his rival) with anger—he
secretes himself and watches. The young Duke Albert disguised as a peasant appears
with his Esquire, who entreats him to leave the place. Giselle appears and finds her
lover—his love is tested through virtue of the Daisy. Hilarion discovers himself and
reproaches Giselle. She rejects him with ridicule. The peasants appear for Giselle to
go to her work—She refuses, and persuades her companions to join her in the dance.

WALTZ BY GISELLE, LOYS, AND PEASANTS.

The Mother of Giselle appears and reproves her for Dancing, and tells her she will
die with dancing and become a Wilies; but live or die, Giselle will dance. Signal
of the Chase is heard, and Loys leaves in fear of being discovered. Hilarion, determined to discover the secret of his rival, steals into the cottage of Loys. Arrival of
the Prince of Courand and Bathilde, his daughter; they seek repose at the cottage
of Giselle. Giselle inimitates her coming Marriage and promises to accompany and
dance at the Marriage of Bathilde. Hilarion has discovered the Duke's secret, and
threatens to expose him.

FESTIVAL !

GRAND PAS DE DEUX . . . BY . . . GISELLE AND LOYS

"Hilarion uses stratagem, and calls the Prince's followers by a signal. Giselle discovers that her lover is a Duke,—and the shock proves too great; she loses her
reason, and Dies of a Broken Heart."

during November 1847. The ballet formed part of a program that included two plays, *Teddy the Tiler* and *The Bronze Horse*. Miss Vallée does not appear to have outshone her predecessors, nor did Julia Turnbull, who offered her interpretation at the Bowery on December 6, 1847. One of the critics took a high tone with Miss Turnbull, an American dancer who had appeared in New York previously, complaining that her dancing had not improved. Charles Burke, a popular comedian, produced, also at the Bowery, a burlesque of the ballet, called *La Chiselle,* during the Christmas season. According to a contemporary critic, this was "a source of innocent merriment during that happy, trying time." Augusta also offered *Giselle* during the same season at Palmo's Opera House, where she had a bad supporting cast. A partial critic found her performance so charming that he urged the public to attend in spite of the deficiencies of the production.

In August 1849 a season of Italian opera and French ballet began at the Broadway Theater. The ballet repertoire included *La Vivandière, L'Almée, L'Illusion d'un Peintre,* and *Giselle*. The *première danseuse* of this company was Hermine Blangy. Performances were well attended, and the singing of the prima donna, Fortunata Tedesco, attracted favorable notices from the critics. *Giselle* appeared in better company here than in theaters devoted primarily to drama, where it had some very odd program mates indeed.[9] During the Broadway Theater season it was paired with *Norma* and *Lucia di Lammermoor*. *Giselle* was also revived for Augusta during 1849, at the Park Theater, a critic calling her performance "the perfect embodiment of the poetry of motion."

[9] *Giselle* was presented many times by groups of dancers in most of the cities of America that were visited by touring companies. The ballet was sometimes given in even stranger company than we have seen in New York. One program really deserves a blue ribbon. It was presented at the Theatre Comique in Boston, date unspecified:

1. El Nino Eddie (child wonder).
2. Pip and Flip, trained dogs introduced by the Snow Brothers.
3. *La Giselle,* ballet divertissement by G. W. Smith.

In this version of *Giselle* the title role was danced by Mlle de Vere. A high point of the proceedings was a *pas de quatre* danced by Wilfred, Bathilde (spelled Batild on the program) Myrtha, and Bertha—a combination that would have staggered Coralli and Perrot.

This was by no means the whole of the evening's entertainment. There were also a play, an exhibition of tightrope walking, and "classical groupings." Only one of the big commercial "hours" on the radio could compete with it.

The Rousset family (Jean and his four sisters, Caroline, Adelaide, Theresine, and Clementine) arrived in New York for an engagement at Niblo's in 1851. Caroline quickly established herself as a favorite with the public in *Catarina ou la Reine des Bandits*. "She is agile and graceful, and accomplishes many feats on the 'light fantastic toe,' which have not been performed by any danseuse that we have seen in some time. Her sisters are very clever in their art and Miss Adelaide, who assumes the male character in the ballet, dresses for the part with judgment." It was only a matter of time until Caroline was seen as Giselle, though by October 8, when it was presented, the Roussets had moved to the Lyceum Theater. Here an awful thought arises: did Miss Adelaide, who "assumed the male character" in *Catarina,* appear as Albrecht? Let us avert our eyes and hurry on to the next Giselle to be seen in New York—Léontine Pougoud at the Bowery Theater on May 16, 1853. Five years later *Giselle* turned up on a program at the Stadttheater, with Celestine Franck (Giselle) and George Washington Smith (Albrecht), along with two plays in German.

Giselle had by now declined in popularity, not even its vitality being able to withstand the strange and variegated treatment to which it had been subjected. Also, artists of the caliber of Augusta were no longer to be seen in New York. Lola Montez, trying to salvage her battered fortunes by an American tour, had a habit of interpolating a *pas seul* from *Giselle* in her programs—a thought almost as horrifying as that of Adelaide Rousset as Albrecht.

On March 14, 1864, at the American Theater the following program was presented: *The Rival Artisans, or the Shipwrecked Sailor, The Black Statue,* and *Giselle.* The cast of *Giselle* included Lizzie Schultze, Millie Flora, Ida Ross, Frank Nixon, Annetta and Lottie La Point, and Jenny Lorraine. Who had the role of Giselle is not made clear, but I am inclined to favor Lizzie Schultze because her name leads the rest. If so, Lizzie was versatile, for she also appears in *The Rival Artisans.*

The last recorded performance of *Giselle* in nineteenth-century New York took place under superior auspices. Katti Lanner, daughter of the Viennese composer, and later for many years chief choreographer at the Empire Theatre in London, arrived in New York for a season at the Grand Opera House. In July 1870 *Giselle* was presented with a cast that included Katti Lanner (Giselle), Bertha Lind

Galina Ulanova as Giselle and Alexander Yermolayev as Albrecht (Bolshoi Theater, Moscow)

Alicia Markova as Giselle and Anton Dolin as Albrecht
GISELLE

GISELLE (scene of the Wilis, Sociedad Pro-Arte Musical, Havana, 1945)

GISELLE Alicia Alonso as Giselle and Fernando Alonso as Albrecht (Sociedad Pro-Arte Musical, Havana, 1945)

GISELLE Alicia Alonso as Giselle and Fernando Alonso as Albrecht (Sociedad Pro-Arte Musical, Havana, 1945)

(Myrtha), and G. de Francesco (Albert). It is reasonable to suppose that *Giselle* bowed itself out of the theater with an elegance and dignity worthy of its beginnings.

Giselle was not seen again in New York until October 15, 1910, when it was revived at the Metropolitan Opera House by Anna Pavlova and Mikhail Mordkin in a version that, according to Carl Van Vechten, then critic of the *Times,* was freely cut. A waltz from Glazunov's *Raymonda* was interpolated in the first act, which, in the words of the same critic, "was very much as if some conductor had performed *Also sprach Zarathustra* somewhere in *Fra Diavolo.*" It is difficult to imagine why this was considered necessary, today's audiences finding Adam's score entirely adequate. Probably the producers were following the custom of Russian producers of ballet, who thought little of ballet composers and arranged and rearranged to suit their own ideas or those of the ballerina. Pictures of this production in a souvenir program indicate that the period had been advanced from the German Renaissance to the eighteenth century, and the *tutu à la Taglioni,* traditionally worn by the Wilis in Act II, had been exchanged for draperies suggestive of graveclothes.

New York critics were not in agreement about the dramatic values of *Giselle*. The *Globe,* probably represented by a bored music critic, called the ballet "tiresome." Van Vechten, a critic who knew his subject (a rarity then as now), criticizing only the liberties taken with the music, said: "Mlle. Pavlova yesterday revivified this honeyfied and sentimental score of Adam's, full of the sad, grey splendour of the time of Louis Philippe. Grisi is said to have been gently melancholy in it, but Pavlova was probably more than that. Her poetic conception of the betrothed girl's madness . . . came very close to being tragic. It is almost impossible to describe the poetry of her dancing in the second act."

New York was not quite ready for a romantic or a classical revival in ballet. Pavlova's *Giselle,* and later Geltzer's *Swan Lake,* made small impression compared with the neo-romanticism of *Le Cygne* and the Oriental *Legend of Azyiade,* the latter stemming, like *Scheherazade,* from the *Arabian Nights,* though considerably less lusty and voluptuous in content than the Fokine ballet. Indeed, after this production, I can find no further record of *Giselle* being performed in New York until June 1934, when it was given at Radio City Music Hall, in a condensed version (performance time, twenty minutes) with choreography by Florence Rogge. Nina Whitney was the over-worked Giselle. It must have been sweated labor to perform a role of such emotional intensity several times a day.

In 1937 *Giselle* was revived by Mikhail Mordkin for the Mordkin Ballet with a cast that included Lucia Chase (Giselle), Leon Varkas (Albert), Dimitri Romanoff (Hilarion, called Hans in this production), and Viola Essen (Myrtha). This presentation retained some of the pantomime that has been omitted from recent *Giselles,* notably a scene in which Berthe gathers the peasant girls around her and tells them the legend of the Wilis. Mordkin, a master of pantomime, set this scene in a convincing and dramatically vivid manner. Another memorable, though less admirable feature was the costumes of the Wilis: strange, modernistic headdresses and draperies of cellophane that crackled in a most disconcerting manner.

When the Ballet Russe de Monte Carlo began its career in America, its first performance, given at the Metropolitan Opera House on October 12, 1938, consisted of those extremes of balletic art, *Giselle* and *Gaité Parisienne.* The program offered the following information about *Giselle:* "Scenario by Theophile Gautier on a theme by Heinrich Heine; music by Adolphe Adam; restaged by Serge Lifar; scenes and costumes after Alexandre Benois." The original choreographers and librettist were not mentioned. The cast was as follows:

GISELLE	*Alicia Markova*	THE DUKE OF COURLAND	
COUNT ALBRECHT	*Serge Lifar*		*Vladimir Kostenko*
BERTHE	*Rosella Hightower*	THE PRINCESS	*Jeannette Lauret*
HILARION	*Marc Platoff*	WILFRED	*Marcel Fenchel*
		MYRTHA	*Alexandra Danilova*

◇◇◇◇◇◇◇◇◇◇◇◇◇◇◇◇◇◇◇

This restaging of *Giselle* missed many fine points in both choreography and pantomime, and though the performance of Markova was a revelation, one had to be exceptionally alert to catch its subtleties. The sad truth was that the much publicized performance of Lifar as Albrecht was one of the most appalling exhibitions of ham acting ever seen on the stage of the Metropolitan, where ham acting is endemic. At least two New York critics placed their opinions of his ridiculous antics on record. A third, who had obviously read and been influenced by Lifar's fluent praise of Lifar (published as treatises on ballet), hailed his performance in extravagant terms, brushing aside Markova's lyric and lovely interpretation as "not sufficiently spiritual or danced with enough expertness to carry complete conviction."

It was at this time that a new phenomenon became noticeable on the audience side of the footlights—ballet had become fashionable. The first-night performance of the Ballet Russe de Monte Carlo was attended in force by café society in its smartest and most spectacular raiment, a manifestation that rather irked the more modest ballet-lovers who had been quietly supporting ballet for as long as there had been any to support. If this was because of presence in the company of Serge Lifar, a social lion in the European branch of café society, then it was the only service he rendered to ballet in America, as the attending publicity awakened a more general interest in an art considered too precious for popular consumption.

Giselle remained in the repertoire of the Monte Carlo Ballet for several seasons, the egregious Lifar being replaced by that superb *danseur noble,* Igor Youskevitch.

The most recent, and up to now the definitive, revival of *Giselle* in New York was presented by Ballet Theatre for the first time on January 12, 1940 at the Center Theater. This was a restaging by Anton Dolin, "after the original choreography by Jean Coralli; scenario by Theophile Gautier based on a theme by Heinrich Heine; music by Adolphe Adam, orchestrated by Eugene Fuerst; scenery and costumes by Lucinda Ballard." This production claimed to be a recreation by Anton Dolin of the authentic Russian version, first produced in Moscow on December 18/30, 1842. This was, in everything but the absence of Markova, far superior to the Lifar version. Pantomime and incidents that had been obscure and doubtful of interpretation in the previous presentation became clear, and there was a genuine feeling for the romantic style of the original conception. While there were no names as lustrous as those of Markova and Danilova in the cast, it was a worthy presentation of a great classic. Later, when Markova joined Ballet Theatre, the audience for the first time saw her incomparable Giselle in a setting choreographically worthy of it, on November 27, 1941 at the Forty-fourth Street Theater. True, the stage was small, and ballet never appears completely at home in the atmosphere of the commercial theater, but the one thing wanting—the stage of the Metropolitan Opera House—was available the following season. *Giselle,* entering its second century of performance, began to make new dance history.

The plot of *Giselle,* as presented by Ballet Theatre, follows:

The story takes place in the Rhineland, during the season of the vintage.

Act I. The scene is an open space in a village, across which two cottages face each other. High on a hill in the distance a castle may be seen.

As the curtain rises, a group of peasants are on their way to the vintage. The door of the cottage on the right opens, and Albrecht enters with his squire, Wilfrid. Albrecht, the owner of the distant castle, has assumed a peasant name (Loys) and disguise, and come to live in the village, the better to further his suit for Giselle, the daughter of a peasant woman who lives in the neighboring cottage. In spite of his humble garb, Albrecht wears a knightly sword, which he takes off and gives to Wilfrid. Wilfrid tries to dissuade him from his caprice, but is dismissed by Albrecht. He leaves, first going into the cottage with the sword.

Albrecht knocks at the door of Giselle's cottage, hiding before his summons can be answered. Giselle comes to the door and looks around, puzzled. When she is on the point of going back into the house, Albrecht comes out from his hiding-place. Giselle greets him with shy pleasure (this is by no means their first meeting), but confides that she has had a dream that has shaken her confidence in his love. When Albrecht smiles at her fears, she picks a flower from the border growing by the cottage, and tries by the time-honored ritual to divine whether he truly loves her. Impatiently she throws the flower to the ground. Albrecht picks it up and triumphantly demonstrates that he is really faithful.

Their pleasure is rudely interrupted by the entrance of Hilarion, a gamekeeper from the near-by forest and a rejected suitor of Giselle's. He tries to reinstate himself in her affections forcibly. Albrecht firmly sends him away. As he leaves, he calls down curses on both of them.

Peasants returning from the vineyards now join Giselle and Albrecht. Berthe, Giselle's mother, breaks into their gay dance, warning the girls that no good will come of their addiction to dancing.

As a punishment for too much dancing while they were alive, they will, when they die, certainly turn into Wilis, condemned to dance all night in the forest and hound to death all who cross their path. Berthe orders Giselle into the cottage and sends Albrecht from the scene. The villagers also go on their way.

Hunting horns are heard in the distance. Wilfrid enters, leading a file of huntsmen, who are followed by the Duke of Courland with his daughter Bathilde and her ladies. Berthe comes out of her cottage to greet the party. Requested by Wilfrid to provide the party with refreshments, she complies with much fussing and bobbing of curt-sies. Giselle's friends carry out a table and chairs for the Duke and Bathilde, who seat themselves. Giselle appears to pour the wine. Admiring Bathilde's dress, Giselle surreptitiously touches the fabric. Bathilde notices the pretty peasant girl and questions her about her life. Giselle answers that she spins, loves to dance, and expects soon to marry her lover. Bathilde removes a gold chain that she is wear-ing and, first asking her father's permission, gives it to Giselle. The Duke takes off his hunting horn, hangs it on a projection of the cottage wall, and, with his daughter and her ladies, goes into the cottage to rest. Wilfrid sends the huntsmen away, and the scene is left vacant.

Hilarion enters. Taking advantage of the absence of observers to search Albrecht's cottage, he emerges triumphantly with the in-criminating sword—a weapon that no peasant could possibly own. Hiding it in a convenient place, Hilarion indicates his intention of using it to expose Albrecht.

The harvesters return carrying baskets of grapes. They also have a special bunch of grapes decorated with a pine cone for Giselle. They clap their hands to summon her. Berthe appears instead and angrily tells them to go away. Giselle, running out, begs her mother for permission to dance with her friends, to which Berthe unwill-ingly consents. Albrecht also rejoins the group. When the merriment is at its height, Hilarion rushes in and rudely separates Giselle and Albrecht. When Albrecht tries to drive him away, Hilarion snatches the Duke's hunting horn and blows a signal. The Duke and his party come out of the cottage. Bathilde, in amazement, recognizes her fiancé, Count Albrecht, in the young man whom the peasants know as Loys. Concealment is at an end, and Hilarion clinches the truth by producing the sword, which Albrecht seizes, then drops. Giselle, shocked at this revelation, becomes frenzied. She tries to prevent Albrecht from kissing Bathilde's hand, pointing to her betrothal ring. Bathilde answers that she too has a ring. At this, Giselle's reason gives way. Seizing Albrecht's sword, she describes a great circle on the ground, and as the horrified spectators fall back, she stabs herself. Trembling with the chill of approaching death, Giselle re-enacts in a pitiful dragging tempo the gay incidents and dances of her happy day. Accusingly she points at Albrecht and falls dead. Albrecht, deeply affected, forces Hilarion to view the results of his plotting, then kneels by Giselle's body in an agony of self-recrimination.

Act II. The scene is a clearing in the forest by the side of a lake. Giselle's lonely grave, surmounted by a cross, is on a rise to the left of the stage.

It is night, and a shadowy form, veiled and mysterious, is seen. The moon rises and the veil disappears, disclosing Myrtha, Queen of the Wilis. The Wilis are the spirits of young girls who in life loved dancing too much. They are condemned to haunt the forest, dancing nightly as a punishment for their frivolity. Myrtha summons her ghostly band to the tomb of Giselle, who is to become one of them. At the Queen's command, Giselle rises from her tomb. The veil that covers her dissolves. Slowly she descends from the mound to stand before the Queen. At a touch from the Queen's flowery scepter, she is possessed with ghostly animation. The Wilis disperse to pursue their task of hounding belated travelers to death.

Albrecht comes to mourn at the tomb of Giselle. He is accompanied by Wilfrid, who implores him to leave the sinister spot. Failing, he reluctantly leaves Albrecht alone. While Albrecht is kneeling at the tomb, Giselle flits by him. Incredulous, he pursues her as she appears and disappears.

Hilarion, wandering in the forest, becomes the prey of a band of Wilis. They torment him until in despair he drowns himself in the lake.

Albrecht returns, still following the elusive Giselle. He is confronted by the Queen, who orders Giselle to lure him to his death. Giselle, not yet detached from her earthly love, defies the Queen, drawing Albrecht to her tomb, whose protecting cross has a power that causes the Queen's scepter to break. Albrecht is not proof against his love for Giselle, who is forced to dance for him. He leaves the tomb, exposing himself to the Wilis' power.

At the point of exhaustion, Albrecht is saved from sharing Hilarion's fate by the coming of day, when unholy powers grow weak and the Wilis return to their graves.

During its many years of existence *Giselle* has been modified by the changing tastes of generations. Much of the mime has been lost, and passages corresponding to the dry recitative of opera have been eliminated. The story is admirably designed for balletic purposes. As it is currently performed, just enough pantomime is left to give the audience an illusion of seeing a period piece without exposing it to the rigors of long mimed passages. These were easily understood by ballet-lovers of the nineteenth century, but it is a matter for conjecture how many of the contemporary audience know that when Bathilde, after seeing Giselle for the first time, turns to the Duke and makes a circular gesture in front of her own face, she wishes to convey the idea that Giselle is pretty. Giselle answers Bathilde's inquiries with a series of arbitrary gestures, plain as words to an audience conversant with the idiom, but today almost meaningless unless one takes the trouble to find out what they indicate.

Many details of production have been changed. Flying Wilis on wires and strategically placed seesaws were a feature of the early performances, and were, according to those who saw them, startlingly effective in the flickering gas lights of the era. Theater-goers of past generations have many times claimed that true romance fled the theater with the advent of electricity. Certainly, Wilis on wires would appear more acrobatic than phantomlike in the steady glow, however subdued, of modern stage lighting. Beaumont tells how the original producers of the ballet planned that the lake in Act II be made of mirrors, placed in such a manner that the passage of the Wilis would be reflected in them. The management found this project too expensive, though in a revival at the Opéra twenty years later the mirrored pool was used to good effect. Originally Giselle did not return to her grave, but sank into a bank of flowers. These are but a few of the changes noted by Beaumont in his fascinating *Ballet Called Giselle,* probably the most exhaustive history of a single ballet ever published.

The story of *Giselle* has also been subject to modification through the years, as a reference to the original libretto will demonstrate. The basic story, however, remains unchanged and in its simplicity is probably all the more acceptable to the modern audiences, unacquainted with the complexities of the ballet books of the past.

Anton Dolin's reconstruction of *Giselle* has its foundation in the ballet as performed in the Russian lyric theaters, in whose repertoires it has remained active from the time of the first performance in 1842 till the present day. To quote the invaluable *Ballet Called Giselle*: "Most, if not all, contemporary English productions are the work of Nicholas Sergeyev, formerly *regisseur* at the Maryinsky Theatre, St. Petersburg, and are probably based on the ballet as performed there from 1884–1887, during which years Marius Petipa finally revised the standardised version, which Perrot produced at St. Petersburg in 1851, and which he himself subjected to many modifications during his service with the Imperial Russian Ballet." In his autobiography, *Ballet Go Round,* Dolin speaks of Sergeyev being brought from Paris to rehearse the Markova-Dolin Ballet in *Giselle,* so that it is reasonable to assume that Dolin's admirable revival of *Giselle* for Ballet Theatre owes something to Sergeyev.

The dances in Act I are interspersed among many pantomimed scenes, which unfold the story in a manner that is clear and easy to follow. The first *pas de deux,* performed by Giselle and Albrecht, exploits *ballotés* and *jetés,* which they perform in unison, with hands joined. The corps de ballet moves in simple patterns, at one point forming a long line that wheels around the stage in a circular pattern. Giselle's solo variation is characterized by balances *en arabesque, pirouettes en attitude,* the high light being a diagonal progress from upstage right to downstage left, in which she hops on point performing *ballonés,* and *attitudes en avant* without change of feet. This variation finishes with Giselle running to her starting-point, repeating the diagonal in a series of *degagé* turns, *pirouettes en dedans,* a series of *chaînés,* and a pose in fourth position. There is a *pas de quatre* (sometimes a *pas de six*) for the friends of Giselle. This might be called a precision number, and is made up of *assemblés, pas de cheval, glissades,* and *jetés* performed in unison.

Act II abounds in fascinating dance patterns, and there is a minimum of pantomime except for the unhappy Hilarion. It begins with a magnificent solo for Myrtha, who makes a series of entrances in *grands jetés,* not unlike the solo mazurka in *Les Sylphides,* though the mood is somber, unlike the gentle melancholy of the Fokine ballet. It has an *adage* featuring *penché arabesques,* balances *en atti-*

tude, and *entrechats six.* It concludes with a spectacular series of *demi-fouettés en l'air, jetés en tournant, sauts de basque,* and *chaînés* performed with the arms in fifth position *en haut.* This solo is as demanding as anything in the entire range of ballet, and the artist who can perform it with the necessary grandeur has executed the balletic equivalent of the exacting dramatic coloratura of *Norma.*

After her evocation from the tomb, Giselle descends from the mound, her movements indicating the yet unawakened spirit. A touch from the Queen's scepter sets her into brilliant motion. She executes multiple *pirouettes en arabesque,* the *enchaînement* concluding with a series of *emboité* turns and *grands jetés.* There is a fascinating succession of entrances in the first scene with Albrecht that suggests the materializing phantom, too tenuous for the human eye to perceive for more than a few seconds. During the last of these appearances Giselle plucks lilies from the border of the lake. Tossing them into the air at the height of a *grand jeté* to Albrecht, she eludes him once more as he leaps to catch them.

Later, when Giselle in obedience to the Queen has been forced to entice Albrecht away from the tomb, there is a *pas de deux,* conventional enough with its pirouettes and poses *en arabesque.* It contains, however, some of the most beautiful lifts to be seen in ballet of any period. They are executed in the slowest possible tempo, producing an effect of airy, thistledown flight that is breath-taking. Giselle's solo variation concludes with a sequence of *entrechats quatre,* performed while traveling upstage at dazzling speed. Albrecht's solo features double *cabrioles en avant,* the high point being a diagonal progess by means of *chassées, assemblé,* double *tour en l'air,* and *pirouettes en dehors.* The last pirouette leads directly without a transitional step into a double *tour en l'air,* in which the dancer twists his body in mid-air until it is horizontal to the ground, to which he falls.

The corps de ballet is called upon to display considerable versatility as well as virtuosity in both acts of *Giselle.* In Act I they are peasants making merry at a vintage festival and later appalled spectators of a tragedy. In Act II they are pale and sinister phantoms. In the ensembles during and following the Queen's variation they perform complicated choreographic patterns in unison. There is a notable passage in which they travel in opposing lines across the stage in arabesques. At the conclusion of the opening ensemble they per-

form, with the Queen, a *grand porte de bras* with a back-bend that
is a public denial of the accusation that they are lacking in flexibility
—a statement often made by detractors of the worth of ballet training, usually proponents of other systems. After the scene with
Hilarion the corps de ballet follow the Queen from the scene in
groups, performing *glissade, jetés* from side to side, and two *grands
jetés*—an *enchaînement* admirably expressing the idea of flight. At
various times in the course of the action, they form a decorative
background, usually posed in *arabesques par terre.*[10]

Admirable though the choreographic re-creation of Ballet Theatre's *Giselle* undoubtedly is, it leaves something to be desired on the
scenic side. Lucinda Ballard's décor for Act I appears to be an attempt to visualize the ballet in the manner of a print of the romantic
period. It is not without charm, but I feel that a ballet with the status
of *Giselle* in the history of the dance deserves treatment less mannered and patronizing. The Act II setting is moderately successful.
Probably the answer to this problem is the projected décor by Eugène
Berman, sketches for which have been exhibited at the Museum of
Modern Art.

Any designer of costumes for *Giselle* has one fixed point of departure—the Wilis must wear the romantic tutu associated with, and
probably designed by, Marie Taglioni, though Eugène Lami is
credited with its invention, truly a stroke of genius. Photographs of
the 1910 production at the Metropolitan display the Wilis in costumes suggesting Duncan tunics that someone had hacked at with
scissors. They may have looked well in motion—in pictures they
are merely untidy. The Mordkin Wilis resembled a Broadway line in
a production number celebrating the virtues of cellophane. Act II
of *Giselle* does not need any bright ideas. The long tutu, the simple
wreath, are the very symbol of the romantic ballet, as well as the
most becoming costume ever designed for dancers.

The original Act I costumes, by Paul Lormier, are theatrical adaptations of the costumes seen in paintings by Dürer. The Monte Carlo
Ballet's costumes, based on designs by Alexandre Benois for a revival
at the Paris Opéra in 1924, suggest a similar source. Lucinda Ballard's
conception favored French Renaissance for the dress of the Duke's
party. The 1910 production, which featured Wilis in more or less

[10] There is a complete choreographic script of *Giselle* as performed by the Markova-
Dolin Ballet in Beaumont's *Ballet Called Giselle.*

Greek tunics, favored late eighteenth-century for its first act décor —
a most unsuitable milieu for a romantic legend. Olga Spessivtzeva
introduced an innovation into this act by wearing a short tutu much
like those worn in current productions of *Coppélia*. This may have
been becoming to Spessitzeva, but is certainly out of keeping with
the spirit of the ballet and the style of the dancing.

The score of *Giselle* by Adolphe Adam, though considerably cut
in modern revivals of the ballet, retains much of its charm. Apparently this is communicated more easily to present-day audiences
than to those who saw the 1910 revival, when the producers seem to
have been afraid to trust it without reinforcements. It is possible
that the full circle has been described, and the artless flow of melodies
and the simple rhythms of 1841 appear less dated than the more
complicated music of composers closer to our day in time, though
not in feeling. Both musically and choreographically *Giselle* is less
old-fashioned than *Scheherazade,* which completely overshadowed
it in the Diaghilev season at the Paris Opéra in 1910. Adam composed much church music, a number of operas (*Le Postillon de
Longjumeau* is the best-known), and scores for fourteen ballets, of
which *Giselle* is the sixth. It was favorably received by the music
critics, who commended it for its originality and the success with
which the composer underlined with orchestral color the fantastic
atmosphere of the second act. The score continues to exercise its
modest charm in a most effective manner, making no demands for
itself and admirably supporting the action and maintaining the
mood, at first gay, then tragic in Act I, eerie in Act II. Other ballets
of the romantic age charmed the audience and the critics, inspiring
artists to record their impressions in paint and on stone, yet have
failed to survive. It may well be that Adam's score was the deciding
factor.

The role of Giselle is unsurpassed for the dramatic opportunities
it offers the ballerina. In Act I she may be as charming or as coy as
her conscience permits. The mad scene has unlimited scope. In Act
II the mixture of womanly tenderness and ghostly remoteness present
an unusual problem. Few ballerinas have achieved a perfect performance in both acts. It would seem that the earthly charm of the
peasant and the spiritual quality of the Wili are not easily recon-
cilable.

A list of the ballerinas who have danced Giselle would be a for-

midable one and would include the great names of several generations. Carlotta Grisi, its creator, has been memorialized in many
prints and lithographs as well as in the writings of Théophile
Gautier. Marie Taglioni, Lucile Grahn, Fanny Cerito, and Fanny
Elssler were among Grisi's contemporary rivals. Closer to the cur-
rent generation, the names of Anna Pavlova, Thamar Karsavina, and
Olga Spessivtzeva head the list. Vera Nemchinova, Margot Fonteyn,
Galina Ulanova, and Alexandra Danilova [11] are among the ballerinas
of today whose interpretations have not yet been seen in New York.
Since the revival in 1910 at the Metropolitan Opera House, New
York has seen performances by Alicia Markova, Mia Slavenska,
Lucia Chase, Nina Whitney, Alicia Alonso, Nana Gollner, Tamara
Toumanova, Patricia Bowman, and Annabelle Lyon.

As Giselle, the *prima ballerina assoluta* of New York is Alicia
Markova. The announcement that she will appear in the ballet has
livened up a flagging season before this. Her performance is not
only great dancing; it is also first-class theater that may be recognized by people who know nothing whatever about ballet but are
sensitive to that communication that is the essence of all great interpretations. She approaches the role with a deep understanding of its
romantic style and an artistic humility that does not permit her to
interject any of the meaningless tours de force danced for the sake
of personal display that characterize performances by less intelligent
dancers. It would be idle to deny the fact that as the peasant lass of
Act I she is a trifle less than perfection, not because of any technical
shortcomings, but because she is physically too elegant to look natural
as anything less than a princess or an elemental. Her mad scene is in
the best tradition of the romantic theater. In Act II she is a creature
of the air, appearing to travel above the stage rather than on it. There
are few contemporary dancers who do not appear earthbound compared with her. Anyone who has seen Markova's transcendant performance of the Wili has witnessed one of the greatest re-creations
the contemporary theater has to offer and certainly one of the greatest
interpretations of the role in all its period of existence.

At least two other artists who have performed Giselle in New York
must be mentioned. Annabelle Lyon, Ballet Theatre's first Giselle,
was ideal in Act I. Her peasant girl was simple and believable, charming and gay, until the shock of her betrayal, when she appeared to

[11] The west coast, however, has had the privilege of seeing Danilova's Giselle.

recede from reality and die of a wounded spirit rather than a self-inflicted injury. In this act her interpretation achieved a pathos not excelled by any other performer of the role in New York. Alicia Alonso, with something of Markova's ethereal quality, gives in both acts an acceptable, though still tentative, performance that may well mature into greatness if she is allowed opportunities to grow into the role.

The role of Albrecht, while it has more importance than many male roles in romantic ballet, is nevertheless overshadowed by the title role—a defect that some dancers have done their best to correct. It was created by Lucien Petipa, brother of the more famous Marius Petipa, chief choreographer of the Russian Imperial Ballet for many years. Lucien achieved more modest fame as a choreographer at the Paris Opéra, with a number of ballets to his credit. He had the onerous and thankless task of trying to satisfy Wagner's exigent ideas when *Tannhäuser,* with the ballet considered necessary by the French opera-goer, was produced in Paris. Apparently he failed to please either Wagner or the Jockey Club. Vaslav Nijinsky and Mikhail Mordkin are among his most famous successors in the role of Albrecht. Anatole Chujoy, in an article in *Dance* (1941), has admirably expressed his opinions of the three best-known contemporary interpreters of the role, and as I am in perfect accord with them, I cannot do better than quote the following: "The role of Albrecht has been danced here [New York] by Anton Dolin, Igor Youskevitch, and Serge Lifar. Dolin is the finer and more convincing actor; Youskevitch, the more exciting dancer, the greater technician; Lifar is the fellow who would create the impression that the ballet is *Albrecht,* not *Giselle.*"

Adèle Dumilâtre, the first Myrtha, was the subject of a number of lithographs by contemporary artists. Critics of the time thought her cold, but that does not seem an undesirable characteristic in the interpretation of a ghostly Queen with a sinister mission. This role has also been overshadowed by that of Giselle, but in the hands of an artist may assume its proper importance. The Monte Carlo Ballet production boasted the presence of Alexandra Danilova, who gave a brilliant performance. Ballet Theatre's Rosella Hightower, more recently seen in New York, meets every technical and emotional demand of the part, and has on occasion saved the ballet from disaster when a lesser artist than Markova has attempted the title role.

The corps de ballet plays an important part in any production of *Giselle*. The absence of a really outstanding ballerina in Ballet Theatre's original performances was somewhat palliated by the remarkable corps de ballet, who danced the difficult second-act ensembles with the precision of Rockettes and a disciplined artistry that has no parallel in the contemporary theater (possibly like a group of coloratura sopranos singing cadenzas in unison). The original members of this admirable group have in many instances achieved distinction in the ballet world. It is sad to relate that their successors are less co-operative in spirit, and display a tendency to carelessness that must not be allowed to develop if the high standards of Ballet Theatre's *Giselle* are to be maintained.

Giselle, now launched on its second century of performance, shows no sign of diminishing vitality or loss of popularity with the public. It has been included in the repertoire of the Sadler's Wells Ballet since 1934, when it was revived for Alicia Markova, then a member of that company. Pictures of Galina Ulanova of the Soviet Ballet, taken during a performance, hint at her dramatic power. As long as there are ballerinas of their artistic gifts to perform the role, *Giselle* will remain in the active repertoires of the dance theaters. It may well live to celebrate its bicentenary.

Ballet Theatre, for its 1946 season at the Broadway Theater in New York, is planning a revival of *Giselle* using the Berman décor. Alicia Alonso and Igor Youskevitch head the cast.

GRADUATION BALL

Ballet in one act by David Lichine; music by Johann Strauss, compiled, arranged, and orchestrated by Antal Dorati; choreography by David Lichine; scenery and costumes by Alexandre Benois.

G RADUATION BALL was first performed by the Original Ballet Russe at the Theatre Royal, Sydney, Australia, on February 28, 1940. The first New York presentation took place at the Fifty-first Street Theater on November 6, 1940, with the following cast:

THE HEAD MISTRESS *Borislav Runanine* [1]	LEADER OF THE JUNIOR GIRLS *Tatiana Riabouchinska*
THE OLD GENERAL *Igor Schwezoff*	LEADER OF THE JUNIOR CADETS *David Lichine*

DIVERTISSEMENT

1. "The Drummer": *Nicolas Orloff*. 2. "Giselle and the Scotsman": *Tatiana Stepanova* and *Michel Panaieff*. 3. "Impromptu Dance": *Tatiana Leskova*. 4. "Dance-step Competition": *Alexandra Denisova* and *Genevieve Moulin*. 5. "Mathematics and Natural-History Lesson": *Marina Svetlova, Irina Zarova, Maria Azrova*. 6. "Perpetuum Mobile": *Tatiana Riabouchinska* and *David Lichine; Anna Leontieva, Tatiana Bechenova, Kira Bounina*.

◇◇◇◇◇◇◇◇◇◇◇◇◇◇◇◇◇◇◇◇◇

The curtain rises on the drawing-room of a girls' school in Vienna, complete with gilt furniture and crystal chandelier. Junior students in white frocks and blue pinafores are running in and out in a state of high ebullience. It is graduation time, and the cadets of a neighboring military academy are to be guests at a ball. Senior girls, aloof and superior, watch the feverish activities of the juniors condescendingly. One of the latter has acquired a large swan's-down powder puff, which she is persuaded to pass around among her friends. While they are experimenting with it, the Head Mistress arrives twittering with excitement. She snatches the powder puff disapprovingly, but cannot resist the temptation to try its effect on herself.

[1] Grotesque female roles in ballet are traditionally performed by male dancers. Examples in the repertoire include the Mother in *La Fille Mal Gardée*, the Fairy Carabosse in *Sleeping Beauty*, and the Wicked Sisters in *Cinderella*.

Military music heralding the cadets' approach puts an end to the confusion. The girls line up in two decorous rows. The cadets enter in formation, led by the General, tremendous in gold braid and side whiskers. Formal greetings over, the General escorts the Head Mistress from the ballroom. The students are free to dance, but there is a difficulty. They are all much too shy to make the first move. In the pause a junior girl, whose earlier behavior has been very tomboyish, is so entranced by the sight of the uniforms that she leaves the line and moves toward the boys in a bemused manner. They click heels and bow, frightening the young miss, who sits down suddenly on the floor. Two cadets assist her to her feet and lead her back to the others.

Flushed with the success of this maneuver, one of the escort party looks around triumphantly at his fellows. To his horror, they unanimously elect him to open the ball. They shove him forward. In an agony of embarrassment he advances. The young ladies are not at all upset, and one of them glides into his arms. They whirl away in a fast Viennese waltz, the cadet waving exultingly to the others. The ice is broken. Boys and girls pair off for the dance.

Head Mistress and General return for the formal part of the entertainment. A *divertissement* is performed, interrupted only by the tomboy, who, enthralled by the romantic beauty of a *pas de deux,* undertakes an impromptu solo of her own.

While these events are taking place, the Head Mistress and the General are becoming more and more absorbed in each other. When the students leave the ballroom for supper, they remain behind for a private dance varied by flirtation. The returning young people catch them in an embrace. They take advantage of this to throw off all pretense of decorous behavior. They romp merrily until Head Mistress and General remember their duties and declare the ball at an end. Cadets march out, girls wave farewell, and lights are extinguished.

One of the young guests, coming back for a quiet good-by to his partner, is put to flight by the Head Mistress. The fun is over.

As first performed by the Original Ballet Russe, *Graduation Ball* was a charming outpouring of high spirits, marred only by being somewhat too long. There were delightful performances by Tatiana Riabouchinska and David Lichine. The *divertissements* were original and very well executed. The high point of these was the oddly named Giselle and the Scotsman—more correctly La Sylphide and the Scotsman. This was an enchanting miniature tribute to one of the jewels of the romantic age of ballet. The man's solo variation, based on the characteristic steps of Scottish national dances, was ingeniously devised. The costumes—romantic tutu and kilt—recalled the mezzotint by F. Gérard. Its moonlit sentiment provided a striking and necessary contrast to the lively antics that preceded and followed it.

The Dance-step Competition was actually a competition in that most exciting of ballet steps, the *fouetté,* varied by pirouettes of various kinds. Genevieve Moulin performed a series of alternating *attitude* and *arabesque* turns that were breath-taking in their virtuosity. The Mathematics Lesson, a humorous trifle, included an arabesque that would probably have caused Cecchetti to have apoplexy.

The score, made up of largely unfamiliar music by Johann Strauss, was the result of research by Antal Dorati and David Lichine among manuscripts in the library of the State Opera in Vienna. It was a source of amazement to many that so much charming Strauss music had not been heard before. Unfortunately, this score was not recorded before the ballet was revised.

When the Original Ballet Russe left New York, and rumors of strife floated back, it seemed that *Graduation Ball* would join the Fafner's hoard of "frozen" ballets owned by Colonel de Basil. Fortunately, *Graduation Ball* was a captive that escaped. With some changes it was revived for Ballet Theatre by David Lichine.

After being produced on the west coast, the new version of *Graduation Ball* was given its first New York performance at the Metropolitan Opera House on October 8, 1944. There were new scenery and costumes by Mstislav Dobujinsky. The cast was headed by Tatiana Riabouchinska and David Lichine in their original roles. The remainder of the cast was as follows:

HEAD MISTRESS   *Alpheus Koon* | GENERAL   *John Taras*

DIVERTISSEMENT

1. "The Drummer": *John Kriza*. 2. "Pas de Deux": *Alicia Alonso* and *Richard Reed*. 3. "Dance Impromptu": *Rosella Hightower*. 4. "Competition": *Marjorie Tallchief* and *Margaret Banks*. 5. "Tyrolian Boy": *Harold Lang*. 6. "Perpetuum Mobile": *Tatiana Riabouchinska* and *David Lichine; Barbara Fallis, June Morris, Fern Whitney*.

To members of the audience who had seen the original production, the new one was a disillusioning experience. The settings and costumes, while following the general outlines of Benois's, seemed too garish. Riabouchinska and Lichine projected their particular brand of charm, and other members of the cast were equal (even superior [2]) to the original group, but much of the charm had evaporated. The substitution of a *pas de deux* of enormous technical difficulty, performed to brassy music for La Sylphide and the Scotsman, was unfortunate: though interesting in itself, it provided no contrast in mood to the rest of the action, which had become boisterous and a little tiresome. The Tyrolian dance was Tyrolese only in its costume, and that might very well have been mistaken for a suit belonging to the wearer's little brother.

When the engagements of Riabouchinska and Lichine (guest artists and not members of Ballet Theatre) terminated, their roles were assumed by Janet Reed and Harold Lang, both of whom gave pleasing performances. The Tyrolian dance was then performed by André Eglevsky, wearing a newly designed costume. This variation, an error in the first place, seemed even more out of place in *Graduation Ball* when danced by Eglevsky, who was scarcely a plausible schoolboy.

On the whole, the revival left a strong impression that fluorescent lighting had replaced candles in the crystal chandelier.

Graduation Ball was revived by the Original Ballet Russe at the Metropolitan Opera House on September 29, 1946, with Olga Morosova (Mistress of Ceremonies), Vladimir Dokoudovsky (Junior Cadet), and Roman Jasinsky (Drummer). This was the original version, and included the charming *pas de deux,* still miscalled "Giselle and the Scotsman."

[2] Notably the Drummer, whose variation, with newly added technical difficulties, was brilliantly performed by John Kriza.

THE GREAT AMERICAN GOOF

William Saroyan's A Number of Absurd and Poetic Events in the Life of The Great American Goof, a Balletplay: music by Henry Brant; choreography by Eugene Loring; scenery and costumes by Boris Aronson.

THE GREAT AMERICAN GOOF was first performed by Ballet Theatre on January 11, 1940 at the Center Theater, New York. The cast, with the descriptions of the characters as they appeared on the program, presumably in Saroyan's own words, is as follows:

THE GREAT AMERICAN GOOF, the naïve white hope of the human race
Eugene Loring

THE WOMAN, the bright potential
Miriam Golden

THE DUMMY, tradition and the ordinary
Antony Tudor

POLICEMAN, orderly idiocy
Gregor Taksa

OLD MAN IN PRISON, ignorance, age, and naïveté *Dimitri Romanoff*

A LITTLE GIRL, wisdom not yet educated and spoiled *Lucia Chase*

WOMEN, sex
Audrey Castello, Maria Karniloff, Nora Koreff, Kirsten Valbor

WORKERS, misfits
David Nillo, Jack Potteiger, Charles Ewing, Peter Michael, Richard Reed, Oreste Sergievsky

Riotous Livers, the dying [1]

A STUDENT OF KARL MARX, an opium addict *Hubert Bland*

PRIEST, capitalism
Vladimir Dokoudovsky

DRUNKARD, a religious man
Harold Haskin

PRAYING BOY, a dreamer of kites and fishes *Leonard Ware*

BEARDED OLD MAN, a boy of fourteen discovering Poetry *Donald Saddler*

GIRL DANCING, his fever
Annabelle Lyon

OLD WOMAN, DYING, one of the living *Dorothy Lysaght*

IMMIGRANT, DYING, one of the living *Oreste Sergievsky*

BOY WITH A FEVER OF 105, one of the living *Hubert Bland*

Passers-by, Passers-by [1]

◆◆◆◆◆◆◆◆◆◆◆◆◆◆◆◆◆◆

After a lapse of several years, it is impossible to detail the action, not clear in the first place, of *The Great American Goof*. William

---

[1] These groups engaged the efforts of any members of the company not otherwise occupied.

Saroyan wrote program notes in which a great many words add up to nothing in particular. He ends the preamble with the following:

"What this ballet says is that you need six or seven thousand years to get this place out of the idiot nightmare it's in now. By that time for all we know there may be a place in which it will be possible for the living really to live, instead of having all the Shakespearian fun they're having all the time.

"In addition to this balletplay, I have written another. It is called The Poetic Situation in America Since Alexander Dumas. . . . It is something that can be read for itself. I plan to continue writing for this form. . . ."

It is fortunate for ballet in America that William Saroyan has found other outlets for his talents. The ballet public is perverse enough to prefer the classic beauty of *Swan Lake,* the poignant realism of *Pillar of Fire,* even the gay nonsense of *Bluebeard,* to the dull cuteness of *The Great American Goof,* which steered people to the lounge of the Center Theater in droves. One performance of it was more than enough for the lifetime of almost any ballet-lover who is by nature a repeater.

It was not the startling originality of *The Great American Goof* that upset people. Indeed, any of the audience old enough to have suffered through the little-theater movement saw every stale "arty" cliché repeated and magnified beyond life size in front of projected scenery, in itself an unsuccessful theatrical experiment. The dancers were called upon to recite[2] lines in chanting voices. Probably this was necessary to back up the program description of this dreary hodge-podge as a balletplay. The lines in themselves were not interesting, even when they were audible.

Choreographically *The Great American Goof* was in the processional style used by Eugene Loring in *Billy the Kid* and *City Portrait.* In the former it had point and meaning, but a repetition of the trick is monotonous. The individual performers walked around the stage competently enough. It must have been a restful interlude between ballets in which they were called upon to dance. Miriam Golden's sumptuous beauty in the role of the Woman is all that one could wish to remember of this anti-ballet, *The Great American Goof.*

---

[2] Training for ballet and maintaining that training are a full-time occupation. Dancers do not, or should not, have time for learning the technique of voice projection.

HELEN OF TROY

Ballet in prologue and three scenes by David Lichine and Antal Dorati;
music by Offenbach, arranged and orchestrated by Antal Dorati; scenery
and costumes by Marcel Vertès; choreography by David Lichine.

H<small>ELEN OF TROY</small>, produced in Mexico by Ballet Theatre, was given its first New York performance at the Metropolitan Opera House on April 3, 1943, with the following cast:

PARIS	*André Eglevsky*	HELEN	*Vera Zorina*
LAMB	*Jean Hunt*	AJAX I	*Richard Reed*
HERMES	*Jerome Robbins*	AJAX II	*John Kriza*
APHRODITE	*Maria Karnilova*	CALCHAS	*Donald Saddler*
HERA	*Rosella Hightower*	ORESTES	*Yura Lazovsky*
PALLAS ATHENA	*Lucia Chase*	THE FAUN	*Nicolas Orloff*
MENELAUS	*Simon Semenoff*		

Sheep, Flower Girls, Ladies of the Court, People of Sparta

◇◇◇◇◇◇◇◇◇◇◇◇◇◇◇◇◇◇◇

Prologue. When the curtain rises, a flock of sheep huddled together becomes visible. They separate, revealing their shepherd, Paris, who rises to his feet. He is fond of his charges and they romp together. This pastoral episode is interrupted by Hermes, who strolls in, tossing a golden apple. He throws it to Paris, explaining that Paris has been chosen to judge a beauty contest, in which the apple is the prize. Hermes beckons and the three contestants appear. Actually there is very little competition, Hera being a rather muscular lady and Pallas Athena the intellectual type. Aphrodite, the third entry, not only is very lovely indeed but quite unfairly offers to lead Paris to her earthly counterpart if he will award her the prize. This he does without hesitation. Aphrodite maliciously waves the apple under the noses of her defeated rivals and starts Paris on the way to his reward. The sheep, who have been timid observers of this episode, disappear, but Paris' pet Lamb follows him. Hermes, left with the angry losers, succeeds in getting rid of them by a trick.

Scene 1. The Court of King Menelaus. Hermes, who has joined

Paris and the Lamb, manages to enlist the aid of Calchas in obtaining admission to the court of King Menelaus, whose wife, Helen, the most beautiful woman in the world is Paris' promised reward. Menelaus, fat, senile, and ridiculous, is no mate for Helen, with whom Paris at once falls in love. As she is surrounded by the court and people of Sparta, Hermes has a difficult task to provide Paris with an opportunity to advance his suit. Fortunately, Calchas covets Paris' pet Lamb. He orders the two Ajaxes to capture her. She escapes. The crowd pursues her from the scene, leaving Paris, Hermes, and Menelaus, who has fallen asleep with his head on Helen's shoulder. Hermes deftly slips into Helen's place, and the field is clear. Losing no time, Paris begins his campaign. Helen is not at all unwilling, and very soon they reach an understanding.

The courtiers, giving up their efforts to corner the Lamb, return. Hermes has to think up some new stratagem to secure privacy for the lovers. Calchas has a splendid idea. He goes into a prophetic trance and announces to Menelaus that the gods wish him to go to war. He sends for sword, shield, and chariot and ruthlessly urges the poor old man to depart. He goes accompanied by the crowd.

Hermes persuades Helen to give Paris the key to her room. Paris, left alone, triumphantly holds this pledge on high.

Entr'acte. Orestes beguiles Helen's chief maid into lending him a dress so that he may gain admittance to Helen's apartment. After much coaxing she yields and helps him into the disguise.

Scene 2. Helen's Apartment. Helen, with the assistance of her maids, is preparing to retire. The clumsy antics of the disguised Orestes so exasperate Helen that she orders him to leave, whereupon he tears off his masquerade and tries to embrace her. Hermes, arriving in the nick of time to get rid of this importunate suitor, tells Helen that Paris is waiting. She feigns coyness. Hermes, not deceived, admits Paris, but chases the Lamb, who tries to follow her master. Helen's coyness quickly vanishes when she sees Paris. A little bored by the love-making, Hermes knits to pass the time. When the tender passages reach a certain intensity, Hermes serves propriety by putting a screen around the lovers, not noticing that the Lamb, who has managed to creep unobtrusively into the room, is hiding behind it.

Much to everyone's annoyance, Menelaus, who has returned home, comes to visit his wife. Clad in a white nightshirt and a red lace-trimmed cap he looks more ridiculous than ever. Hermes does his best to prevent him from seeing Paris, while the lovers are doing their best to help themselves. Suddenly Paris tiptoes from behind the screen, followed by a woolly figure on all fours, whom Menelaus eyes with suspicion. He makes a grab at it and finds that it is Helen dressed in the Lamb's skin. In the ensuing struggle the screen crashes to the floor revealing the unfortunate Lamb shivering nakedly. Paris tries to make an inconspicuous exit, but is followed by Menelaus and the entire court, who suddenly appear on the scene. Hermes directs traffic until everyone has gone but Helen and the exhausted Menelaus, who falls on the floor. Hermes spreads the lambskin over him while Helen strikes a derisively triumphant attitude.

Entr'acte. Menelaus weeps bitterly for his sad plight. Six court ladies come to sympathize, but remain to be of practical assistance. His handkerchief is so wet with tears that it is useless. They wash and iron it and give it back to him.

Scene 3. The Beach. The court ladies are enjoying life at the beach. One of them comes in leading a Faun on a leash. When the leash is removed it becomes evident that the Faun is not quite domesticated. He escapes, first frightening the ladies out of their wits.

The entire court assembles. A ship arrives and Menelaus, Hermes, and Helen go on board. They are joined by Paris, who is disguised in the robes of Calchas. At the last moment Menelaus is tossed into the arms of the courtiers. The ship sails away carrying Paris, Helen, and Hermes to Troy.

Helen of Troy passed through a number of vicissitudes before reaching final production. It was originally designed by Michel Fokine as a companion piece to *Bluebeard*. Unfortunately this great choreographer, stricken with the illness that caused his death, was unable to finish his work. The completion was entrusted to David Lichine with none too happy results. The elegance and light touch that have endeared *Bluebeard* to countless audiences are nowhere visible in *Helen of Troy*. Viewed in its entirety, it bears the same relation to *Bluebeard* that *Hellzapoppin* does to *Iolanthe*. It does not lack good moments. The miniature pastorale danced by Paris and the sheep is charming and, as it opens the ballet, gives one high hopes of what is to come. It does not take long for the hope to fade before the onslaught of low comedy and even burlesque clichés. There is a brief revival of true comedy in the third scene, in which the episode of the ladies and the Faun is a really hilarious parody of *The After-noon of a Faun.*

The character of Hermes, created by Jerome Robbins, a dancer of outstanding comic as well as dramatic ability, is conceived in an idiom that might be called pure Flatbush. He strolls with supreme self-assurance from episode to episode on excellent terms with the audience and himself. He unites the offices of night-club master of ceremonies and Greek chorus, occasionally taking a hand in events when they seem to lag. It is too bad that the drama is really not worth bothering about. Hermes deserves a more interesting setting —possibly a ballet based on *Amphitryon 38.*

With the exception of Paris, the other characters of *Helen of Troy* lack even the slight dimensions necessary for musical comedy. Menelaus is a figure of not very much fun although the role has em-ployed the energies of such excellent dancers as Simon Semenoff and Dimitri Romanoff. Calchas, created by Donald Saddler, was merely a sketch and a rather incomprehensible one. When John Taras took it over, he unobtrusively remedied the choreographer's neglect, fill-ing in the outline with amusing and significant touches.

The role of Helen, danced in New York by Vera Zorina (it had been designed for Irina Baronova), made the transition from musical comedy to ballet easy for this star of stage and screen. Maria Kar-nilova and Nana Gollner have offered versions more acceptable to the ballet public, but it will never be a gem in any ballerina's crown.

André Eglevsky as Paris shares with Jerome Robbins the credit for whatever popularity *Helen of Troy* may enjoy. The part was de-signed to exploit Eglevsky's breath-taking pirouettes and remarkably fluid style of dancing. Without these two artists the ballet would be a shambles.

It is possible that *Helen of Troy* could be pulled together and be-come a worthy part of the repertoire. New costumes (Vertès nodded on this occasion), elimination of the more obvious low-comedy clichés, and line routines with style would do wonders for it, the basic idea being not without merit.

THE HUNDRED KISSES

The Hundred Kisses (Les Cent Baisers): libretto by Boris Kochno after the fairy tale by Hans Andersen; music by Frederic d'Erlanger; choreography by Bronislava Nijinska; scenery and costumes by Jean Hugo.

THE first performance of *The Hundred Kisses* was at the Royal Opera, Covent Garden, London, on July 18, 1935. The American première, by Colonel W. de Basil's Ballet Russe, took place at the Metropolitan Opera House, New York, on October 18, 1935, with the following cast:

THE PRINCESS	*Irina Baronova*	THE GARDENER	*Roman Jasinsky*
THE KING	*Edouard Borovansky*	THE BIRD-CATCHER	*Georges Lazovsky*
THE PRINCE	*David Lichine*	THE SWINEHERD	*Vania Psota*

THE MAIDS OF HONOR: *Nina Verchinina, Vera Zorina, Tamara Grigorieva, Olga Morosova, Edna Tresahar, Lisa Serova, Mira Dimina, Vera Nelidova, Sono Osato, Galina Razoumova, Tamara Tchinarova, Anna Volkova*

The story which has borrowed its theme from Hans Christian Andersen's story "The Swineherd," is as follows:

The scene is a pleasant meadow before the gates of a castle that is seen in the distance. A Princess lovely, vain, and erratic, has been sought in marriage by a neighboring Prince. He is coming to pay his first formal visit to her. Accompanied by her Maids of Honor, she comes to meet him. He arrives with two favorite retainers, a Gardener and a Bird-catcher. Each in turn dances for the pleasure of the Princess and presents her with a gift on the Prince's behalf. These are simple things—a rose and a songbird. The sophisticated Princess is offended at the idea that such childish trifles are considered suitable offerings for a King's daughter. She laughs and leads her Maids through the castle gates, which close behind them.

The Prince sends his retainers away. Alone, he mourns for a lost illusion, having discovered that the beauty of the Princess is a mask for shallowness and conceit.

His grief is brought to an abrupt pause by strange music made by a wandering Swineherd, who is playing a most unusual instrument. He is scraping the inside of a bowl with a spoon. So merry is the tune produced that melancholy cannot live in its neighborhood and feet seem to dance of their own accord. The Prince tries to buy it with gold. The Swineherd has no wish for money, but he is willing to exchange his rough peasant garb for the Prince's velvet and feathers and throw in the bowl for good measure. Cutting a strange figure in his splendor, he capers off, leaving the Prince the owner of the wonderful bowl.

The Prince disguises himself in the Swineherd's discarded garments and makes a few tentative scrapes with the spoon. The Maids of Honor, lured by the odd sound, look over the castle wall. Unable to resist the spellbinding music, they dance out of the gate, followed by the Princess, who, coming to investigate, is also caught by the magic. Whirling madly, they dance until they fall exhausted to the ground.

The Princess is delighted with the new toy and bargains for it with the disguised Prince. His price is a hundred kisses. The Princess is properly horrified at the thought of kissing a lowly peasant and offers her Maids of Honor as substitutes. When this is refused, she disdainfully consents to pay the price in person. Calling the Maids to surround her and protect her from prying eyes in the castle, she begins to pay her debt.

The King, attracted by the commotion, comes to find out what is going on. Peering over the heads of the Maids, he is shocked and revolted by the spectacle of his daughter kissing a common swineherd. In a rage, he orders the Maids into the castle. When the confused and embarrassed Princess follows them, he shuts the door in her face. The Prince takes off his disguise and slowly goes on his way.

The Princess, having scorned true love and bartered her kisses for a toy, is left desolate before the castle gates.

In *The Hundred Kisses,* Hans Andersen's simple tale takes on a very modern sophistication achieved by subtle character-drawing. This Princess, far from being the conventional figure of a fairy tale, is certainly the graduate of a progressive school and in training to be an ornament of café society. Her haughty bad manners are an amusing comment on the behavior of a certain section of prewar society.

The other characters of this small drama are more conformable to the accepted idea of a fairy tale, but the moods and actions of the Princess set the atmosphere of the ballet.

Choreographically, *The Hundred Kisses* is full of invention. Bronislava Nijinska used to the fullest extent the abilities of a fine cast and a remarkable corps de ballet. The variations for the Gardener and the Bird-catcher were suggestive of these pastoral occupations. The Prince's solo, designed to express a mood rather than the dancer's virtuosity, was a forerunner of the more technically difficult Beggar's solo in *Devil's Holiday*—a classic of grief and frustration. The Swineherd's brief appearance had a heavy-footed gaiety appropriate to the character.

The role of the Princess was a nice blend of character and difficult technical dancing. The Maids of Honor were required to follow the Princess's lead in steps that exploited pirouettes and *fouettés* in bewildering succession and variety. The payment of the hundred kisses was amusingly portrayed in a *pas de deux* with many original lifts and poses.

The Hundred Kisses was fortunate in its original cast. David Lichine was an ideal Prince, archetype of romance to anyone who had ever read Andersen or Grimm. As the Princess, Irina Baronova indicated the shallowness of the character, looked enchantingly pretty, and danced with precision the appallingly difficult steps—a feat of dramatic balance that no other performer of this role ever quite managed.

The score of *The Hundred Kisses* was specially composed for this ballet by Frederic d'Erlanger. Without any particular charms of its own (it will never appear as a concert suite), it was adequate for its purpose and evoked a suitable atmosphere.

The ballet was less well served by its décor. The setting was conventional and uninteresting. The costumes of the corps de ballet, well designed, with details suggesting the sixteenth century, were carried out in hard and unpleasant colors. The Princess's costume was quite another matter. Black with white details, it caught the eyes of artists and photographers in the audience. For several years afterwards it turned up in reminiscent paintings and sketches.

Looked back on, *The Hundred Kisses*, not seen in New York for five years, seems to be one of the last really effective works by Bronislava Nijinska. Short and to the point, it tells an old story with a modern and worldly twist. Viewed in contrast to *Bolero*—a movie prologue resurrected from pre-talkie days—the intellectually pretentious *Pictures at an Exhibition,* and the inept and repetitious *Brahms Variations,* it takes on the properties of an authentic, though slight, work of art.

JARDIN AUX LILAS

Jardin aux lilas (Lilac Garden): ballet in one act by Antony Tudor; music by Ernest Chausson; designed by Raymond Sovey, after sketches by Hugh Stevenson.

J*ARDIN AUX LILAS* was originally performed by the Ballet Club at the Mercury Theatre, London, on January 26, 1938. The American première, by Ballet Theatre, took place at the Center Theater, New York, on January 15, 1940, with the following cast:

CAROLINE (the Bride-to-be)		THE MAN SHE MUST MARRY	
	Viola Essen		*Antony Tudor*
HER LOVER	*Hugh Laing*	AN EPISODE IN HIS PAST	
			Karen Conrad

FRIENDS AND RELATIONS: *Maria Karnilova, Nora Kaye, Mimi Gomber, David Nillo, Hubert Bland, Donald Saddler, John Schindehitte*

◇◇◇◇◇◇◇◇◇◇◇◇◇◇◇◇◇◇

The scene of the ballet is a garden surrounded by lilac trees. It is a moonlit evening at the turn of the century. A party is in progress. Caroline, escorted by the man to whom she is engaged, has a longing to take leave of the man she loves. Her desire is thwarted by the passage of other guests through the garden and the presence of a jealous woman with whom her fiancé once had an affair. In spite of interruptions and frustrations her Lover manages to give Caroline a spray of white lilacs, but not the farewell kiss for which she yearns.

Jardin aux lilas was the first work by Antony Tudor to be seen in America. To an audience that had learned to associate personal intensity and subjective emotion in the dance with bare feet, lank hair, and no technique, it was a startling revelation and quite as important as anything that has happened in a decade of dance history. The opening programs of Ballet Theatre—coltish versions of the classics varied by the dreary ineptitudes of *The Great American Goof*—had not seemed especially promising. Here, following a bad start, was an authentic and original work of art with a simplicity and directness that had an almost universal appeal.

No program notes are necessary for a complete understanding of *Jardin aux lilas*. The characters are clearly defined, never blurred by the exigencies of theatrical presentation. The possessiveness of the fiancé, the resigned acquiescence of Caroline, the controlled despair of the Lover, and the watchful jealousy of the ex-mistress are never lost to view and need no words to explain them. The interplay of these varying intensities, interrupted by the entrances of the guests, tells the story without a single unnecessary movement.

The choreographic style of the ballet is conditioned by the costumes, which are a simplified version of those in vogue in the early part of the century. There are no beats, but turns of various kinds (*attitude, arabesque,* and *à la seconde*) are employed. There are a number of beautiful and original lifts. Tudor employs less colloquial gesture in this work than he was later to use in *Pillar of Fire* and *Undertow*.

The ballet is admirably served by the music—Ernest Chausson's *Poème* for violin and orchestra, a far from obvious choice for ballet music. Its delicate emotionalism supports and underlines the mood of the touching little tragedy.

The costumes and setting, copied from the English originals by Hugh Stevenson, are simple and suitable, never interfering with the action, and calling no attention to themselves. Indeed *Jardin aux lilas* could be performed in practice clothes and still make its points.

There have been many changes in the cast since the ballet was first performed in America in 1940. Hugh Laing and Antony Tudor retain their original roles. Caroline has been assumed by Annabelle Lyon, Nora Kaye, and Alicia Markova. None of these dancers has conveyed quite the young poignancy that Viola Essen communicated. It remains her finest performance in ballet up to the present time. The ex-mistress has been a vehicle for Maria Karnilova and Alicia Alonso. Hugh Laing's Lover was his introduction to American audiences, who were at once aware that Ballet Theatre had acquired a dancing actor of distinction and remarkable powers of projection. His performances in *Pillar of Fire, Romeo and Juliet,* and *Aleko* demonstrate his versatility.

Jardin aux lilas was transferred from the tiny Mercury Theatre in

London to the vast stage of the Center with no diminution of intensity or theatrical power. It has entranced huge audiences at the Lewisohn Stadium and remains a beloved part of Ballet Theatre's repertoire. It is safe to claim that this ballet is a true classic of the modern dance drama.

THE JUDGMENT OF PARIS

*Satiric ballet in one act; scenario by Hugh Laing; music by Kurt Weill;
designed by Lucinda Ballard; choreography by Antony Tudor.*

THE JUDGMENT OF PARIS was first performed in London
by the Ballet Club.[1] The American première took place at the Center
Theater, New York, on January 23, 1940, with the following cast:

Juno	*Viola Essen*	Minerva	*Lucia Chase*
Venus	*Agnes De Mille*		

Antony Tudor and Hugh Laing

◇◇◇◇◇◇◇◇◇◇◇◇◇◇◇◇◇◇◇

The scene is a *boîte de nuit* (French for clip joint) in Paris. Two
tables are visible. At one of them lounge two female entertainers. At
the other a third keeps the Waiter company. An air of profound
boredom hangs over the place like a cloud. Suddenly the pall is
lifted. The Waiter is galvanized into activity. He drives the girls
from the tables and hobbles to meet an incoming customer as fast as
his fallen arches will carry him. This Customer has an air of slightly
naïve opulence about him. He is none too sober, but not nearly so
drunk as he is going to be. He orders a bottle of wine. While the
Waiter goes to get it, the entertainment arrives. All signs of lassitude
have vanished. The girls are out to make a conquest, and as the best
woman will undoubtedly win, each is keyed up for action. They go
through a simple line routine together before performing their solo
specialties.

First Juno. She is young and not too experienced. She ingrati-
atingly displays her gauche young charms. With a black lace fan she
makes gestures that might be obscene if they had not also a rather
touching innocence. No doubt she would win hands-down if the
Customer were sober. As it is, she finishes her dance without attracting more than a reasonable amount of attention.

[1] This performance took place in July, 1938, at the Westminster Theatre, London,
with a cast that included Agnes De Mille, Charlotte Bidmead, Therese Langfield,
Hugh Laing, and Antony Tudor. It was performed as a curtain-raiser for a Gogol
play.

Now Venus advances to the fray. Buxom and self-assured, she has a mop of coarse tow-colored hair and a bright blue satin costume set off with an enormous bow over the derrière. Her props are two pink hoops, which she alternately waves in the air and passes over the leg with which she is performing a double *ronde de jambe*. This must be her favorite step, as she does it to right and left several times. The Customer likes it too. Her tour de force consists in raising both hoops over her head and pulling them down over her body to her feet (modestly turning to face her audience when they become involved with the bow on her bustle). She steps out of them with an air of triumph that might indicate doubt whether she really thought she could make it. Her slightly ample charms make it likely that a new and more capacious set of hoops are on order. The Customer, quite pleased with her, has a drink sent to her table.

Minerva is tired with the awful weariness of the middle-aged lady of alleged pleasure whose triumphs, if any, are far behind her. Nevertheless, habit forces her to compete with her colleagues. Her aid to entertainment is a faded pink feather boa that is nearly as tired as its owner. She blows on it to restore some semblance of its vanished curl before she begins her act. It is not at all easy. Her back hurts and her knees creak. The Waiter, not entirely unsympathetic, gets her a drink, which she hastily gulps before exhibiting her special stunt— the splits. With a mighty effort she slowly begins. Halfway down, she looks at the Customer for approval. Finding that he is not even bothering to look, she hauls herself upright and tries some close tactics. Going to his table, she indicates with her finger the steps she is going to perform. Nagged into it, the Customer gives her his attention. Encouraged, she gives up dancing, puts her elbow on the table, and, cupping chin in hand, gazes at him with whatever ardor she is capable of. He imitates her attitude and with a derisive grin knocks her elbow off the table. This is the end. She walks slowly back to the entertainers' table, her feather boa trailing on the floor.

By this time the Customer is as drunk as an owl, but not too drunk to make a choice. He orders another bottle of wine and beckons Venus to join him. A moment after she reaches his table he passes out cold. In one second flat he is surrounded; the three entertainers and the Waiter snatch his wallet and jewelry. To Venus goes the watch, which she puts down her front, first making sure that it is ticking.

The Judgment of Paris is straight out of Toulouse-Lautrec, costumes and all. It ought to be very funny, but there is an underlying mood that renders it not much more comic than a death-bed scene. However it may have been intended, there are times when it seems unbearably tragic. This is largely due to the fine characterization of Minerva by Lucia Chase, one of the more compelling performances in the contemporary theater. Only the insensitive can find anything humorous about it. This impersonation has many times moved at least one of the audience close to tears. Possibly one ought not to become sentimental about the sordid sorrows of an aging bawd, but Miss Chase's characterization has a strong emotional impact that is impossible to experience with indifference.

Viola Essen, Ballet Theatre's original Juno, conveyed the proper degree of tentativeness. Her portrait of the freshman floozy had a certain youthful charm. One felt that this girl would not linger long in such a *milieu*. Maria Karnilova and Janet Reed have also performed this role, with technically excellent interpretations, but lacking the bouquet of Viola Essen's.

Agnes De Mille danced the part of Venus, which she had created in London. Later it passed to Janet Reed and presently to Shirley Eckl. All have been satisfactory, although Miss Reed has not quite the physique necessary to display the costume.

Antony Tudor may still be seen in his original role of the Customer. There have been several Waiters since Hugh Laing relinquished the part—John Taras, Alpheus Koon, and Regis Powers.

The mood of this little gem of the gutter is set by the music drawn from Kurt Weill's *Dreigroschenoper*. It is not reassuring music. It goes through the motions of gaiety, but always a feeling of insecurity is present and desperation is never far behind. It is a perfect choice for *The Judgment of Paris*.

The Judgment of Paris bears the unmistakable stamp of Antony Tudor's genius. Presented without a setting, against black curtains, it makes its points. With a background to match the costumes inspired by Toulouse-Lautrec, it would be infinitely more effective. Will someone bring this project to the attention of Ballet Associates?

LES NOCES

L*ES NOCES,* Igor Stravinsky's dramatic cantata, holds a position in the ballet world comparable to that of *Le Sacre du Printemps;* it is seldom performed because the complexities of the score offer difficulties too great for the average ballet organization to overcome. The requirements of *Les Noces*—a quartet of solo singers, a chorus, four pianists, and an assortment of percussion instruments[1]—are too much for the repertory company to cope with unless the presentation is sponsored by a musical organization. Even the Diaghilev Ballet, with its unusual resources, delayed the production of the ballet. Although the music had been completed in 1918, the first performance of *Les Noces* did not take place until June 13, 1923, when it was given at the Théâtre de la Gaîté Lyrique, Paris. It did not reach London until three years later, when it was performed at His Majesty's Theatre on June 14, 1926.

Les Noces, an artistic success in Paris, received a mixed reception in London, one slightly dazed critic expressing his bewilderment thus: "The rhythms are hammered into one's brain until one hardly knows what is happening. Three in a bar, four in a bar, seven in a bar—the more it changes the more it sounds to me exactly alike." It became the subject of considerable controversy. Ernest Newman and Alfred Kalisch, eminent critics and musicologists, attacked the work; Osbert Sitwell and, oddly enough, H. G. Wells defended it. At the height of the argument Wells wrote an open letter to the press praising *Les Noces* to the skies.

The score of *Les Noces* was first heard in New York on February 14, 1926, when it was performed under the auspices of the International Composers' Guild at Aeolian Hall.

On April 25, 1929 the League of Composers, under the direction of Leopold Stokowski, staged *Les Noces* at the Metropolitan Opera House, New York, on a program that also included Claudio Monteverdi's opera *Il Combattimento di Tancredi e Clorinda. Les Noces* is described in the souvenir program as "Russian choreographic scenes

---

[1] Four timpani, xylophone, bell, cymbals, tambourine, triangle, side drum, snare drum, drum without snare, small cymbals, and bass drum.

with singing and music by Igor Stravinsky." The solo singers were
Nina Koshetz, Sophie Braslau, Gabriel Leonoff, and Moshe Rudinov.
The pianists, all of whom have achieved fame as composers, were
Aaron Copland, Louis Gruenberg, Marc Blitzstein, and Frederick
Jacobi. The choreography was by Elizaveta Anderson-Ivantzoff.
There must have been some changes or substitutions among the
dancers, for the souvenir program is not quite in accord with the
performance program. The latter lists the following dancers: Valen-
tina Koshuba, Juliette Mendez, Rina Nikova, Emily Floyd, Rose
Marshall, Harold Hirsch, Jacques Cartier, Don Oscar Becque, and
George Volodin. There was also a corps de ballet.

Sergei Soudeikine was responsible for the stage settings and costumes, which are described as in the "feeling of the primitive wood
sculpture that almost every Russian can do with an axe. The costumes also are in this feeling—except those of the bride and groom,
which reflect the ancient Russian Eros-cult. The colors of the costumes and stage set represent Slavic peasant life—the color of wood
—wheat—clay—flax—beer—honey—and the old ikons of Nov-
gorod."

Seven years later, almost to the day, Colonel W. de Basil's Ballet
Russe revived *Les Noces* under the supervision of Bronislava Nijinska, the choreographer of the original version. The settings and costumes by Nathalie Gontcharova were those designed for the Paris
production. This production took place under the auspices of the Art
of Musical Russia, all singers, pianists, and the conductor, Eugene
Fuerst, being members of that organization.[2] The role of the bride,
created by Felia Doubrovska, was performed by Tamara Grigorieva.
Irina Baronova led the women, and Yurek Shabelevsky the men.

Les Noces with Nijinska's choreography differed considerably
from the version presented by the League of Composers. Its lines of
uniformly clad dancers—the women in black jumpers and white
blouses, their hair drawn tightly back under headcloths, the men in
conventional Russian peasant costume, also carried out in black and
white—offered a stark contrast to the riot of color one might reasonably expect at a Russian-ballet wedding feast. The rigid evolutions
and grim expressions of the performers suggested funereal rites, or
participation in human sacrifice, evoking an atmosphere not wholly

[2] The solo singers: Jeanne Palmer, Helena Shwedova, Ivan Velikanoff, Vasily Roma-
koff. The pianists: Pauline Gilbert, Hannah Klein, Joan Blair, Alfred Theilecker.

in agreement with the words (not devoid of a suspicion of *joie de vivre*) sung by soloists and chorus. This conclave of mourners might very well have been a group in a conquered country gathered to take leave of a hostage about to be shot. No faint gleam of happiness was permitted to appear even momentarily. It is difficult to accept the idea that any wedding could be attended by such profound misery as was here portrayed.

Stravinsky's own ideas about *Les Noces* were quite at variance with Nijinska's. In his autobiography he says:

"The stage production of *Les Noces,* though obviously one of talent, did not correspond with my original plan. . . . It was not my intention to reproduce the ritual of peasant weddings, and I paid little heed to ethnographical considerations. . . . I wanted all my instrumental apparatus to be visible side by side with the actors or dancers, making it, so to speak, a participant in the whole theatrical action.[3] For this reason I wished to place the orchestra on the stage itself, letting the actors move on the space remaining free. The fact that the artists in the scene would uniformly wear costumes of a Russian character while the musicians would be in evening dress not only did not embarrass me, but, on the contrary, was perfectly in keeping with my idea of a *divertissement* of the masquerade type. . . . As I did not feel that I had a right to jeopardize the performance since, after all, the scenic realization did not compromise my work, I very reluctantly consented to Diaghilev's staging."

The 1936 production of *Les Noces* was a *succès d'estime* with the critics if not with the average ballet-goer. John Martin, reviewing it in the *Times* said:

"Nijinska . . . has couched her composition in terms of the starkest design, and her movement is characterized by a general inhibition which only serves to mark the bits of violence which break through from time to time . . . overcast with profound mysticism, almost with a kind of terror for the solemnity of the occasion. That the total result is barren, ugly, geometrical and above all intellectual and emotionless, has been a common verdict on the work ever since its first production in 1923. . . . There is, to be sure, no emotionalizing by the dancers; it is in the responsive mechanisms of the audience that the emotion is brought into being."

Some of the audience found *Les Noces* intensely moving, but the greater part were frankly bewildered. The 1929 public was musically sophisticated and appreciated the complicated rhythmic structure of

[3] A method of presentation used in *L'Histoire d'un Soldat,* an earlier work by Stravinsky.

the score, and there is reason to believe that Mme Anderson-Ivant-zoff's choreography was of a slightly cheerier character than that of Nijinska. The audience in 1936, more interested in ballet than music, found little to hold their interest, and the ballet was scarcely a popular success. To a public that was fascinated by the charm of the "baby ballerinas," the complete absence of glamour and obvious appeal was disconcerting. The only virtuosity in *Les Noces* lay in the exact performance of complicated patterns of rhythmic movement by groups of dancers almost anonymous by virtue of the uniform costumes.[4] The ballet was given a fine performance by singers, dancers, and instrumentalists. Music-lovers were grateful for an opportunity to hear the seldom played score. *Les Noces* was presented several times that season, but has not since been seen in New York.

[4] The audience's state of mind was such that when Shabelevsky performed a single pirouette, he was loudly applauded, which must have surprised him very much indeed. They missed a really difficult feat by Baronova—*jetés* executed with arms in fifth position *en haut*.

ORPHEUS AND EURYDICE

Opera in two acts (four scenes); music by Christoph Willibald von Gluck; stage production by George Balanchine and Paul Tchelitchev; costumes designed by Paul Tchelitchev.

ORPHEUS AND EURYDICE was first presented as an opera-ballet by the American Ballet during the Metropolitan Popular Season at the Metropolitan Opera House, New York, on May 22, 1936, with a dual cast of dancers and singers:

	Singers	Dancers
ORPHEUS	*Anna Kaskas*	*Lew Christensen*
EURYDICE	*Jeanne Pengelly*	*Daphne Vane*
AMOR	*Maxine Stellman*	*William Dollar*
Shepherds and Nymphs)		
Furies and Ghosts from)	*Chorus of the*	*American Ballet*
Hades, Heroes from Elysium,)	*Metropolitan Opera*	*Ensemble*
Followers of Orpheus)		

The story of *Orpheus and Eurydice* follows the familiar myth, differing only in that it has a happy ending.

Orpheus, singer and musician, goes to seek his wife, Eurydice, victim of untimely death, in the underworld. Encouraged by Amor, he descends to the region of the infernal spirits, who, softened by his sweet singing, allow him to pass through their domain to the Elysian Fields, whence he will be allowed to rescue Eurydice from death if he can recognize her without looking at her. He passes this test, and a further condition is imposed. On his journey upward he may not look upon her face. If he does, she will die anew. Orpheus starts on his way, followed by Eurydice, who cannot understand his coldness. He yields to her reproaches, turns to look at her, only to see her sink lifeless to the ground. His wild grief reaches Amor, who appears and restores Eurydice to life. A scene of general rejoicing follows, in which Orpheus and Eurydice are welcomed back to the world of the living by their friends.

The success of the pantomime version of *Le Coq d'Or,* one of the most imaginative and attractive operatic presentations ever offered at the Metropolitan, was probably the inspiration of this production of *Orpheus and Eurydice*. Unfortunately, it was staged and choreographed in a manner that would have been hard for even an audience inured to advanced ballet to take, and no one has ever suspected the opera audience of advanced tastes of any kind for opera or ballet. No one will deny that the American Ballet and its directors had the highest possible ideals, but, in true American Ballet style, they completely disregarded the kind of audience they were playing to.

Lincoln Kirstein, in his *Blast at Ballet* says: "We saw Hell as a concentration-camp with flying military slave drivers lashing forced labor; the Elysian Fields as an ether dream, a dessicated bone-dry limbo of suspended animation, and Paradise as the eternity we know from a Planetarium arrayed in the astronomical patterns of celestial science." What was neglected to make these ideas convincing was to supply *Orpheus and Eurydice* with a new score, the emotional content of Gluck's being completely disregarded. The opera had not been heard in New York for many years, but the music was familiar even to music-lovers who had not heard the Toscanini revival, through arias and excerpts heard in concert, as well as the fine recording (nearly complete) of the opera. One cannot challenge any choreographer's right to use music as he sees fit. Audiences have an equal right to reject such conceptions if they are as widely at variance with their own ideas as this production of *Orpheus and Eurydice* was.

Balanchine's hellish concentration camp, separated from the footlights by a grill up and down which the dancers climbed, was uncommonly like a gilded monkey cage, inspiring more mirth than pity or terror. The idea was no doubt a valid one, but it simply failed to come off. Surely the drama in Gluck's magnificent music for this scene is realized more appropriately by the methods used in the 1938 revival of the opera at the Metropolitan, with its great masses of singers and dancers banked solidly almost to the top of the stage. The thunderous *"Non!"* hurled at the descending Orpheus sent shivers down the spine of the least imaginative person who heard it.

The scene in the Elysian Fields presents many problems, some of which might be solved by the Massine of the third movement of the *Symphonie Fantastique*. It has never been adequately performed at the Metropolitan, least of all in the spun-sugar setting devised for the American Ballet's presentation, which distracted the eye from the choreography. Gluck's Happy Spirits may have achieved a state of nirvana, but that was no reason for presenting them as faceless ghosts, clad in costumes trailing bits and pieces along the ground that definitely interfered with the dancers' movements.

Much was made of the fact that the traditional assignment of the roles of Orpheus and Amor to women was going to be disregarded in this production. Was it to make the change less abrupt that Lew Christensen was clad in an epicene costume which included black fingerless elbow-length gloves more appropriate to a crinolined belle of the fifties than to the protagonist of a classical tragedy? Of course, there may have been some deeply concealed symbolism, or even an archæological precedent for these curious accessories. If so, the bewildered audience was not taken into the secret.

There were several *pas de deux* and *pas de trois* in Balanchine's most tangled style occurring from time to time in the course of the action, but they were like puzzles whose baffling complexities seemed designed to display the ingenuity of the dancers rather than any expression of emotion. It is fair to say that the intricate dance patterns were beautifully performed by the dancers. Lew Christensen made a fine and dignified Orpheus in spite of his silly costume. William Dollar, not physically suited to the role of Amor, was further handicapped by being brought in on a wire, a naïve contrivance much used in the romantic ballet. Wires are plausibly employed in the underwater scene in *Das Rheingold,* where they are concealed in the general gloom. In *Orpheus and Eurydice* the all too visible wire gave the audience one more excuse to laugh.

The staging of *Orpheus and Eurydice,* in spite of a reasonably good presentation conducted by Richard Hageman, was a flat failure, disappearing after two performances. It was not doomed by the fact that the Metropolitan audience resented opera presented in ballet or pantomime form. *Le Coq d'Or* held its place in the repertoire for seven seasons, for a total of forty-two performances, a record by no means equaled by "straight" productions of the opera. The production of *Le Coq d'Or,* however, was at one with the spirit of the music, arising out of the music and not arbitrarily imposed on it—a fact recognized by the audience, obtuse though they may be about ballet in general.

PAGANINI

Fantastic ballet in three scenes by S. Rachmaninoff and M. Fokine; music by Serge Rachmaninoff (Rhapsody for Piano and Orchestra on a Theme by Paganini); choreography by Michel Fokine; scenery and costumes by Serge Soudeikine.

PAGANINI was first produced at the Royal Opera House, Covent Garden, London, on June 30, 1939. The first New York performance took place at the Fifty-first Street Theater on November 8, 1940, with the following cast:

PAGANINI	*Dimitri Rostoff*	GUILE	*Tamara Grigorieva*
THE DIVINE GENIUS		SCANDAL	*Yura Lazovsky*
	Alexandra Denisova	GOSSIP	*Alberto Alonso*
A FLORENTINE BEAUTY		ENVY	*Tatiana Leskova,*
	Tatiana Riabouchinska		*Tatiana Bechenova*
A FLORENTINE YOUTH	*Paul Petroff*	SATAN	*Borislav Runanine*

Evil Spirits, Ghosts, Phantoms, Paganini's Rivals, Their Sponsors, Florentine Maids, Florentine Youths, Divine Spirits, Paganini's Doubles

◆◆◆◆◆◆◆◆◆◆◆◆◆◆◆◆◆◆◆◆

At first glance, a violinist would seem an unlikely figure upon which to pin the plot of a ballet. However, the Hoffmanesque cloud of myth and fantasy that surrounds the career of Nicolò Paganini is the stuff of which romantic ballets are made. His many inventions in the technique of violin-playing seemed to envious rivals inspired by the Devil. Lesser musicians believed that only supernatural aid, and that not of angels, could possibly produce such virtuosity. His many amorous adventures seemed to indicate devilish art in love as well as music. All his life he was plagued by envy and scandal, mocked by inept imitators capable of copying only his most superficial aspects. When death from cancer seemed near, he passed his dying hours improvising on his violin.

To quote the program notes: "In the ballet three episodes are taken from the life of the artist: (a) Paganini on the concert platform; (b) Paganini amongst the people; and (c) Paganini in his solitude."

Scene 1. Paganini is seen on the concert platform surrounded by an audience of sensation-seekers. We see Paganini through their eyes. The devil, many-armed, and masked like a goat, leans over Paganini and plays for him. Envy, Scandal, and Gossip run gibbering below the platform while Guile, a more attractive though none the less destructive figure, mounts it to stand beside him.

Scene 2. In a pleasant landscape high above Florence, youths and maidens join in a fete. The leader, a beautiful girl in a pink dress, is partnered in the dance by her lover. Paganini enters carrying a guitar. He plays and the girl in pink follows his rhythms in her dancing. Faster and faster grows the pace. She dances in delirious ecstasy until she drops unconscious. The young people are horror-stricken and drive away the sinister figure who has caused this tragedy.

Scene 3. Paganini is alone in his study, a large room with a staircase in the rear. He is improvising, inspired by the Divine Genius, who bends tenderly over him. She is driven away by his tormentors, figures of impostors who are dressed and masked to imitate him exactly. They are led by Satan, who also wears Paganini's aspect. They hound him until he falls lifeless. The Divine Genius, with a company of Spirits, returns and the forces of Satan fade before her. She calls Paganini, whose soul, leaving the helpless body lying on a bier, rises and follows her as she floats up the staircase.

Paganini was hailed by the critics [1] with unusual acclaim—"unmistakable masterpiece," "a great work has come to enrich the treasury of ballet masterpieces." The public agreed with the critics' estimate. It was indeed something new, though expressed in dance terms familiar to the ballet audience. One might complain of the psychological shift in the second scene. In the first and third scenes Paganini is represented as rising in aloof grandeur above spiritual torment and the malice of his enemies. In the second scene he is somewhat less than noble when driving a happy young girl to delirium and exhaustion. This charge is probably a little childish, as the situation was the excuse for one of the most brilliant solos ever devised by Fokine, the high point of the ballet, choreographically speaking. It was per-

[1] A music critic complained that the "familiar sounds of the piano emerge from the orchestra pit. Had the choreographer never heard a guitar?" One might expect this from a dance critic notoriously more interested in movement than in the sounds supporting it. Was he suggesting that Rachmaninoff rescore his Rhapsody for a guitar?

formed with coruscant speed by Tatiana Riabouchinska. At first a lovely Tanagra-like figure glowing with happiness, she became a maddened creature demoniacally possessed. This must be one of the most hectically paced solos in the history of ballet. It is difficult to imagine who could have replaced Riabouchinska in this part.[2]

The role of Paganini was conceived solely in terms of mime. It was admirably and forcefully performed by Dimitri Rostoff, who seemed made by nature for this impersonation. Competent enough as a character actor in other ballets, he was distinguished as Paganini.

Sergei Rachmaninoff's Rhapsody for piano and orchestra, provided by the composer with a new ending, was a flawless choice of music to underline the drama. A more obvious selection might indicate a composition for violin and orchestra. It becomes apparent on second thoughts that no violinist at the service of a ballet company's orchestra could match the visual illusion with an auditory one.

Settings and costumes by Serge Soudeikine were effective for their purpose without being really outstanding, except in the pastoral scene—a charming landscape peopled with figures dressed in flower-like colors. The Divine Spirits wore headdresses that resembled those of celestial Red Cross workers. Here the romantic tutu as in *Les Sylphides* would surely have been more appropriate. However, this is a small issue to raise in the presence of one of Michel Fokine's last masterworks.

Paganini formed part of the opening program presented by the Original Ballet Russe at the Metropolitan Opera House in the fall of 1946. Vladimir Dokoudovsky performed the title role, Genevieve Moulin was the Florentine Beauty, and Nina Stroganova the Divine Genius. These dancers in no way equaled their predecessors in the roles.

[2] Recasting ballets is a favorite sport of ballet-lovers.

PAS DE QUATRE

THE first intimation of an event of the highest importance in the annals of the romantic ballet was a modest announcement in the *Illustrated London News,* dated July 5, 1845, in which Signor Puzzi respectfully informed "the Nobility, Subscribers to the Opera, his Friends, and the Public" that his benefit would take place on July 10, at Her Majesty's Theatre. The promised attractions included Donizetti's *Anna Bolena* and selections from Rossini's *Pietro l'Eremita.*[1] This already massive program was to conclude with "Entertainments in the Ballet Department," including "the combined talents of Mdlle. C. Grisi, Mdlle. Lucile Grahn, and Mdlle. Cerito; M. Perrot, M. Gosselin, and M. St. Leon. In addition to which, Signor Puzzi has the honour to announce that he has effected an arrangement by which he has secured the assistance of Mdlle. Taglioni."

The *Illustrated London News* does not review this performance—gargantuan to us, but apparently a commonplace to the hardy operagoers of the first half of the nineteenth century—therefore I am not certain whether Signor Puzzi's benefit was graced by the presence of Taglioni. A week later, however, there appeared in the same periodical an advertisement for Mlle C. Grisi's benefit to take place on July 17. The promised program, including Mozart's *Così Fan Tutte,* offered in addition the combined talents of the same illustrious group of dancers, this time the honor roll being led by Mlle Taglioni. A "new Pas de Quatre, between Mdlle. Taglioni, Mdlle. C. Grisi, Mdlle. Lucile Grahn, and Mdlle. Cerito. To conclude with the second act of 'La Giselle.' "[2]

The first performance of *Pas de Quatre* took place, according to C. W. Beaumont, on July 12, 1845, so that it is more than likely that persons who attended Signor Puzzi's benefit did not have the pleas-

---

[1] This was actually *Mose in Egitto,* provided with a new libretto in deference to English objections to the appearance of Biblical characters in theatrical productions.

[2] "Applications for Boxes, Pit, Stalls, and Tickets, to be made at the Box Office, Opera Collonade. Doors open at Seven, the Opera to commence at Half-past Seven." (*Illustrated London News,* July 12, 1845.) One wonders at what hour carriages were to be called!

ure of seeing Taglioni with her illustrious colleagues. The performances are reviewed in glowing terms by the *Illustrated London News*.

"The past week's performances at Her Majesty's Theatre have been signalised by an event unparalleled in theatrical annals, and one which, some two score years hence, may be handed down to a new generation by garulous septuagenarians as one of the most brilliant reminiscences of days gone by. The appearance of four such dancers as Taglioni, Cerito, Carlotta Grisi, and Lucile Grahn, on the same boards, and in the same *pas,* is truly what our Gallic neighbours call 'un solemnité theatrale,' and such a one as none of those who beheld it are likely to witness again. It was therefore as much a matter of curiosity, as of interest to hurry to the Theatre to witness this spectacle; but every other feeling was merged in admiration when the four great dancers commenced the series of picturesque groupings with which this performance opens. We can safely say we have never witnessed a scene more perfect in all its details. The greatest of painters, in his loftiest flights, could hardly have conceived, and certainly never executed, a group more faultless and more replete with grace and poetry than that formed by these four *danseuses*: Taglioni in the midst, her head thrown backwards, apparently reclining in the arms of her sister nymphs. . . . No description can render the exquisite, and almost ethereal grace of movement and attitude of these great dancers, and those who have witnessed the scene may boast of having once, at least, seen the perfection of the art of dancing, so little understood. There was no affectation, no apparent exertion or struggle for effect on the part of these gifted *artistes;* and though they displayed their utmost resources, there was a simplicity and ease, the absence of which would have completely broken the spell they threw around the scene. Of the details of the performance it is difficult to speak. In the solo steps executed by each *danseuse,* each in turn seemed to claim pre-eminence. Where everyone in her own style is perfect, individual taste alone may balance in favour of one or the other, but the award of public applause must be equally bestowed; and, for our own part, we confess our *penchant* for the peculiar style, and our admiration for the dignity, the repose, the exquisite grace which characterise Taglioni, and the dancer who has so brilliantly followed the same track (Lucile Grahn), did not prevent our warmly appreciating the charming archness and twinkling steps of Carlotta Grisi, or the wonderful flying leaps and revolving bounds of Cerito. Though, as we have said, each displayed her utmost powers, the emulation of the fair dancers was, if we may trust appearances, unaccompanied by envy. . . . The house crowded to the roof, presented a concourse of the most eager faces, never diverted for a moment from the performance; and the extraordinary tumult of enthusiastic applause . . . imparted to the whole scene an interest and excitement that can hardly be imagined."

The reviewer was so carried away by the emotions which the performance of *Pas de Quatre* aroused that he could scarcely spare more than a word or two for the singers, who included such a brilliant array of stars as Giulia Grisi (a cousin of Carlotta), Giovanni Matteo Mario, and Luigi Lablache.

On Thursday night, July 17, the performance was attended by a glittering audience "including her Majesty, Prince Albert, the Queen Dowager, etc." The tradition that *Pas de Quatre* was arranged at the request of Queen Victoria seems to be invalidated by two facts: first, the Queen's presence at the third performance (surely the première would have been timed for her visit to the theater); second, the *Illustrated London News* makes no reference to any such thing. It would seem reasonable that Benjamin Lumley, manager of Her Majesty's Theatre, having secured so many fine singing stars, would be equally assiduous, in an age when ballet was crowding opera for first place in the musical theater, to make his ballet department outstanding. Whatever his reasons, the *Pas de Quatre* was an event that even the masterful vocabularies of the modern Hollywood press agents would be strained to describe. A quartet of contemporary ballerinas with standing in the ballet world equivalent to that of the 1845 danseuses would include Alicia Markova, Alexandra Danilova, Margot Fonteyn (Sadler's Wells), and Galina Ulanova (People's Artist, U.S.S.R.).

The music for *Pas de Quatre,* familiar to the present-day ballet audience, was by Cesare Pugni, who later became an official composer of ballet scores for the Imperial Theaters of Russia. He is remarkable chiefly for the vast amount of ballet music that he produced, most of which is said to be devoid of anything resembling inspiration or dramatic power. So little of his music is heard today that any opinion of it must be derivative in origin. Certainly the music for *Pas de Quatre* has the charm one finds in an early Victorian *bibelot* or an antique lace-edged valentine.

Lumley in his *Reminiscences of the Opera,* published many years after the event, relates a story of his difficulties in arranging the *Pas de Quatre* that does more credit to his imagination than his respect for his readers' intelligence. It is a typical tale of artistic temperament. He tells how the choreography was arranged with a careful attention so that each danseuse would have an opportunity to shine, but not outshine her colleagues—arrangements that came to nought because of the reluctance of Grisi, Grahn, and Cerito to take second place to anyone but Taglioni. This debacle is said to have occurred on the day of the performance—a most unlikely event, as it is impossible to believe that a ballet of such importance would be subject to last-minute whims, or indeed in such a tentative state that it could be affected by them. Dr. A. Michel has pointed this out with corroborative detail in a most informative article in *Dance* (July 1945).

There is no doubt at all that Jules Perrot, who was the choreographer of *Pas de Quatre,* did not find his task particularly easy. Working with four such eminent artists must have strained his capacity for tact and diplomacy to the utmost. That he succeeded is witnessed by the many memorials of the event surviving in the charming lithographs of Chalon and the enthusiastic accounts in the contemporary press and memoirs. Perrot, in addition to being a very fine dancer (Gautier called him "the male Taglioni"), was a choreographer of outstanding abilities, at least one of whose ballets, *Esmeralda,* is still part of the active repertoire of the Soviet ballet theaters. He is also credited with arranging several solos in *Giselle,* the title role of which was created by Carlotta Grisi, his wife.

The undeniable *ballerina assoluta* of *Pas de Quatre* was Marie Taglioni, who made her debut in Vienna in 1822. Her individual style of dancing, which concealed a strong technique under a flowing simplicity of movement, was something entirely new in the dance world. She was already an artist of note when she appeared in *La Sylphide,* the first full-fledged romantic ballet, with choreography by her father, Filippo Taglioni. In *La Sylphide,* Taglioni wore for the first time the costume forever afterward associated with the romantic ballet and still to be seen in the neo-romantic *Sylphides*. From that point on, ballet cut entirely loose from its courtly background of classical mythology and found subjects for librettos in folk stories and fairy tales. Taglioni's fluid style and unusual elevation made her the ideal interpreter of the sylphides, nymphs, and naiads of the new dispensation. Her position in the artistic world became that of supreme artist of the dance until her retirement in 1847, when legends began to gather around her name. Her floating elevation became a part of the mythology of the dance, much as Nijinsky's was to do many years later. The maddening impossibility of ever really knowing the true quality of a dancer of the past is in the case of Taglioni

GRADUATION BALL
(Alicia Alonso
and
Richard Reed)

PAS DE QUATRE (Nora Kaye, Alicia Markova, Rosella Hightower, Annabelle Lyon)

PAS DE QUATRE (1845), after the Chalon lithograph (Carlotta Grisi, Marie Taglioni, Lucille Grahn, Fanny Cerito)

PILLAR OF FIRE (Nora Kaye as Hagar)

PRINCESS AURORA (John Kriza as the Bluebird)

mitigated by the many accounts that her contemporaries have written of her. The critic of the *Illustrated London News* says: "There is an ease and repose about Taglioni, which marks more than anything else, her peculiar talent and style of dancing. The difficulties she executes are attained by almost all first-rate *ballerine;* her peculiarities in other respects may be imitated, and are now become, in fact, the standard of the best style of dancing; but the quietness, the facility, and the total absence of effort, remarkable in her performance, are the true characteristics of genius, and belong only to the greatest among her rivals." This would indicate that Taglioni's tours de force, like those of Markova and Pavlova, were the product of that concealed virtuosity which bears no relation to the circus tricks beloved by the unperceptive among the ballet audience.

Taglioni is said to have imparted the secret of her remarkable elevation to her favorite pupil, Emma Livry, for whom she devised the choreography of the ballet *Le Papillon,* produced at the Paris Opéra to music by Jacques Offenbach in 1861. Emma Livry's performance was greeted with superlatives by the critics and she was hailed as the successor of Taglioni, who had trained her to that end. A year later this dancer was dead as the result of burns sustained when her costume caught fire during a rehearsal of *La Muette de Portici.* She was one of a number of dancers to meet a similar fate in the era before electricity eliminated the fire hazard from the theater along with the glamorous flickering of the gaslights.

Lucile Grahn, to whom the critic of *Pas de Quatre* was partial, had a shorter career in the dance theater than her colleagues. She created roles in *Catarina, ou La Fille du Bandit* and *Eoline, ou La Dryade,* and was a notable Giselle, but illness and accident interfered with her success. Of her the *Illustrated London News* said: "she has been gradually gaining ground in public estimation. She is now an acknowledged favourite, and deservedly so. Her refined and poetical style of dancing, her remarkable grace and agility, combine to render her one of the first dancers of the day." Her dramatic abilities appear to have been impressive, and she is the subject of a number of lithographs.

Fanny Cerito, according to her contemporaries, was a dancer of the forceful, impetuous variety, with a style that would appear to be far more easily found in the dance world of the present decade than the ethereal elegance of Taglioni and Grahn. She is associated with roles in *Ondine* (famous for the *Pas de l'Ombre,* a pose from which inspired the balancing feats performed by Tudor's Italian Ballerina), *La Vivandière,* and *La Fille de Marbre.* The critic of the *Illustrated London News* (without whom, it becomes increasingly apparent, this account of *Pas de Quatre* and its personalities could never have been written) scores her for her lack of precision and neatness when he reviewed her performance in a ballet called *Manola,* though her appearance in *Pas de Quatre* was praised.

The fame of Carlotta Grisi, favorite dancer of Théophile Gautier, is second only to that of Taglioni. The creator of Giselle, she is celebrated in many contemporary accounts and memorialized in some of the most charming lithographs of an age that specialized in them. Her reputation is not dependent on *Giselle* alone. She created roles in many ballets—*Esmeralda, La Filleule des Fées, Paquita,* and *Le Diable à Quatre,* to name but a few. Gautier said of her: "She is happy to dance for sheer love of it, like a young girl at her first ball; and, however difficult the thing she has to do, she does it as though it was the merest trifle, which is as it should be; because in the arts nothing is so disagreeable as a difficulty obviously overcome." [3]

The success of *Pas de Quatre* led to its revival in a later season with Carolina Rosati replacing Grahn. At least three other ballets were produced exploiting a similar idea though more elaborately. *Le Jugement de Paris* [4] (1846; Taglioni, Grahn, Cerito) had a plot that employed a supporting cast including Arthur St. Léon (Paris) and Jules Perrot (Mercury). *Les Éléments* (1847; Grisi, Rosati, Cerito) anticipated Massine's *Seventh Symphony* in having a group of dancers impersonating the Earth. *Les Quatre Saisons* (1848; Grisi, Rosati, Cerito, Taglioni the younger) reverted to the simplicity of *Pas de Quatre* though the cast lacked the luster of the original. All of these ballets were arranged by Perrot, and performed at Her Majesty's Theatre, London, during Lumley's fabulous opera seasons.

In 1936 Keith Lester reconstructed the *Pas de Quatre* for the Markova-Dolin Ballet. He was assisted in this project by C. W. Beaumont, the greatest authority on ballet in the English-speaking world, and Leighton Lucas, who transcribed the original musical score, which was discovered in the British Museum. Molly Lake, Diana

---

[3] Quoted by C. W. Beaumont in *A Miscellany for Dancers.*
[4] This was revived by Keith Lester for the London Ballet in 1939, as *La Pas des Déesses,* the name of a *divertissement* in the original ballet.

Gould, Kathleen Crofton, and Prudence Hyman formed the cast of the restaging, which was as close to the original as the experts' combined knowledge, based on contemporary reviews and pictures, could make it. The ballet remained an important item of the repertoire of the Markova-Dolin Ballet until its dissolution.

During the 1941 season of Ballet Theatre at the Majestic Theater, New York was introduced to *Pas de Quatre,* which appeared on the program with the following credits: "choreographic re-creation by Anton Dolin; music by Cesare Pugni, transcribed by Leighton Lucas, especially orchestrated by Paul Bowles." Just how much this version owes to Keith Lester is not mentioned. Dolin in his autobiographical *Ballet Go Round* is critical of Lester's arrangement, finding it too long drawn out for its content. Photographs of Lester's version are similar to groups in Dolin's, but as their points of origin lie in the Chalon lithographs, duplication may be expected.

Dolin's re-creation of *Pas de Quatre* was performed by Nana Gollner (Taglioni), Nina Stroganova (Grahn), Alicia Alonso (Grisi), and Katharine Sergava (Cerito). It was a pleasant enough work, and competently danced, though Alonso was the only member of the cast who displayed a perception of the romantic style.

The true revelation of the charm of *Pas de Quatre* came when Alicia Markova danced Taglioni with her incomparable style in a manner that recalled the ecstatic century-old reviews of the original performance. These might have served without a change of a superlative to describe Markova's interpretation. The other roles were assumed by Irina Baronova (Grahn), Nora Kaye (Grisi), and Annabelle Lyon (Cerito). This delightful event took place at the Forty-fourth Street Theater during the 1941 season of Ballet Theatre.

Choreographically, *Pas de Quatre* is contrived with artful simplicity. When the curtain rises, the dancers are seen in a pose that duplicates the most famous of Chalon's lithographs. They dance together, weaving in and out in simple patterns, resuming a tableau, after which three of the dancers (Taglioni, Grisi, and Cerito) curtsy and leave the stage. The first two variations have changed places in the program several times. As originally presented, the first variation is technically the most brilliant, with steps of distance and elevation. The high point is a series of *jetés en tournant,* with *entrechats cinq* in a large circle. This solo finishes with multiple *entrechats quatre,* with the dancer turning slightly first to one side and the other. This has been brilliantly performed by Karen Conrad and Rosella Hightower.

At the end of her variation, each dancer acknowledges the applause and then with a graceful *port de bras* directs the attention of the audience to the next soloist.

In the second variation (sometimes performed first) the dancer travels in a diagonal with small steps on point in fifth position, leading always with the same foot. It includes *brisés* and a single *fouetté en tournant* executed very slowly, concluding with a double *pirouette en dedans*. Nora Kaye and Rosella Hightower have at various times been seen to advantage in this solo.

At this point the series of variations is interrupted by a brief *pas de deux,* performed by Taglioni and usually the dancer impersonating Grahn, which serves to introduce the third variation—a solo in waltz time. This is characterized by *balancés en tournant,* poses, *jetés en tournant,* and ends with the dancer leaving the stage in a *grand jeté.* The charm of this variation depends greatly on a fluid style and musical phrasing, both of which Annabelle Lyon brought to her interpretation of it. Her successors in the role have failed to efface the impression that she made on those lucky enough to have seen her.

The fourth variation, performed by Taglioni, is based on a close study of the lithographs of this great dancer. It includes many poses, notably arabesques with stylized *port de bras* that are the very essence of these charming studies. There is a Cecchetti *assemblé* that is identical with the one in the Prelude in *Les Sylphides.* The high point is a series of *cabrioles* and *brisés* executed in constantly changing directions. The solo ends with the characteristic Taglioni arabesque and a kneeling pose. Only Markova, with her complete understanding of the romantic style, can properly perform this variation, and there ought to be an injunction to prevent any other dancer from attempting it.

The final ensemble is brisk in tempo, and the choreographic highlight is a series of *echappés* performed by the dancers, who join hands in an outside circle. At the conclusion the dancers resume the original pose.

Pas de Quatre has the enchantment of a true period piece. It is unpretentious, charming, and direct in its appeal to the audience. Properly cast (this means Markova), it cannot fail in its effect. It has been part of Ballet Theatre's repertoire since 1941.

PETER AND THE WOLF

Ballet in one act; choreography by Adolph Bolm; story by Sergei Proko-
fiev; music by Sergei Prokofiev; scenery and costumes by Lucinda
Ballard.

PETER AND THE WOLF had its world première at a matinee
performance given by Ballet Theatre at the Center Theater, New
York, on January 13, 1940, with the following cast:

PETER	*Eugene Loring*	FIRST HUNTER	*Harold Haskin*
BIRD	*Viola Essen*	SIX HUNTERS:	*Charles Ewing, Jack*
DUCK	*Karen Conrad*		*Potteiger, Donald Saddler, Oreste*
CAT	*Nina Stroganova*		*Sergievsky, Richard Reed, Leonard*
GRANDFATHER	*Edward Caton*		*Ware*
WOLF	*William Dollar*		

The ballet begins with the voice of a narrator, who introduces the
characters and their corresponding instruments in the orchestra.

The curtain rises on a meadow, dominated by a large tree. To the
left is a garden gate leading to Peter's house. To the right is a small
duck pond and the beginning of a grim forest.

To the sound of gay music, Peter runs in. He is rosy-cheeked, has
a shock of yellow hair, and is dressed in overalls. He greets the Bird,
who chirps with pleasure. The Duck follows Peter out of the garden
gate, which he has left open. She engages in an altercation with the
Bird. The Duck is contemptuous of a feathered creature who can't
swim. She demonstrates her gifts by diving into the pond. While the
Bird is fluttering around, arguing the point, the Cat appears. The
Bird hastily takes refuge in the tree. The Cat prowls below.

Grandfather enters, angrily waving his stick. He knows that the
Wolf lurks in the forest, but he cannot convince Peter, and anyway
Peter is not afraid of wolves. Grandfather drags him inside the gate
in spite of his protests. As soon as they have gone, the Wolf appears.
Duck, Bird, and Cat are much agitated, but only the Duck loses her
head and gets within his reach. She is seized by the Wolf, who car-

ries her into the forest for the kill. He returns looking satisfied, but apparently the Duck does not agree with the Wolf, for he has hiccups.

Meanwhile Peter has been laying plans. He gets a long rope and climbs with it to the garden wall, where he is joined by the Cat. He manages to lasso the Wolf with the aid of the Bird, who, descending from the tree, dazzles the Wolf by pecking at his eyes. Peter ties the rope to a tree, and the Wolf's frantic efforts to get away pull the rope tighter. This is definitely a stalemate until the Hunters arrive. With a good deal of misgiving, they agree not to shoot the Wolf, but to bind him securely and take him away to a zoo.

Peter has his moment of triumph, but is careful to award credit to his able assistants, the Bird who helped actively, and the Cat who gave moral support. Grandfather is still angry, no doubt foreseeing a series of similar episodes and not caring for the prospect.

The Chief Hunter leads the bound Wolf (no longer dangerous), the rest of the Hunters, and Peter in a grand procession to the zoo. The Bird, caroling merrily, brings up the rear.

There is an epilogue in which the narrator draws a moral and the characters of the story wave good-by to the audience.

Peter and the Wolf, an Orchestral Fairy Tale, was composed by Sergei Prokofiev, and was given a first performance at a children's concert in Moscow on May 2, 1936. Its purpose was to teach children how to distinguish the various instruments of the orchestra. This worthy object did not keep it from being very entertaining indeed. It would be quite impossible to take the music seriously, or even in an ironic spirit—a mistake made with the *Lieutenant Kijé* suite, which was used for the tragic ballet *Russian Soldier* by Michel Fokine. Unfortunately Mr. Bolm has not realized all the humor implicit in the score, though his ballet has given far more pleasure to matinee audiences than critics or the more informed section of the ballet public will believe.

The dancers do their best within the limits set by the choreographer, and have added touches of their own as they grew into their roles. This is not ordinarily a commendable practice, but in the case of *Peter and the Wolf* it has worked very well. There have been changes in the cast, many for the better. Yurek Lazovsky was a delightful Peter. Hugh Laing hid his dark glamour behind Grandfather's whiskers for several seasons, and demonstrated that he is a character actor of impressive abilities. The choreography called upon the Bird to rise from a full *plié* on point to an attitude, a difficult feat that weaker dancers were able only to approximate, but that Nora Kaye performed beautifully and smoothly. Jean Hunt added the Duck to her amusing gallery of birds and beasts. Nina Stroganova's Cat has remained without a rival to date. Dancers who have emerged from the ranks of the Hunters to stardom frequently revert to them in an emergency.

The setting by Lucinda Ballard is in the style made familiar by the Chauve-Souris. The costumes, save for Grandfather's bathrobe—a very remarkable garment—are nondescript, but serve their purpose.

Peter and the Wolf has had no vacation from the repertoire of the Ballet Theatre. It does not expect one until a new children's ballet is born.

PETROUCHKA

PETROUCHKA, that extraordinary product of the collaboration of Stravinsky, Fokine, Benois, and Diaghilev, was performed for the first time in the United States at the Century Theater, New York, on January 25, 1916 by Sergei de Diaghilev's Ballet Russe. The cast included Lydia Lopokova (Dancer), Léonide Massine (Petrouchka), and Adolph Bolm (Blackamoor), none of whom had appeared in the original Paris production.

The Diaghilev Ballet that came to America in 1916 was something less than the assemblage of virtuoso dancers that had startled Paris in 1909. Then and for several seasons thereafter Diaghilev had drawn his dancers from the State Theaters of Russia, engaging them for the Paris season and the yearly tour of Europe when the Russian theaters were closed. The dismissal of Vaslav Nijinsky from the Imperial Russian Ballet following an incident, the details of which are obscure, forced Diaghilev to organize a permanent company. This company had been more or less disrupted by the outbreak of World War I. When the invitation to tour America came, Nijinsky had been interned in Hungary as an enemy alien; Karsavina, because of domestic responsibilities, was unable to make the journey; other dancers declined to brave the hazardous Atlantic crossing at the height of the U-boat menace. Nevertheless, Diaghilev managed to assemble a company of dancers, engaging Lydia Lopokova in New York. This talented dancer, who had joined his company in 1911, left it to pursue a dramatic career in America. The new company disappointed those of the New York audience who had seen the Diaghilev Ballet abroad in its golden age (1909–14). The untraveled ones felt no such sentiment. They could not compare the Diaghilev Ballet with anything but itself, ballet being noticeably absent from the New York theatrical scene.

Nothing that New York had ever seen in the theater prepared it for *Petrouchka*—the startling score (one of the turning-points in the history of modern music), the imaginative décor, the free style of dancing, were something entirely new. The critic of the *Times* wrote in his review of the first performance:

"*Petrouchka* which was given for the first time here, is called 'burlesque scenes in four tableaux' and is altogether one of the most extraordinary products of the contemporary Russian school, both in its pictorial effects: the phantasmagoria of color, of Russian carnival characters, costumes, and boisterous action, and in the music, equally a phantasmagoria of incomparable verve and brilliancy, fitting and illustrating in every detail for the ear what is presented to the eye. Both are of an indescribable fascination."

Vaslav Nijinsky joined the company some time later, having been released from his internment. He assumed the role that he had created, appearing in *Petrouchka* at the Metropolitan Opera House on April 13, 1916. It was remarked that in addition to revealing his incomparable interpretation of the title role he had clarified details of the choreography which had become obscured.

In 1919 the Metropolitan Opera staged a revival of *Petrouchka* under the direction of Adolph Bolm, who appeared in the title role. Rosina Galli (Dancer), and Giuseppe Bonfiglio (Blackamoor) were also in the cast. The settings and costumes were by John Wenger. The principal reason for this offering was the presence in the company of the conductor Pierre Monteux, who had been associated with the Diaghilev Ballet for several years and had conducted the original performance of *Petrouchka* in Paris. There were five repetitions of the ballet at the Metropolitan that season.

There was a further revival of *Petrouchka* at the Metropolitan in 1924. The cast was almost identical with that of the 1919 production, and new settings and costumes were designed by Serge Soudeikine. Tullio Serafin conducted and Wilfred Pelletier played the piano solo. At various times *Petrouchka* was paired on double bills with *Cavalleria Rusticana, Pagliacci,* and at least once with Montemezzi's *Giovanni Gallurese. Petrouchka* was performed ten times during this and the succeeding season, and then dropped from the repertoire.

As early as March 1916 the Neighborhood Playhouse presented a version of *Petrouchka* that probably owed little beyond the general idea to the original ballet. In this production, performed for the first time on March 11, 1916, the cast included Ivan Lezvinov (Petrouchka), Lillie Lubell (Ballerina), Philip Rossiter (Blackamoor) and Frank J. Zimmerer (Charlatan—called "the showman" on the program), who also designed the décor. This production was revived from time to time during that barren period when dance in New York meant the line routines of Broadway, pupils' recitals in dance academies, and the offerings of small group movements more concerned with theories than theater. The Neighborhood Playhouse, with its colorful and varied dance programs, reminded audiences that the dance was a branch of theatrical art. The performances may have lacked something technically, but were never to be mistaken for revival meetings or political gatherings—an error easily made by a stranger straying into recitals given by insurgent groups that busied themselves in freeing the dance from the awful error of being theatrical.

Colonel W. de Basil's Ballet Russe performed *Petrouchka* for the first time in America on January 12, 1934, at the St. James Theater, New York. Tamara Toumanova (Dancer), Leon Woizikowsky (Petrouchka), and David Lichine (Blackamoor) headed the cast. The curtain, scenery, and costumes were by Alexandre Benois. The choreography was said to be "after Fokine."

Petrouchka formed part of the repertoire of the Ballet Russe de Monte Carlo. This production also had a Benois décor, and choreography "by Michel Fokine" which did not vary perceptibly from the de Basil version, which was "after Fokine."

In 1940, Fokine was invited by the Original Ballet Russe to restage his great work. This, as far as may be ascertained the first performance of *Petrouchka* to be given in America under·the direction of the choreographer, took place at the Fifty-first Street Theater, New York, on November 21, 1940. Details of the production follow:

Petrouchka, a burlesque in four acts; book by Alexandre Benois and Igor Stravinsky; music by Igor Stravinsky; choreography by Michel Fokine; curtain, scenery, and costumes by Alexandre Benois.

THE DANCER	*Tamara Toumanova*	THE GAY MERCHANT	*Dimitri Rostoff*
PETROUCHKA	*Yura Lazovsky*	THE GYPSIES	*Tatiana Lipkovska,*
THE BLACKAMOOR	*Alberto Alonso*		*Sono Osato*
THE OLD CHARLATAN	*Marian Ladre*	THE STREET DANCERS	
THE CHIEF NURSEMAID			*Anna Leontieva,*
	Lara Obidenna		*Anna Volkova*
THE HEAD COACHMAN			
	Serge Ismailoff		

Nursemaids, Coachmen, Grooms, Masqueraders, Peddlers, Officers, etc.

◇◇◇◇◇◇◇◇◇◇◇◇◇◇◇◇◇◇◇◇

Act I. The Carnival. The scene is Admiralty Square in St. Petersburg. The square is surrounded by stalls and showmen's booths,

erected for a carnival. A heterogeneous mob—working people, soldiers, cadets, fine ladies attended by their servants—in fact, a cross-
section of the city's population—has assembled to enjoy Butter Week,
the traditional fling that precedes the bleak forty days of Lent. A man
with a music box wanders through the crowd. A street dancer spreads
her carpet and demonstrates her tricks, providing her own accompaniment on a triangle. A rival sets up shop, amazing the bystanders
by performing the splits. Two tall attendants who have been standing guard in front of a curtained booth move forward to clear a
space, crowding the people back from the center of the square.
Through the curtains appears the Charlatan—a strange, bearded
figure, wearing a tall turban and a cloak patterned with cabalistic
symbols. The crowd, awed, waits breathlessly while he produces a
flute out of thin air. He plays an exotic melody, holding his hearers
silent. The effect is, indeed, almost hypnotic, one little shawled working girl being irresistibly drawn forward until ordered back into
line by the policeman. Suddenly the Charlatan ceases his tune. A
wave of his arms causes the curtains of the booth to fly open, revealing three cells, each inhabited by a limp figure suspended on an
iron frame. One by one the dolls are animated by the Charlatan's
fluting and they dance, still supported by the frames. At their
master's command, they leave their cells and are revealed to the
crowd as traditional puppets strangely brought to life—the Blackamoor, dressed in a rich Oriental costume; the Dancer, gay in red
tutu, striped pantalettes, and a chic cap; Petrouchka, the clown, in
white scalloped jacket and red and yellow trousers. Surrounded by
the people, they go through their routine, dancing to a frenzied
rhythm and enacting a simple bit of drama, in which Petrouchka
resents the Blackamoor's flirtation with the Dancer and belabors
him with a baton held under his arm. The turn ends with a fast and
furious dance, which ends with all three puppets sitting cross-legged
on the ground.

Act II. Petrouchka's Cell. The cell is black and gloomy. There are
a few scattered stars for decoration and a grim portrait of the Charlatan hangs on the wall, ever present reminder of who is master. The
door opens and the Charlatan roughly thrusts Petrouchka into his
cell to wait for the next performance. Petrouchka is the least carefully contrived of the three puppets. His mouth is crooked and his
hands mere blobs of rag. Unfortunately for him, he is also the most

nearly human, and his imperfections trouble him. His miserable reflections are interrupted by the entrance of the Dancer—a very elegant doll indeed, beautifully made and smartly dressed. Petrouchka adores her perfection. Her appearance in his gloomy cell fills him with a frenetic delight that frightens her away. Alone, he yields to his bitterness, gesturing his defiance at the Charlatan's portrait. He tries to get out, but his useless hands will not open the door. Frantically he beats on the flimsy wall, which gives away, allowing the gay tumult of the carnival to be heard. His agony is of no avail. His glimmering of a soul is hopelessly imprisoned in a silly clown's body. Overcome by despair, he sinks to the ground.

Act III. The Blackamoor's Cell. The gay colors and comfortable divan in the Blackamoor's cell are in marked contrast to the bare gloom of Petrouchka's. The Blackamoor is gorgeously dressed in semi-Oriental style, and he has not been spoiled in the making. His grotesquerie is indigenous to his species, not the result of careless workmanship. The Charlatan's art has endowed him with movement, but few intimations of a human spirit disturb his repose. He is amusing himself as a baby might, tossing a coconut in the air and catching it with his feet. He rolls off the divan, rises, and with his scimitar tries to split the coconut. The failure of his clumsy strokes inspires him with the idea that the coconut is an invulnerable fetish. Prostrating himself, he worships it. A lively staccato air is heard. The Dancer enters blowing a toy trumpet. The Blackamoor, forgetting the coconut, turns to this new source of entertainment. They dance together—the Blackamoor awkward and heavy, the Dancer crisp and taut. Finishing the dance, the Blackamoor makes crude love to the willing Dancer. They sit on the divan, where Petrouchka, who has somehow managed to break out of his cell, finds them. The intrusion annoys the Dancer and infuriates the Blackamoor, who, sword in hand, drives Petrouchka away. Again the Blackamoor sits on the divan. With an authoritative gesture he orders the obedient Dancer to join him.

Act IV. The Carnival. The passage of time has not abated the exuberance of the crowd. A bevy of ornately dressed nursemaids adds even more color to an already brilliant scene. Encouraged by the bystanders, they dance, at first alone, then with a group of coachmen. Itinerant salesmen peddle their wares. Girls swoop down on a sleigh laden with gay scarves and ribbons. A Bear-leader induces his clumsy charge to perform. Two gypsy girls, with a drunken Merchant in tow, make a disorderly entrance. The Merchant's pockets are bulging with money, which he carelessly flings about, to be snatched by anyone within reach. As the level rays of a low sunset appear, a few flakes of snow begin to fall. Maskers, some in travesty, some in grotesque animal masks, leap through the crowd. One in the costume of a horned devil terrifies the girls, who enjoy the sensation. The curtains of the Charlatan's booth are shaken by a sudden disturbance. The Blackamoor pursues Petrouchka out of one side and into the other, followed by the protesting Dancer. Again Petrouchka rushes out, seeking protection among the crowd. The Blackamoor overtakes him, ruthlessly strikes him down with his sword, and disappears. Silenced by the horror of this swift violence, the merrymakers gather round Petrouchka, who dies, convulsively reaching for something above that only dimly exists in his poor limited mind.

One of the mob calls the Policeman, who hurriedly hobbles away in search of the Charlatan, with whom he returns. With his magician's cloak and turban laid aside, the Charlatan is a much less impressive figure than at his first appearance. His black cloak and battered top hat reduce him to the status of an ordinary old man. The angry reproaches of Policeman and spectators he answers by picking up the corpse, demonstrating to all that it is merely a sawdust-stuffed effigy, not worth their anger or sorrow. Relieved, they begin to drift home by groups and couples, leaving the Charlatan alone in the dark deserted square. The old man trudges away, dragging the doll behind him by one arm.

Suddenly a thin triumphant screech is heard. Startled, the Charlatan turns to see Petrouchka above the booth, stretching to the sky with exulting gesticulations. As the Charlatan looks unbelievingly from the limp object at his feet to the transfigured creature in the air, Petrouchka dies once more. The vitality of the faint humanity within him has been exhausted by this final gesture.

The critics were delighted with this production of *Petrouchka*. John Martin began his review in the *Times* (November 22, 1940) by stating flatly,

"Last night at the Fifty-First Street Theatre the Original Ballet Russe put on the best performance of *Petrushka* that has been seen in these parts for twenty-five years. Under the direction of its creator, Michel Fokine,

this modern classic assumed something of its true shape after many seasons of brutal treatment and quite justified the old balletomanes who have
stoutly maintained its greatness for a generation in spite of all the evidence.

"To say that last night's presentation did full justice to the work would
be to make false claims, for this is a work that demands genius from top
to bottom. There are no more Nijinskys, no more Imperial Ballets. There
are still, however, a Fokine, a masterpiece of the choreographic theatre and
plenty of talent and it is wonderful what results can be obtained from
such a combination.

"For the first time in many a year the opening scene with its crowds
of carnival merrymakers emerged from the department of utter confusion
and focussed the attention where it belonged. The final scene . . . built
steadily to a rousing climax and showed itself as an integrated dramatic
episode instead of a melange of milling about and minor interludes.

"The three chief characters, whose magnificently conceived styles one
had almost despaired of ever seeing again, took on individuality and importance, and their tragedy became a thing of emotion and suspense in its
inhibited puppet-like metier . . . these scenes took on a form and dramatic concentration they have long lacked."[1]

Less impressed by the solo performances than by the general effect,
Mr. Martin, with more than his customary sympathy for ballet (he
makes no secret of his preference for the "modern" dance), recognized the soundness and promise of the several interpretations. Indeed, for Toumanova (a dancer of extraordinary power when her
addiction to tours de force is held under by strict discipline) he had
nothing but praise. Yura Lazovsky, since given an opportunity to
grow into the difficult title role, has demonstrated that as Petrouchka
he is at least the equal of any contemporary dancer.

It is difficult to understand why Fokine, long a resident of New
York, had not been asked to supervise a production of *Petrouchka*
by any of the ballet companies that had been manhandling this great
dance drama for the previous six years. There had indeed been fine
individual performances of the solo roles—Danilova's Dancer, Massine's Petrouchka, and Franklin's Blackamoor come to mind. These
individual triumphs did not, however, atone for slovenly, spiritless
ensembles and careless productions.

When Ballet Theatre added *Petrouchka* to the repertoire in 1942,

---

[1] To demonstrate that this was not a minority report, the dance critic of the
Herald Tribune (the only New York daily except the *Times* that considers it worth
while to employ a dance critic) wrote: *"Petrouchka* has been given some downright
insulting productions in the past . . . under Fokine's personal supervision the work
emerged in all its brilliance and poignancy."

Michel Fokine directed the production, in which the title role was performed by Yura Lazovsky, then a member of Ballet Theatre. The cast also included Irina Baronova (Dancer), Richard Reed (Blackamoor), and Simon Semenoff (Charlatan). In this revival Yura Skibine made the Head Coachman a more than ordinarily interesting character, from both a dancing and an acting point of view.

Ballet Theatre also offered a performance of *Petrouchka* in which the four leading dancers were Americans—Lucia Chase (Dancer), Jerome Robbins (Petrouchka), Richard Reed (Blackamoor), and John Taras (Charlatan). Although the Dancer is an ungrateful role for Miss Chase, its staccato style emphasizing her lack of rhythmic continuity, the three male members of the group were beyond doubt equal to any European cast seen on the Metropolitan stage since 1917. Jerome Robbins's interpretation was a highly original one. His Petrouchka had shed some of its pathos for a spirit of protest. Where other Petrouchkas looked with sad submission at the pathetic rag-doll hands with which the malice or carelessness of the Charlatan has endowed him, Robbins's puppet had an angry bitterness that displayed nothing of resignation. There was little that was invertebrate about this Petrouchka. It was a new and fascinating revelation of a familiar character.

Choreographically, *Petrouchka* is designed in the freest possible style. The crowds behave as crowds do everywhere. Coachmen and nursemaids dance in the manner that their prototypes in real life might very well choose. Only the two street dancers perform *sur les pointes,* and that with stylized circus vulgarity. The movements of Petrouchka and the Blackamoor make little reference to the classic style. The Dancer displays all the clichés of the *danse d'école* performed in a delicately satirical manner, her *pas de deux* with the Blackamoor being the *reductio ad absurdum* of classicism. After seeing *Petrouchka,* and keeping in mind the fact that it has been performed by practically every important ballet company since 1911, one wonders what more the alleged reformers of ballet and exponents of freedom in the dance thought they could achieve. *Petrouchka* and *Les Sylphides,* in their highly various ways, are freer than anything produced by the insurgents, most of whose work is quite free from anything resembling a knowledge of dancing technique and theatrical quality.

The evolution of *Petrouchka* from a fantasy for piano and orchestra to the ballet score is an interesting one. Stravinsky has told the story in his autobiography.

"Before tackling *Sacre du Printemps* . . . I wanted to refresh myself by composing an orchestral piece in which the piano would play the most important part—a sort of *Konzertstück*. In composing the music, I had in mind a distinct picture of a puppet, suddenly endowed with life, exasperating the patience of the orchestra with diabolical cascades of arpeggios. The orchestra in turn retaliates with menacing trumpet blasts. The outcome is a terrific noise which reaches its climax and ends in the sorrowful and querulous collapse of the poor puppet. . . . I struggled for hours . . . to find a title that would express in a word the character of my music and, consequently, the personality of this creature.
"One day I leapt for joy. I had found my title—Petrouchka, the immortal and unhappy hero of every fair in all countries."

Diaghilev, delighted with the idea, persuaded Stravinsky to expand the idea into a ballet, and worked with him on details of the plot. Benois contributed dramatic ideas as well as the superb décor. The ballet was put into rehearsal with Vaslav Nijinsky as Petrouchka and Thamar Karsavina as the Dancer. The production reached the stage of the Théâtre du Chatelet, Paris, on June 13, 1911. Though it did not have the influence on the minor decorative arts that *Scheherazade* did, and the chic audience found nothing in it equivalent to the *frisson* produced by *L'Après-midi d'un Faune, Petrouchka* is a far more sound and enduring work of art, still holding a valid place in the repertoire.

The music of *Petrouchka* is unrivaled among twentieth-century ballet scores for popularity and influence. A suite arranged from the ballet is a staple of the concert hall. Countless modern composers have been inspired by it. The atmosphere of the carnival is evoked by the lusty rhythms of folk tunes. There is cynical comment on Petrouchka's woes and an occasional gleam of pity. Lush Oriental rhythms underline the passages for the Blackamoor. The delicate pizzicato for the Dancer at once proclaims her daintiness and complete lack of human warmth. After the boisterousness of the first carnival scene it would seem to be impossible for Stravinsky to go any further. And yet, incredibly, he does. The milling and confusion of the scene surge through the orchestra in waves of massive sound. An auditor who had never heard of the ballet would have small difficulty in imagining the crowded scene. The heavy brass chords that announce the Bear, the thudding of the Coachman's dance, the weird music for the maskers, and the thin piping of Petrouchka's triumph build up to an incomparable picture, painted in the colors of the orchestration.

Many famous dancers have interpreted the title role of *Petrouchka*: Vaslav Nijinsky (of him Beaumont says that his Petrouchka was "a puppet that sometimes aped a human being"), Adolph Bolm, Léonide Massine, Stanislas Idzikowsky, Nicholas Zverev, Léon Woizikowsky, Yurek Shabelevsky, Yura Lazovsky, and Jerome Robbins. The Dancer has enlisted the talents of Thamar Karsavina, Lydia Lopokova, Bronislava Nijinska, Lydia Sokolova, Rosina Galli, Alexandra Danilova, Alicia Markova, Irina Baronova, and Tamara Toumanova. The Blackamoor, created by Alexander Orlov and associated in this country with Adolph Bolm, has been performed by Giuseppe Bonfiglio, David Lichine, Frederic Franklin, André Eglevsky, and Richard Reed. The original Charlatan was Enrico Cecchetti. New York has seen Ottokar Bartik, Marian Ladre, Simon Semenoff, and John Taras.

Although more than thirty years have elapsed since *Petrouchka* was first performed, its position as one of the greatest of ballets remains unassailed. Its perfect fusion of music, choreography, and décor, and its theme—the timeless tragedy of the human spirit—unite to make its appeal universal.

PILLAR OF FIRE

Ballet by Antony Tudor; music by Arnold Schönberg ("Verklärte Nacht"); settings and costumes by Jo Mielziner.

PILLAR OF FIRE was given its world première by Ballet Theatre at the Metropolitan Opera House, New York, on April 8, 1942, with the following cast:

The Family			THE FRIEND	*Antony Tudor*
ELDEST SISTER	)(	*Lucia Chase*	THE YOUNG MAN from the House	
HAGAR	)(	*Nora Kaye*	Opposite	*Hugh Laing*
YOUNGEST SISTER	)(	*Annabelle Lyon*		

LOVERS-IN-INNOCENCE: *Maria Karnilova, Charles Dickson, Jean Davidson, John Kriza, Virginia Wilcox, Wallace Seibert, Jean Hunt, Barbara Fallis*

LOVERS-IN-EXPERIENCE: *Sono Osato, Rosella Hightower, Muriel Bentley, Jerome Robbins, Donald Saddler, Frank Hobi*

MAIDEN LADIES OUT WALKING: *Galina Razoumova and Rozsika Sabo*

◆◆◆◆◆◆◆◆◆◆◆◆◆◆◆◆◆

The time is the turn of the century; the place, an open space across which two houses face each other. As the curtains rise to the opening strains of the music, Hagar is seen sitting alone on the doorstep of the house on the right. It is early evening, and the gloom is lit only by the lights in the two houses. There is much coming and going of the young people of the neighborhood, their quiet companionship contrasting with Hagar's loneliness. The Maiden Ladies promenade, primly holding their trains. The Eldest Sister looks disapprovingly at Hagar, but is all affection to the Youngest Sister, obviously the Benjamin of the family. When the Friend appears, Hagar rises eagerly to meet him. He is intercepted and claimed by the Youngest Sister, who appears to regard Hagar's tense mood as an occasion for slightly malicious teasing. The Friend does not resist the flattering attentions of the Youngest Sister, but joins her in a walk. Hagar, left alone, reflects on her dismal lot. Her Eldest Sister, smug, old-maidish, and cold to everyone except her favorite sister, obviously expects Hagar to be content with the same dreary existence that she herself finds quite satisfactory. The Friend, who had given her some hope of escape, has been attracted to the superficial charm of the Youngest Sister, whose childish demeanor covers a grasping and malicious nature. Hagar, in her solitary meditations, is tormented by her active imagination. The walls of the house opposite become transparent to reveal the earthy love-making of its inhabitants. At once appalled and attracted, she falls a ready victim to the brutal seduction of one of the young men who live there. As she goes into his house with him, a group of men and women emerge. They are very different from the quiet boys and girls whose evening walk Hagar watched so enviously. The women are blowsy, with streaming hair and gaudily colored skirts, the men lusty and vulgar.

When Hagar leaves the strange house, she is overcome by a feel-ing of guilt. She has acquired experience, but no love or affection to fill the void in her life, or to palliate what her training and back-ground force her to consider as an irretrievable sin, even though she was driven to it by desperation. Faces that appear to accuse her are all around. Scorned by the members of her own society, she is rejected by the outcasts. The evening draws to a close. Her Youngest Sister returns with the Friend. Her Eldest Sister calls her family into the house, bidding a formal good-night to the Friend.

In a forest clearing, surrounded by great trees, Hagar sees all the inhabitants of her world—both her worlds—come and go. Again she meets the scorn of her sisters and the contempt of the slatterns. Making a feeble attempt to call back her seducer, she is crushed by his non-recognition. When the Friend appears, she runs from him in shame and terror, to be caught and held with understanding gentle-ness. Together they walk into the forest, Hagar's troubled soul at peace at last in his love and companionship.

Pillar of Fire is Antony Tudor's unquestioned masterpiece. Not a case history like *Undertow,* nor a delicate evocation of drama in high society as in *Jardin aux Lilas,* it is a painting, in dramatic chiaroscuro, of the tragedy of the tormented soul of an individual. Hagar is as real as the girl next door, and her tragedy is no period piece. It arises out of bitter frustration and desperation—emotions felt by al-most every human being to a greater or less degree, and therefore universally understood. There is a moral lurking behind the story: sexual experience alone will never bring surcease to the loneliness of the unloved.

Hagar is an individual, but she is not the only character with dimensions in this ballet. The Eldest Sister unfortunately belongs to no time or place but may be encountered everywhere. She is prim and of her period, in high collar, leg-o'-mutton sleeves, and train, but her arid philosophy also finds refuge under a dress bought yesterday at Macy's and worn self-righteously to Red Cross or P. T. A. meeting. Not necessarily a spinster, she can cast her blight over her children as well as over her sisters.

The Youngest Sister is the archetype of the petted, pampered brat grown to thoroughly unpleasant young girlhood. With carefully camouflaged malice, she goes through life making it hell for the sensitive neurotic whose miseries are none the less real for being occasionally auto-induced.

These two women are so real that one can become indignant about them—a rare reaction to characters in a ballet.

The Young Man is a simple child of nature, his evil quality being as absolute as the holiness of a saint, and about as accidental. In spite of the strong dramatic projection of the role, built up with a wealth of colloquial gesture, he remains a symbol rather than a real person.

The groups of innocent and experienced lovers are the Greek chorus who comment on events as they happen. The good boys and girls are grave, gentle, and shadowy. As in real life, the sinners are far more interesting and vivid.

Choreographically, *Pillar of Fire* is stated in Antony Tudor's highly individual adaptation of classical technique. There is little that can be named in the terminology of the classroom, all the steps being performed with characteristic modifications. Movements from everyday life are introduced with dramatic impact: the Young Man's removal of his coat; the way he flexes his legs; Hagar's pull at her high collar, and her anxious fussing with her braids; the prim lift of the train, characteristic of the Eldest Sister; the blowsy girl's drag at her shoulder strap. All these gestures, introduced quite realistically without any attempt at ballet stylization, tell volumes about the characters who perform them. The Lovers-in-Innocence are seen in more or less classical terms: at their first entrance the boys perform double *tours en l'air;* in the second scene the girls travel in *bourrées*.

There are two *pas de deux* for Hagar, the first with the Young Man, the second with the Friend. The first of these is really spectacular and includes a brilliant lift that is an expansion of the supported *grand jeté*. In classical ballet the cavalier supported the ballerina around her waist.[1] In *Pillar of Fire,* Hagar is caught by the inside of the thigh and held high in the air, her arms being in fifth position *en haut.* The *pas de deux* is fast and daringly acrobatic, at times appearing to draw its inspiration—undoubtedly dramatically appropriate—from an apache dance. The second *pas de deux,* gentler in character, includes strange, almost inverted poses, symbolic of Hagar's mental conflict and abased mood. There is an incident in the second scene when one of the Lovers-in-Experience does a slow *développé à la seconde* and, while holding the pose, is slowly turned to face her partner. It is a noble movement, and probably indicates that earthy love also has its moments of grandeur. When Hagar, in this scene, moves from group to group, seeking a friendly face, she does so by means of single *sauts de basque.* The classic base of Tudor's vocabulary of movement is at all times evident, though it would probably have puzzled Petipa to find the words in the terminology of the *danse d'école* to describe the steps.

Nora Kaye, as Hagar, gives a performance that has become a legend in the dance theater, even while the ballet still forms a very active part of an active repertoire. In *Pillar of Fire* her intensity and tragic earnestness tear at the heartstrings of the least impressionable member of the audience. Never for a moment does she forget the characterization; the most difficult step, the most complicated lift, are an integral part of the drama, and technical difficulties are never allowed to deflect the mood. She moves through the ballet in a controlled, dedicated frenzy, for which there is only one parallel in the theater—Rose Pauly's interpretation of Electra. Until the première of *Pillar of Fire,* Nora Kaye was one of a group of talented young dancers. At that performance a great dramatic ballerina was revealed to the ballet audience. It is gratifying to realize that she is the product of American ballet schools and learned her stagecraft in a predominantly American ballet company. Her unquestioned status as bal-

[1] Part of the new freedom introduced into ballet by Fokine was the breaking down of the proprieties formerly observed in the classical ballet. In a *pas de deux* it was permissable to support the ballerina only by the hand or arm, and waist. She might also be carried on her partner's shoulder. A lift like the one in *Pillar of Fire* would probably have caused a stampede from the theater in 1890.

lerina is honestly earned—not the result of press-agentry, influence, or managerial whims.

Lucia Chase, in the Eldest Sister, has one of her finest roles, ranking with her Minerva in *The Judgment of Paris*.

No one has realized all the implications in the character of the Youngest Sister since Annabelle Lyon left Ballet Theatre. Lyon had the proper amount of surface charm, through which the subtle malice of the true nature appeared. Her successors—Jean Hunt and Janet Reed—are far too sweet. As performed by them, the Youngest Sister's actions appear to be the result of childish heedlessness rather than the calculated mischief intended by the choreographer. *Pillar of Fire* is one of the infinitesimal number of ballets in which the dramatis personæ may be imagined as having a future. Annabelle Lyon's Youngest Sister was undoubtedly an incipient hellion, and one was even more pleased to see Hagar escape from her than from the more direct Eldest Sister. Lately this point in the drama has become invalidated by the more conventionally sweet childishness of Lyon's successors.

Hugh Laing as the Young Man projected a dark, subtly brutal earthiness that made a sharp contrast to Antony Tudor's Friend. There are many times when Laing is called upon to make a dramatic point without the aid of dancing steps or stylized movements—at one point simply by walking across the stage. Only Massine, in the contemporary dance theater, has equaled this characterization for intensity of personal projection.

Sono Osato as a Lover-in-Experience gave an outstanding performance, missing no angle of the character. She managed to look blowsy, with a stylized sluttishness that was real without being realistic. She was sorely missed in the role until the versatile Alicia Alonso was assigned to it.

The décor in the first scene is a perfect background for the brooding intensity of the ballet. The costumes of the Family and their friends reproduce the styles of the period, modified where necessary to meet the requirements of dancing. The dresses of the female Lovers-in-Experience add a note of strong color to the *mise en scène* —deep, rich reds and purples. These costumes were cleverly designed to indicate a sort of decorative sluttishness—skirts suggesting the flounced silk petticoats popular at the turn of the century, worn with white tops that looked like corsets and camisoles. The loose hair and dishabille contrasted sharply with the wrenlike neatness and meek grays and browns of the dresses worn by their good-girl counterparts.

The second scene, following the first without interruption, was less striking in its décor. It must be said that the ending, with the lovers walking up a ramp into a spotlight, has a touch of Hollywood about it. There is a well-founded rumor that the choreographer had other ideas, and was forced to compromise on the customary grounds of economy.

The critics who enjoy quibbling about even the finest ballets were unable to raise a single dissent, in the face of the really overwhelming ovation that greeted the première of *Pillar of Fire*. There were at least twenty-six authentic curtain calls.[2] The clamor might have gone on for the rest of the evening except for the fact that there were two more ballets on the program. The *Times* called it "a tremendous achievement," and the *Herald Tribune* said: "Superlatives are inadequate in describing this ballet, for its tremendous dramatic power results from that rare and perfect fusion of inspired artistry and knowing craftsmanship."

When Arnold Schönberg composed *Verklärte Nacht,* he had in mind a definite program, based on a poem by Richard Dehmel, whose romantic, sometimes erotic poetry has an attraction for composers, several of whom have set his lyrics to music. The poem *Verklärte Nacht* tells of the agony of a woman who confesses her unfaithfulness to the man she loves. He comforts her, reassures her of his love and protection, and together they walk in the transfigured night. Antony Tudor's program for *Pillar of Fire* grew out of this poem, preserving the basic idea, while expanding it to allow a variety of characters and incidents. At no time is the prevailing spirit of the ballet at odds with the mood of the music. No more perfect fusion of music and choreography exists in the entire range of ballet. Schönberg set his seal of approval on the work, by conducting a performance during a west-coast season of Ballet Theatre.

Pillar of Fire has a weakness that is shared by other modern dance dramas. The leading role is so closely identified with its creator that the imagination quails at the task of recasting it. Other roles in the

[2] As opposed to the kind when a few relatives and friends of the ballerina (usually a guest artist with little appeal to the real ballet audience) try to make as much noise as an honestly enthusiastic audience.

ballet have been performed more or less adequately by substitutes. Choosing a new Hagar is a mental puzzle that might well be substituted by ballet-loving insomniacs for the traditional sheep-counting. It is scarcely a soporific, but will undoubtedly serve to pass the time.

Pillar of Fire continues to be an active part of Ballet Theatre's repertoire. Its drama and intensity have not been surpassed in any branch of the contemporary dance theater.

A note on the performance given by Ballet Theatre at the Metropolitan Opera House, New York, on April 8, 1942:

Anyone who was fortunate enough to be present at the opening performance of *Pillar of Fire* saw not only the unveiling of a masterpiece, but the high point of the renaissance of ballet in New York. There can exist in the annals of the New York stage few such exhilarating occasions. The program opened with *Swan Lake,* danced by Alicia Markova. Sometimes the habit of using the classics for warming up results in a spiritless performance, but this was one of those magic evenings when nothing could go wrong. *Pillar of Fire* came next, to be greeted by thunderous applause that would have toppled on its foundations any Broadway theater (where six tepid curtain calls rate a mention in *Variety* of a terrific ovation). When the riot was quelled by a firm refusal to raise the curtain for the twenty-seventh time, it did not seem possible that the rest of the evening could be anything but an anticlimax. However, that enchanting choreographic joke *Pas de Quatre,* superbly performed by Alicia Markova, Karen Conrad, Rosella Hightower, and Annabelle Lyon, brought just the proper note of contrast. *Princess Aurora,* the concluding ballet, found Baronova at the top of her form. Partnered by Yura Skibine, she gave a fine interpretation of the title role. To add to the already overflowing measure, there was Ian Gibson, superlative Bluebird, whose soaring flights brought gasps of amazement from the audience. A new "Ah, but—" school was born on the spot. Ballet Theatre's inability (due not only to war-time exigencies, but to other and more remediable causes) to hold a fine company together offers no immediate prospect of another such truly gala performance.

PRINCE IGOR

PRINCE IGOR (the *Polovtsian Dances* from Act II of Alexander Borodin's opera *Prince Igor*) was arranged by Michel Fokine for the first season of the Diaghilev Ballet in Paris. The dances were not presented out of their context, as is the current practice, but as an opera-ballet with the accompanying choruses. *Prince Igor,* given for the first time at the Théâtre du Chatelet, Paris, on May 19, 1909, proved to be one of the most sensational features of the repertoire. The cast included Sophie Fedorova (a Polovtsian Girl), Helen Smirnova (a Polovtsian Woman), and Adolph Bolm (a Polovtsian Warrior).

The Paris audience was completely bowled over by the first performance, which Haskell says was "the undoubted success of the season." Ballet in Paris had descended from its high estate. The classic perfection of the eighteenth century had hardened into static formulas. The only legacy remaining from the romantic revival of the early nineteenth century was the lost prestige of the male dancer, who had degenerated into a mere *porteur* for the ballerina, tolerated because necessary. The corps de ballet had become a background, grouped decoratively to take the empty look off the stage while the star performed. *Prince Igor,* with its ensemble of male dancers, each one able to perform feats of incredible virtuosity, was something so entirely new that there was not even a tradition in French ballet to make it imaginable. It is not to be wondered at that it was received with tumultuous acclaim, which contemporary memoirs have built up into a legend.

Prince Igor has a plot only in relation to the story of the opera. The dances in Act II are commanded by the Polovtsian Chief for the entertainment of the captive Prince Igor, with whom he wishes to make a peace treaty. The dances are a kind of competition in which seasoned warriors vie with the boys of the camp, the women with the young girls. It ends with a mass of madly leaping figures, the men tossing bows in the air. When performed with the necessary savage energy, it can be thrilling, music, décor, and choreography uniting to produce an overwhelming effect.

New York first heard the choruses and dances from *Prince Igor* performed in concert, by the MacDowell Chorus and the Philharmonic Orchestra, under the direction of Kurt Schindler, on March 3, 1911. When the Metropolitan Opera, inspired by the success of *Boris Godunov,* wished to add another Russian opera to the repertoire, *Prince Igor* was chosen. It was prepared by Toscanini, who, however, had left the Metropolitan by the time the opera was produced. The first performance took place on December 30, 1915, under the direction of Giorgio Polacco. The ballet (called on the program "incidental Tartar ballet") was arranged by Ottokar Bartik, and if the critic of the *Times* may be trusted, it compared favorably with the later presentation by the Diaghilev company.

The ballet was performed by Rosina Galli, Giuseppe Bonfiglio, sixteen Tartar male dancers, and the entire corps de ballet.

The sequence of the dances is as follows:

1. Polovets Dance—The corps de ballet.

2. Kingdal (Sword) Dance—Tartar male dancers.

3. Uzundara Dance—Rosina Galli, Giuseppe Bonfiglio, and the Tartar male dancers.

4. Tartar Ballabile[1]—Rosina Galli, Giuseppe Bonfiglio, Tartar male dancers, and corps de ballet.

Prince Igor was first performed in the United States with Fokine's choreography by the Diaghilev Ballet, at the Century Theater, New York, on January 18, 1916. The cast included Lubov Tchernicheva, Sophie Pflanz, and Adolph Bolm. This production lacked the element of surprise, New York having seen the Metropolitan performance less than a month previously. The *Times* critic said in part:

"The dances of Mlles. Tchernikowa[2] and Pflanz, and of M. Bolm, as well as those of the various groups into which the subordinate members of the ballet were divided, were spirited and pictorial. It was not overpowering, however, perhaps because advance laudation had built up an imaginary picture impossible to be lived up to. In fact, the recent production at the Metropolitan, though inferior as to setting and costuming had more real

---

[1] *Ballabile,* a term used in classical ballet, is applied to the evolutions of the corps de ballet (usually, though not always, in waltz time), the purpose of which is to permit the ballerina to rest, or change her shoes or costume. An example is the "Sweet Rosy O'Grady" number in *Swan Lake. Ballabile* seems rather a mellifluous word to apply to the savage goings-on in *Prince Igor.*

[2] New York knows her better as Tchernicheva.

thrill in its savagery than this one, especially to the extent it was provided there by individual dancers and their contrast with the group work." [3]

At the Metropolitan, *Prince Igor* was given nine times in three seasons. The ballet made sporadic appearances during the twenties, several times under the direction of Adolph Bolm.

Colonel W. de Basil's Ballet Russe presented *Prince Igor* (in strict ballet form, without the accompanying choruses) in its first American season. It was performed for the first time at the St. James Theater, New York, on January 10, 1934. The cast included Leon Woizikowsky (Polovtsian Warrior), Tamara Grigorieva (then known as Sidorenko), and Tamara Toumánova. It was given no less than forty times that season, in New York and on tour.

After the departure from the company of Leon Woizikowsky, whom Beaumont considers one of the two outstanding interpreters of the Polovtsian Warrior, the other being Adolph Bolm, the role was performed by David Lichine and Yurek Shabelevsky. Lichine's performances were scarcely memorable, but Shabelevsky was a worthy successor to Woizikowsky. His interpretation had a sinister, savage quality, which, allied to a superb dancing technique, resulted in a performance that lived up to the best traditions of the role and added some new ones. Toumanova, who was not happy as the Polovtsian Girl, was replaced by Vera Nelidova, a dancer with remarkable elevation. These fine performers brought a certain vitality to a ballet that had become a dusty souvenir of a past era.

Ballet companies seem reluctant to drop *Prince Igor* from the repertoire. After all, it is a good concluding number, the curtain descending on a stage full of whirling figures, which theoretically sends the audience home in an exhilarated frame of mind. Actually, most performances of *Prince Igor* as currently presented are depressants, but the theory is a good one and managers cling to it. Therefore it was not surprising to find *Prince Igor* among the offerings of the Ballet Russe de Monte Carlo. It was given by this company for the first time at the Metropolitan Opera House on October 19, 1938. The

[3] This review would have been instructive for the "Ah, but—" school of self-appointed critics who used to be quite vocal in the lobbies during intermissions at the beginning of the current revival of ballet in America. According to this select group, anyone who had not been present at the 1916-17 Diaghilev season in this country had no idea of what ballet or dancing could be. A little research among newspaper critiques of the period provided a number of answers to these rhapsodists.

cast was led by Frederic Franklin (Polovtsian Warrior), Jeanette
Lauret (Polovtsian Woman), and Lubov Roudenko (Polovtsian
Girl). This performance was no worse than some that had pre-
ceded it.

The décor of the Diaghilev production of *Prince Igor* by Nicholas
Roerich was a remarkable picture of the primitive camp of a nomadic
tribe. This, somewhat the worse for its long service in the theater,
was used by the de Basil company. The Monte Carlo Ballet had a
setting by Constantin Korovine, which differed little from the familiar Roerich backdrop. The new costumes, particularly those of the
women slaves, were a novel note. The de Basil slaves were dressed in
identical short skirts and brassières of orange red. The Monte Carlo
group wore individually designed costumes with many strings of
beads and bracelets, while the Polovtsian Woman glittered in cloth
of silver. All together, they livened up the scene considerably.

Prince Igor, except when performed as part of the opera, has become a period piece. No one is particularly interested in it, and it
receives perfunctory performances. The sensation of 1909 is a profound bore today. It should not be performed at all unless it can be
produced in a manner commensurate with its importance as one of
the first ballets with a sound ethnographic background. Otherwise
it had better be shelved, thus allowing the historically minded members of the audience to keep their illusions.

The performances of *Prince Igor* offered by the Original Ballet
Russe at the Metropolitan Opera House during its 1946 season did
nothing to change these opinions. We have seen more savage abandon at a Sunday School picnic than the Tartar warriors exhibited.

THE PRODIGAL SON

The Prodigal Son (Le Fils Prodigue): scenes in three tableaux by Boris Kochno; music by Sergei Prokofiev; choreography by David Lichine; scenery and costumes by Georges Rouault.

THE PRODIGAL SON was first presented by the Original Ballet Russe at the Theatre Royal, Sydney, Australia, on December 30, 1938. The first New York performance took place at the Fifty-first Street Theater on November 26, 1940, with the following cast:

THE PRODIGAL SON	*David Lichine*	THE COMPANIONS of the Prodigal Son	
THE FATHER	*Dimitri Rostoff*	*Boris Belsky, Lorand Andahazy*	
THE SIREN	*Sono Osato*	THE VAGABOND	*Alberto Alonso*
THE SISTERS of the Prodigal Son			
Ludmilla Lvova, Sonia Orlova			

Friends of the Prodigal Son

Scene 1. The Prodigal Son's character is established as that of a youth whose strongest desire is to please. He does not really wish to hurt his Father or his two devoted Sisters, but the persuasions of his Companions induce him to leave his quiet home for a more lively scene.

Scene 2. The Prodigal Son and his Companions come to an inn. The people there, learning that he has gold, plot to get it away from him. The Siren is brought in, borne high on a shield. She wears a long train, which is carried by the Vagabond. The shield is lowered; the Siren steps down and detaches her train. She begins a dance of seduction, designed to woo the Prodigal Son's gold from his pockets. In a detached manner, she exhibits her array of charms and gives him wine to drink. The gold is not produced quickly enough for the bystanders. Seizing the Prodigal Son, they shake him until the gold runs from his clothing. Removing his festive garments, they cast him aside and turn their attention to the Siren, whose cold sensuality has aroused their passions. They sweep over her like a forest fire, while the Vagabond capers madly. They carry her away. The Prodigal Son is left with the chill aftermath of debauchery in which he has lost all and gained not even a momentary pleasure.

Scene 3. The Father and the Sisters grieve for the absent one. The Sisters keep watch and when they see him coming, go to meet him. The Prodigal Son cowers before his Father's approach. The Father with a tender gesture covers him with his cloak and carries him into the house.

The Prodigal Son was originally produced by the Diaghilev Ballet at the Théâtre Sarah-Bernhardt, in Paris, on May 21, 1929. This version had choreography by George Balanchine. The cast, headed by Felia Doubrovska (the Siren) and Serge Lifar (the Prodigal Son), included Anton Dolin and Leon Woizikowsky. The Prokofiev score and the Rouault décor were commissioned by Serge Diaghilev for this production. It was one of the last offerings in the last season of the Diaghilev Ballet's existence.

The revival of *The Prodigal Son* was entrusted to Lichine, who is said not to have seen the ballet in its first form. In any appraisal of works produced during the current renascence of ballet in the United States, *The Prodigal Son* would stand close to *Pillar of Fire* as a work of art. Its adult psychology and the absence of choreographic clichés are not easily paralleled in a *ballet d'action* except possibly in *Billy the Kid,* though the latter was flawed by a confused plot. In ballet no one should have to read program notes to understand what the action is meant to depict. *The Prodigal Son* had this desirable clarity to a marked degree. In fact there were events on the stage that could not have been put into words at all in the modern theater and that needed no words to explain them.

The opening and closing scenes in *The Prodigal Son* were mimed with touching simplicity, the choreographic ingenuities being reserved for the scenes in the inn. The entrance of the Siren was spectacular, but was merely a preliminary to several groups that, far from being simply decorative as in the classic or even the modern symphonic ballets, had a definite functional purpose. The most memorable of these was that when the Siren at the apex of a pyramid poured wine down a pipeline formed of human hands into the mouth of the Prodigal Son, who was seated on the ground at the base. There was a dramatic moment when the limp body of the Prodigal was hoisted high in the air and shaken until gold rolled in all directions.

The performance of the entire group of dancers in *The Prodigal Son* was outstanding. The miming of Dimitri Rostoff as the Father, stern at first, tender and protective in the last scene, was profoundly touching. It is difficult to forget the beautiful gesture with which he lifted the abject Prodigal and covered him with his cloak. Every member of the corps de ballet performed difficult evolutions precisely, yet spontaneously.

In the Siren, Sono Osato had the most important and the finest role of her career. Her exotic beauty and elegance of line were admirably displayed by the revealing costume, and her dancing gave promise of a great career in ballet. That this did not eventuate is no fault of Osato's. Overlooked and neglected by choreographers, who had a pearl for their use, she has turned to musical comedy—a bitter loss to ballet, where fine technicians with both personality and the power to project it are rare indeed. A genuine American ballerina was lost to ballet, where, in spite of press agents and personal cults, few true American ballerinas exist.

David Lichine gave a very fine performance as the Prodigal Son,[1] a role created by Anton Dolin. For Lichine this ballet was a threefold triumph, as choreographer, actor, and dancer. It is difficult to believe that the banal line routines of *Helen of Troy*[2] could have emerged from the same brain.

The score by Sergei Prokofiev was spare and lean, in a mood similar to that of the music for the movie *Alexander Nevsky*. Possibly it might have seemed less impressive in the concert hall, but for *The Prodigal Son* it was ideal.

The décor by Georges Rouault had the dark rich tones and simple masses of early stained glass. This illusion was intensified by the heavy black lines suggesting leading in both sets and costumes.

The Prodigal Son was one of those fortunate enterprises in which music unites with décor and choreography, all subservient to one purpose—the creation of a complete and balanced work of art.

[1] In the Balanchine version of *The Prodigal Son* this was Serge Lifar's role. Many purple passages have been written about his wonderful interpretation. Be that as it may, nothing that Lifar vouchsafed to his audiences in America left the smallest impression that he could act or dance save in an unintentionally comic manner.

[2] A contentious New York daily newspaper justified its dull existence by heading a review of *Helen of Troy* with "Once Too Offenbach."

RODEO

Rodeo, or The Courting at Burnt Ranch, by Agnes De Mille; music by
Aaron Copland; scenery by Oliver Smith; costumes by Kermit Love.

RODEO was performed by the Ballet Russe de Monte Carlo at
the Metropolitan Opera House, New York, on October 16, 1942, with
the following cast:

THE HEAD WRANGLER	THE COWGIRL	*Agnes De Mille*
Casimir Kokitch	THE RANCHER'S DAUGHTER	
THE CHAMPION ROPER		*Mlada Miladova*
Frederic Franklin	THE CALLER	*Anton Vlassoff*

Easterners from Kansas City, Cowhands, Womenfolk

◇◇◇◇◇◇◇◇◇◇◇◇◇◇◇◇◇◇◇

Scene 1. Rodeo: Saturday afternoon. The Corral. The cowhands
have gathered for their weekly rodeo, their customary Saturday
afternoon recreation. Their display of riding and roping is con-
tinually being interrupted by the efforts of the Cowgirl to equal or
even surpass the men at their games. This shocks the Rancher's
Daughter, who has come out to watch the fun with her Eastern
friends from Kansas City, and incidentally flirt with the Head
Wrangler. The Cowgirl also admires the Head Wrangler, though it
is obvious that her hoydenish ways can offer no competition to the
feminine charm of the Rancher's Daughter.

The rodeo over, the girls walk together in the early evening. The
Cowgirl has no friends—her tomboy behavior makes her unaccept-
able to the womenfolk and does not endear her to the men. Her
efforts to attract companionship are overlooked or brushed aside.

Interlude. Retrospect. A running square dance is performed to the
rhythms of clapped hands.

Scene 2. Ranch House: Saturday night dance. A tinny piano plays
for the dance that is going on inside the ranch house. The Cowgirl,
not yet recovered from the depression of the afternoon, sits on a
bench. She is still dressed in the pants and red shirt that she wore at
the rodeo. Keeping her company, and equally lost in gloom, is the

Champion Roper, who has an eye on the Rancher's Daughter. Up to now he has had no success with her, as she is attracted by the Head Wrangler.

There is much flitting backwards and forwards on the part of the girls, sometimes followed by the men. The Champion Roper, who has troubles of his own, tries to cheer the Cowgirl and tidy her up a bit. When the dancers transfer their activities to this part of the house, she is ignored and fails to get a partner. She disappears, not missed by anyone.

The dancing continues, Head Wrangler and Champion Roper competing for the favors of the Rancher's Daughter. Suddenly the Cowgirl reappears. Her entrance causes a sensation. She is neatly dressed in gay blue and yellow, her hair tied with a large bow. She is embarrassed by the stares, not all hostile, and tries to hitch up her pants. With a determined effort she advances to take her place among the dancers. As it is quite evident that she is as attractive as any girl present, besides possessing the charm of novelty, she has no lack of willing partners. Wrangler and Roper vie for the privilege of dancing with her. She is torn between the two, deciding in favor of the Roper, whose attitude of fellow sufferer has abruptly changed to that of would-be lover.

Rodeo is a genuine contribution to American ballet. It has reached a wider audience than *Filling Station*. Its uncomplicated plot and straightforward presentation make it easier to follow than *Billy the Kid*. No program notes need be read for a perfect understanding of *Rodeo*. Girl gets boy is the easiest story in the world to grasp, with or without words.

Choreographically, *Rodeo* owes much to *Billy the Kid,* notably an adaptation of Eugene Loring's processional style in the evening stroll that brings the first scene to a close, as well as in the riding and roping pantomime. More important original elements include the characteristic running square dance, a lively Western version of the more leisurely square dance performed in Southern and Eastern states. Agnes De Mille's close observation of colloquial gesture joins ballet steps and lifts to produce movement that is varied and at all times interesting. *Rodeo* is not an adaptation of musical comedy or a photographic reproduction of a country dance. It is a genuine ballet, using folk dance in the spirit in which it was used by classical choreographers, the difference being that this material happens to be American.

The settings by Oliver Smith form a perfect background for the action of the ballet, suggesting the illimitable space and flat horizon of the ranch country. The men's costumes are more successful than those of the women. The latter belong to no identifiable period and are sloppy and unbecoming.

The music by Aaron Copland is rhythmic and its skillful use of Western melodies and dance tunes would provoke nostalgia in an audience that had never been west of Weehawken. Composed especially for *Rodeo,* it may well live long after the ballet has been forgotten.

When Agnes De Mille produced *Rodeo* for the Ballet Russe de Monte Carlo, she was called upon to work with a veritable league of nationalities. Frederic Franklin's Champion Roper and Casimir Kokitch's Head Wrangler were entirely successful in spite of the fact that both of these dancers learned their art far from the United States —a tribute to the catholic character and application of a sound ballet technique. Agnes De Mille, creator of the Cowgirl, relinquished this role to Lubov Roudenko, in whose hands the characterization did not suffer. In fact, Roudenko gave a more restrained performance, which fitted neatly into the framework of the ballet and held no lingering atmosphere of the personal projection of the dance recital —Agnes De Mille's more usual métier.

Currently *Rodeo* is suffering from careless performances. The pantomime has become broad and obvious and the patterns blurred. The principal roles have been assigned to dancers lacking in authority and stage presence. *Rodeo* is too valuable a part of the truly American contribution to ballet repertoire to be allowed to fall into desuetude.

ROMEO AND JULIET

The Tragedy of Romeo and Juliet: narrative ballet in one act by Antony Tudor, based on the play by William Shakespeare; music by Frederick Delius; scenery and costumes by Eugène Berman.

ROMEO AND JULIET was presented by Ballet Theatre in a partial performance on April 6, 1942. Later in the week, on April 10, it was given in its entirety. Both performances took place at the Metropolitan Opera House, New York, with the following cast:

Heads of two houses at variance with each other:

MONTAGUE) (*Borislav Runanine*
CAPULET) (*John Taras*
ROMEO, son to Montague
     Hugh Laing
MERCUTIO, friend to Romeo
     Nicolas Orloff
BENVOLIO *Jerome Robbins*
TYBALT, nephew to Lady Capulet
     Antony Tudor

FRIAR LAURENCE *Dimitri Romanoff*
PARIS, a young nobleman
     Richard Reed
LADY MONTAGUE *Miriam Golden*
LADY CAPULET *Galina Razoumova*
JULIET, daughter to Capulet
     Alicia Markova
ROSALINE *Sono Osato*

KINSMEN OF THE MONTAGUES: *Hubert Bland, Rex Cooper, Stanley Herbertt*
KINSMEN OF THE CAPULETS: *John Kriza, Donald Saddler, Michael Kidd, Robert Lindgren, John Duane*
LADIES AT THE BALL: *Muriel Bentley, Jean Davidson, Virginia Wilcox, Mimi Gomber, Rozsika Sabo, Shirley Eckl, Barbara Fallis, Albia Kavan, Georgia Hiden*
TOWNSPEOPLE: *Rosella Hightower, Borislav Runanine, Nicolas Vassilief, June Morris, Hilda Wagner*
THE ATTENDANTS: *Jean Hunt, Billie Wynn*

◈◈◈◈◈◈◈◈◈◈◈◈◈◈◈◈

(Each paragraph in the following narrative corresponds to a scene in the ballet, which is presented without pauses.)

The action begins on the forepart of the stage, when Romeo enters, followed by Rosaline. This lady, cold and beautiful, parries Romeo's caresses, ostentatiously smoothing her hair and dress as she does so. She vanishes through the curtained doorway. Romeo lingers for a moment, stamps his foot petulantly, and follows her.

The rival factions, the Montagues, led by Mercutio, and the Capulets, led by Tybalt, enter from opposite sides of the stage. An angry demonstration is prevented from becoming open violence by the appearance of the heads of the opposing clans with their ladies. Their followers, only slightly subdued, are persuaded to depart.

Romeo and Mercutio linger behind, to encounter Rosaline, who beckons them to follow her.

A ball is in progress in the house of the Capulets, ladies and gentlemen moving through the measures of a stately dance. Capulet and his wife enter accompanied by Paris, whom they have in mind as a suitable husband for their daughter, Juliet. Accompanied by her Nurse, Juliet appears. Her father wishes to present Paris to her, but ignoring him, she runs to Tybalt, who persuades her to accept Paris as her partner in the dance. Romeo, present with Mercutio and his friends, is greatly moved by Juliet's beauty. He also joins the dance, maneuvering so that he stands next to her in the chain of dancers. As it proceeds on its formal rounds, he is eventually able to take her hand. Juliet, becoming aware of Romeo, has no eyes for anyone else. At the end of the dance the guests go to the banquet hall. Juliet eludes them and is at once claimed by Romeo. They are alone until Tybalt notices her absence. Returning for her, he finds her with a son of the hated Montague. At once the thinly veiled hostility breaks out anew. Romeo and his friends are compelled to leave the ball to avoid open conflict.

Night has fallen. Romeo and Mercutio, accompanied by their friends carrying torches, linger in the orchard of the Capulets. Mercutio holds forth at some length on the beauty of the night. Eventually they go on their way without Romeo, who loses himself in the darkness.

Two of the young guests emerge from the house, to vanish into the shadows after a tender scene. Juliet, on the balcony of her room, sees Romeo in the garden below. Twice their communion is interrupted: the Nurse comes out for a breath of air, yawning and rubbing her back; Tybalt and Paris walk through the garden talking of some grave matter. Romeo is forced to leave, but not before he has received Juliet's promise to meet him at Friar Laurence's cell.

Romeo arrives at the friar's cell. His impatience is evident in his nervous pacing and anxious appeals to the monk. When Juliet ar-

rives, he rushes to meet her. His ardor is restrained by the friar until
their betrothal is blessed by the proper forms of the church. They
part after a prolonged embrace. Juliet leaves, engaging to communi-
cate with him by the Nurse, who is waiting for her.

A street crowded with members of the rival parties, townspeople,
and an occasional beggar becomes the scene of horseplay, then of
disorder. First the minor members of the clans, then Tybalt and
Mercutio are involved. Romeo coming on the scene, still in a happy
daze from his meeting with Juliet, desires nothing but peace. Unfortunately, his effort at interference enables Tybalt to catch Mercutio off his guard and kill him. Tybalt prudently slips away. A girl
who had loved Mercutio trips in, quite unconscious of the events in
progress. The sight of Mercutio dead stops her gay approach. As she
collapses on her dead lover's body, Romeo, maddened by the sight
of her grief, forgets his hopes of peace and starts for Tybalt, who has
reappeared. They fight it out while their respective factions look on.
Romeo kills Tybalt, first knocking him down, then stabbing him in
the back. Romeo is urged by his friends to take flight, but he is reluctant to leave without the promised word from Juliet. Juliet and
her Nurse, on their way home, come upon the body of Tybalt.
Grieved for the loss of a kinsman, Juliet nevertheless remembers to
send the Nurse to Romeo with a token. The bodies are removed from
the scene of the carnage. Beggars and townspeople venture out of the
corners where they have taken refuge.

The first rays of the rising sun illuminating Juliet's room have
awakened her. Romeo is still asleep, and shortly he, too, awakens to
the realization that not only must he leave Juliet, but as an outlaw
he must leave his native city as well. After a tender scene he says
farewell to her, fearing to look back as he goes lest his resolution
weaken.

Lady Capulet and the Nurse come to awaken Juliet. In a moment
or two they are followed by a group of young girls and Capulet himself. This is to be the day of Juliet's wedding to Paris, hastened because of the disturbed state of the city, and her father has come to
make the announcement himself. Numb with misery and shock,
Juliet allows herself to be arrayed in bridal attire by the attending
girls. Friar Laurence, hovering anxiously, tries to reassure her. Seizing a moment when they are unobserved by Juliet's parents, who

have gone to conduct Paris to meet his bride, he gives Juliet a vial, telling her to drink the drug it contains. Juliet in her desperation swallows the drug, falling senseless just as the bridegroom enters.

Before a frieze of mourning figures Juliet's bier is carried high on the shoulders of the Capulets. Father, mother, and bridegroom follow. Romeo comes in and, seeing the funeral cortege, dashes madly away.

Juliet is seen lying on her tomb in the Capulet vault. Sunk in grief, Romeo enters. Sorrowfully he looks at his dead beloved and takes poison. The effect of the drug that Juliet has taken begins to wear off. She stirs, awakens, and, catching sight of Romeo, turns to him joyfully. He can scarcely believe his eyes on seeing her living, and his joy meets hers until a poison-induced paroxysm seizes him. He takes her place on the tomb. As the full realization of what has happened dawns on Juliet, she stabs herself with Romeo's dagger.

The mourning parents are seen grouped on either side of the tomb, reconciled by the bitter sorrow they share.

The tragic story of *Romeo and Juliet* has had much attention from musicians. At least seven operas are based on it, one an ambitious attempt by an English composer named Barkworth to set the entire text of Shakespeare's play.[1] Berlioz and Tchaikovsky have used the plot for a dramatic symphony and a fantasy overture respectively. In 1926 the repertoire of the Diaghilev Ballet included a *Romeo and Juliet* with music by Constant Lambert and choreography by Nijinska. As Haskell calls it a "surrealiste manifesto; a very temporary joke," it would appear to have been *Romeo and Juliet* in name only. In 1939 a ballet based on Shakespeare's play was produced at the Royal Hungarian Opera House in Budapest, with choreography by Gyula Harangozó, and a musical score by Tchaikovsky, probably the orchestral work mentioned previously. Another *Romeo and Juliet,* with a specially composed score by Sergei Prokofiev and choreography by Leonid Lavrovsky, was produced at the Kirov State Theater of Opera and Ballet, Leningrad, in 1940. Photographs of this production are of considerable interest; they display a lavish décor, and suggest that Galina Ulanova is a Juliet of striking beauty and dramatic ability.

[1] These operas appear in pairs, chronologically speaking; they are by Steibelt (1783); Zingarelli (1796); Vacaja (1832); Bellini (1833); d'Ivry (1864); Gounod (1867); Barkworth (1920); Zandonai (1922).

At least one critic claimed that Antony Tudor's *Romeo and Juliet* was "heavily chained to Shakespeare." Obviously, this gentleman had forgotten his high-school struggle with the text of the play. The ballet certainly derives its inspiration from the lovely lyric flights in the play, but presents the plot with swift economy, utilizing only those scenes that lend themselves to dancing and pantomime, omitting everything extraneous to a simplified exposition of the tragedy. Certain episodes are amplified: Rosaline, a character who is described, but never actually appears in the play (unless as a mute personage in the ballroom scene), is introduced at the beginning of the ballet; the street scene in which the brawl takes place becomes a crowded canvas with townspeople and beggars wandering in and out; Juliet is not found apparently dead in her bed, but takes the potion after she has been arrayed in her wedding dress. Far from being chained to Shakespeare, Tudor had ranged freely through the tragedy, choosing and occasionally rearranging scenes for balletic purposes. He remains, however, quite true to the spirit of the play, the only important liberty taken being one that is a change for the better: Romeo is a much stronger personality in the ballet than he is in the play. He wastes no time weeping over Rosaline's coldness. Far from indulging in such silly and neurotic behavior, he stamps in justifiable annoyance at her antics, following her from the scene with an air that indicates that he has had enough of her. Mercutio is less dominating in the ballet, and quite distinctly belongs to the Montague faction, instead of being neutral until he takes up a personal quarrel with Tybalt, as in the play. Tybalt emerges as a strong, rather dour character in the ballet, and not quite the dandified "King of Cats," as conceived by Shakespeare. Little of the lusty humor of the Nurse is apparent, though it is referred to in the street scene. Certain characters are suppressed entirely—notably the Prince and the various obtrusive and talkative servants. Paris is a shadowy figure, appearing only when the plot cannot proceed without him, and not at all in the tomb scene.

Choreographically the ballet leans to dramatic pantomime, dancing in the usual sense of the word taking a secondary place. Appropriately, Juliet (and her company of bridesmaids, who are figures straight from Botticelli's *Primavera*) is the exception to this rule. The rest of the dramatis personæ move in characteristic stylized patterns that tell the story in the manner of a series of Renaissance paintings.

The dancing in the ballroom scene is grave and dignified, probably an adaptation of a courtly *basse danse*. The Queen Mab scene, complete with torchbearers, follows the ballroom scene instead of preceding it. Partly mimed and partly danced, it is a charming evocation of Mercutio's whimsical declamation. When Romeo eludes his friends in the shadows, Benvolio's single gesture carries the impact of " 'Tis in vain to seek him here that means not to be found." This scene, which in its entirety comes closest to being chained to Shakespeare (it is a condensation of two scenes, one preceding, one following the ball), is delightfully carried out and has the true flavor of the play. There is a *pas de deux* performed by two unnamed guests in the orchard scene that draws its choreographic inspiration from the *basse danse* performed by the ensemble. The balcony scene presents difficulties that are not quite overcome. At this point speech becomes almost necessary to bridge the gap in the two planes on which the action takes place. The fight is in terms of wrestling rather than the expected sword play. This lends variety to the scene, as it employs interesting lifts and falls, in which some observers detected a resemblance to judo, though it is more probably a stylized use of ballet lifts. This series of movements was attacked on the grounds that it was inappropriate to Renaissance Verona, yet it makes for a scene of brawling violence that no introduction of prop swords could possibly effect. In fact there is a pleasant absence of these clattering accessories throughout the action, the stabbing of Tybalt and Juliet's self-immolation being achieved satisfactorily with imaginary weapons. The scene in Juliet's room is a passionately tender *pas de deux*. This *pas de deux* has a lift that, as performed by Markova, is a movement of rarely beautiful grace. As she is held high in the air, she does a stylized *demi-fouetté,* changing her direction with a lovely floating quality that is breath-taking. The dressing of Juliet for her wedding is accomplished in an exquisite dance sequence by a group of girls costumed after Botticelli, in movements that recall that painter at his finest. The funeral procession, before a mourning frieze of the same girls holding a drapery falling in heavy folds, achieves a grandeur out of proportion to the economy of the means employed. The tomb scene, shorn of all characters save the protagonists of the drama, has a final *pas de deux* (Romeo's poisoned draught is slower in its working than in the play) of tragic intensity.

When the production of *Romeo and Juliet* was first considered by

Ballet Theatre, Salvador Dali was asked to design the décor. His ideas, however, while they were fascinating examples of this artist's wildly individual approach to the subject, were not in line with Tudor's intention to produce the ballet in a unit setting that would permit the action to flow uninterrupted by the pauses necessary to make scene changes. This was perhaps fortunate, as there are many who regard Dali as something less than serious. At all events, the décor and costumes designed by Eugène Berman for this presentation are in themselves beautiful enough to make a less soundly constructed ballet memorable. His unit setting enables the drama to progress without pauses, the lifting of the drop at the beginning of the action and the lowering of a frame for the tomb scene taking place unobtrusively. The setting is a three-sided double colonnade, with curtains that are drawn or pulled aside at the appropriate moments by two attendants whose sympathetic interest in events sometimes replaces the missing chorus. The architecture is early Renaissance, forming a perfect background for the costumes, simplified adaptations of period dress as seen in contemporary paintings. Juliet's costume for her entrance is purely Botticelli, even the floating quality being achieved in some miraculous manner. The whole décor of *Romeo and Juliet* seems likely to become a classic of ballet design, and indeed is worthy to stand beside anything in the contemporary theater. It is the last ballet décor to be produced with all the resources of prewar splendor, and the materials in which the costumes are carried out are worthy of their fine design.

The performances in *Romeo and Juliet* were of a very high order. Alicia Markova was the perfect Juliet, looking as though indeed "she had not seen the change of fourteen years." For once, there was a Juliet who made Romeo's quick reactions believable. Her light darting steps barely seemed to touch the ground. It is possible that her characterization may have appeared understated to devotees of the full-voiced, buxom ladies of the theater who have at times most unsuitably played Juliet. Markova's deerlike shyness in the first scene, her tragic, controlled despair, the exquisite movement of her hand as she wakes up in the tomb scene, all are unforgettable in their subtlety. Her accurate sense of style kept every motion and gesture within the period frame designed by the choreographer, yet no facet of the characterization was ever allowed to suffer because of the stylization. Nora Kaye, Markova's successor in the role, gives a dramatically intense interpretation that is individual and affecting, but it undeniably lacks the poetry of Markova's conception.

Hugh Laing, framed by nature to be the ideal interpreter of Romeo, is warm and believable. He is limited, however, by the choreographic characterization, less completely realized than Juliet's. Nicolas Orloff's Mercutio, Jerome Robbins's Benvolio, and Sono Osato's Rosaline were memorable. The last mentioned role has never been adequately performed since Sono Osato left Ballet Theatre.

The music, an arrangement of several orchestral pieces by Delius, is scarcely an obvious choice for ballet music, except possibly for Tudor, who appears to prefer music that states a mood rather than music of a marked rhythmic structure. This arrangement supports the moods and action of the ballet admirably, and may even make friends for Delius, a much underrated composer.

Romeo and Juliet lives up to its choreographer's reputation for unique style, psychological penetration, and theatrical skill. It is also one of the most surpassingly beautiful pageants to be seen in the contemporary theater.

ROUGE ET NOIR

Rouge et Noir (Red and Black): ballet in four movements and one scene; music by Dmitri Shostakovich (First Symphony); choreography by Léonide Massine; scenery and costumes by Henri Matisse.

R*OUGE ET NOIR* was first produced at the Théâtre de Monte Carlo, Monte Carlo, on May 11, 1939. The first American performance took place at the Metropolitan Opera House on the evening of October 28, 1939, with the following cast:

WOMAN	*Alicia Markova*	LEADER OF THE BLACK GROUP
MAN	*Roland Guerard*	*Marc Platoff*
LEADER OF THE RED GROUP		LEADER OF YELLOW GROUP
	Frederic Franklin	*Nathalie Krassovska*

Eleanora Marra, Rosella Hightower, and *Lubov Rostova* had solo roles in the various groups

◆◇◆◇◆◇◆◇◆◇◆◇◆◇◆◇◆

The following is quoted from the program:

1st Movement (Agression): Man, symbolizing the poetic spirit, is pursued and overtaken by brutal forces.
2nd Movement (Field and City): The men of the city encounter the men of the field and bear them off.
3rd Movement (Solitude): Woman parted from man is tormented in her solitude by an evil spirit.
4th Movement (Destiny): Man eludes the brutal forces and finds woman again. But joy is shortlived, for in freeing himself from his worldly enemies he is conquered by destiny.

The most exciting feature of *Rouge et Noir* is the décor by Henri Matisse. The setting consists of a backdrop and several flat arches painted in primary colors, in front of which dancers dressed in suits of fleshings in red, blue, yellow, and black, with headdresses that covered their hair (with the most important group, including Man and Woman, in white), ebbed and flowed in changing patterns. It was extraordinarily effective scenically, though best seen from a distance, Matisse having placed almost too much faith in the ability of identical costumes to reconcile the vagaries of the human form. The groups formed and came apart, making wonderful blocks of color like an abstract painting set in motion.

As long as Alicia Markova was Woman, *Rouge et Noir* had a strong emotional impact. A very abstraction of womanhood, yet she wrung the heart with her magnificently understated agony in the face of loss and adversity—a symbol and precursor of the hell that was already breaking out in Europe, to spread all over the world. As she was succeeded in this role by a dancer of considerably less (to put it charitably) artistic stature, *Rouge et Noir* lost any interest except as a piece of stage decoration.

Massine had taken a lot of criticism of previous symphonic ballets on the subject of the unballetic scurrying of dancers on their way to form one of his famous architectural tableaux. To a certain extent this criticism was justified, and he answered it superbly in *Rouge et Noir,* where the groups (many and fascinating) click into position as though placed there by a gigantic hand working a jigsaw puzzle.

Frederic Franklin as Leader of the Red Group had the most interesting movements from the choreographic point of view—not intrinsically, but because they had been found appropriate for a serious role in a tragic ballet. They included tap steps and "bumps," more familiar to revue than ballet audiences. The part was performed with ingratiating directness and remarkable technical skill by Franklin.

As the controversy over the propriety of Massine's use of symphonies for ballet music seems to have died a natural death, no one appears to have questioned his employment of the Shostakovich First Symphony for *Rouge et Noir.* To quote Nicolas Slonimsky: "The success of this youthful work is explained by a combination of ingenuous melodic invention and a natural sense of rhythm. It is sufficiently modern to be interesting and sufficiently academic to be agreeable." This might also serve as an encomium on the ballet it inspired.

LE SACRE DU PRINTEMPS

LE SACRE DU PRINTEMPS, with a score by Igor Stravinsky, was Vaslav Nijinsky's third ballet. Clouds of controversy obscure the details of its creation, contrary claims being advanced by his associates in the work on one hand, and his wife on the other. Stravinsky stated flatly that "his ignorance of the most elementary notions of music was flagrant," complaining that he had to teach Nijinsky the rudiments of music as they worked together on the choreography. In her fascinating, though unreliable biography of her husband Romola Nijinska gives him all the credit for an entirely new approach to balletic art. Other authorities claim that Nijinsky was in constant difficulties during the many rehearsals required (one hundred and twenty, according to Beaumont). Unable to make his orders clear to the dancers, his authority had to be bolstered by the constant presence of Diaghilev at rehearsals.

One fact emerges quite distinctly from the haze: the original conception of the ballet was Stravinsky's. He was haunted by the image of the most beautiful virgin of a primitive tribe ritually chosen to sacrifice herself to ensure the well-being of her people. He carried his idea to Nicholas Roerich, who was deeply interested in pictorial reconstructions of primitive Russia. Together they worked out a program for the musical composition. Diaghilev became interested in the work and agreed to produce it. To Stravinsky's dismay, he entrusted the choreography to Nijinsky, whose first work, *L'Après-Midi d'un Faune,* had been a *succès de scandale,* and whose second, *Jeux,* had been greeted very tepidly. Both of these ballets were small-scale affairs and by no means an adequate preparation for an attempt to solve the titanic difficulties presented by Stravinsky's complicated score.

After an unprecedented number of rehearsals, *Le Sacre du Printemps* was performed for the first time at the Théâtre du Champs-Élysées, Paris, on May 29, 1913, Pierre Monteux conducting. Its reception has been compared to that which greeted *Hernani* for tumult and riot. The fashionable audience, bewildered by the massive sonorities of the music and the strange evolutions of the dancers, both in defiance of the accepted canons of musical and balletic art, lost their heads completely and behaved themselves as only a Paris mob can. The dancers, although frightened by the unexpected violence of the outbreak (not completely hostile, as admirers of Stravinsky conducted a counterdemonstration), carried on with the ballet, the tumult being finally stilled by the superb performance of Marie Piltz in her solo of sacrifice which concludes the ballet. The producers were completely taken by surprise, as the audience composed of critics and other guests who had been invited, according to Parisian custom, to the dress rehearsal had received the ballet with approval.

At subsequent performances the audience was calm enough and even began to appreciate the work, but its appalling difficulties caused it to be presented only six times. At least two of the repetitions took place in London before a public that was, according to Haskell, "amazed, but polite."

Stravinsky, far from pleased with Nijinsky's choreography, called it "a very labored and barren effort rather than a plastic realization flowing simply and naturally from what the music demanded." Nijinsky's conception negated every rule of the classic ballet, substituting angular, heavy, turned-in movement for the traditional steps of elevation and turn-out of the *danse d'école*. He also attempted to turn to practical use some of Jaques-Dalcroze's theories, one of which demanded a movement from the dancers to correspond with every note of the musical accompaniment.[1] It is quite unlikely that Dalcroze had ever contemplated the application of his theories to a work so complicated as the score of *Le Sacre du Printemps*. Nijinsky was scarcely an innovator in his use of *en dedans* steps. In *Petrouchka,* in which he had created the title role, Fokine had employed angular, turned-in steps and gestures to express the agony of Petrouchka's fragment of a soul. Nijinsky applied this vocabulary of movement to the ballet as a whole. The result, in spite of Stravinsky's dissatisfaction, impressed many with its primitively fanatical atmosphere and the almost hypnotic pounding of its savage rhythms. Very shortly after its first production it had become a theatrical legend.

Le Sacre du Printemps was not seen again until 1920, although the music was occasionally heard in concert, not as an orchestral suite, but exactly as played for a ballet performance. When a revival was

---

[1] A critic found this an evidence of industry on the part of the choreographer rather than of a real feeling for music.

considered, it was impossible to produce it in the form that Nijinsky had created. No one could remember the strange complexities of his choreography, and the original company had been scattered by the first World War. Léonide Massine, at that time first dancer and choreographer of the Diaghilev Ballet, was called upon to create a new ballet. As he had never seen the original version, his approach grew out of his own reactions to the music. This time Stravinsky was better pleased, declaring that Massine "accomplished his task with unquestionable talent." He approved of much of Massine's conception, finding beauty in the Chosen Virgin's solo, as well as some of the group movements, but complaining that at times the rhythmic subtleties of his score had been disregarded. André Levinson, comparing the two versions (and not caring much for either), said: *"Les danseurs de Nijinsky étaient harcelés par le rythme; ceux de Massine jouent maladroitement avec lui."* Lydia Sokolova, as the Chosen Virgin, in what is generally agreed to be the longest and most exhausting solo in the history of theatrical dance, won everybody's approbation, including Stravinsky's. This version of *Le Sacre du Printemps* remained in the repertoire of the Diaghilev Ballet for several seasons, gradually winning calm acceptance from the ballet public.

The musical public of America had an opportunity to hear the score of *Le Sacre du Printemps* several years before the ballet was performed in this country. Leopold Stokowski conducted the Philadelphia Orchestra in the first American performance of *Le Sacre du Printemps* on March 3, 1922 at the Academy of Music, Philadelphia. Other performances followed, the reactions of the audiences being mixed. The conservatives were upset, many leaving before the conclusion of an early performance in Carnegie Hall.[2] *Le Sacre du Printemps* has followed the path of many another controversial musical masterpiece—hailed with extravagances from friends and curses from enemies, succeeded, little by little, by an acceptance that receives it into the company of Beethoven and makes it one of the musical family. *Le Sacre du Printemps* has even been streamlined for popular consumption in the movies, appearing with accompanying cartoon in Disney's *Fantasia*.

[2] A story that may belong to musical folklore is told about a Carnegie Hall performance of *Le Sacre du Printemps*. An elderly gentleman wearing an old-fashioned ear trumpet sat listening to the mad pounding. A look of complete incredulity came over his face. Removing the ear trumpet, he looked at it doubtfully, shook it, and put it back again, with a resigned expression.

Le Sacre du Printemps reached America in ballet form under the auspices of the League of Composers. It was performed for the first time in Philadelphia on April 11, 1930. The first New York performance took place at the Metropolitan Opera House on April 23, 1930. The scenery and costumes by Nicholas Roerich closely approximated those designed by this artist for the Paris production. Léonide Massine, master of the revels at Roxy's, was director of choreography (by courtesy of S. L. Rothafel, as the program was careful to explain). The cast included Martha Graham (Chosen Virgin), Gould Stevens (Sage), Anita Bay (Witch), and a corps de ballet of thirty-seven. The Philadelphia Orchestra, under the direction of Leopold Stokowski, played for this production as well as for Arnold Schönberg's *Die Glückliche Hand,* which formed the other half of the program.

The prospect of seeing the ballet *Sacre du Printemps* aroused a great deal of anticipatory interest. The musical public, having had an opportunity to hear the score and to read several fascinating accounts of the historic first night (a notable one was written by Carl Van Vechten), looked forward with enthusiasm to a great emotional experience. It is more than likely that if Marie Piltz and the veterans of the hundred and twenty rehearsals had been on hand to perform Nijinsky's original choreography in all its savage intensity, the production would have seemed pale and anemic in comparison with the frenzied orgies that imagination (and the score) had conjured up. One critic called it a "colorful, virile, aggressive spectacle but by no means horrendous or appalling." Oscar Thompson, writing in *Musical America,* said: "The stage performance of 'Le Sacre' tended to clarify the Stravinsky score. Much that by reason of its bludgeoning sonorities and its uncouth rhythms had been perplexing to those who could feel its power but not grasp its scheme, was unriddled. Perhaps certain extravagant and rapturous comments on this work would never have been written if familiarity with the music in its stage form had preceded experience with it in the concert hall." Samuel Chotzinoff, in the New York *World,* remarked that "Mr. Leonide Massine had (by courtesy of Mr. Roxy) devised rites so innocent that they would not have offended the Daughters of the American Revolution. . . . Miss Graham wound up proceedings with a bit of solo grotesquerie." It is only fair to add that another critic found Martha Graham a more ecstatic Chosen Virgin than either Marie Piltz or Lydia Sokolova. The general consensus of opinion was that from a

ROMEO AND JULIET
(Nora Kaye and Hugh Laing)

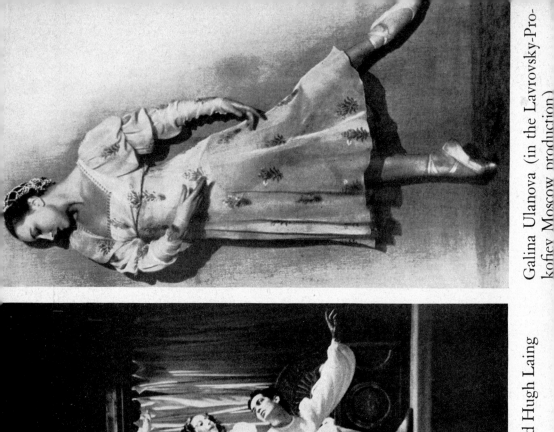

Galina Ulanova (in the Lavrovsky-Prokofev Moscow production)

Alicia Markova and Hugh Laing

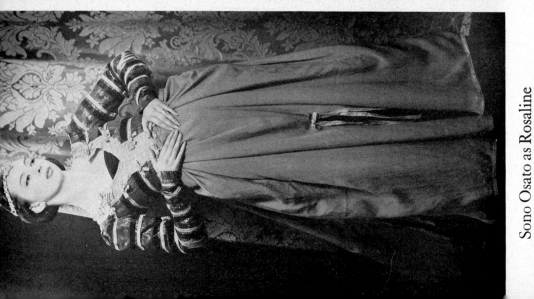

Sono Osato as Rosaline
ROMEO AND JULIET

Ritual of the Ancestors

Martha Graham
as the
Chosen One

LE SACRE DU PRINTEMPS (League of Composers, New York)

THE SLEEPING BEAUTY (Olga Larochinskaya and unnamed partner) dramatic point of view *Die Glückliche Hand,* performed by the Humphrey—Weidman group, was in all ways superior.

The action of the ballet, according to the League of Composers' program, is as follows:

Part 1. The Adoration of the Earth. Introduction—Harbingers of Spring, Dances of the Adolescents—Mock Abduction—Spring Rounds—Games of the Rival Tribes—The Procession of the Sage—Dance of the Earth.

Part 2. The Sacrifice. Introduction—Mystical Circles of the Adolescents—Glorification of the Chosen One—Evocation of the Ancestors—Ritual of the Ancestors—The Sacrificial Dance of the Chosen One.

Le Sacre du Printemps has not been seen in New York since the performance sponsored by the League of Composers. At least one souvenir program of Colonel W. de Basil's Ballet Russe listed it as part of the repertoire, but nothing was ever heard of its being performed by that organization. Its formidable difficulties probably discourage attempts at revival. Indeed, one quails at the thought of the treatment the magnificent score would be bound to receive at the hands of a ballet orchestra. *Le Sacre du Printemps* as a ballet may better survive in legends than face the cold realities of inadequate routine performances.

ST. FRANCIS

St. Francis (Nobilissima Visione): choreographic legend in one act and five scenes by Paul Hindemith and Léonide Massine; music by Paul Hindemith; choreography by Léonide Massine; scenery and costumes by Paul Tchelitcheff.

S*T. FRANCIS,* under the title of *Nobilissima Visione,* was first performed by the Ballet Russe de Monte Carlo at the Drury Lane Theatre, London, on July 21, 1938. The American première took place at the Metropolitan Opera House, New York, on October 14, 1938. The cast, substantially the same as the original, was as follows:

ST. FRANCIS	*Léonide Massine*	THE KNIGHT	*Frederic Franklin*
	(*Michel Panaieff*	THE POOR MAN	*Nicolas Ivangin*
THREE COMPANIONS	(*Roland Guerard*	POVERTY	*Nini Theilade*
	(*Marcel Fenchel*	OBEDIENCE	*Jeanette Lauret*
ST. FRANCIS' FATHER	*Simon Semenoff*	CHASTITY	*Lubov Roudenko*

Rosella Hightower, Yura Skibine, Charles Dickson, and others were also in the cast

◆◆◆◆◆◆◆◆◆◆◆◆◆◆◆◆

Scene 1. The shop of Pietro Bernadone. Francis and his three Companions are spending an idle hour in the shop belonging to Pietro Bernadone, Francis' Father. Richly colored silks and brocades are displayed in profusion. Many purchasers come and go. Occasionally Francis lends a hand in the business of the shop, waiting on those customers who promise to be interesting. A beggar comes in seeking alms. Francis thoughtlessly rebuffs him. When the beggar turns away with a despairing gesture, Francis, touched, follows and gives him a gift. Francis is depressed by this reminder of the darker side of life, but his mood is brightened by the arrival of a splendid Knight, who, attended by two squires, is on his way to war. Francis tries a friendly passage of arms with him and is worsted. The Knight invites him to join his train, persuading him that the pursuit of military glory is the only way of life for a young man. Francis follows him, dreaming of honor on the battlefield.

Scene 2. A country road. Francis watches the Knight's followers performing a military drill. He is learning the technique of war. Travelers are seen approaching. The Knight, overlooking no chance of plunder, orders his men to attack the unarmed group, many of whom are women, unable to defend themselves. The soldiers carry off the women and whatever loot they can seize. Francis' vision of the warrior's life does not comprehend such sordid greed and wanton brutality. Refusing to obey the Knight's command to resume the march, he takes off his helmet, ungirds his sword, and, kneeling on the ground, prays for guidance. Three heavenly apparitions, Poverty, Obedience, and Chastity, appear. Obedience and Chastity vanish. Poverty remains. His prayer finished, Francis follows her from the scene.

Scene 3. The house of Pietro Bernadone. The house is splendidly decorated. A banquet celebrating the return of Francis is in progress. The guests are gay, dancing and drinking. Francis, troubled and moody, participates in a half-hearted manner. A band of beggars, attracted by the festivity, enters unobtrusively. Francis, overcome by their wretchedness, impulsively gives them the golden vessels from the table. At this moment Francis' Father comes in. Furious at this high-handed disposition of his property, he strikes his son. Francis accepts with meekness his Father's anger. Removing his festive garments, he lays them at his Father's feet and leaves the house.

Scene 4. A country hillside. Francis by renouncing possessions has found peace. Clad in rags, he lives as a hermit. He dances to express his intense joy, waving two leafy branches which he forms into a cross. A group of peasants fleeing from a wolf who has caught one of their number interrupts his solitude. He goes to meet the wolf. Unable to withstand the saint's mystic power, the wild creature allows itself to be tamed and led away by the country folk. Now the three Companions of Francis' worldly life come to join him. They too have donned the livery of poverty. He welcomes them, but when they wish to add some little comforts to his bare existence he forbids them. As he sleeps on the ground, the lady Poverty appears. Francis, awakening, welcomes her as his bride. They exchange girdles and with the three Companions celebrate a marriage feast of bread and water.

Scene 5. A landscape with a great rock in the distance. A throng of monks and nuns pace in. Poverty leads Francis to the summit of the rock while the sky blazes with light.

St. Francis was not an unqualified success with the critics, most of whom were more familiar with folklore than hagiology. Nevertheless it was a sincere attempt to convey a mystical experience in terms of the dance. It won many admirers among that portion of the audience who, finding their appetite for the adventures of enchanted princesses and dancing dolls easily cloyed, welcomed an appeal to more adult emotions. The score by Paul Hindemith, though lacking in dramatic power, commanded the attention of lovers of contemporary music. However, wanting virtuoso performances, the ballet failed to hold the interest, through repeated presentations, of those ballet-lovers who can witness a hundred *Swan Lakes* and find something new in the hundred and first.

Americans accustomed to the starkly serious work of Martha Graham and other modern dance artists welcomed *St. Francis* more wholeheartedly than did London. John Martin in an enthusiastic review called it "one of the great dance works of our day." He said further: "Let it be stated at once that this is a work that is not to be judged by any of the ordinary standards, nor described in any conceivable way to make its power and its beauty understandable in advance."

The choreographic patterns of *St. Francis* are based on a profound study of medieval Italian painting, particularly the first three scenes. The stylized movements of hands and bodies are an evocation of the thirteenth century as its painters defined it for succeeding generations. In the fourth scene the movements are free and plastic, owing much to the contemporary dance. The apotheosis reverts to the original style and is a living fresco almost Byzantine in character.

Massine in the role of St. Francis gave a deeply moving performance. His interpretation, lacking something of the essential gaiety of Francis in the earlier scenes, made much of the mystical intensity and joyous asceticism of the saint. Poverty impersonated by Nini Theilade had the disembodied quality of a vision. This dancer, now remote from the world of ballet, had a little of the lightness and effortless grace that characterize Alicia Markova.

For many the most notable feature of *St. Francis* was the music composed for it by Paul Hindemith. This has outlived the ballet and has an occasional hearing as a concert suite. Some of the melodies employed are based on medieval songs and may even have been known to the historical St. Francis, who in his worldly days was not unacquainted with the art of the troubadour. The score has what one critic called "a noble asceticism." It creates atmosphere, but lacks the dramatic climaxes necessary to support the action of the ballet.

The settings and costumes by Paul Tchelitcheff are the least interesting aspect of *St. Francis*. The designs in themselves were sound. Unfortunately they were carried out in unsuitable materials and clashing colors. An exaggerated use of stripes proved monotonous and at times distracting. It is interesting to speculate on how Eugène Berman, with his fine sense of period, might have used this opportunity.

St. Francis deserves a high place in the all too brief list of truly adult ballets. It has not been seen for several years, owing, it is said, to a managerial prejudice. It is not a work that could be performed many times in a season. Along with *Dark Elegies* it should have a permanent place in the repertoire.

SCHEHERAZADE

SCHEHERAZADE is one of the earliest products of the wave of romanticism that swept the dance world during the first decade of the twentieth century. In the Tchaikovsky-Petipa ballets the *danse d'école* achieved a perfection that could no more be improved upon than the operas of Mozart. Repetition of the formula by less inspired choreographers to the routine scores of the official hack composers could only lead into an artistic *cul de sac*. Fortunately, fresh winds were blowing. Michel Fokine, trained in the Imperial Schools of Russia, and the American Isadora Duncan, working from opposite directions and with an entirely different object in view, brought a new freedom into an art in which traditions had become fetters. It was Duncan's avowed aim to destroy an art in which she saw only the superficial aspects—undoubtedly repulsive to her undisciplined spirit. Fokine chose to work within the structure of the classical ballet, using its admirable system of training and discarding the rigid conventions that inhibited progress.

It is debatable just how much Fokine owes to Duncan. Admirers of the latter claim that she was his direct inspiration. It is more likely that he arrived at his conclusions unaided. Quite certainly, Fokine showed no inclination to cut loose from his academic background. One of the earliest works to demonstrate his new ideas was *Le Cygne* (1905), which was projected before Duncan's visit to Russia. *Le Cygne,* probably performed more often than any single solo in the history of balletic art, was designed for Anna Pavlova and closely associated with her during her career. It was included in practically every program in which this great dancer appeared. Choreographically, *Le Cygne* was in the freely romantic style that Fokine later expanded for *Les Sylphides.*

Fokine's ideas were regarded with suspicion by the officials of the Imperial Theaters and most of his opportunities for expression were confined to ballets arranged for the pupils' annual performances and charity performances. His first work for official presentation at the Marinsky Theater was *Le Pavillon d'Armide,* in which Alexander Benois, friend and close associate of Sergei Diaghilev, collaborated, supplying the libretto as well as the décor. This was probably the most artistically satisfying ballet produced in Russia since *Sleeping Beauty*. It was included in the first program of Russian ballet presented to western Europe by Diaghilev in 1909. The overwhelming success of the first season of Russian ballet to be given *en grand tenue* in Paris (there had been previous minor invasions of European capitals by small groups of Russian dancers) led to plans for a further season, the programs of which were to consist of ballets by Fokine, with a single exception, *Giselle. Scheherazade,* composed for the 1910 season, was the most immediately successful presentation of the repertoire.

Scheherazade, based on the prologue to *The Arabian Nights,* is one of many ballets with an Oriental background. It was the first, however, in which choreographer and designer united to produce a genuinely Eastern atmosphere. *La Bayadère* and *La Fille du Pharaon,* to name two of a number in the repertoire of the Imperial Theaters, were ballets in which the action had a Hindu and an Egyptian locale respectively. The ballerinas were dressed in tutus decorated with Hindu or Egyptian designs decoratively applied, blocked shoes of conventional pink satin, and hair arranged after the fashion of the moment. The costumes of the male dancers were much less conventional. They performed surrounded by decorative groups of non-dancing supers dressed in authentic period costumes, in realistic architectural settings of the type later used by David Belasco. The corps de ballet were dressed to conform to the principal dancers. Choreographically the ballets followed a conventional pattern. If performed in practice clothes, they would have been stylistically indistinguishable from ballets with an Occidental flavor.

Fokine and Bakst, working in close collaboration with Diaghilev, completely changed this rigid scheme. Bakst's setting, far from being archæologically correct, evoked a genuine *Arabian Nights* atmosphere, with its piles of cushions, exotic lamps, and heavy draperies. A dancer in tutu and blocked shoes would have looked ridiculous in such a background. Bakst's costumes, based on descriptions of those worn by the characters in the tales told by Scheherazade, were daringly designed in rich colors and unusual fabrics. The choreography was equally unconventional. The dancers moved in rhythms that were theatrical adaptations of Oriental dances. Steps of elevation were used in the dance patterns for the men, but anything in the nature of the formal variations and *pas de deux* of the classic ballet was entirely missing.

The musical score was adapted from Rimsky-Korsakov's *Scheherazade* suite, Part I serving as an overture and Parts II and IV for the action of the ballet. Musicologists were less disturbed by the omission of Part III than they were by the change in the program of the music.[1] The suite, while written to illustrate several episodes in *The Arabian Nights,* was not specifically composed for the violent and bloody prologue that is the basis of the libretto of the ballet. The Rimsky-Korsakov family also raised a protest against what they considered a violation of the composer's intentions. Time is on the side of the producers of the ballet. It would be safe to assume that when the *Scheherazade* suite is played in concert, the majority of the hearers picture a performance of the ballet rather than the events detailed in the program notes.

The first performance of *Scheherazade* took place at the Paris Opéra on June 4, 1910, with the following cast:

ZOBEIDE	*Ida Rubinstein*	SHAH ZEMAN	*Basil Kissilov*
FAVORITE SLAVE	*Vaslav Nijinsky*	CHIEF EUNUCH	*Enrico Cecchetti*
SHAHRIAR	*Alexis Bulgakov*	ODALISQUE	*Sophie Fedorova*

◇◇◇◇◇◇◇◇◇◇◇◇◇◇◇◇◇◇

The story of the ballet, adapted from the prologue to *The Arabian Nights* by Léon Bakst, is as follows:

As the curtain rises, a setting of colorful splendor is revealed. Important to the action are three blue doors at the rear of the stage and a staircase to the left. Zobeide, King Shahriar, and his brother, Shah Zeman, are sitting on a divan surrounded by the ladies of the harem and slaves. An all-pervading atmosphere of lassitude and boredom is not dispelled by the dancing of three odalisques. Shah Zeman stares at the wives distrustfully and whispers his suspicions to his brother. He persuades Shahriar to start on a hunting expedition in spite of the protests of the wives and the sulky petulence of Zobeide. The Chief Eunuch and the lesser wives assist the brothers to put on their armor, bidding them a ceremonial farewell. Zobeide ignores these

---

[1] In a later revival of *Scheherazade* a portion of Part III was included to accompany a long, romantic, and atmospherically unsuitable *pas de deux*. This has not been included in any of the revivals of the ballet presented by the de Basil or Monte Carlo Ballets.

preparations, but at the last moment follows the brothers to bid them good-by.

Immediately there is a change of mood. The pall of tedium vanishes. Wives and slaves become animated. Some of the wives produce jewel-boxes and mirrors and help one another arrange their ornaments to the best advantage. Another group, leaving the scene, comes back with the Chief Eunuch. They coax him to open the doors. When he refuses, one of them steals his keys while the rest distract him. He snatches the keys away from the impudent thief, but it is plain that most of his indignation is assumed. When approached with gifts of jewels, he makes a proper show of reluctance, and opens two of the doors.

Blinking in the unaccustomed light, dark-skinned male slaves enter. Their assured manner makes it clear that this is an old story. With little delay, each finds his lover.

Zobeide returns and looks upon the orgiastic spectacle. Far from disapproving, as the remote elegance of her manner might indicate, she summons the Chief Eunuch and orders him to open the third door. This time his disinclination is not assumed. He remains adamant until Zobeide throws a magnificent string of pearls at his feet. Greed overcomes his fear of his master, and he opens the door.

There is a tense pause. The Favorite Slave leaps in and embraces Zobeide. He is splendidly dressed in gold, which emphasizes his blackness and animality. After the first raptures are over, Zobeide commands a feast. Slaves with flagons of wine and platters of fruit appear, followed by dancers with tambourines. A mad orgy begins, changing to a dance. While Zobeide watches, her Favorite climbs the stairs for a better view. Unable to resist, he leaps into the dance, leading it into wilder and wilder rhythms.

Suddenly the dancers on the right stop, sinking to the floor. The two kings have returned with guards and are about to exact a jealous vengeance. The dancers scatter, but the guards overtake them and swords flash. The Chief Eunuch falls by the hands of his underlings, and there is a world of petty tyranny endured in the satisfaction they take in the deed. The Favorite Slave appears, hotly pursued by soldiers. Eluding them for a moment, he is cornered. As they strike him with their swords, he hurls himself into the air, twisting like a hooked fish, and falls dead.

All the guilty are dead but one. Zobeide has watched the massacre in frozen horror, and now it is her turn. She rises, goes to Shahriar, and for a moment it seems as though her charms will prevail over her husband's desire for vengeance. Shah Zeman advances to kick the body of the Favorite Slave, which gives a final convulsive shudder. Shahriar resigns Zobeide to the group of eagerly waiting eunuchs. Snatching a dagger from one of them, she stabs herself, falling at her husband's feet, and clutching his hand with her last dying strength. Shahriar bows his head in sorrow as the curtain falls on a scene of desolation.

The original cast of *Scheherazade* was, with one exception, a dazzling array of virtuoso artists.[2] The ballet, a scene of unbridled passions presented in a free plastic style by a first-rate cast, could not fail to be an immediate success. Nijinsky's brilliant dancing, Rubinstein's beauty, and the complete departure from the accepted canons of balletic art became topics of conversation and subjects to be memorialized by painters and writers. The most striking feature of the production, however, was the dazzling décor, which had a far-reaching and almost unparalleled effect on decorative arts everywhere. Carl Van Vechten, writing several years later, said:

"The Russian ballet on its decorative side is entirely responsible for the riot of color which has spread over the Western world in clothes and house furnishings. . . . George Bernard Shaw did not stretch the truth when he said that for the past five years the Russian Ballet has furnished the sole inspiration for fashions in women's dress. . . . And so we might go back year by year to the season when Bakst's *Schéhérazade* launched the Oriental craze which is still making itself felt in the hamlets on the Great Lakes.[3]

Scheherazade reached New York a little more than a year after its première at the Paris Opéra. The first American performance took place at the Winter Garden on June 14, 1911. Produced by Gertrude Hoffman and staged by Theodore Kosloff, it shared a program with

[2] Ida Rubinstein, who created Zobeide, was not a dancer. She was an amateur of ballet, whose financial aid helped to promote the 1910 season of Russian ballet in western Europe when an official subsidy was withdrawn owing to the intrigues of Diaghilev's enemies. The role of Zobeide, involving very little dancing, was designed to exploit her striking beauty and mimetic ability.

[3] As an inhabitant of a hamlet on the Great Lakes during this period, I can testify, if not to an Oriental craze, at least to the fact that the Bakst influence on colors considered suitable for interior decoration was both far-reaching and beneficial. Muddy drabs, sickly greens, and frightened crimsons began to vanish before a tide of pure, vibrant color.

Cléopâtre and *Les Sylphides*—three Fokine ballets originally performed in western Europe in the Diaghilev seasons of ballet in 1909 and 1910. They were launched in New York with no acknowledgment of any indebtedness to original choreographer or producers.[4] The cast of *Scheherazade* included Gertrude Hoffman (Zobeide), Lydia Lopokova (Odalisque), Theodore Kosloff (Favorite Slave), and Alexis Bulgakov (in the role he had created). The souvenir program (entitled *Album Souvenir*) displays a reproduction of the Bakst décor for *Scheherazade*. Photographs of the set indicate that Bakst's ideas were carried out in a manner that can only be called road-company, his masses of clear, glowing color being overlaid with a profusion of busy pattern. It seems likely that Fokine's choreography met a similarly fussy treatment. An amusing feature of the plot as detailed in the *Album Souvenir* is the reiterated insistence on the fact that the amorous slaves who invade the harem are Arabs—no doubt an attempt to parry any criticism that might arise on the grounds of racial issues.

Gertrude Hoffman's *La Saison Russe* does not appear to have been entirely successful, as a further program which would have included *Carnaval, Prince Igor,* and *Fire Bird* failed to eventuate. It is possible that New York's interest in the balletic Orient (less then than it was later to become) had been satiated by Mikhail Mordkin's *Legend of Azyiade,* in which he and Anna Pavlova performed the leading roles. This was produced during the 1910–11 season at the Metropolitan Opera House. It was performed several times, once at least as a curtain raiser to *Cavalleria Rusticana.*

In January 1916 Diaghilev arrived in New York with his company of dancers to present a season of ballet at the Century Theater, later moving to the Metropolitan Opera House. Nijinsky, arriving late to join the company, appeared in his original role of the Favorite Slave in a performance of *Scheherazade* at the Metropolitan on April 15, 1916. The Catholic Theatre Movement had protested against *Scheherazade* during the initial run at the Century. It is probable, however, that the Metropolitan audience saw an unbowdlerized version.

Scheherazade has been given many times and in many versions since these inaugural performances. It has been the inspiration for uncounted Oriental fantasies, acts in vaudeville and revue, and pupils'

[4] I base this assertion on an examination of newspaper publicity and the souvenir program. I have not seen a performance program.

recitals, most of them performed by players whose dancing technique, if it existed at all, was rudimentary. When Massine was ballet master at Roxy's, it received a production, in 1929, complete with elephants and Roxyettes, that should have given it the *coup de grâce*. This was by no means the case. It was just beginning a new lease on life. Between the Roxy production and the revival by Colonel W. de Basil's Ballet Russe there were performances at Radio City and the Lewisohn Stadium.

The de Basil ballet performed *Scheherazade* for the first time in New York on October 9, 1935, at the Metropolitan Opera House. The cast included Lubov Tchernicheva (Zobeide) and Yurek Shabelevsky (Favorite Slave). Owing to an accident to Shabelevsky (sustained, according to rumor, in the leap from the stairs), Massine assumed the role of the Favorite Slave at a number of repetitions during the 1935 season. These early performances by the de Basil company, while but pale reflections of the originals, did have a wintry gleam of the intensity that must have informed the original performances if contemporary critics are to be trusted. Tchernicheva, Massine, and Shabelevsky were in touch with the traditions of their roles, and neither emotional implications nor technical problems were beyond them.

Since the 1935 season there have been other revivals of *Scheherazade,* by the Monte Carlo Ballet and the Original Ballet Russe. With the principal male role in the hands of dancers less experienced than Massine and Shabelevsky the ballet is chiefly remarkable for the miming of Zobeide by such distinguished dancers as Alexandra Danilova, Jeannette Lauret, and Irina Baronova.[5]

The glory has departed from *Scheherazade*. Bakst's glowing colors have receded behind grey veils; from being an object for persecution by busybodies, it has become an acceptable item on Saturday matinee programs, traditionally devoted to children; the choreography once so daring, seems dated beside that of *Giselle,* which it completely overshadowed during the 1910 season. For newcomers to ballet who may have read a biography of Nijinsky, *Scheherazade* may retain some of its glamor, though only an act of faith can perceive it in contemporary performances.

[5] I once saw a performance of *Scheherazade* at the Lewisohn Stadium in which Zobeide and her Favorite were performed by Patricia Bowman and Paul Haakon. This production included the romantic and interminable *pas de deux*. The whole thing was strongly reminiscent of kittens pretending to be tigers.

SEBASTIAN

A ballet in one act and three scenes, based on a story by Gian-Carlo Menotti; choreography by Edward Caton; music by Gian-Carlo Menotti; scenery by Oliver Smith; costumes by Milena.

SEBASTIAN was given its première by Ballet International at the International Theater, New York, on October 31, 1945, with the following cast:

A COURTESAN	*Viola Essen*	SEBASTIAN	*Francisco Moncion*
THE PRINCE	*Kari Karnakoski*	A Fortune Teller, Pages, Amazons,	
His Sisters:		Courtiers, Peasants, Doge, Bishop,	
FIORA)	(*Lisa Maslova*	Accolites, etc.	
MADDALENA)	(*Yvonne Patterson*		

The scene is laid in Venice at the end of the seventeenth century. The story is of a conflict between two sisters, Fiora and Maddalena, whose possessive love for their brother, the Prince, will not allow him to find happiness with his mistress, the Courtesan. Constantly they spy on his meetings with her, until they are able to gain possession of her veil, which, according to the rules of witchcraft, gives them power over her. They make a wax image of the Courtesan, cover it with her veil, and in a frenzy of evil stab the image with arrows, causing her to suffer agony with each blow. Their intention of bringing about her death is thwarted by the humble adoration their Moorish slave, Sebastian, who has long loved the Courtesan from afar. Removing the wax image, he stands in its place, covered with the veil, receiving in his own body the deadly wounds intended to destroy the Courtesan. The black magic, thus diverted from its intended object, reacts against the sisters. The way for the Prince's happiness with his beloved is opened by the selfless devotion of Sebastian.

The action of *Sebastian* takes place amid a swirl of pageantry. There is a street scene in which all the picturesque characters that fancy can devise pass in processions, both religious and secular. The first scene, with its perspective of the Square of St. Mark, is an admirable backdrop for the brilliant costumes that are fantastic approximations of historical originals.

The score by Gian-Carlo Menotti, which seems after one hearing to have its melodic basis in Scarlatti, is dramatic and suggestive of the period. There are times, however, when there is too much music for a given situation and the choreographer is forced to spin out the action by repetition. This could have been avoided by closer co-operation between composer and choreographer, and will no doubt be remedied when the ballet is revived.

The performances in *Sebastian* had varying degrees of intensity, no doubt owing to the personalities of the dancers. A choreographer cannot fail to be influenced by the idiosyncrasies of the dancers with whom he works. As he cannot always choose his cast, particularly in a small company, this imposes certain handicaps. Kari Karnakoski as the Prince, was a shadowy sort of person to have aroused such bitter passions. No doubt a dancer of more personal force would make the Prince plausible. Viola Essen was far from the accepted type of courtesan, resembling rather a timid debutante. Her pathos was undeniable, but one could not help wondering how she had become a member of the oldest profession in the first place. The two sisters, mimed by Yvonne Patterson and Lisa Maslova, dancers of considerable powers of projection, were figures of an evilness that made believable their wicked schemes and savage possessive love. As Sebastian, Francisco Moncion emerged as a dancing actor of the Hugh Laing type, with an ability to make every movement count in the drama, even when the scenes in which he was involved seemed unduly prolonged. This is the first role in his dancing career to make use of his real abilities, and it is to be hoped that the dissolution of Ballet International will not deprive him of future opportunities. His is a talent rare enough in the dance theater and should be given a chance to develop.

Sebastian is the first important choreographic work by Edward Caton, whose career in ballet has included such diverse roles as the Bluebird and Mother Simone in *La Fille Mal Gardée*. *Sebastian* shows a freshness of approach and is theatrical in the best sense of the word. His method was termed by a critic "a dance stylization of fragmentary pantomimic suggestions." It has certain weaknesses and at times seems long drawn out. Cuts in both music and action will increase the dramatic tension. If the shortlived Ballet International reorganizes, doubtless these *longueurs* will be corrected.

THE SEVENTH SYMPHONY

Music by Beethoven; theme and choreography by Léonide Massine; scenery and costumes by Christian Bérard.

THE SEVENTH SYMPHONY was first performed by the Ballet Russe de Monte Carlo at the Théâtre de Monte Carlo on May 5, 1938. The American première took place at the Metropolitan Opera House, New York, on October 15, 1938, with the following cast:

First Movement: The Creation
THE SPIRIT OF CREATION
     Frederic Franklin
THE SKY   Mia Slavenska
THE STREAM Nini Theilade
THE PLANT Nathalie Krassovska
THE DEER
  Marina Franca, Yura Skibine
THE BIRD Tania Grantzeva
THE SERPENT T. Robert Irwin
THE SUN Casimir Kokitch
THE FISH Rosella Hightower
THE WOMAN Jeannette Lauret
THE MAN George Zoritch

Second Movement: The Earth
THE ADOLESCENT Charles Dickson
THE INNOCENT Max Kirbos
THE WOMAN Nini Theilade
Third Movement: The Sky
THE GODS
  Mia Slavenska, Igor Youskevitch

Fourth Movement: The Destruction
BACCHANALE Nini Theilade, Lubov
  Rostova, Frederic Franklin
CUPID Dorothy Etheridge
THE FIRE Igor Youskevitch

First Movement: *The Creation*. Under the guidance of the Spirit of Creation, chaos becomes an orderly habitation for plants, animals, birds, and fish. Finally Man and Woman appear, with the menacing Serpent beside them.

Second Movement: *The Earth*. Hate and violence have made their appearance on earth. A group of men and women mourn for the Adolescent, who has been murdered.

Third Movement: *The Sky*. Gods and Goddesses of the air, untouched by the turbulence that rages on earth, hold a joyous revel.

Fourth Movement: *The Bacchanale and the Destruction*. Man has sunk into weakness and debauchery. The Gods, angered by the sight of the evil parody of their own Olympian pleasures, destroy the world by fire.

The Seventh Symphony, the fourth of Massine's symphonic ballets, is the least successful of his ventures into that genre. After all, it is an ambitious project to attempt to depict the creation of the world in terms of the theater. Even Wagner was more modest: he merely asked that the Rhine overflow its banks while Valhalla blazed—stage directions modified out of recognition in Metropolitan productions of *Die Götterdämmerung.* Massine's ballet was not the first to approach this difficult theme. Darius Milhaud composed *La Création du Monde* for the Swedish Ballet. It was produced with choreography by Jean Börlin in Paris in 1923, the style being strongly influenced by African Negro sculpture, which had recently come into artistic vogue. The same score was used by Ninette De Valois for a new version presented by the Vic-Wells Ballet in 1931. Antony Tudor performed the role of Man in this ballet.

The Seventh Symphony, employing Beethoven's Seventh Symphony in A, was entirely different in its attack on the subject, involving a mixture of Greek mythology and the Bible (both Old and New Testaments), in a confusing manner. It had certain interesting features. The first movement had several arresting moments: the entrance of the Deer (Marina Franca and Yura Skibine, later Lubov Roudenko and André Eglevsky), whose delightful progress across the stage often woke up those of the audience who had been thrown into a coma by the amorphous maneuverings of the groups representing various elements and forms of plant life; the Serpent was a fascinating creature, who made his first entrance slithering down a track formed by a number of dancers clumped together in a solid formation. The Spirit of Creation was alternately performed by Frederic Franklin and Marc Platoff. An irreverent critic called this part "a role which is rather suggestive of a conjurer waving his wand and producing rabbits out of a hat with as much dignity as possible." A curious feature of this movement was the backdrop representing a spacious plain with ruins and broken columns. Was this a whimsy of the artist, or an indication that an old world was being remade?

The second movement was composed in the manner of the Andante in *Chorearteum,* with its balletic employment of the central-European style of free plastic dance. Those of the audience who were not offended by the allusion to the Descent from the Cross found this section of the ballet moving and by far the most interesting of the four. There was an odd figure (the Innocent) in the mourning group who might have been invented by Dostoyevsky.

The third movement, conventional in its choreographic content, served to introduce that superb classical dancer Igor Youskevitch to New York audiences. The quality of this scene was improved when Alicia Markova assumed the role that she had created in Europe, her ability to suggest a goddess of the air being more inherent than Mia Slavenska's.

The fourth movement began well, with some fine groups based on Greek vase drawings. Dorothy Etheridge's Cupid was the first of many pleasing characterizations by this young artist. The Bacchanale was more successful than many attempts to make scenes of riotous festivity theatrically plausible. Unfortunately, the destruction by fire was decidedly on the naïve side. Fluttering red rags, without the aid of the smoke screen provided for Metropolitan performances of *Die Walküre* and other fiery Wagnerian operas, were far from credible as destructive agents. Many uneven dramatic presentations have been saved by a thrilling last act. *The Seventh Symphony* cannot be included in the number; it trailed feebly to an inept conclusion.

The music critics who had so bitterly attacked *Les Présages* and *Chorearteum* should have held their fire for *The Seventh Symphony,* a much more vulnerable target. As little was heard from them, it is probable that their fire power had been weakened by Ernest Newman's heavy artillery.

For several years Massine has achieved nothing in the symphonic ballet except *Rouge et Noir* and *Aleko*. It is not safe to say that he has exploited all the possibilities of this form. Massine's artistic demise has been announced several times. However, he has a habit of confounding those critics who are hardy enough to state that his choreographic genius has atrophied. Some of his most memorable works were accomplished after several years of purely commercial productions for revues and movie palaces. It is possible that he may even recover from the arid period which produced as its climax *The Moonlight Sonata*.

SLEEPING BEAUTY

SLEEPING BEAUTY and *Swan Lake,* collaborations by Petipa, together share the pinnacle of achievement in the classic ballet. *Sleeping Beauty* had a more auspicious beginning than *Swan Lake,* which, given a poor production in Moscow by second-raters, passed into an oblivion that might have become permanent had not Marius Petipa, choreographer of *Sleeping Beauty,* been attracted by the score and revived it with all the resources that the Marinsky Theater could command.

Sleeping Beauty, Tchaikovsky's second ballet score, was commissioned by Ivan Alexandrovich Vsevolozhsky, director of the Imperial Theaters, who sent the composer a libretto, based on Perrault's fairy tale *La Belle au Bois Dormant.* Tchaikovsky, pleased with the libretto, found no difficulties in composing music to fit the choreographic outline supplied by Marius Petipa. It is unbelievable that such enchanting, spontaneous melodies could result from a pattern as rigid as a stencil.[1]

Sleeping Beauty was given a production of great magnificence with a first-rate cast at the Marinsky Theater in St. Petersburg. On January 14, 1890 the dress rehearsal was attended by Alexander III and his court. Accustomed to the banal routines of the official composers whose music did no more than provide the dancers with a rhythm to which they might perform, the glittering audience was a little nonplused by Tchaikovsky's beautiful score, which actually dared to call attention to itself. The public also gave the ballet not much more than a polite reception. *Sleeping Beauty,* retained in the repertoire in spite of these tepid reactions, eventually achieved a degree of popularity that has kept it in the active repertoires of the Russian musical theaters from that day to this.

The original cast included Carlotta Brianza (Princess Aurora), Paul Gerdt (Prince Desire, later Prince Charming), Enrico Cec-

[1] Petipa's program for the ballet which he sent to Tchaikovsky appeared in four successive issues of the *Dancing Times* from December 1942 to March 1943. He frequently specifies the time, the number of bars, and the mood of the music required for a given episode. For example: "For Aurora's entrance—abruptly coquettish ¾. Thirty-two bars. Finish with 16 bars, ⁶⁄₈ forte."

chetti and Varvara Nikitina (the Bluebird and the Enchanted Princess). Cecchetti was also seen as Carabosse, the evil fairy. As this personage appears only in the first scenes of the ballet, Cecchetti was able to throw off the grotesque trappings of the role and assume the glamorous costume of the Blue Bird for the *divertissement* act.

Sleeping Beauty has been given at least two new productions in the Russian theater since 1890: one, some time before 1921, with a décor by Constantin Korovine; one in 1936, with some choreographic revisions, and a new décor by Isaak Rabinovitch.

Probably the first excerpt from *Sleeping Beauty* to be performed in western Europe was the Bluebird *pas de deux*, included in the *divertissement* ballet *Festin*. This was a pastiche, the score of which included the finale of Tchaikovsky's Second Symphony, the Bluebird music, a hopak by Mussorgsky, as well as selections from Glinka and Glazunov—in fact, a sort of Russian salad. *Festin* formed part of the 1909 repertoire of the Diaghilev Ballet, and was dropped after the first season.

Another excerpt, a *pas de deux* called on the program *Aurore et le Prince,* was performed by Mathilde Kchesinska and Vaslav Nijinsky in London during the 1911 season at Covent Garden. This was probably the *grande adage* that has become familiar to audiences in *Aurora's Wedding* (Col. W. de Basil's Ballet Russe), and *Princess Aurora* (Ballet Theatre).

New York was introduced to *Sleeping Beauty* in 1916, when Anna Pavlova and her company appeared in it at the Hippodrome. This production, supervised by Ivan Clustine, with Anna Pavlova (Princess Aurora) and Alexandre Volinine (Prince Charming), vied for the audiences' attention with the customary Hippodrome attractions. André Olivéroff, in his *Flight of the Swan,* describes it: "What a hodgepodge it was! A kaleidoscope panorama of spangles—spangled dancers, spangled divers, fliers in spangles, some fifty or sixty of them, suspended on wires. . . . Singing sirens emerged dripping from the spacious pool. . . . There was the flying piano act. . . . The clowns . . . the elephants . . . and throughout all this a vast orchestra, the brasses predominating, boomed out tune after reckless tune." Somewhere in the midst of the confusion *Sleeping Beauty* struggled for recognition—a vain battle. Before long it was cut beyond recognition, a series of Pavlova's solo variations being substituted for the excisions.

In the same year the Diaghilev Ballet made its journey to America and, along with the Fokine ballets, presented the Bluebird *pas de deux,* now called *La Princesse Enchantée,* in a setting by Léon Bakst, described by a critic as "a crimson landscape from no existing land . . . devised for an ordinary *pas de deux* . . . lifts it out of the ordinary immediately and almost suggests that the title means something which it does not." One wonders how even the least discerning critic could call the Bluebird *pas de deux* ordinary, unless the standards of execution were considerably lower than that of contemporary dancers. It is fair to say, however, that this review was written before Nijinsky joined the company. Xenia Maclezova, probably the first Enchanted Princess to be seen in this country, was said by Carl Van Vechten to be "very nearly lacking in those qualities of grace, poetry, and imagination with which great artists are freely endowed." According to the same critic, Lydia Lopokova, also appearing in this role, "had charm as a dancer, whatever her deficiencies in technique. . . . As . . . *La Princesse Enchantée,* she floundered hopelessly out of her depth." The Bluebird was probably danced by Bolm or Gavrilov, although contemporary critics do not mention the fact.

Sleeping Beauty (called *The Sleeping Princess*) made its real debut in western Europe in a production of unparalleled magnificence at the Alhambra Theatre in London, on November 2, 1921. The cast assembled by Diaghilev was a fabulous roll-call of the great names of ballet, and in minor roles appeared many who were later to achieve distinction. Princess Aurora, danced at the opening performance by Olga Spessivtzeva, was alternately assumed by Lubov Egorova, Lydia Lopokova, and Vera Trefilova. Pierre Vladimiroff (Prince Charming), Ludmilla Schollar (White Cat), Felia Doubrovska (Fairy of the Pine Woods), Lydia Sokolova (Cherry-Blossom Fairy), Bronislava Nijinska (Fairy of the Humming-birds), Vera Nemchinova (Carnation Fairy), Lydia Lopokova (Lilac Fairy), Lubov Tchernicheva (Fairy of the Mountain Ash), Jean Jazvinsky (Cantalbutte), Leon Woizikovsky (Indian Prince), Anatole Vilzak (Spanish Prince), and Stanislas Idzikowsky (Bluebird) are highlights of the cast, names known to every ballet-lover. Anton Dolin, hidden behind a Russianized substitute for his real name—Patrick Healy-Kay—was one of the royal pages.

A link with the Marinsky production was the presence of Carlotta Brianza, the original Princess Aurora, as the Fairy Carabosse. Later in the season Enrico Cecchetti appeared in this role, which he had created, to celebrate his fiftieth anniversary as a performer of leading roles.

This production of *Sleeping Beauty* was a labor of love to Diaghilev and his colleagues. Stravinsky, who worked with him, speaks of it in his autobiography:

"Diaghilev had worked at it passionately and lovingly, and once more displayed his profound knowledge of the art of the ballet. He put all his soul, all his strength, into it, and in the most disinterested way, for there was here no question of enhancing his reputation as a pioneer or appealing to the curiosity of the public by new forms. In presenting something classical and dignified he demonstrated the greatness and freedom of his mentality together with a capacity to appreciate not only the values of today and of remote periods, but also—and this is an extremely rare quality—the values of the period immediately preceded by our own."

Stravinsky took an active part in the production of *Sleeping Beauty*, which differed in several particulars from the original. He orchestrated music, existing only in manuscript or the piano score, that Diaghilev wished to use, and provided certain musical connective tissue that the exigencies of the production made necessary. The choreographic details were under the direction of Bronislava Nijinska, who also created additional numbers, notably "The Three Ivans," still to be seen in the surviving *Auroras* familiar to American audiences.

For all the lavish magnificence of the décor and costumes by Léon Bakst, the superb cast, and the loving care that went into this revival, it was a failure with the London audiences, who had been conditioned by previous ballet seasons to expect the variety that the more usual three-ballet programs could provide. A failure of stage mechanics at the opening performance, causing delays, distracted the critics, who were unable to appreciate the austere beauties of unadulterated classicism. Diaghilev might have been saved from impending bankruptcy if *Sleeping Beauty* had run for at least six months. At the end of three months it closed, and an ill fate attended the production even into the warehouse where the costumes were stored. They were hopelessly damaged, though fortunately Bakst's beautiful sketches survived.[2]

[2] There are very few photographs of this production surviving out of the morgues of newspapers and files of periodicals, the evil star extending its baleful influence even to the official photographer of the sets. His studio, where all his negatives were stored, was burned.

Cyril W. Beaumont in his *Complete Book of Ballets* gives a detailed account of both rehearsals and performances of *Sleeping Beauty*. He was fortunate enough to have seen almost every performance during the three months' run. He writes of it from the heart and it is impossible to read his report without envy. Apparently all that was wrong with this production was that it was many years in advance of its time, the proof being that the 1939 revival at Sadler's Wells—a pale approximation of the original—was an outstanding success.

In 1922 a one-act *divertissement* ballet was salvaged from the remains of *Sleeping Beauty*. Called *Le Mariage d'Aurore,* it was performed in Bakst's décor for Act I, Scene 1 of the London production. Some new costumes were designed by Nathalie Gontcharova, and others were borrowed from the discontinued *Pavillon d'Armide*. This proved highly successful and continued in the repertoire of the Diaghilev Ballet until it came to its end in 1929. The final performance given by this company in London took place at the Royal Opera, Covent Garden, on July 26, 1929. The last ballet on this program was *Le Mariage d'Aurore,* with Alexandra Danilova as Aurora, and Alicia Markova and Anton Dolin in the Bluebird *pas de deux*. Many dancers are associated with the ballet: Vera Nemchinova as Aurora was partnered by Anatole Vilzak and, surprisingly, by George Balanchine; Alice Nikitina and Anton Dolin, Vera Savina and Stanislas Idzikowsky, were associated with the Bluebird *pas de deux;* Alicia Markova performed one of her first solo roles as Red Ridinghood; Ninette de Valois, now director of the Sadler's Wells Ballet, danced the "finger" variation, during her two years with the Diaghilev Ballet.

Le Mariage d'Aurore was presented in America by the De Basil Ballet. The first performance was given while the company was on tour, the first New York showing taking place at the Majestic Theater on March 21, 1935. There had been one at the Academy of Music, Brooklyn, on March 19. The program for the Majestic Theater performance lists the following:

1. Prelude.
2. Polonaise, performed by an ensemble of twelve men and twelve women.
3. Dance of the Seven Ladies of Honor. (This was the *pas de sept* from Act I, Scene 1 of the Alhambra production.)

4. Scene and Dance of the Duchesses, performed by five men and five women.

5. Farandole, by the ensemble.

FAIRY TALES

6. Florestan and his Sisters . . . Vera Zorina, Lubov Rostova, and Roman Jasinsky.

7. Little Red Ridinghood . . . Lisa Serova and Jean Hoyer.

8. The Bluebird . . . Tatiana Riabouchinska and David Lichine. (Roland Guerard in Brooklyn.)

9. The Porcelain Princesses . . . Eugenie Delarova, Tatiana Chamie, and Vania Psota. (This was an interpolation from *The Nutcracker*.)

10. The Three Ivans . . . Yurek Shabelevsky, Marian Ladre, and Narcisse Matouchevsky. (This was an original addition to the Alhambra production by Nijinska, performed to the music of the coda of the *pas de deux* that follows.)

11. *Pas de deux* . . . Irina Baronova and Paul Petroff. (This was not the complete *pas de deux,* which would include solo variations and a coda, but the opening *adage*.

12. Mazurka, by the entire cast.

When the De Basil Ballet had its first season at the Metropolitan Opera House in October 1935, *Le Mariage d'Aurore* was included in the opening program. Five variations had been added following the *pas de sept*. These included the "finger" variation (third in order of performance) and the Sugarplum Fairy's variation from the *pas de deux* in the last act of *The Nutcracker,* the latter being Aurora's solo. During the 1937 season a sixth variation was introduced.

Le Mariage d'Aurore was easily one of the most popular ballets in the de Basil company's repertoire. It was usually performed on opening and closing programs, following a tradition of the Diaghilev Ballet. *Le Mariage d'Aurore* frequently caused the critics pain, but invariably pleased the audiences.

Irina Baronova and Tamara Toumanova were closely associated with the role of Princess Aurora. They alternated in the part and each had legions of admirers. One could choose Toumanova's dark beauty and brilliance of technique (thrilling, though not always dependable), or Baronova, fair and sculptured, with a rhythmic continuity that some found too fluid for a true classic style. Both were charming interpretations, both promised more than they were later to fulfill. Toumanova was at her best in the "finger" variation, and Baronova excelled in the Sugarplum Fairy solo.

David Lichine and Tatiana Riabouchinska were firmly associated in the public mind with the Bluebird *pas de deux*. Neither of these dancers was, by any stretch of the imagination, a good exponent of the *danse d'école,* but by skillful showmanship they managed to convince audiences that each performance was ideal: Riabouchinska by her charm and dramatic approach, Lichine by his brilliant *batterie* and thrilling elevation. Roland Guerard, an American dancer in the same company, offered a far more academically correct version of the male variation, but, lacking the projection of Lichine's, it was overlooked. Several critics raised a cry that a superior American artist was being neglected and discriminated against in a Russian company. Possibly, but ballet audiences, lacking appreciation of the fine points of technique, unmistakably preferred Lichine's robust performance technique and glamorous personality.

Alexandra Danilova gave a few performances of Princess Aurora with her customary authority and elegance of line. As a rule, however, she was content to allow the "baby ballerinas" to shine as Aurora, although her interpretation of the role, as well as an occasional "finger" variation, was a delight to the more sophisticated part of the audience.

When the De Basil Ballet ceased to visit America in 1938, there were many who missed *Le Mariage d'Aurore* more than any other single item in their repertoire.

In the meantime an American company had turned its attention to *Sleeping Beauty.*[3] It was produced in a prologue and three acts with choreography by Catherine Littlefield. The first performance took place at the Academy of Music, Philadelphia, by the Philadelphia Ballet, on February 12, 1937. The most important roles and their performers follow:

CANTALBUTTE	*Lasar Galpern*	PRINCE FROM THE SOUTH	
FAIRY OF BEAUTY	*June Graham*		*Thomas Cusmina*
FAIRY OF GOODNESS	*Dania Krupska*	PRINCE FROM THE EAST	
FAIRY OF HAPPINESS	*Joan McCracken*		*Jack Potteiger*
FAIRY OF SONG	*Karen Conrad*	PRINCE FROM THE WEST	
FAIRY OF DANCE	*Miriam Golden*		*Carl Littlefield*
FAIRY OF HOPE	*Dorothie Littlefield*	PRINCESS AURORA	
CARABOSSE	*Edward Caton*		*Catherine Littlefield*
PRINCE FROM THE NORTH		PRINCE DESIRÉ	*Alexis Dolinoff*
	Thomas Cannon		

[3] Mikhail Mordkin also revived *Sleeping Beauty* in 1936. First performed in his New York studio, it was later shown in near-by towns. It was not performed in a New York theater. The music was a two-piano version of the Tchaikovsky score.

The Fairy Tale *Divertissements* included:
  Puss in Boots and the Little White Cat, *Rudolph d'Alessandro* and *Betty Kerns.*

BLUEBIRDS	*Edward Caton* and *Marion Ross*	RED RIDINGHOOD AND THE WOLF *Norma Gentner* and *Nickolai Popoff*

The costumes for this production were designed by Lee Gainsborough, the décor by the Jarin Scenic Studios.

⟡⟡⟡⟡⟡⟡⟡⟡⟡⟡⟡⟡⟡⟡⟡⟡

The Philadelphia Ballet performed *Sleeping Beauty* at the Lewisohn Stadium, New York, on July 29 and 30, 1937. It is scarcely fair to judge any ballet by its performance at the Stadium, where a number of insuperable handicaps present themselves: primitive lighting equipment, a stage floor unsuitable for dancing, and the necessity, destructive to illusion, of beginning performances by daylight. Two pleasant features of the presentation were the opportunity of hearing considerably more of Tchaikovsky's enchanting score than the one-act *Le Mariage d'Aurore* afforded, and the presence in the Philadelphia Ballet of a number of young American dancers of promise. Among these were Miriam Golden and Karen Conrad, later of Ballet Theatre, and Joan McCracken, who has made a successful career on Broadway.

Catherine Littlefield in the principal role was undistinguished, offering little competition to the Auroras already in the field, although her lack of dramatic projection might have been due to the difficulties of performing at the Stadium. Edward Caton, like Enrico Cecchetti in the original production, doubled the roles of Carabosse and the Bluebird, displaying his fine command of mime and the *danse d'école.*

Later when the Philadelphia Ballet toured, a one-act version of *Sleeping Beauty* was included in the repertoire.

When the Ballet Russe de Monte Carlo succeeded Colonel W. de Basil's Ballet Russe as the foremost touring ballet organization in America, its classical entries during the first season were confined to *Swan Lake* and *Coppélia.* In 1939 it presented the Bluebird *pas de deux* as a *divertissement.* Performed before a pale setting, with nothing to distract the eye from the dancing, it was a welcome addition to the repertoire. Alicia Markova and Mia Slavenska as the Enchanted Princess, Igor Youskevitch and Roland Guerard as the Bluebird, all presented more technically correct performances than New

York had been accustomed to, although Slavenska's earthbound style of dancing was not suited to the role.

In 1940 the Original Ballet Russe, identical in repertoire with the De Basil Ballet although there had been some changes in personnel, returned to New York. It began its long engagement at the Fifty-first Street Theater on November 6 with *Aurora's Wedding*,[4] the first ballet on their opening program. The smaller stage of the Fifty-first Street Theater (the rechristened Hollywood) did not permit the use of the familiar Bakst setting with its Bibbiena-inspired columns and perspectives, and another, less spacious, also by Bakst, was substituted. It was evident that other changes had crept in. The "baby ballerinas" had grown up, but they had not advanced in artistic stature. Toumanova as Princess Aurora was even more beautiful than formerly, but her technique had acquired a circus overtone that was, as John Martin justly expressed it, "brassy" and "strident." Riabouchinska danced the Enchanted Princess with her customary dramatic flair, partnered by Roman Jasinsky, who as the Bluebird was capable, though not exciting. New York had seen Alicia Markova and Igor Youskevitch dance this brilliant *pas de deux* and had learned to demand higher standards of execution. The number of variations had been reduced to three, which also detracted from the interest. Nevertheless, *Aurora's Wedding* was welcomed back to New York, and later performances had several pleasant surprises. Baronova's Aurora had much of its old glamour, and her variation continued to be enchanting. Alexandra Denisova, in a single performance as Princess Aurora, gave promise of a brilliant future as a classical dancer—a promise unfortunately not fulfilled. Lichine as the Bluebird several times demonstrated that his fine elevation and exciting personal projection were a more than adequate substitute for technique in the eyes of audiences—at least until they had time to think it over.

When the Original Ballet Russe folded its tents and stole away, it seemed as though *Aurora's Wedding* was doomed once more to oblivion. However, fortunately for those who cherish it, Ballet Theatre stepped into the breach with a delightful reconstruction of the *divertissement* act, this time called *Princess Aurora*. The program called it "a *ballet divertissement* in one act by Anton Dolin; choreography by Anton Dolin, after Marius Petipa; scenery by Michel

---

[4] Up to this time the ballet had appeared on programs as *Le Mariage d'Aurore* (*Aurora's Wedding*).

Baronoff, after original designs by Léon Bakst; costumes by Barbara Karinska, after original designs by Léon Bakst." This version varied a good deal from that offered by the two de Basil companies, both musically and choreographically. With a long score and a five-act ballet to range through, there was no artistic reason why the choice should light on the same features that had characterized other presentations.

Princess Aurora, first performed in Mexico, had its New York première at the Forty-fourth Street Theater on November 26, 1941, with the following cast:

PRINCESS AURORA	*Irina Baronova*	THE KING	*David Nillo*
PRINCE CHARMING	*Anton Dolin*	MASTER OF CEREMONIES	
THE QUEEN	*Jeannette Lauret*		*Duncan Nobl*

ENTRANCES:

"Pas de Sept."

"Seven variations" *Rosella Hightower, Karen Conrad, Lucia Chase, Sono Osato, Nora Kaye, Annabelle Lyon, Irina Baronova*

"Pas de Trois" *Nora Kaye, Rosella Hightower,* and *Charles Dickson*

"The White Cat and Puss in Boots" *Lucia Chase* and *Simon Semenoff*

"The Bluebird" *Karen Conrad* and *Ian Gibson*

"The Three Ivans" *Yura Lazovsky, Nicolas Orloff,* and *Hubert Bland*

"The Rose Adagio" *Irina Baronova, Anton Dolin, Dimitri Romanoff, Yura Skibine,* and *Donald Saddler*

◇◇◇◇◇◇◇◇◇◇◇◇◇◇◇

Princess Aurora was the most beautifully mounted classic revival yet to be seen in New York. From the moment Duncan Nobl in the magnificent trappings of the Master of Ceremonies made his entrance on the stage, it was evident that this was to be no semi-resurrection in bargain-basement costumes, but a full-dress production worthy of the ballet's status in the history of the dance. The presence of the King and Queen, in costumes that perfectly reproduced the Bakst sketches, made the stage seem more populous than the larger numbers of dancers used in former revivals, and provided a sensible reason for the pomp and circumstance.

Choreographically this revival had many interesting features. The greater part of the variations were new. The White Cat and Puss in Boots would have been an agreeable substitute for Red Ridinghood (who with the passage of time had become a dismal bore) if one of the roles had not been ludicrously miscast. The Three Ivans was all that remained of the Diaghilev-Nijinska interpolations. The Rose

Adagio was an exciting problem in balance to be solved by the ballerina with the aid of her four partners. The only fault one could find with the production was that the décor seemed underpainted.

The performances were in most cases excellent, and in one at least as exciting as anything seen up to date in the contemporary dance theater. Irina Baronova as Aurora looked beautiful, danced her difficult variation (no longer borrowed from *The Nutcracker*) with ease, and held her long sustained balances in the Rose Adagio in a manner that was balletic and not of the circus. The "finger" variation, unaccountably danced first (its dramatic brilliance should place it fourth or fifth on the program), was beautifully presented by Rosella Hightower. Sono Osato, Annabelle Lyon, and Nora Kaye were memorable in their solos. But the most thrilling performance was that of Ian Gibson as the Bluebird. Here was the ideal Bluebird, with the neat, crisp technique of Guerard and an elevation that was even more startling than Lichine's. If he lacked something of the practiced stagecraft and glamour of the latter, it was not missed. Gibson had the unique ability to project, not personality nor characterization, but the fine points of classical technique. He had already displayed his ability to soar in the character role of Alain in *La Fille Mal Gardée,* but as the Bluebird he exhibited a command of the *danse d'école* not surpassed and seldom equaled in the contemporary dance theater.[5] Karen Conrad, his partner in the *pas de deux,* was an adequate performer, but scarcely his equal as a dancer.

Alicia Markova and Nora Kaye have also performed Princess Aurora. It is not one of Markova's better roles (although she performs it superbly), her exquisite airy quality being lost in the poses and balances of the Rose Adagio. Nora Kaye sometimes gives an exciting interpretation that serves the purpose of keeping in the public mind the classic background of her Hagar (*Pillar of Fire*) and Caroline (*Jardin aux Lilas*).[6]

[5] The critical mind is at all times hard for the layman to fathom. In a period when the critics were greeting with hysterical delight the performances of any American male dancer who could get through a classical *pas* without falling flat on his face, Ian Gibson's superb achievements in this most difficult of dancing styles were passed over in cold silence, or with a mere mention that he was appearing in the cast. Was it because he was a Canadian, trained in Vancouver and Paris?

[6] There are few roles in the "modern" dance that Nora Kaye could not perform at least as well as their creators. It would require quite an effort of the imagination to visualize any of these self-appointed geniuses in one of the great roles from the classic dramas that are the heritage of the dance theater.

With the arrival of Toumanova in Ballet Theatre, the *grand pas de deux* was revived for her. It would have been more of a delight to see again if Toumanova's approach to it had become any less strident with the passage of time. Unfortunately, it recalled the circus more vividly than ever. It is a mystery why this dancer's predilection for holding balances to the edge of absurdity was not used to some legitimate purpose in the Rose Adagio. Other modifications have found their way into *Princess Aurora*. The man-power shortage is felt as much in the ballet world as in industry. No longer can a dancer of David Nillo's status be spared to make a single entrance as the King. Ballet Theatre's Peter Rudleys (this name is its equivalent of the theatrical George Spelvin), lacking the grand manner, bustle in, overwhelmed by Bakst's gorgeous costume. The Mazurka is danced with little feeling for style, and the four boys performing it wear their helmets at four different angles, all unconvincing. The number of variations has been reduced, although the "finger" variation remains obstinately first. The Cats have quite unnecessarily disappeared, there being several young dancers in the company who could perform the female role acceptably, and one misses the enchantingly feline music. On the whole, *Princess Aurora,* after a superb start, has run down, needing critical attention from the *régisseur* and more care in the casting—a fate that befalls many ballets, particularly classic revivals, after they have been in the repertoire for more than two or three seasons.

The variations in *Princess Aurora,* in some cases borrowed from the scene in the first act in which the good fairies come to endow the baby Princess with their own good qualities, have many interesting features. There is little of the various aspects of the *danse d'école* that they leave unexplored in their presentation. In the Russian ballet theaters they were regarded as test pieces for the aspiring dancer. One who achieved the rank of ballerina (not then applied to any dancer performing in a ballet company, or Broadway musical), appearing as Swan Queen or Aurora, had almost invariably made her way from Red Ridinghood and the White Cat through the variations before she was accounted ready for the star's role.

Among the ballet audience there are some who are interested in the technicalities of the dancing. When the dancer performs a brilliant step, they would like to know what to call it. In endeavoring to set down the more obvious features, I am not trying to compose a handbook from which a future revival of *Princess Aurora* may be constructed. In all the following choreographic details, there are many transitional steps and repetitions omitted. I would not advise an aspiring dance duo to perform the Bluebird *pas de deux* from reading this sequence of steps. This is a very simple attempt to name the more easily recognizable steps for those who would like to know the dancer's terminology. The official language of ballet is French, just as the official language of music is Italian. Readers who are not interested may skip the following paragraphs.

As performed by Ballet Theatre, the solos begin with the "finger" variation, so called because of the hand movements that characterize it. The dancer enters from the right with a *pas de cheval* and, making a dramatic pause, poses with arms outstretched and pointing fingers. There are four principal steps: a stylized *balloné, bourrées, degagé pirouettes, grands jetés,* and a series of *chaînés,* all performed with great rapidity, and accompanied by characteristic arm and hand movements. It ends with an *arabesque.* As originally presented by the De Basil Ballet, this variation was considered second only to Aurora's in importance and was performed by one of the ballerinas of the company, usually Danilova or Toumanova. Striking and dramatic, it is worthy of any ballerina's best efforts. In the Original Ballet Russe it was neglected, being assigned to a secondary dancer who performed the steps with deadly conscientiousness. Although badly placed in *Princess Aurora,* it received spirited performances by Rosella Hightower, who later resigned it for the Enchanted Princess in the Bluebird *pas de deux.* It has not been properly performed since then.

The second variation is grave and dignified. In the original production this was the solo of the Lilac Fairy, Aurora's godmother. The entrance from the upstage left is made with a *grand rond de jambe en l'air,* a fifth position, and a step into *arabesque,* a large and beautiful movement. The solo ends with a *pas de chat* and a kneeling pose. It demands from the dancer impeccable line and the ability to sustain its slow rhythm with fluid grace. Tamara Grigorieva (De Basil Ballet) and Sono Osato and Alicia Alonso (Ballet Theatre) have met its requirements admirably.

The third variation is swift and birdlike. The dancer runs in with little steps on point, with arms behind her back, fingers fluttering. This is the simplest of the variations and depends for its effect on the charm of the dancer performing it. It was included in *Aurora's Wedding,* usually danced by Vera Nelidova. Rozsika Sabo is associated with it in Ballet Theatre.

The fourth variation exploits a greater variety of steps than the previous solos. It was originally danced by Aurora in an earlier scene in which she describes her growing up from childhood, using a stylized *port de bras* beginning with a small movement and expanding the gesture until her arms are high over her head. The steps include *chassée* turns in a circle, followed by a *développé à la seconde.* Performing a series of *chaînés* of increasing velocity, she ends in a fourth position. Nora Kaye has given striking performances of this variation, and it is possibly her finest single performance in the classical vein. This was not included in *Aurora's Wedding.*

The fifth variation is one of the gayest in the whole of classical ballet as we know it. It includes very fast *passées* on point, each *passée* gaining height. From an *entrechat trois* she steps into an *arabesque.* She hops on point with tiny steps, finishing with a *relevé* into *attitude en avant.* This also was new to the Ballet Theatre audience, who will not forget Annabelle Lyon's performance. Subsequent dancers merely executed the steps without Lyon's inimitable sparkle.

Aurora's variation concludes the series. Difficult and ungracious, it may acquire a certain grandeur from a fine performance, but at least one member of the audience considers it a waste of the ballerina's energy. Aurora runs on, as though greeting the guests, bowing slightly to the King and Queen. She does a *glissade, arabesque,* and, using a transitional step (*failli*), poses *en attitude,* arms in fifth position *en haut,* followed by a fourth position with expanding *port de bras;* again *glissade, arabesque, bourrée* moving diagonally, *rond de jambe, retiré;* hops *en attitude en avant.* She retraces her diagonal with fifth position *emboîtés,* does a preparation leading to a *pirouette* ending with a large fourth position. The next sequence begins with *glissade, arabesque,* and continues with a circle of *piqué* turns covering the entire stage. The variation ends with *chaînés* and a *pas de chat* into a fourth position, with arms outstretched. Any charm that this variation may have comes entirely from the ballerina's ability to phrase her steps musically. Baronova and Markova both performed it beautifully, although it seemed to chain the latter's aerial elegance to the ground.

The *pas de trois* varies in many particulars from the de Basil version, which was originally performed in New York by Vera Zorina, Lubov Rostova, and Roman Jasinsky. The passage of time has blurred the details, but one or two features emerge from memory. There was a series of *grands jetés* performed by the dancers in a big circle around the stage. At the conclusion the male dancer knelt on one knee, the girls supporting themselves in *penché arabesques,* with one hand on his shoulder. Ballet Theatre's *pas de trois* includes *demi-fouettés en l'air* and supported *grands jetés* by the girls. While the male dancer does *entrechats six,* the girls perform *fouettés en tournant.* He supports the girls in poses *en arabesque* together, and *pirouettes* separately. The whole ends in a classical group with one of the girls kneeling in front. This *pas de trois* has been performed by several combinations of dancers, its success depending on perfect co-ordination and timing. The original Ballet Theatre group (Nora Kaye, Rosella Hightower, and Charles Dickson) solved all its problems, setting a standard seldom equaled by their successors.

The Bluebird *pas de deux* (more correctly the Bluebird and the Enchanted Princess [7]) is probably the most renowned duet in the entire range of classical ballet. This may be due to the unusual brilliance and variety of the man's variation—the high point of male virtuosity in the dance. It is often presented out of its context, and no production of *Sleeping Beauty,* however fragmentary, omits to present it in its entirety. New York was familiar with the version (one that slurred over many fine points in the choreography) offered by the de Basil company. Ballet Theatre's revival, staged by Anton Dolin, who had been a notable Bluebird in the Diaghilev Ballet, restored much that had been previously passed over.

The Bluebird *pas de deux* follows the strict classical form: *adage,* two solo variations, and a coda.

The *adage* begins with the entrance of the Enchanted Princess. She pauses in an *arabesque,* then kneels in the characteristic pose (*épaulé* with arms crossed over chest). As the music repeats the opening strain, the Bluebird enters in a *cabriole derrière* (sometimes *sauté*) with *entrechat cinq.* He pauses in a *soussus* pose, advances, and sup-

---

[7] The original story, by Perrault, *L'Oiseau bleu,* has a plot of great complexity. It involves a King who loses his dearly loved wife and marries a wicked woman who is unkind to his daughter, the Princess Florine. Described as *"douce et spirituelle,"* Florine is loved by a King who comes to her disguised as a bluebird. After many adventures they are married.

ports the girl in a *pirouette*. Using his right arm for support, she takes an *attitude*, in which he promenades her. Still supporting her, he makes a small and quick turn to her downstage side, where he stands in a *plié arabesque à terre*, while she again supports herself on his shoulder in an *arabesque*, balances, and holds the pose. They part, making opposite semicircles to meet facing each other at the center of the stage. She raises her leg to a second position, in which pose he promenades her, then gives her the impetus for a *fouetté pirouette*, ending in an *arabesque* with characteristic birdlike fluttering. In unison they move: *glissade, arabesque, jeté en tournant*. She promenades, performing *petits battements en avant*. He supports her in multiple finger *pirouettes*, then a *développé au quatrième devant*. She moves downstage in *glissade, arabesque* which changes to a pose *au quatrième devant* on point. She runs to the Bluebird, who lifts her so that she lies across his shoulder. He carries her upstage and lowers her to the floor. He repeats his opening step, the *entrechat* being followed by a *tour en l'air*, his arms in fifth position *en haut*. She joins him performing *glissade, pas de chat*, and *pirouettes*, which end in an *arabesque en face*. This is repeated three times, ending in an *arabesque* in profile to the audience. Again they walk in opposite semicircles to the center of the stage. They meet, and while he supports her, standing off to one side, she does a slow *développé à la seconde*, in which she balances. This is followed by a repetition of the lift to the shoulder. She then assumes the characteristic kneeling pose, while he stands behind her *en arabesque*.

For his solo variation the Bluebird walks to the left side of the stage and performs a step of elevation that dancers seem to have as much difficulty in naming authoritatively as performing.[8] In a downstage diagonal he performs what might be called a *cabriole en avant* with *entrechat quatre*. This, repeated three times, brings the dancer to the opposite downstage corner, where he performs an *assemblé, entrechat six*, double *tour en l'air*, and a pose *en arabesque*. A preparation, *glissade*, and *jeté en tournant* carry him to the upstage corner, where he begins another diagonal crossing, this time performing *temps de poisson, assemblé, entrechat cinq*, repeated three times and concluding with the same sequence of steps that brought the first

---

[8] I have asked many dancers, including two who have appeared in the role of the Bluebird, what the step is. They all become very involved, but reach no conclusions. A highly informal description is that he sits in the air and twinkles his feet.

diagonal to a close. Two *jetés en tournant* bring him to the upstage center. He advances to the footlights, performs a series of *entrechats six,* a *soussus,* a double *tour en l'air,* concluding with a characteristic pose.

This variation, composed largely of steps of elevation, at least one of which may have been specially composed for the occasion, can be a pedestrian affair when performed by a dancer without the necessary *ballon* and elevation. Among the dancers seen in New York, Ian Gibson alone met all its requirements. Several dancers have given theatrically acceptable performances. Lichine's admirable elevation deceived many into believing his performance much finer than it really was. André Eglevsky, physically unsuited to the allegro aspects of classical technique, is a naturally slow-moving dancer, with a broad rather than a high jump, enjoying a fame built on his ability to perform unlimited pirouettes. As the Bluebird, he executes the steps with academic accuracy, although he sometimes gives the impression that he does not know what to do with his hands. John Kriza has given some promising interpretations, which may improve with time. Igor Youskevitch and Roland Guerard, though no longer seen in the role, are remembered favorably. There are a number of dancers who go through the routine in a passable way, completely failing to grasp the essential masculine simplicity of its classic style.

The solo variation of the Enchanted Princess begins with a pose in fourth position *épaulé,* with hands crossed at wrist. To the opening bars of the music, she flutters back and forth. Her first step *à la seconde,* with birdlike arm movements, is followed by a fifth position *bourrée* in place. After a repetition, she performs *demi-fouettés* on point, alternately to right and left, followed by *emboîtés, échappés,* hops *en arabesque.* The high point is a series of *chaînés* with characteristic *port de bras* to right and left, followed by *dégagé* turns, which begin and end in *chaînés.* After an *arabesque* she sinks to the floor in the *épaulé* kneeling pose that is associated with her.

Technically this variation is comparatively simple. It carries certain dramatic implications, however, that may be overlooked by its executants. The music that accompanies her *chaînés* to right and left has a delicately stormy quality that seems to blow the resisting Enchanted Princess to and fro. At this point a dainty indication of stylized fright does not come amiss. Some dancers ignore this completely, depriving the performance of its charm. Tatiana Riabouchinska made the most of this aspect of the variation. Her physical loveliness, allied to her dramatic flair, made her Enchanted Princess a delightful impersonation in spite of her deficiencies in technique. Karen Conrad, a dancer of remarkable elevation and such quickness of movement that she often anticipated the music, made little of the characterization. Rosella Hightower gives a warm and spirited performance, technically perfect and musically phrased.[9]

The coda begins with the entrance of the Bluebird. He takes a pose that is a preparation for a series of *brisés volés*. He performs three *changements,* and multiple *pirouettes en dehors,* waiting in a fifth-position pose with hand over heart for the entrance of the Enchanted Princess. She enters in a sequence of single *piqué* turns, followed by double *piqué* turns. When she reaches the opposite corner she does several *ronds de jambe en l'air* and *pas de bourrée,* advancing with arms outstretched to her partner. She *chaînés* away into double *pirouettes* and an *arabesque à terre.* They join briefly, separating for a momentary fourth position *épaulé,* with *plié,* performed in opposite directions. He does a *cabriole* while she poses *en arabesque.* Making semicircles, they meet in *grands jetés.* She places her hand on his shoulder, and together they traverse a diagonal in *brisés* and low *arabesques* until they reach the downstage corner. She does supported *pirouettes en dehors,* ending in a back bend over his arm. She leaves the stage in a *grand jeté.* He does a *double tour en l'air* and follows her, also in a *grand jeté.*

The Rose Adagio, spectacular in performance, is a problem in balance. The Princess Aurora performs a variety of *pirouettes,* supported by her partners, concluding with a repetition of the long-sustained *attitude,* which she maintains while the four cavaliers promenade her in turn. This *adage* belongs in the second act (or first if the christening scene is called the prologue), where it has dramatic point and meaning. The cavaliers are four princes come to seek her hand in marriage, and her even distribution of smiles and graciousness indicate her state of mind, still untouched by love. In *Princess Aurora* it does not wear as well as the *pas de deux* that it replaced. There are times when it has the atmosphere of a sporting event. Both Markova and Baronova performed it with superb aplomb, but it is

[9] Alicia Alonso is reported to be an excellent Enchanted Princess. I have not seen her performance, but her lovely line and classic demeanor make it more than likely that the reports are correct.

a style of dancing that does not permit the former to display her unparalleled lightness and is a waste of that supreme quality.

The *pas de deux,* the choreography of which is said to have certain features added by Nijinska, is less spectacular than the Rose Adagio, though it makes a much better climax to a *divertissement* ballet. Nana Gollner, partnered by Paul Petroff, performs it charmingly, making light of its technical difficulties. It includes the various supported *pirouettes* and poses that make up the vocabulary of the classical *adage.* Its more spectacular features include a low *révérence à terre,* from which the ballerina rises to an *attitude sur le point,* and a series of lifts (called "fish") in which she jumps into her partner's arms assuming a classical pose as she lands. Sometimes it concludes with a lift (in which the dancer is supported on her partner's slightly bent knee) that seems a complete defiance of the laws of gravity.

It is an unfortunate truth that a revival of *Sleeping Beauty* could only be achieved by robbing all existing ballet companies of their ranking artists. Irina Baronova once promised to be an ideal Aurora. After a year in a Broadway musical she appears to have lost her command of the niceties of classical technique. Toumanova, who gave many thrilling performances as a very young dancer, has acquired unfortunate mannerisms since reaching maturity. Markova, Giselle and Sylphide *par excellence,* is somehow not a convincing Aurora— it is like asking a coloratura soprano to sing Brünnhilde. Possibly by the time that the wise producer who realizes that the public is ready for a full-dress classical revival gets around to it, the ideal Aurora may have emerged from whatever classroom she is working in at this moment.

Rosella Hightower, most enchanting of Enchanted Princesses, will make the perfect Lilac Fairy when that happy day arrives. There are a number of fine young classical dancers available for the other roles: Alicia Alonso, Annabelle Lyon, Mary Ellen Moylan, Marie-Jeanne, Maria Tallchief, and Nana Gollner are outstanding names that come to mind. It might be possible to rotate the important roles, as was done in the historic Alhambra production. Someone has said that ballet is the only branch of the theater where understudies and alternate casts are greeted with enthusiasm. Informed audiences (as opposed to the kind who make one visit to the ballet to see some press agent's pet who may have made an appearance in a movie or musical comedy) are delighted to see as much variation in casting as possible, especially in the classical ballets. Whatever mysterious deity arranges the programs for the New York seasons of ballet is singularly stupid on this point. In a recent season, a great classic role was danced almost exclusively by one highly press agented star with all the *élan* of a wooden Indian, while at least three other members of the company who far surpassed her were given one or two performances at the most. Ballet is not supported by the casual ticket-buyer who saw the ballet three years ago and thinks that enough time has elapsed to make it seem new again. Choosing his evening because Madame Anonymous, star of stage and screen, is on the program, he buys his ticket, sees the performance, and stays away for another three years. The ballet audience from whom support comes is quite a different matter. It is made up of people who attend not single performances but entire seasons; who go to see ballet, performed by ballet dancers; who know that Madame Whatnot's stay in Hollywood has made her useless to ballet, unless she is willing to spend at least a year in solid work under strict discipline; who do not give a damn about novelties or troupes of Spanish dancers, or anything else that interferes with the presentation of ballet; and, lastly (because we have to stop somewhere, not because we have run out of grievances), who would like to receive some consideration from the arrangers of programs. This tirade, purely spontaneous, has carried one indignant member of the audience far from *Sleeping Beauty*. Let us return to the subject in hand.

A first-class production of *Sleeping Beauty* (provided a good Aurora can be found) is easily possible in New York, where several of the dancers who had important roles in the Diaghilev revival are available to direct it—notably Pierre Vladimiroff and Anatole Vilzak, though there are others. Anton Dolin has many memories of that historic production. Elizaveta Anderson-Ivantzoff danced several roles in this great classic before she gave her interpretation of Princess Aurora at the Bolshoi Theater in Moscow. A committee of these informed authorities (always supposing they could be induced to work together) would be capable of producing a revival that not only would add a brilliant chapter to ballet history in America, but would provide an unparalleled stimulus to ballet training for a whole generation of dancers.

The revival of *Sleeping Beauty* (called *The Sleeping Princess*) by the Sadler's Wells Ballet in London in 1939 was eagerly welcomed by a public that had neglected the Diaghilev revival eighteen years previously. The current production, along with the complete *Swan Lake,* has maintained an honored and popular place in the repertoire of England's national ballet. Margot Fonteyn (Princess Aurora) and Robert Helpmann (Prince Charming) headed the cast, which included June Brae (Lilac Fairy), Pamela May (Rose Fairy), and John Greenwood (Carabosse). The settings and costumes by Nadia Benois, as far as one can tell from photographs, appear to be in the spirit of those by Bakst. Oliver Messel is said to be designing new costumes, which seems to indicate that the production is not going to be shelved in the immediate future. The choreographic details of the revival were supervised by Nicholas Sergeyev who as a child had performed the role of one of Carabosse's attendant rats in the first Marinsky performance in 1890, and as a mature artist appeared in many subsequent performances. If Sadler's Wells ever makes its long-promised visit to America, it is to be hoped that its classic revivals, which include *The Nutcracker* and *Coppélia* as well as *Swan Lake* and *The Sleeping Princess,* will be included in its repertoire thus ensuring ballet audiences in this country at least one opportunity of seeing them in their entirety, with choreography that at least makes an attempt to approximate the originals and not something dreamed up by the local boys and girls.[10]

It is impossible to overestimate the place of *Sleeping Beauty* in the history of ballet. André Levinson, most celebrated of modern ballet critics, says of it: "This work . . . is most truly representative of the heroic period of Russian ballet." In the production of the Tchaikovsky-Petipa ballets the *danse d'école* reached the ultimate. There was nothing new to be done along those lines, perfection not being susceptible of improvement. Repetition of the formula, lacking the inspiration of great music, became more and more automatic, until it froze into a catalepsy comparable to that of the Princess Aurora in the ballet. Fokine was the Prince Charming who awakened the dormant beauty with the warmth of new ideas, opening the way, not only to modern ballet, but to other forms of dance as well. This, however, did not mean that the classic ballet was dead. One does not banish Mozart to oblivion because one admires Beethoven. Classic,

[10] *Swan Lake* with choreography by William Christensen; *Sleeping Beauty* with choreography by Catherine Littlefield. *Aurora's Wedding* and *Princess Aurora* were arranged by producers with less confidence in their ability to improve on Petipa.

romantic, and modern ballet set each other off, leading to the perception of new beauty in all forms. It is a basic truth, however, that a firm grasp of the classic technique is the one foundation for all forms of the art of the dance—a fact that has dawned on the exponents of the "modern" dance, who send their disciples to ballet schools to acquire the fundamentals that they themselves scorned as a matter of principle. Once acquired, everything else becomes easy for the artist. Unless the classics are maintained as a living tradition, the dance as an art form will be a dead thing, consigned to the uses of a Broadway line routine. *Swan Lake* and *Sleeping Beauty* are the keystones of ballet. As long as they are cherished and kept alive by adequate and frequent performances, ballet will maintain its proper position as the fountainhead of all forms of theatrical dancing.

In its 1946 season at the Metropolitan Opera House, the Original Ballet Russe presented *Aurora's Wedding* in a manner entirely unworthy of the traditions established in earlier seasons. The variations, except when occasional performances were given by guest stars, were executed in a manner that could have been bettered in any local student recital; the choreography had become confused; the costumes and scenery showed the ravages of five years of touring. On the whole, it was a sorry spectacle.

LE SPECTRE DE LA ROSE

LE SPECTRE DE LA ROSE shares with *Les Sylphides* and *Le Cygne* (*The Dying Swan*) a unique place in the history of ballet. In these works Michel Fokine made use of classical technique in a hitherto unknown way. Anything resembling those passages in ballet which correspond to the dry recitative of opera were eliminated. Movements became fluid and the mechanics of the supported adagio were hidden from the audience. *Le Spectre de la Rose* is essentially a *pas de deux,* but it bears little resemblance to the classical *pas de deux* as devised by Petipa and other choreographers who preceded Fokine. The strictly classical *pas de deux* followed a fixed pattern: a supported adagio, a solo variation for the male dancer, a solo variation for the female dancer, and a coda in which both participants displayed their virtuosity. Comparison of this formula with *Le Spectre de la Rose* demonstrates how far Fokine had left accepted conventions behind.

Le Spectre de la Rose has a simple story, for which the inspiration was a poem by Théophile Gautier. The music is Carl Maria von Weber's *Invitation to the Dance,* and the settings and costumes were designed by Léon Bakst.

❖❖❖❖❖❖❖❖❖❖❖❖❖❖❖❖❖

The scene is a bedroom, simply furnished and decorated in a color scheme of blue and white. It has two windows set at angles on opposite sides of the stage. To the left is a bed in a curtained alcove and in the foreground a chair upholstered in white. A Young Girl enters. She is dressed in a white muslin party frock, a light cape,[1] and a bonnet tied with a bow. She has come home tired from her first ball. In her hand she carries a souvenir—a red rose. She sits in the chair to recall the pleasures of the evening. Falling asleep, she dreams that the rose has assumed human form. They dance together. He kisses her and leaps out of the window. She awakens, lingering for a

---

[1] At the Paris Opéra performances she is accompanied by a maid, who removes the cape and leaves.

moment on the borderline of sleep. Saddened, she realizes that it was an illusion and crushes the rose to her lips.

Le Spectre de la Rose was first performed at the Théâtre de Monte Carlo in 1911 by Thamar Karsavina and Vaslav Nijinsky. It was an immediate success. Critics and public lost themselves in a maze of adjectives in their efforts to describe the transports with which they viewed Nijinsky's sensational leaps and effortless execution of the difficult steps.

The fame of *Le Spectre de la Rose* preceded it to New York, where it was first performed by Lydia Lopokova and Alexandre Gavriloff at the Metropolitan Opera House on April 3, 1916. This presentation was greeted with modified rapture. Lydia Lopokova was, no doubt, enchanting as the Young Girl, but this is not a woman's ballet. The New York audience was waiting for the much publicized Nijinsky leap. Nijinsky made his first appearance in America in this ballet on April 12, 1916, and no one was disappointed. For once, advance publicity was not exaggerated.[2]

The subsequent history of *Le Spectre de la Rose* closely parallels that of *Scheherazade*. Designed to exploit the unique personality and technical pre-eminence of Nijinsky, it has never been satisfactorily performed since he retired. There have been many revivals in Europe and America. In New York, David Lichine and Paul Haakon have given creditable performances.

In 1941 Ballet Theatre revived *Le Spectre de la Rose* with Ian Gibson and Annabelle Lyon. Ballet audiences who had been astonished by Gibson's remarkable performance in the Bluebird *pas de deux* expected a revelation. His clear-cut and precise classical technique, however, were not adapted to the fluidity and romanticism of the Fokine style. This experiment was dropped after the 1941 season.

In the first performances of *Le Spectre de la Rose,* Thamar Karsavina's interpretation of the Young Girl was almost as much lauded as Nijinsky's more spectacular feats. It is possible that she danced for a more discriminating audience. Currently this character of the little

[2] One critic raised a dissenting voice, complaining that there was "a discordant note in a super-refinement of gesture and posture that amounted to effeminacy . . . as did certain technical details of the dancing, such as dancing on the toes, which is not ordinarily indulged in by male dancers" (*New York Times,* April 13, 1916).

drama has become the forgotten woman of ballet, though it usually receives a better performance than the role of the Spectre. Irina Baronova and Tatiana Riabouchinska, as "baby ballerinas," gave touching and wistful renditions of the Young Girl. These could scarcely be equaled in charm by a mature artist. Something of what Karsavina achieved by artistry was recaptured by these very young dancers through the enchantment of youth. With the passage of time these performances became much more routined.

It is unfortunate that *Le Spectre de la Rose* has degenerated into a stunt ballet. Audiences sit relaxed until the moment comes for the leap (not always executed in the manner prescribed by the choreographer),[3] which, however ineptly performed, is greeted with storms of applause. One must conclude that this acclaim is not for the dancer they have just seen, but a tribute to the past glories of the ballet.

[3] The leap was done originally as a *saut de chat,* executed with the forward leg bent. It gave the illusion of flight and the dancer's downward progress was not seen by the audience. In most current performances the Spectre makes his exit in a *grand jeté.*

SWAN LAKE
AND
THE MAGIC SWAN

CLASSICAL BALLET, evolving and expanding for three hundred years, reached its highest point in the Tchaikovsky-Petipa ballets —*Le Lac des Cygnes* (*Swan Lake*) and *La Belle au Bois Dormant* (*Sleeping Beauty*).

Swan Lake had a modest beginning. In 1871 Tchaikovsky spent a summer vacation with his sister Alexandra Davidova. For the amusement of her children he composed a miniature ballet called *Swan Lake*. Several years later, when commissioned by the Bolshoi Theater in Moscow to compose a ballet score, Tchaikovsky included this music along with a fragment from his opera *Undine* in the score of *Swan Lake*. It is said that Vladimir Petrovich Begichev, the director of the theater, himself suggested the subject of *Swan Lake,* but it seems likely that Tchaikovsky, in view of his previous interest in a story of that name, had some hand in the composition of the legend, the locale of which is *Allemagne dans le temps fabuleux des Contes*.[1]

Misfortune dogged the first production of *Swan Lake*. The direction of the Bolshoi, accustomed to the commonplace rhythms of the official composers who, spiritual ancestors of the Hollywood musical craftsmen of today, kept music[2] of all kinds on hand ready to be tailored to the measure of a dancer's abilities, found Tchaikovsky's delightful score beyond their comprehension. They had no compunction whatever about slashing it here and there, inserting excerpts from other ballets, which they considered more danceable. *Swan Lake* was first performed at the Bolshoi on March 4, 1877, with choreography by Julius Reisinger and as Swan Queen a dancer called Karparkova—names otherwise unknown to fame in western Europe. There is no doubt at all that the ballet was a dismal failure. Tchaikov-

---

[1] A stage direction from the score of *Swan Lake*.

[2] It was known as "drawer music" as it was composed in advance and kept neatly filed, ready to produce at a moment's notice.

sky with his usual humility attributed this to shortcomings in his score, which he promised to revise. Fortunately the opportunity to keep this promise never arose.

Tchaikovsky composed two more ballets, *Sleeping Beauty* and *The Nutcracker,* for the Marinsky Theatre in St. Petersburg. These, given elaborate and choreographically sound productions, were popular with the public if not with officialdom. After Tchaikovsky's death, in 1893, Marius Petipa, becoming interested in the score of *Swan Lake,* determined to produce it at the Marinsky. The habit of presenting *Swan Lake* piecemeal began at once and Act II (that portion of the ballet most familiar to American audiences) was performed on February 29, 1894 at a memorial concert of Tchaikovsky's work. Petipa, unable to give his full attention to the choreography, sketched his plans, entrusting the details of the production to Lev Ivanov.

On January 27, 1895, *Swan Lake* reached the stage of the Marinsky in its complete form with the celebrated Italian ballerina Pierina Legnani in the exacting dual role of Odette-Odile. This time the ballet was an artistic and popular success, the *réclame* of which was not at all damaged by the fact that it contained an unusual choreographic feature that became a subject for controversy.

In the third act of *Swan Lake* there is a *pas de deux* of formidable technical difficulty for the Prince and Odile. The coda of this *pas de deux* included the thirty-two *fouettés* [3] *en tournant,* a feat of virtuosity that was executed by Legnani. This was the first appearance of multiple *fouettés* in serious ballet and many connoisseurs were appalled by what they held to be an exhibition of pure acrobatics. Others were carried away by the brilliance of the exploit, thrilled by the skill and superb balance of the executant. This faction would assemble at every repetition of *Swan Lake* and count the turns to be quite certain that the canonical number had been duly performed — a procedure not unknown more than half a century later.

As this is what might be termed the first legal appearance of multiple *fouettés,* it may serve as an excuse for a digression on this phenomenon. Writers on ballet sometimes find it necessary to apologize for it. Granted that it is acrobatic, surely with fifty years of artistic tolerance, if not benediction, it can be taken for granted as part of the legitimate choreographic vocabulary. Arnold Haskell says that

[3] The *fouetté* is a turn on one leg. Traction is obtained partly by a *relevé* of the supporting foot, partly by a whipping movement of the other leg.

"it became a commonplace to . . . young dancers. . . . They could perform thirty-two, sixty-four, and more, if necessary, and they did it with ease and precision." Possibly they did, and one would like to have seen it. This breed of dancer is rarer, however, than Mr. Haskell's words would indicate. It is one thing to perform multiple *fouettés* in the classroom. It is quite another to execute them in the coda of a difficult *pas de deux,* and there are few enough dancers who are equal to the achievement. They should not be denied their meed of appreciation.

Swan Lake has remained in the active repertoires of the theaters of Russia since its Marinsky production. Countless ballerinas have danced it since Legnani—Pavlova, Karsavina, Kchesinska, Preobrajenska, among the most famous. Americans detailed to Moscow during World War II will testify that it is still a living issue there, the merits of the rival ballerinas Semenova and Ulanova being hotly debated.[4] One correspondent suggested decorating veterans of twenty-five performances with a silver swan.

Swan Lake reached London in 1911. It was performed there for the first time at the Royal Opera House, Covent Garden, on November 30, 1911, with Mathilde Kchesinska and Vaslav Nijinsky in the principal roles. This production was by the Diaghilev Ballet, Kchesinska appearing as a guest artist. There is an improbable story about this performance to the effect that Mischa Elman left a recital he was giving at Albert Hall on that evening to play the violin solos for the *adages.* Actually there were four performances of *Swan Lake* during the season and Elman played for all of them. In no case did the dates of the performances conflict with any of his professional engagements. Diaghilev, in employing a violinist of Elman's standing, was carrying out a custom of the Marinsky Theater, where Leopold Auer usually played the solos. The thought of Elman dashing madly from recital to opera house and back again, possibly tuning his violin in a hansom cab on the way, is fascinating. Unfortunately it isn't true.

New York also saw *Swan Lake* in 1911. It was presented at the Metropolitan Opera House on December 19, 1911, at a matinee, with Katerina Geltzer and Mikhail Mordkin. The Music Division of the New York Public Library maintains a file of Metropolitan perform-

[4] Let me confess at once to a partiality for Ulanova, arrived at after seeing both of these artists perform excerpts from *Swan Lake* in the movies.

ance programs, but to the unknown mastermind who edited the 1911 collection for the bindery what may have been the first performance of *Swan Lake* in the Western Hemisphere was of no importance and the program is not included in the volume for that year. By some weakness or inadvertence a later program is available, revealing the cast to be as follows:

ODILLIA)
ODETTA)   *Katerina Geltzer*
(Prima Ballerina from the Imperial Opera, Moscow)
SIEGFRIED   *Mikhail Mordkin*
BENNO, his friend *Alexander Volinine*

WOLFGANG, SIEGFRIED'S TUTOR
      Kiprion Barboe I
QUEEN   *Mlle Pantaliewa*
VON ROTHBART (Sorcerer)
      M. Trojanowski

◆◆◆◆◆◆◆◆◆◆◆◆◆◆◆◆◆◆◆

It was described as a fairy-tale ballet; music by Tchaikovsky; adapted for the ballet by Marius Petipa and rearranged by Mikhail Mordkin.[5] The settings by James Fox, staff artist of the Metropolitan Opera House, pleased the critics, but the flight of the swans [6] did not. Mme Geltzer was praised for her brilliant dancing, although exception was taken to her muscular development. Very few dancers could stand comparison with Pavlova, who had danced at the Metropolitan the previous season in *Giselle*. Her elegance of line gave succeeding dancers competition that was almost unfair. *Swan Lake* was repeated at the Metropolitan in its complete form, but more often given one act at a time—Act III on December 21, and Act II on December 29. This precedent has been faithfully adhered to by ballet companies in America ever since.

Possibly the severe classicism of *Swan Lake* failed to attract dancers or producers. It was not included in the Diaghilev company's repertoire in America. In the wave of ballet revivals that followed this tour and those of Pavlova, emphasis seems to have been placed on the exotic and romantic aspects of the dance. Oriental dancers flourished, dying swans drooped sadly in every pupils' recital, but it requires more than a costume and a desire to dance *Swan Lake*.

In 1930 Act II of *Swan Lake* was revived at the Chicago Civic

[5] A note in the souvenir program for these performances states: "Mr. Mordkin has taken certain liberties in condensing the acts to comply with American conceptions of stagecraft."

[6] Corps de ballet on wires? Or could it have been an apotheosis of stuffed swans from *Parsifal*?

Opera by Laurent Novikoff with Ruth Pryor and Edward Caton. A critic—one William Yates—who apparently did not like Tchaikovsky, remarked: "Laurent Novikoff's arrangement of dances, especially in view of the mediocre music, was especially fine." It is fortunate for Mr. Yates that he enjoyed the dancing. Otherwise he must have had a painful evening. *Swan Lake* was presented on this occasion in a double bill with *Le Jongleur de Notre Dame*. If he found the music of *Swan Lake* mediocre, what could he have thought of the other half of the program? Mr. Yates refers to a dance in *Swan Lake* as a "composition of three." If this is an attempt to translate the language of ballet into English, it is rather an awkward substitute for *pas de trois*. This *pas de trois* was danced by three girls. Was this the popular *pas de quatre* (dance of the little swans) reduced in numbers, or just something fancy dreamed up by Mr. Novikoff for the occasion?

Colonel W. de Basil's Ballet Russe presented their version of *Swan Lake* (Act II) on March 9, 1934, with Alexandra Danilova and David Lichine. This was the beginning of *Swan Lake* as a hardy perennial of the repertoire. Of the major ballet companies in the United States, only the now moribund American Ballet omitted it from the repertoire.

When the Ballet Russe de Monte Carlo began its career as a touring organization in 1938, it followed a precedent established by Diaghilev, adding to Act II a *pas de trois* from Act I, thereby enhancing the interest and leaving undisturbed such fragments of plot as are visible. This feature, highly popular with audiences, was the cause of a major *"scandale"* [7] in the ballet world. Serge Lifar, who had excellent reasons for avoiding comparison with other dancers of the company, insisted that the *pas de trois* be eliminated. When the management (it cannot always be wrong) rightly refused to heed this demand, he departed for Paris in a huff. Audiences who had seen him hamming his way through *Giselle* (the dancing equivalent of the Italian tenor who sobs and gulps an aria) and his outsize performance in *Swan Lake* were delighted. [8] A company that included such accomplished dancers as Igor Youskevitch, Frederic Franklin,

---

[7] Any incident that disturbs the routine of a ballet company—missing an entrance, a personal quarrel, a fit of temperament—is known as a *scandale*.

[8] Some who had turned in to the box office tickets purchased in advance of the opening of the season took heart and bought them back again.

and Roland Guerard was not likely to miss that exploiter of past glories, Serge Lifar.

Ballet Theatre produced Act II of *Swan Lake* in a restaging by Anton Dolin, who omitted the *pas de trois* on the ground that it interfered with the artistic unity of the ballet. A note in the program stated: "The *pas de trois* which is so often seen in this act belongs to the Prologue (called Act I by Beaumont) and has no real place in the romantic scene, its presence making the ballet a series of *divertissements* instead of a connected scene." On those grounds the *pas de quatre* might also be omitted, as, though it is undeniably part of the original choreography, its lively rhythms are in almost comic contrast to the adagio that immediately precedes it. Dolin was later induced to restore the *pas de trois* at a special performance at the Majestic Theater, New York, on February 27, 1941, when Vera Nemchinova made a guest appearance in *Swan Lake*. However, he placed it at the beginning of the act as a sort of curtain-raiser—a far from satisfactory arrangement. As dancers must warm up before performing variations of such technical brilliance, so the audience must be warmed up to appreciate them. This innovation has been dropped and Ballet Theatre currently presents *Swan Lake* without the *pas de trois*.

Since 1934 America has seen coveys of Swan Queens—Alexandra Danilova, Alicia Markova, Irina Baronova, Tamara Toumanova, and Mia Slavenska head the list of European importations; Patricia Bowman, Nana Gollner, Nora Kaye, Karen Conrad, and Rosella Hightower are among the Americans.

Every ballet-lover has his favorite Swan Queen. Arguments for and against the various interpretations can attain a violence that is almost enough to break up friendships. There are some who prefer the warm femininity of Danilova, others the ethereal aloofness of Markova. Both are enchanting; both expositions of the role are valid. Their partisans find it possible to enjoy both performances—with reservations, of course. Danilova's superb line and thrilling execution of the coda are unforgettable. Markova's imponderable elegance and delicate *petits battements* have their own charm. One can only make a choice by the light of personal prejudice. Baronova, Toumanova, and Slavenska also have their adherents. Baronova has a warm romantic approach to the role. Toumanova's borders on the

LES SYLPHIDES (Alicia Markova and Anton Dolin) Barbara Fallis in background

LE MARIAGE D'AURORE (*Aurora's Wedding*). Tamara Toumanova and David Lichine. Paul Petroff and Nathalie Branitzka, Sergei Ismailov and Anna Adrianova, Marc Platoff, Alexandra Danilova and Yurek

as Odette in *Swan Lake*

ALEXANDRA DANILOVA

as the Sugarplum Fairy in *The Nutcracker*

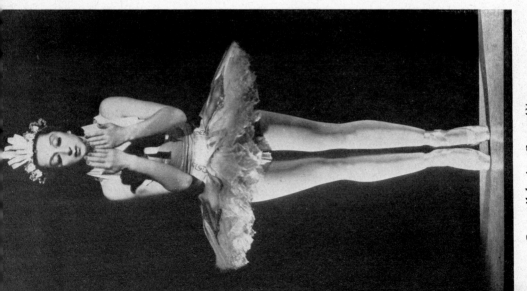

as Swanilda in *Coppélia*

ROSELLA HIGHTOWER (*penché arabesque in Swan Lake costume*)

athletic. She delights in executing multiple pirouettes and long-sustained balances on point, which are frequently displayed with very little regard for the rhythm and tempo of the music, but which enchant the more circus-minded members of the audience.

Among American Swan Queens, Rosella Hightower has the true classical approach. As a very young dancer with the Monte Carlo Ballet she attracted the attention of the serious ballet-lover when she danced in the *pas de trois*. Her exquisite line, neat precise technique, and musicality proclaimed the classical ballerina in the making. That promise has been fulfilled by the sensitive elegance of her Swan Queen, presented by Ballet Theatre. Unfortunately, Miss Hightower is merely a dancer of high artistic gifts—not a refugee from musical comedy or Hollywood. Naturally she has been passed over when performance schedules are made out. Podunk and Pottsville have more opportunity to see this genuine American ballerina (as opposed to the press agent's product) than New York. In a recent season at the Metropolitan she gave exactly one performance of *Swan Lake* and that was at a Sunday matinee. It was small satisfaction to have it called the best of the season by a discerning critic.

Patricia Bowman and Karen Conrad, technically excellent, were lacking in the authority necessary for a Swan Queen. Nana Gollner has good line, but her powers of projection are scarcely equal to the vast spaces of an opera house. Conservative members of the audience find her divagations from the accepted choreography, however artistically warranted, somewhat disturbing. Recently Nora Kaye, outstanding dramatic ballerina, has tried her hand at *Swan Lake*. Her interpretation, still tentative, is indicative of future brilliance.

On the whole, America can take legitimate pride in her native Swan Queens.

The role of Prince Siegfried is a thankless one—his principal task is to support the Swan Queen through her *adages*. It calls for a dancer with a sound classical technique (he has one variation), the ability to project the mimed passages without making them seem ridiculous, and a self-effacing disposition. Igor Youskevitch, Anton Dolin, and André Eglevsky have managed this difficult combination of requirements with simple dignity. Too many others regard the part as a chore that must be got through somehow, and in the resulting lack of balance the ballet suffers. Benno frequently receives a better performance. As this role is usually performed by a young dancer on his promotion, it is taken seriously and enhances the romantic overtones of the *conte des Fées* atmosphere.

In the original production of *Swan Lake,* Von Rothbart, the enchanter, spied on the meeting of Prince and Swan Queen in the form of an owl. Ballet Theatre's first production of *Swan Lake* made a reference to this by giving the enchanter an owl mask to wear. This was not a successful experiment; Von Rothbart looked more like a character who had wandered in from *Peter and the Wolf* than the grim and menacing figure he is meant to be. The owl mask has long since been retired.

The Ballet Russe de Monte Carlo produced a reconstruction of Act III of *Swan Lake,* which they entitled *The Magic Swan,* with choreography by Alexandra Fedorova patterned after the original by Petipa. This was performed for the first time at the Metropolitan Opera House, New York, on October 13, 1941. The cast was headed by Tamara Toumanova (Odile) and Igor Youskevitch (Prince Siegfried). This, the *divertissement* act of the ballet, included a mazurka (led by Eleanora Marra and Marc Platoff), a czardas (led by Lubov Roudenko and Frederic Franklin), *pas de trois* (Leila Crabtree, Dorothy Etheridge, and Roland Guerard), *danse espagnole* (Mlada Miladova and Casimir Kokitch), *tarantelle* (Sonia Woicikowska and Harold Lang). The ballet concluded with the brilliant and once controversial *pas de deux* superbly performed by Tamara Toumanova and Igor Youskevitch. This production paused just before the end to throw in a faint suggestion of plot, when one saw Odette flutter despairingly on the edge of the gay scene and then float unnoticed away.[9] It did not occur to the management to present Acts II and III on the same evening or even during the same season, much as audiences everywhere would have welcomed such a program.

The production of *The Magic Swan* was unworthy of such an important revival. The scenery and costumes by Eugene Dunkel were a third-rate road-company attempt at baroque grandeur. The costumes gave the impression that they had been run up from bargain-basement materials. Toumanova, indeed, looked magnificent in a black tutu glittering with jewels. Later when Slavenska performed

---

[9] Any member of the audience who noticed her probably thought she was one of the local ladies who hadn't been invited to the party.

this role, she added a large pink rose to the black costume—definitely not an improvement.

Though *The Magic Swan* has disappeared from the repertoire, the *pas de deux* continues to be performed. Alexandra Danilova, Tamara Toumanova, and Mia Slavenska have displayed their command of academic technique in it. Tamara Toumanova is at her exciting best in this tour de force, its vertiginous turns and sustained balances exactly suiting her temperament and forceful technique. The man's role can seldom have been performed in any generation more beautifully than by Igor Youskevitch. Who that saw it can forget his breathtaking entrance in the coda at the height of a *grand jeté*, invariably evoking a gasp of amazement from the audience? Experiencing the exhilaration and thrill of this performance, one was frequently led to wonder why anyone had ever felt the urge to reform the classic ballet.

When two or three ballet-lovers congregate to indulge in a session of wishful thinking aloud, if some benevolent genie offered to fulfill their desires, at least one of them would ask for a revival of the complete *Swan Lake*.[10] Dreams do not cost anything and at least one ballet-lover would like to see a full-dress production of this keystone of the classical ballet with two ballerinas—Alexandra Danilova (Odette) and Tamara Toumanova (Odile); Igor Youskevitch as Prince Siegfried; Ian Gibson in the *pas de trois;* the 1940 corps de ballet of Ballet Theatre (the best that has ever been seen in New York); as alternate ballerinas, Rosella Hightower and Alicia Alonso; settings and costumes by Eugène Berman; production by Anton Dolin, or someone with equal taste and knowledge of the true classical tradition. The money that has been squandered on dreary nonsense (*Brahms Variations, The Red Poppy, Helen of Troy,* or name your own) would easily have paid for a really magnificent revival of *Swan Lake.*

For the better understanding of *Swan Lake,* a brief exposition of the story, as related by C. W. Beaumont in the *Complete Book of Ballets,* follows: .

[10] The San Francisco Opera Ballet has produced a complete *Swan Lake* with choreography by William Christensen and a cast that included Janet Reed. The touring range of this company is limited, however, to the west coast, though I believe it once gave some performances in Chicago.

Act 1. The scene is a festival being held to celebrate Prince Siegfried's coming of age. His mother rebukes him for his frivolity, informing him that she expects him to choose a bride from among the ladies she has invited to a ball that she is giving the following evening.

A flight of swans overhead suggesting a midnight hunt, the Prince and his friends leave the festivities.

Act 2. The scene is a moonlit clearing by the side of a lake. A crowned swan is seen floating toward the shore. The Prince's followers, carrying crossbows, enter in time to catch sight of the swan. Pleased at the prospect of a quarry, Benno (the Prince's friend) calls the Prince so that he may have the first shot. The Prince, in a melancholy mood, waves the group away.

This is the hour when Odette—a Queen who has incurred the enmity of the enchanter Von Rothbart—may for a brief time resume the human form of which she has been deprived by her enemy's magic art. Thinking that she is alone, she has come to enjoy her freedom. When she sees the Prince she is terrified. Finding him sympathetic, she tells him her sorrowful story. The ominous figure of Von Rothbart looms up. When the Prince tries to kill him, Odette stands in the line of fire. Her deliverance will not come that way.

Odette's ladies, who share her enchantment, assemble for their hour of liberty. Benno, returning to look for the Prince, sees them and calls the huntsmen, who raise their crossbows to take aim. Odette, rushing to defend her ladies, is followed by the Prince, who commands his followers to withhold their fire, explaining the sad plight of the Queen and her entourage.

The Prince, who has fallen in love with Odette, invites her to the ball, where he proposes to choose her for his bride. She answers that she may not be present until the evil spell is lifted, warning the Prince not only that her death will follow if he breaks his word but that Von Rothbart will do his best to separate them.

With the arrival of dawn Odette and her ladies must change their human forms and again become swans. The Prince leaves, vowing that he will set them free.

(In Act II as performed in the United States, the Prince tries to follow Odette, but is struck senseless by Von Rothbart.)

Act 3. The scene is a magnificent ballroom where guests are assembling. A number of beautiful young ladies dance for the Prince, who remains unimpressed by their charms. Various groups of guests dance a mazurka, a czardas, and other national dances. A fanfare heralds the arrival of a new party — Von Rothbart and his evil daughter, Odile, to whom his magic has given the aspect of Odette. The Prince, deceived, greets them with delight. He dances with Odile, then proclaims her his chosen bride, while the despairing Odette flutters vainly at the castle window trying to warn the Prince of the deception. Von Rothbart vanishes in triumph with Odile. The Prince, realizing that he has been tricked, rushes away in search of Odette.

Act. 4. The scene is again the clearing by the lake, where Odette's friends are waiting for her. She enters grief-stricken at the Prince's failure to remain true to her. When the Prince appears she refuses to speak to him, but forgives him when he explains the enchanter's stratagem.

Von Rothbart, by his black arts, calls up a storm. The lake threatens to engulf them. The Prince, declaring that he does not wish to live without Odette, offers to share her fate. His unselfishness is stronger than the evil magic, and the spell is broken. When dawn comes, Odette and her friends are free.

Choreographically Act 2 of *Swan Lake* may well stand alone. Except for the few mimed passages, now mostly omitted, it is all dancing, and dancing that is arranged in a manner guaranteed to secure the utmost in variety and drama. The Swan Queen's entrance is particularly effective. She runs down a ramp at the rear of the stage and lands in a *pas de chat*. There follows a brief *pas d'action* with the Prince. The corps de ballet has a charming group number accompanied by a melody that every newcomer to *Swan Lake* discovers to his delight is practically identical with *Sweet Rosy O'Grady*. This is followed by the grand *adage* in which the ballerina displays her command of the beautiful slow movements of the *danse d'école,* supported by her partner and framed by the groupings of the corps de ballet. The *pas de quatre* lightens the serious mood. This is performed by the four smallest dancers available. Its swift beats, *entrechats quatre, emboîtés,* and birdlike turnings of the head, executed in unison, make it a very popular feature with audiences. This would seem to be the spiritual ancestor of precision dancing — Tiller Girls, Rockettes, and others. The solo variation for the Prince is characterized by the typical pirouettes, *entrechats,* and *tours* that comprise the conventional male variation. This is succeeded by a thrilling coda in which the Swan Queen enters in a series of *demi-fouettés,* sometimes followed by *échappés.* Danilova is particularly brilliant in this episode.[11] Dancers sometimes vary these steps, as a coloratura soprano chooses her own cadenzas. The dancing ends with the Queen posing *en arabesque,* supported by Benno. The Prince gently lifts her from Benno's grasp, while the music passes from the exciting measures of the coda to the original sad theme.[12]

Act 3 of *Swan Lake* (*The Magic Swan*) except for the *pas de deux* is much less interesting from a choreographic point of view. National dances to be effective must be performed with a fire that is likely to vanish after a few repetitions by the average ballet company. First performances often boast the company's principal soloists as leaders of groups. Later they retire in favor of less accomplished dancers, taking the spirit and animation with them. Nothing is more deadly than an apathetic czardas or a tired mazurka. It is not to be wondered at that *The Magic Swan* was shelved and only the *pas de deux* retained in the repertoire. For the projected dream production of *Swan Lake* the genie must provide a director who will maintain discipline and keep the corps de ballet alert and interested.

As far back as 1934 the Sadler's Wells Ballet of London presented a revival of the complete *Swan Lake,* supervised by Nicholas Sergeyev, with Alicia Markova (Odette-Odile) and Robert Helpmann (Prince Siegfried). The décor by Hugh Stevenson was retired in favor of a new setting by Leslie Hurry in 1943. How long will America have to wait for a similar tribute to one of the greatest of ballets? Does not the popularity of *Giselle* attest to the audience's interest in classical ballet?

[11] I have been told that Danilova's dazzling *échappés* are achieved by performing the *relevé* from *demi-point,* instead of the more usual *relevé* from the foot flat on the floor.

[12] "It is a curious fact that the principal theme of the ballet, which recurs again and again, is practically the same as the 'Mystery of the Name' theme from *Lohengrin,* the notes to which Lohengrin sings, *'Nie sollst du mich befragen.'* Now, Tchaikovsky visited Bayreuth in 1876, the year he wrote the ballet. Of course, *Lohengrin* was not sung at Bayreuth before 1894, however." (Carl Van Vechten in the *Evening Globe,* December 20, 1911, reprinted in *Dance Index,* September-October-November 1942.)

LES SYLPHIDES

LES SYLPHIDES is a suite of dances with choreography by Michel Fokine, music by Frédéric Chopin, and costumes in the romantic style originated by Eugène Lami for *La Sylphide,* Taglioni's most famous vehicle. The setting for the first Paris production was by Alexandre Benois.

Les Sylphides is called on the program "a romantic revery," but it had to suffer many changes before it reached its present abstract form. At first known as *Chopiniana,* it was created by Fokine for a special performance by artists of the Imperial Ballet in St. Petersburg. This version had a plot that, as detailed in C. W. Beaumont's *Complete Book of Ballets,* sounds like a preliminary sketch for *Paganini* (1939). A second production, arranged for a Pupils' Annual Performance presented by the students of the Imperial School of Ballet in St. Petersburg on April 6, 1908, was closer to the final form as the contemporary audience sees it.

Renamed *Les Sylphides,* the ballet had its first performance in western Europe at the Théâtre du Chatelet, Paris, on June 2, 1909. The cast included Anna Pavlova, Thamar Karsavina, Maria Baldina, and Vaslav Nijinsky. A pale anemone blooming delicately amid the colorful violence of *Scheherazade, Cléopâtre,* and *Prince Igor,* it has survived triumphantly through all changes in balletic fashion. Few ballet companies dare to omit it from their repertoires.

The action, for plot there is none, is as follows:

The mood of romantic reverie is evoked by the overture—the *Prélude, opus 28, No. 7.*

The *Nocturne, opus 32, No. 2,* is played as the curtain rises to disclose a forest glade. The four principal dancers are posed, surrounded by members of the corps de ballet, who *bourrée* forward and separate to form symmetrical groups as a background for the soloists, all of whom participate in the introduction. It ends with a brief *pas de deux* in which two girls execute *penché arabesques* and *attitudes en avant.*

The first solo is danced to the *Valse, opus 70, No. 1,* by a woman dancer. This is technically very demanding and includes *grands jetés, jetés en tournant,* and *cabrioles.* There are characteristic shoulder movements and turns of the head which impart a warmth to this Sylphide. She is less remote than her sister spirits. The part was originally performed by Thamar Karsavina. In this generation of dancers Rosella Hightower meets all its demands.

The second solo is performed to the *Mazurka, opus 33, No. 3.* This is customarily, though not always, danced by the first lady of *Les Sylphides,* who later takes part in the *pas de deux.* Four times she crosses the stage diagonally in *grands jetés,* following with a series of *relevés en arabesque.* There are characteristic *ports de bras* that are echoed by the corps de ballet. The variation ends with an arabesque on point. This was danced at the first Paris performance by Anna Pavlova. Alexandra Danilova, Irina Baronova, and Alicia Alonso have given beautiful performances of a solo that has many pitfalls for the dancer. It demands effortless elevation and concealed virtuosity. When executed by a dancer who lacks the self-effacing quality of the true Sylphide it may degenerate into an athletic stunt. Dancers whose strenuous jumps are greeted with storms of applause that might better be reserved for the *fouetté* competition in *Graduation Ball* have no appeal for the discriminating ballet-lover.

During the first sixteen measures of the *Mazurka, opus 67, No. 3,* the corps de ballet form a group. They stand in a double row making a close semicircle curving toward the rear of the stage. They hold each others' hands with arms crossed in front—probably the germ of the characteristic Balanchine arm weavings. As the male dancer enters with a *cabriole,* the front line sinks to a kneeling position. The variation that follows has been modified and even changed to suit individual performers. As presently danced, it opens with a stylized mazurka step. It includes three *entrechats six,* a *grand cabriole en avant, pirouettes en arabesque,* ending with a *soutenu* turn and a kneeling pose. In the first Paris performance this was danced by Nijinsky. Not difficult technically, this role makes demands on the dancer's interpretative ability. It calls for a dignified simplicity with no faint suggestion of the epicene. Igor Youskevitch and Yura Skibine are ideal interpreters of the part. Recently John Kriza has given some fine, though still tentative, accounts of it.

The *Prélude, opus 28, No. 7,* introduces a solo that to many ballet-lovers is the high point of *Les Sylphides.* For the first eight measures the corps de ballet form the three groups that Arnold Haskell has called "fountains," the girls kneeling to surround a central figure. These "fountains" are arranged symmetrically to right, left, and center of the stage. The solo dancer runs in and assumes a listening pose. This variation is in the freest style and calls for a rhythmic continuity not possessed by all who attempt it. The steps and arm movements are all stylized, representing a purely romantic approach to classroom technique. There is a *rond de jambe* executed *par terre* and a Cecchetti *assemblé* among the few academic steps. The *ports de bras* are free and the whole is so fluidly phrased that individual steps melt into one another in a manner that must have amazed a generation raised on Petipa and Ivanov. This was originally performed by Maria Baldina. When Alicia Markova dances *Les Sylphides* she usually takes the prelude as her solo, performing it with her customary grace and elegance. Tatiana Riabouchinska is ideal in this part. She seems to listen for the horns of elfland with a feyness that no other dancer brings to the role, evoking a moonlit mood for the whole ballet, however inept the other performers may be.

The *pas de deux* danced to the *Valse, opus 64, No. 2,* opens with one of the loveliest lifts in all ballet. This should begin in the wings so that the woman dancer appears to float into sight in a romantic arabesque pose. Half the effect is lost if the lift is taken, as it sometimes is, in full view of the audience. As her partner carries her diagonally across the stage, she does a single *cabriole.* Dancers lacking in restraint sometimes add movements of their own that are no improvement to the original choreography and destroy the illusion of slow drifting flight. The *pas de deux* is characterized by evanescent poses and lifts that flow smoothly into one another. The mechanics of support are reduced to a minimum and in a first-rate performance are not visible. The partner appears merely to restrain his lady's flight rather than aid it. In this *pas de deux* Alicia Markova's thistle-down lightness is unforgettable.

At the end of the *pas de deux* there is a moment of silence.[1] The stage is empty. To the *Valse, opus 18, No. 1* (*Grande Valse Brilliante*), the corps de ballet enter diagonally in groups. They ebb and flow in waves. Advancing in a forward *balancé,* arms reaching high in air, they surge toward the front of the stage in *grands jetés.* The solo dancers enter singly, performing short variations. These might

---

[1] Members of the audience whom silence and an empty stage embarrass usually seize this opportunity to applaud.

be called allegro versions of their earlier solos. At the end of the coda they resume the positions in which the rise of the curtain found them.

When Gertrude Hoffman presented her *Saison des Ballets Russes* at the Winter Garden, New York, in 1911, the repertoire was composed of three ballets—*Les Sylphides*,[2] *Cléopâtre,* and *Scheherazade.* The company was made up of dancers from the Diaghilev Ballet and various European opera houses. At least one member of the original cast of *Les Sylphides* was included in this group—Maria Baldina. Lydia Lopokova and Alexander Volinine also appeared in this ballet, with a corps de ballet of twenty-two. The opening performance took place on June 14, 1911. All three ballets were staged by Theodore Kosloff and nowhere in the newspaper announcements is there any acknowledgment of indebtedness to Michel Fokine. Even an article in the *Evening Globe* by Carl Van Vechten speaks of *Les Sylphides* as being "arranged by one of the Russian ballet masters." This leads one to the conclusion that it may have made its initial bow to New York in a pirated performance. In whatever form it was presented, it must have provided a charming contrast to the overheated Orientalism of the other ballets on the program.[3]

Sergei Diaghilev's Ballet Russe gave *Les Sylphides* at the Century Theater, New York, on January 20, 1916 with a cast that included Xenia Maclezowa, Lydia Lopokova, Lubov Tchernicheva, and Adolph Bolm. The critic of the *New York Times* called it "a series of divertissements in the strict classical style," and praised the setting and remarkable lighting effects. Later in the season, when the company had moved to the Metropolitan Opera House, Nijinsky replaced Bolm in *Les Sylphides,* appearing for the first time on April 14, 1916, and garnering critical acclaim for his marvelous "rhythm sense," which was compared to that of Pavlova.

It would be impossible to enumerate the many performances of *Les Sylphides* given in the United States. It forms part of every important ballet company's repertoire, and its solos are coveted by every dancer.

Every ballerina has danced at least one role in *Les Sylphides,* not always to the glory of her reputation as a dancer. Many have felt it

[2] It was described as a "romantic revelry."
[3] Present-day ballet-goers might be interested in the price range—fifty cents to $2.50. Smoking was permitted.

necessary to wear costumes made of different material, extra ornaments, strangely placed wreaths—anything to distinguish them from the other soloists and the corps de ballet. Another variety of ballerina tries to introduce her own technical specialty—extra beats, long-sustained balances, exaggerated arm movements, energetic leaps. There is indeed real distinction to be won in this ballet, but only by the dancer with the artistic humility to subordinate her personality to the choreographer's intention.

It is interesting to watch the progress of *Les Sylphides* in a newly formed ballet company. It offers many hazards. If its smoothly flowing solos are danced for display, the atmosphere vanishes. The first mazurka may evoke a vision of Taglioni—or Babe Didrikson. Ballet Theatre's first performances boasted a décor that looked like a platter of scrambled eggs, and dancers who turned the solos into an athletic free-for-all and whose arm movements were reminiscent of the Australian crawl. This lively event was introduced by the crashing strains of the *Military Polonaise*. Time and experience have eliminated these glaring errors of taste.

The ballet-lover has to endure a good deal about the music for *Les Sylphides* from musical purists who brush it aside contemptuously as "orchestrated Chopin." He may ignore these remarks or answer them with "orchestrated Bach," "expanded Gluck," or "rearranged Mussorgsky," none of which seem to keep these same music-lovers away from concert and opera. Let us agree on two facts: *Les Sylphides* has acquired a tradition in almost forty years of performance; some orchestrations are better than others.

It is interesting to learn that the first inspiration for the ballet that eventually became *Les Sylphides* was a suite by Alexander Glazunov called *Chopiniana*—an orchestration of four Chopin piano pieces. As this arrangement dates from 1894, the mayhem committed on Chopin can scarcely be charged to ballet. At most, the choreographer's chief sin is opportunism. Later at Fokine's request Glazunov added another number to the suite—a waltz, which was retained when Fokine revised his original ballet, *Chopiniana*. For this version Maurice Keller made an orchestration of the chosen pieces. There have been many arrangements of the music since that time, Stravinsky contributing to the one used by the Diaghilev Ballet in Paris. More recently versions by Vittorio Rieti (Colonel W. de Basil's Ballet Russe) and Lucien Caillet (Ballet Russe de Monte Carlo) have been heard. During the 1938 season the Ballet Russe de Monte Carlo used what may have been the original Paris arrangement by Glazunov, Stravinsky, and Taneyev. The program for Ballet Theatre's first season modestly suppressed the name of the arranger. This was probably a measure of safety, as some indignant lover of Chopin might have waylaid and murdered him if his name had been made public. Later a more acceptable orchestration was prepared by Benjamin Britten. Ballet International did not hesitate to name Maurice Baron as the perpetrator of their particular outrage on Chopin, although justice requires a statement that in a very small theater amplifiers were used, causing the orchestra to sound like massed bands at a military tattoo. The Rieti and Caillet versions are by far the most satisfactory.

The sequence of the music varies, and sometimes there are substitutions. There are even regrettable instances on record of *Les Sylphides* being heralded by a particularly brassy orchestration of the *Military Polonaise*—fine inspiring music for a flag-raising, but something less than suitable as a prelude to a vision of moonlit nymphs.

Almost as many scenic designers as musicians have served *Les Sylphides*. The original setting was by Alexandre Benois, and the "Ah, but—" school of ballet-lovers sigh sentimentally for its moonlit glamour. Diaghilev himself supervised the lighting, which evoked murmurs of admiration from audiences in the Century Theater in 1916. Photographs of the Benois décor show a parklike landscape with a romantic ruin (called a pavilion by a 1916 critic) in the distance—not an altogether suitable setting for supernatural beings. It is therefore reasonable to suppose that the effect was largely due to the lighting. Other settings by A. Socrate and Léon Zack have been used. The De Basil Ballet presented its admirable *Sylphides* before an adaptation of a landscape by Corot which had no suggestion of the mundane about it. Ballet Theatre's platter of scrambled eggs was designed by Augustus Vincent Tack, who should have known better. Later Eugene Dunkel provided a more appropriate landscape after Corot. His design for Ballet International was less successful—a forest grove, whose trees interfered with the movements of the dancers.

Les Sylphides has been danced in many strange places—a bull ring in Mexico City, a beer garden in Switzerland, in a narcissus field in the south of France.[4] In open-air performances managerial stupidity

[4] These adventures befell the De Basil Company during its early days.

usually places *Les Sylphides* first on the program, thereby making certain that there will be sufficient daylight to spoil the mood. An ideal performance would be lit by the moon, with only enough artificial light to assist, not crowd, nature.

The costumes for *Les Sylphides* have suffered comparatively little change, although dancers do their best. They are simple, beautiful, and universally becoming, even flattering, as they hide faults of line mercilessly revealed by the classical tutu.

Many purple passages [5] have been written to describe the moods evoked by *Les Sylphides.* C. W. Beaumont has succeeded admirably. There are accounts that sound like the effusions of copy-writers for perfume advertisements. *Les Sylphides* must be experienced preferably in a good performance, but something of the magic remains even in an indifferent one.

Choreographically *Les Sylphides* was revolutionary. For the first time academic technique was used in a free and fluid fashion. Contrast the *pas de deux* in *Princess Aurora;* or better still compare the soft poses and fleeting groups of the corps de ballet in *Les Sylphides* with the carefully contrived arrangements and static groupings of the corps de ballet in *Swan Lake.* The difference is immediately apparent. Both styles have their place in ballet, but the breakdown of the rigid formulas of the classical ballet was necessary before *Petrouchka, Le Sacre du Printemps,* and even contemporary ballets like *Pillar of Fire* were possible. Fokine was a one-man revolution in choreography, and *Les Sylphides* was his declaration of independence. Fortunately, having no inclination to throw the baby out along with the bath, Fokine chose to work within the framework of the traditional ballet, expanding and enriching it, rather than establish a personal cult that would die with him. His early ballets contain the germs of practically every choreographic innovation of the last forty years. *Les Sylphides,* fragile and lovely, is also a manifesto of freedom to the art of the dance.

[5] A most amusing one appears in the souvenir program of the 1916 season of the Diaghilev Ballet in the United States: ". . . a lovely old-fashioned nosegay, in which the central male blossom is surrounded by the most fragile rosebuds of the *corps du ballet,* and the whole is set in a *toot* [whatever that may be] of rarest lacework of Chopin's masterpieces." This is the sort of thing that keeps strong-minded people away from ballet.

SYMPHONIE FANTASTIQUE

Symphonie Fantastique (An Episode in the Life of an Artist): chore-ographic symphony; music by Berlioz; choreography by Léonide Mas-sine; scenery and costumes by Christian Bérard.

T HE first performance of *Symphonie Fantastique* was given at the Royal Opera House, Covent Garden, London, on July 24, 1936. The American première took place at the Metropolitan Opera House, New York, on October 29, 1936, with the following cast:

A Young Musician	*Léonide Massine*	The Young Shepherd	
The Beloved	*Tamara Toumanova*		*George Zoritch*
The Old Shepherd	*Marc Platoff*	The Deer	*Alexis Kosloff*
		The Jailer	*Yurek Shabelevsky*

Alexandra Danilova, Anna Adrianova, Nina Verchinina, Olga Morosova, Roman Jasinsky, and *Paul Petroff* were also in the cast

❖❖❖❖❖❖❖❖❖❖❖❖❖❖❖

The action of the ballet is best detailed in Hector Berlioz's own words, which appear in the 1910 edition of the *Symphonie Fantas-tique* published by Breitkopf & Härtel, and were reprinted in the ballet program:

"A young musician of unhealthily sensitive nature and endowed with vivid imagination has poisoned himself with opium in a paroxysm of lovesick despair. The narcotic dose he had taken was too weak to cause death, but it has thrown him into a long sleep accompanied by the most extraordinary visions. In this condition his sensations, his feelings and memories find utterance in his sick brain in the form of musical imagery. Even the beloved one takes the form of melody in his mind, like a fixed idea, which is ever returning, and which he hears everywhere.

"1st Movement—Visions and Passions. At first he thinks of the uneasy and nervous condition of his mind, of somber longings, of depressions and joyous elation without any recognizable cause, which he experienced be-fore the beloved one appeared to him. Then he remembers the ardent love with which she suddenly inspired him; he thinks of his almost insane anxiety of mind, of his raging jealousy, of his reawakening love, of his religious consolation.

"*2nd Movement—A Ball.* In a ballroom, amidst the confusion of a brilliant festival, he finds the loved one again.

"*3rd Movement—In the Country.* It is a summer evening. He is in the country musing when he hears two shepherd lads who play the *ranz des vaches* (the tune used by the Swiss to call their flocks together) in alternation. This shepherd duet, the locality, the soft whisperings of the trees stirred by the zephyr wind, some prospects of hope recently made known to him, all these sensations unite to impart a long unknown repose to his heart, and to lend a smiling color to his imagination. And then she appears once more. His heart stops beating, painful forebodings fill his soul. 'Should she prove false to him?' One of the shepherds resumes the melody, but the other answers him no more . . . sunset . . . distant rolling of thunder . . . loneliness . . . silence.

"*4th Movement—The Procession to the Stake.* He dreams that he has murdered his beloved, that he has been condemned to death and is being led to the stake. A march that is alternately somber and wild, brilliant and solemn, accompanies the procession. . . . The tumultuous outbursts are followed without modulation by measured steps. At last the fixed idea returns, for a moment a last thought of love is revived—which is cut short by the death blow.

"*5th Movement—The Witches' Sabbath.* He dreams that he is present at the witches' dance, surrounded by horrible spirits, amidst sorcerers and monsters in many fearful forms, who have come to assist at his funeral. Strange sounds, groans, shrill laughter, distant yells, which other cries seem to answer. The beloved melody is heard again, but it has its noble and shy character no longer; it has become a vulgar, trivial and grotesque kind of dance. She it is who comes to attend the witches' meeting. Friendly howls and shouts greet her arrival. . . . She joins the infernal orgy . . . bells toll for the dead . . . a burlesque parody of the Dies iræ . . . the witches' round dance . . . the dance and the Dies iræ are heard at the same time."

When Massine first used a symphony—the Tchaikovsky Fifth—for his ballet *Les Présages,* the music critics protested, though faintly. After all, it was only Tchaikovsky, held lightly enough by these learned gentlemen. The success of *Les Présages* led to *Chorearteum,* for which Massine dared to employ the Brahms Fourth Symphony. At once the critical body was aroused—to lay hands on Brahms, music's sacred cow, was too much. Even people who had never seen a ballet took a hand in the controversy, and letters were written to the London *Times.* When these ballets were given in the United States, the reactions were less violent. Unfortunately no one here ever writes letters to the *Times* about anything less than a political issue. If by any chance a letter about the state of music or ballet was received, it would be at once handed to the music department—probably with tongs—and buried in the depths of the Sunday edition. At all events, New York was seeing serious ballet performances for the first time in many years. In the interval there had been occasional dance programs at the Neighborhood Theater, pupils' recitals at the Lewisohn Stadium, the Denishawn Dancers, and the various groups that had arisen in the wake of Mary Wigman's visit, but of genuine ballet there was scarcely a memory. American audiences were too busy getting used to the idea of having ballet to raise many issues about it.

When Massine offered *Symphonie Fantastique* as his third symphonic ballet, the critical guns were spiked. Here was a symphony for which the composer himself had written a detailed plan of action that had been faithfully followed by the choreographer.

From the moment the curtain went up, it was apparent that this ballet was a success. Unlike *Chorearteum,* the *Symphonie Fantastique* offered no novel choreographic material. Employing a vocabulary of movement familiar to his audiences, Massine treated each division of the symphony as though it were a separate ballet, the whole being held together by the figures of the Young Musician and his *idée fixe,* the Beloved.

The first movement, full of visions and delirium alternately checked and intensified by the intermittent appearances of the Beloved, is probably the least interesting of the five divisions of the ballet. There are many architectural groups, and sometimes the means by which they are contrived are too obvious for complete illusion. The costumes of the dancers representing gaiety, melancholy, and other abstractions are none too happy.

The second movement, a ballroom scene, is theatrically very effective. The febrile whirling of the music, matched by the mad waltzing of the corps de ballet, seemed the very evocation of a ball in a dream. The setting, a series of high, narrow red arches with blackamoors holding candelabra standing between them, caught the fancy of New York display-designers and even recently has been seen reproduced in a department-store window. The women's costumes—white frocks of the romantic period, worn with flowered headdresses and black ballet shoes, were extremely successful. It would be safe to say that the headdresses started a fashion, as after the opening performance ladies in the audience were seen wearing flowers in their hair at the exact angle prescribed by Christian Bérard for the corps de ballet. If all this seems too trivial to mention, remember that the same phenomena have been observed in every period in which the art of ballet has enjoyed its greatest popularity.

The third movement is a pastoral scene, and a prophet would have foredoomed it to failure for any balletic purpose. It proved, however, to be the artistic success of the ballet. It is seen through the eyes and mind of the Young Musician, who, seated on a broken column, watches a succession of dream characters pass. First a deer, whose wriggles provide the only touch of comedy in the ballet; then two shepherds, and a picnic party of women, girls, and children. The young shepherd and one of the girls dance together. A child chases a bird. A storm arises and dies away. Simple things in a muted tempo, but in some extraordinary way Massine as the Young Musician, scarcely moving, managed to convey that all these events and people had no existence except as he thought of them—a miracle of theatrical projection. In the London performances the figure of the Beloved, appearing briefly, was suspended on a wire, thus reverting to a practice of the nineteenth century. In New York this was dispensed with, as the use of the same device in Balanchine's *Orpheus* had amused rather than impressed the audience.

The fourth movement, the march to the scaffold, was in marked contrast to the preceding episode and in its own way almost as successful. The staccato movements of the crowd, what Beaumont calls the "horrible jigging of the judges," and the swift violence are almost unbearably vivid. From a psychological as well as a scenic point of view, this episode owes much to Daumier.

The fifth movement, the witches' Sabbath, seems an anticlimax after the preceding scene. Many examples will testify to the fact that witches' Sabbaths and hell scenes generally are rarely adequate on the stage.[1] This episode does, however, have some fine moments. The entrance of the Beloved, gracious and remote till now, transformed into the queen of the Sabbath, with lank hair and dress seared in the fires of hell, is memorable. For the rest, the stage is populated by the more respectable monsters from Brueghel, their antics rather comic than otherwise. Here the music carried the ballet to a triumphant conclusion.

[1] Exception must be made for the underworld scene in Gluck's *Orpheus* as staged —of all places—at the Metropolitan Opera House.

In this and other ballets Massine gave ample proof of his pre-eminence as choreographer. His performance of the Young Musician placed him in an equally high position as actor. His powers of personal projection were never seen to better advantage than in the pastoral episode, which without him lost its rare subjective quality ·and became a pretty interlude without distinction. Massine was the complete embodiment of one of the sentimental firebrands of the romantic revival.

As the Beloved, Tamara Toumanova was absolutely unrivaled. Detached and beautiful through four movements, she was changed in the fifth into a fury whose like has not been seen on the stage since the grand manner passed away. Whatever Toumanova may accomplish in the movies or other fields of theatrical endeavor, she can look back on the Beloved as her most effective role as well as a sound artistic achievement.

A *pas de deux* performed by Nina Verchinina and George Zoritch in the pastoral scene was most interesting from the point of view of pure dancing. Faintly reminiscent of Balanchine, it was marked by original lifts and combinations of steps. Roman Jasinsky alternated with Zoritch in this part, to the advantage of the ballet, Jasinsky having fewer personal idiosyncrasies to interpose between the choreographer's intentions and the audience.

There was a minimum of dancing *sur les pointes* in *Symphonie Fantastique*. This was reserved for the Beloved and some of the dancers representing abstractions.

Symphonie Fantastique has not been seen in New York since January 1941. This is too long to be deprived of one of the few masterpieces of symphonic ballet, which was scheduled for revival during the 1946 season of the Original Ballet Russe, the company having returned to New York after five years largely spent in Latin America.

THE THREE-CORNERED HAT

The Three-Cornered Hat (Le Tricorne): ballet by Martínez Sierra, drawn from a fable by Alarcón; music by Manuel de Falla; choreography by Léonide Massine; scenery and costumes by Pablo Picasso.

LE TRICORNE was first produced by Sergei Diaghilev's Ballet Russe at the Alhambra Theatre, London, on July 22, 1919. The American première, by Colonel W. de Basil's Ballet Russe, took place at the St. James Theater, New York, on March 9, 1934, with Leon Woizikovsky as the Miller. Léonide Massine was seen in this role, which he had created, in a performance given the following week. Programs for these presentations are not available. One dated October 9, 1935, gives the following cast:

THE MILLER	*Léonide Massine*	THE GOVERNOR	*David Lichine*
THE MILLER'S WIFE		THE DANDY	*Michel Katcharoff*
	Tamara Toumanova		

Alguazils, Neighbors

◆◆◆◆◆◆◆◆◆◆◆◆◆◆◆◆◆◆

There is a sound of drums and castanets, and the voice of a singer is heard. Shouts of *ole* and vigorous handclapping precede the rise of the curtain, disclosing the exterior of the Miller's house. At the rear of the stage is an archway through which a bridge may be seen. A deep-blue sky outlines hills and the towers of a distant town. On the wall of the house there is a birdcage and a musket hanging on a bracket.

The Miller stands outside his house watching three men carrying sacks of corn to the mill. When they are gone he turns his attention to the bird, which he encourages to sing. His Wife, flirtatious and pretty, runs in. They engage in a dance that seems to express their delight in each other and the beautiful morning. They go to the well, and while the Miller is drawing water his Wife's attention is attracted by the passage across the bridge of the Dandy, who is a very smart young man dressed with rococo elegance in white and pale green. He is flying a kite, but is quite willing to pause for a little flirtation with the attractive young woman. He blows her a kiss. The Miller, having done with his noisy task, notices him and chases him from the bridge.

The pompous entrance of the Governor accompanied by his wife in a sedan chair and a guard of alguazils causes the Miller to forget his annoyance over this incident for a more immediate cause. The Governor, elderly and decrepit, is not past noticing a pretty woman. He tosses his handkerchief in the direction of the Miller's Wife, who, curtsying deeply, picks it up and returns it to him. The procession passes on.

A girl carrying a pitcher of water on her shoulder strolls by. The Miller, determined to repay his wife for her antics, engages in a little flirtation of his own. His wife, furiously jealous, drives the girl away. The Miller goes into the house, leaving his wife alone.

The Governor comes back to pursue the promising lead given him by the Miller's Wife. Not at all averse to playing a game with him, she teases him with a bunch of grapes and excites him to such exertions that he loses his balance and falls gasping to the ground. The Miller returns in time to laugh at the end of this episode. Realizing that he has been made a fool of, the old man slinks away muttering threats. The Miller and his Wife perform a triumphant fandango before going into their house.

Men and women of the village appear and join in a dance to celebrate an afternoon of festival.

The Miller's Wife makes an impressive entrance. She is wearing a black shawl, which she manipulates in a dramatic manner. She is followed by the Miller, who carries a bundle containing cups and a skin of wine. All drink, the Miller taking his directly from the wine-skin. Throwing it down, he begins the farruca. This dance works up to a tremendous climax accompanied by the rhythmic handclappings of the whole group.

As the afternoon of gaiety is drawing to a close, the pleasant scene is interrupted by the arrival of the alguazils bearing the Governor's warrant for the Miller's arrest. Thrusting the anguished Wife aside, they lead him off to prison. The villagers prudently remove themselves from the scene.

Left alone, the Wife gives way to her grief and desolation, stamping angrily when the voice of the cuckoo, traditional symbol of betrayed husbands, is heard. She falls to the floor in an attitude of despair.

Certain that he will meet little opposition now that the Miller has been disposed of, the Governor struts in with a senile swagger. He cocks his three-cornered hat at a gay angle, flicks his lace ruffles, and advances to make his conquest. The Wife is horrified. Eluding him, she runs to the top of the bridge. He follows her, dropping his cape as he goes. When he reaches the top of the bridge, the Wife gives him such a hearty push that he falls over the parapet. She leaves the bridge, and when the Governor, wet and bedraggled, emerges from the river, she laughs merrily at his plight. As his ardor has not yet abated, she is forced to seize the musket and threaten him with it before she can make her escape.

Once she is gone, the Governor begins to realize that he is old, wretched, and more than a little damp. Removing his coat, he hangs it over the birdcage and goes into the Miller's house to rest.

Meanwhile the Miller has escaped from his jailers and makes for home. Crossing the bridge, the sight of the Governor's cape lends wings to his feet. Snatching it as he runs, he dashes into his house and discovers the Governor. The miserable old man, grotesque in a hooded coat belonging to the Miller, emerges uncertainly. The Miller baits him maliciously, making passes at him *torero* style. Crushed, the Governor cowers to the earth while the Miller draws a rude caricature[1] of him on the wall and runs away.

The Governor cautiously rises from his prostrate position. He is aghast at the vulgar scribble on the wall. Worse is to come. The alguazils, searching for the escaped prisoner, are heard approaching. The Governor again takes refuge in the Miller's house, but cannot hide from the zeal of his jailers, who, failing to recognize their master, drag him out and beat him unmercifully. As they are preparing to take him back to prison, the Miller's Wife returns and, seeing one whom she believes to be her husband being assaulted, tries to defend him. She is quickly undeceived when the Miller, accompanied by friends, comes on the scene. There is a happy reunion. The deflated Governor is glad to make his escape from the scene of his humiliation accompanied by the alguazils, who by now are aware of their mistake.

[1] According to C. W. Beaumont's account of *Le Tricorne,* the Miller writes: "Your wife is no less beautiful than mine." This is in line with the original Alarcón story. In American performances the Miller draws a caricature.

The villagers gather and celebrate the discomfiture of this petty tyrant in a joyous jota, tossing his effigy high in the air.

During World War I (1914–18) the Diaghilev Ballet took refuge in Spain and Switzerland. Switzerland's influence on the dance theater is negligible. The stay in Spain produced one outstanding work of art—*Le Tricorne*. The score, while not written specifically for this ballet (it was composed for a pantomime also based on Alarcón's story), was revised to make it suitable for dancing, and several numbers, including the final jota, were added. Massine, who had produced a number of small and now forgotten ballets employing the Spanish idiom, was ready to work on a larger scale. Falla's magnificent score gave him the opportunity. Massine improved his knowledge of Spanish dance by employing a gypsy dancer named Felix who enjoyed a local celebrity in Seville. This young man provided some of the raw material that Massine organized in a theatrical manner. He was not, as has been said, the true creator of *Le Tricorne*. When Massine took Felix to London, the gypsy, unable to endure the tensions imposed by the unaccustomed way of life, went mad. This story has been many times repeated in a manner discreditable to Massine and Diaghilev. Actually their only crime was an error in judgment. London is not exactly a suitable environment for a Spanish gypsy.

The choreographic style of *The Three-Cornered Hat* might be called Russian ballet Spanish. The steps used are authentic Spanish dance forms—*koradin, sevillanas, farruca, bolero, jota,* and others—but they are assembled in a manner that no Spanish choreographer would dream of. To the non-Spanish audience this is a definite advantage. True Spanish dancing may prove dull to the uninitiated unless he is spiritually attuned to its peculiar wave-length. *Aficionados* of the castanet and heel-beat may flinch at what they may consider the solecisms of *The Three-Cornered Hat*. It must be said, however, that it has always been popular in Spain and formed part of the repertoires of the Russian ballet companies that included Spain in their European tours prior to 1939.

The magnificent setting for *The Three-Cornered Hat* by Pablo Picasso is one of the glories of modern ballet. It evokes the very spirit of Spain and might be studied in conjunction with El Greco's dark and brooding painting of Toledo. These two pictures do much to explain that strange and sometimes incomprehensible country. The costumes are worthy of the scenic background. It seems incredible to read in Walter Propert's *The Russian Ballet* (1931) that "the beauty began to fade with the insistence of these noisy dresses, that never seemed to move with the wearers . . . that looked as if they were cut in cardboard." Maybe time has softened the colors and wilted the buckram, because these strictures sound silly now, the effect of setting and costumes being that of a Picasso of the best period set in exciting motion. There was once an inner curtain representing a bullfight. New York has been denied a sight of this. Has it been lost or is it moldering in some European storehouse?

Massine's performance as the Miller is superb theater and the keystone of the whole production. When New York saw this for the first time, the critic of the *New York Times* called it "an electrifying achievement which elicits bravos from an audience, almost as an irresistible reaction." More than a decade later this statement is still true. Massine's dancing of this role remains one of the outstanding successes of the dance world and is still stopping the show.

The role of the Miller's Wife was created by Thamar Karsavina. Of her, Beaumont says that "the only criticism that could be made is that she was perhaps too elegant for the part." In New York this role was first performed by Tamara Toumanova. Physically she was ideal and in her pre-movie days gave a delightful interpretation. Lately she has forced her effects too emphatically and has lost some of the dignity and reserve that must underlie all Spanish dancing, even the Russian ballet variety.

Several seasons ago a managerial caprice caused Ballet Theatre to make the experiment of casting Argentinita as the Miller's Wife.[2] The results were disastrous. Argentinita, competent enough in her own field, made no attempt to learn the choreography of *The Three-Cornered Hat* and appeared to be carrying out a private project of her own while the ballet swirled around her.

Leon Woizikovsky was the original Governor. American audiences have seen David Lichine, Simon Semenoff, Marc Platoff, and Antony Tudor in this part. In recent years the Dandy has lost his importance. No dancer of the artistic stature of Stanislas Idzikowsky

[2] This experiment had been tried before. Maria Dalbaicin, a Spanish dancer who had been included in a group of Spanish dancers brought to London by Diaghilev to appear in *Cuadro Flamenco,* was cast as the Miller's Wife with no particular success.

has undertaken it. Michel Katcharoff did little more than make an appearance. Ballet Theatre's Michael Kidd has restored some of its significance.

There have been several attempts to capitalize on the popularity of *The Three-Cornered Hat* by producing other Spanish ballets. These have proved profoundly and ineluctably dull. Several come to mind, notably *Capriccio Espagnole,* which united Russian ballet Spanish dancing with Russian Spanish music. The costumes and setting based on Goya's tapestry designs were the only saving grace. Other ballets, *Goyescas* and *Cuckold's Fair,* the latter wasting Danilova's time and energy, serve to pad a repertoire, but do little to attract audiences. *The Three-Cornered Hat* remains the only ballet in which Spanish dancing and atmosphere have a genuine theatrical appeal. Until a trio of artists with the genius of Picasso, Falla, and Massine again collaborate, it is likely to retain possession of the field.

THREE VIRGINS AND A DEVIL

Choreography by Agnes De Mille; scenario by Ramon Reed; music:
Antiche Danze ed Arie, arranged by Ottorino Respighi; costumes de-
signed by Motley; setting designed by Arne Lundborg, after sketches
by Miss Harris.

THREE VIRGINS AND A DEVIL was performed by Ballet
Theatre for the first time on February 11, 1941 at the Majestic Theater, New York, with the following cast:

Three Virgins		A Devil	Eugene Loring
THE PRIGGISH ONE) *Agnes De Mille*		A Youth	*Jerome Robbins*
THE GREEDY ONE) *Lucia Chase*			
THE LUSTFUL ONE) *Annabelle Lyon*			

❖❖❖❖❖❖❖❖❖❖❖❖❖❖❖❖❖

The curtain rises on an open space. At one side a church may be
seen, on the other the entrance to a cave. The three Virgins enter, the
Priggish One dragging her reluctant friends into view. She is bound
for devotions, the others obviously having other ideas. However, the
Priggish One's piety is much stronger than the others' lack of it,
and as usual the one who knows what she wants is getting her way.
She urges them almost to the church door, when she notices the
Greedy One's gay hat and jewelry. The Priggish One insists that they
be put in the alms-box to be sold for the poor. The Greedy One,
reasonably enough, tries to defend her possessions, pointing to the
garland of flowers on the Lustful One's head, hoping to distract the
Priggish One's attention. The argument ends when the Greedy One
has put her finery in the alms-box and the Lustful One has not only
removed her frivolous wreath, but trampled it underfoot. The three
now kneel and pray. The Lustful One's orisons are diverted from
their proper path when she catches sight of a whistling Youth, clad
in crimson, strolling by. Regretfully she turns her glance away from
his gay invitation to join him.

A new hindrance to holiness arrives in the shape of a begging palmer who asks charity of the Greedy One. She passes along the request to the Priggish One, who produces a coin, which the palmer bites mistrustfully before he pockets it. Their curiosity is aroused by his feet, one of which has a peculiar look about it. Suddenly the palmer tosses off his cowled gown and broad hat, revealing himself to be the Devil in person, complete with horns, tail, and cloven hoof. The terror of the three Virgins would propel them from his presence, but they are frozen in their tracks by his black art. Seizing a fiddle standing conveniently by the mouth of the cave, he plays a compelling rhythm that forces even the Priggish One to dance. As the music grows wilder, their steps lose all decorum and they look down at their jerking bodies in terrified amazement at these involuntary convulsions. The Devil drops his fiddle and partners the Lustful One through the measures of a more polite dance, leaving her abruptly to chase the Greedy One when she attempts to play the instrument.

The Youth in crimson retraces his merry path. This time the Lustful One does not refuse to follow him. In fact, she leaps with delighted agility onto his back, to be carried into the cave, which turns out to be a postern gate to hell.

The Devil dangles a gold pendant in front of the Greedy One. The Priggish One saves her for the moment, but before long she, too, has been enticed into the cave.

Free to concentrate his attention, the Devil now goes for the Priggish One in earnest. She is not to be overcome by any ordinary means, so he resorts to guile. He weeps loudly. She tries to make him brace up and be a man in the manner of a mother encouraging a small boy. Refusing to be comforted, he mops his eyes on her dress. Hastily she substitutes the furry tassel on the end of his tail. By degrees she draws him closer to the church. Realizing her intention, he changes his tactics. As gentleness has got him nowhere, he drops all pretense, and resorts to brute force. Snarling, he leaps at her from the top of the church steps and chases her wildly around, confusing her until it is difficult to tell who is chasing whom. He edges closer to the cave, stopping abruptly in front of it, then stepping aside as the Priggish One is carried into it by her own momentum.

With a mockingly triumphant gesture he points to her retreating figure.

Three Virgins and a Devil first made its appearance at the Palace Theatre, London, in 1934, in the review *Why Not Tonight*. The three virgins were danced by Greta Nissen,[1] Elizabeth Schooling, and M. Braithwaite. Stanislas Idzikowski was the Devil. It was danced to music by Walford Hyden. A picture of the three girls posed in front of the setting strongly suggests the kind of movement used in the version arranged by Agnes De Mille for Ballet Theatre.

The second version of *Three Virgins and a Devil* was fitted to new music—the Respighi arrangement of *Antiche Danze ed Arie*. This was an admirable choice. Its measures support every mood and movement of the ballet—the disputes and prayers of the virgins, their mad abandoned dance, the ringing of church bells, the devil's weeping are all plainly to be heard.

The décor is a delightful theatrical adaptation of a Flemish painting. The costumes are in keeping with the period, though it is difficult to reconcile the Priggish One's prim character with the gay red of her dress. Surely the modest gray worn by the Lusty One would be more appropriate. The Youth's crimson costume, with its preposterous hat and fluttering ribbons, is one of the most hilariously funny getups ever seen on the New York stage.

Choreographically *Three Virgins and a Devil* is carried out, for the most part, in the style made familiar by the Jooss Ballet, back attitude turns and extension turns of various kinds being extensively employed. The Devil is almost purely classical, his variation characterized by beats, pirouettes, and *tours en l'air*.

The performances in *Three Virgins and a Devil* were on a high dramatic and technical level. Eugene Loring as the Devil did his best dancing as a member of Ballet Theatre. He was succeeded in this role by Yura Lazovsky. Lucia Chase as the Greedy One displayed her remarkable ability as a character dancer. Annabelle Lyon was charmingly sly as the Lustful One. Agnes De Mille marred her performance of the Priggish One, as she does all her roles by unnecessary grimacing, although otherwise it was effective. Maria Karnilova gives a more subtle interpretation. The Youth in crimson served to introduce the Jerome Robbins of *Fancy Free* and *Helen of Troy* to a delighted audience. Later, when he took over the part of the Devil, John Kriza

[1] Greta Nissen will be remembered for her charming performance in Deems Taylor's ballet-pantomime *A Kiss in Xanadu* in *A Beggar on Horseback*.

was cast as the Youth. Jerome Robbins's Devil, too sinister and serious for comedy, was not one of his most successful characterizations.

With the choreographer's guiding hand removed, *Three Virgins and a Devil* began to lose its incisive outlines. Before it is restored to the repertoire of Ballet Theatre, from which it has been absent for a season or two, it should be restudied.

UNDERTOW

Ballet by Antony Tudor; music by William Schuman; décor by Raymond Breinen.

UNDERTOW was first performed at the Metropolitan Opera House, New York, on April 10, 1945, with the following cast:

THE TRANSGRESSOR	Hugh Laing	NEMESIS	Rozsika Sabo
CYBELE	Diana Adams	POLYHYMNIA	Lucia Chase
POLLUX	John Kriza	PUDICITIA	Cynthia Risely
VOLUPIA	Shirley Eckl	ATE	Alicia Alonso
AGANIPPE	Patricia Barker	HYMEN	Dick Beard
	(Regis Powers	HERA	Janet Reed
	(Stanley Herbertt		(Marjorie Tallchief
SILENI	(Michael Kidd	BACCHANTES	(June Morris
	(Fernando Alonso		(Mildred Ferguson
SATYRISCI	(Kenneth Davis	MEDUSA	Nana Gollner
	(Roy Tobias		

Prologue—The City—Epilogue

◆◆◆◆◆◆◆◆◆◆◆◆◆◆◆◆◆◆

Prologue. In a grim wasteland Cybele endures her travail, giving birth to a son. When she rejects him to seek comfort in the arms of Pollux, he turns away hurt and embittered. The Transgressor has been born.

The City. The growing light discloses a street suggestive of the dockside of some northern city—Copenhagen or Edinburgh. One knows that it is a city where the sun is cold and the present an interval between fog and rain. Volupia, a coldly commercial streetwalker, stands at one side ready to bid joylessly for the custom of the first passer-by. The Transgressor enters with his child companion, Aganippe. Volupia looks at him invitingly. He ignores her, but although he continues his game of catch with Aganippe, it is plain that he is conscious of her presence.

The first of the Sileni—a disreputable character in a derby hat—strolls in. After some preliminary skirmishing he becomes Volupia's first customer of the evening and follows her from the scene.

The Satyrisci—a group of tough adolescents—make a boisterous entrance. They wrestle, rough-and-tumble fashion, and disappear.

The second of the Sileni—an elderly pot-bellied person—appears just in time to encounter Volupia, who has returned to her beat. He declines her advances out of sheer indecision, his furtive gestures indicating that he would like to follow her if he dared. His refusal arouses her ill temper, which frightens him into a hasty shambling exit.

Nemesis and Aganippe come in, pursuing some childish game. The latter attracts the attention of the first Silenus. He is driven off by the Transgressor, whose manner has shown a mounting tension and disgust throughout the preceding episodes.

Polyhymnia, an uplifter beaming with sanctimonious sweetness and the urge to conduct prayer meetings, enters. Pudicitia and Pollux, neighborhood boy and girl out for an evening stroll, join the group. Ate, in search of mischief, follows them. Polyhymnia annoys her and she expresses herself emphatically, although the others are tolerant enough. Ate attempts to interest the Transgressor. Failing, she runs after the Satyrisci.

Hymen and Hera, bride and groom, dance merrily in. They are young and in love, and their exuberance knows no bounds. The Transgressor looks after them sadly as they dash away.

Three Bacchantes, harridans of the lowest class, reel drunkenly forward, pausing to sing a hymn with alcholic fervor before they stagger off in different directions.

Ate returns with her group of louts. Viciously she eggs them on until they drag her out of sight. Returning alone, with dress disheveled, she is seized by the Transgressor, who with Aganippe has been a tense observer of this episode. Terrified, Aganippe runs away as his hands close about Ate's throat. The entrance of Nemesis leading one of the drunken women causes him to hesitate long enough for Ate to escape. The Transgressor, left alone, broods darkly.

Lithe and eager, Medusa emerges from the shadows seeking amusement. Since she is no commercial siren, her purpose is less obvious than Volupia's, less innocently vicious than Ate's. If she cannot attract Pollux, who appears presently with Pudicitia, she will have the Transgressor. For a moment she is thwarted by Polyhymnia, who has gathered a following for a corner prayer meeting. The Transgressor, shaken by the emotions awakened by Ate's behavior, would

gladly join them. Polyhymnia tries to induce Medusa to participate.
When she thinks she has succeeded, Medusa suddenly unleashes her
fury and drives the little band from the scene.

The suppressed hate and passion of the Transgressor are completely unveiled. At first he seems to respond to Medusa's amorous
advances, but his violence terrifies her. She tries to get away, but
there is no escape for her. He plays on her fear cat-and-mouse-fashion.
At length completely beside himself, drawing her into an embrace, he
strangles her.

Epilogue. In a lonely plain dominated by a cloud-filled sky the
Transgressor awakens to consciousness. At first he feels a release of
tension; then an awareness of his frightful crime begins to dawn.
People begin to wander by. When they stop to look at him, pointing
accusingly, he knows beyond doubt what he has done and goes to
meet the inescapable consequences.

Undertow is a courageous attempt to relate a case history in terms
of dance. Unfortunately, it lacks clarity. Presented without program
notes and with a cast of characters whose names with one exception
are drawn from Greek and Roman mythology, it managed to be-
wilder a large part of the audience from the moment of the curtain's
rising or even from the first look at the program. The strained attitudes and strange evolutions in the first scene failed to convey the
idea of birth and gave some who saw it the idea that Antony Tudor
had taken a leaf out of one of Balanchine's older books and placed
his dancers in a three-cornered predicament with no significance but
a decorative one.[1]

When the lights rise on a scene that could very well be contemporary and Aganippe turns out to be a small child in a white pin-
afore, confusion really begins. Volupia is undoubtedly a suitable
name for a lady of the evening, Sileni and Satyrisci are descriptive of
elderly roués and young delinquents, but it is scarcely fair to call a
pigtailed child Nemesis. Ate, archetype of nasty little girls who
play behind barns or in box cars with equally nasty little boys, may
be a modern goddess of discord. Hymen and Hera have lost their
high estate and become the slum proletarian bridal couple, gay in

[1] More than one ballet-goer of long experience fell into this trap, notably Mr. Carl
Van Vechten, who was writing ballet criticism before some of the current crop of
critics were born.

rented wedding clothes, enjoying their one-day honeymoon. Pollux [2] and Pudicitia are an ordinary boy-and-girl twosome. The Bacchantes become three riotiously drunken scrubwomen. Medusa's mythological prerogative of turning the beholder to stone suffers a change. Far from petrifying the Transgressor, she arouses in him a feverish passion to possess and destroy.

It is not strange that the reviews ranged from plaintiveness through flippancy to disappointment. Much was expected from the creator of *Pillar of Fire* — a simple direct story of love frustrated, betrayed, and transfigured, always clear in its intention and statement. Ballet could go no further in those particular directions. The audience at *Undertow* did not know what was coming, but it did not anticipate obscurity, which had never been present in the previous works of this great choreographer. If the subject had been less serious, one might have guessed that he was having his little joke.

The individual performances in *Undertow* are of a high order with one or two exceptions. Alicia Alonso (Ate) and Nana Gollner (Medusa), two fine dancers in the classical tradition, testified to their ability to create moods far removed from the serene emotions of Swan Queens and Sylphides. Marjorie Tallchief (Bacchante) demonstrated a talent for characterization that foretells a brilliant future. Hugh Laing as the Transgressor holds the dramatic focus without ever appealing for a sympathy that would be out of place extended to a homicidal maniac.

Choreographically the ballet is in the style made familiar in Tudor's earlier works. He uses ordinary actions and colloquial gesture in a balletic manner — not superimposed on a ballet routine, but fused with the steps to form an individual style. The role of Pollux, beautifully danced by John Kriza, is almost purely classical, characterized by *pirouettes en attitude,* and *grands ronds de jambe* — the latter a favorite step of the choreographer. Ate is also seen in classical terms, her role having many academic steps and poses. Volupia angles for business posing in a conventional fifth position *sur les pointes.* The long solo for the Transgressor in the epilogue is strange and staccato. The idea of mental disturbance becomes clear as one watches the spasmodic and incomplete movements. This is not the

[2] Confusion is not at all lessened by having Pollux appear in the prologue as the father and lover, later as an ordinary young man squiring Pudicitia.

passé (stylized)

attitude, seen from side

ROSELLA HIGHTOWER

arabesque with *plié, par terre*

attitude en avant

passé (transitional movement)   third arabesque

ROSELLA HIGHTOWER

fourth position *sur les pointes*,
seen from three-quarter angle   *sauté en arabesque*

grand jeté   *penché arabesque*

TODD BOLENDER (in *Commedia Balletica* costume)

cabriole (shadow) and leap   arabesque

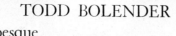

sauté in fifth position   TODD BOLENDER   *sauté* in *passé position*
(shadow) and stylized arabesque

soussus   ALPHEUS KOON   *saut de chat*

photographic reproduction of the tics that may accompany paranoia as seen in *Mad Tristan,* but a subtle conveyance of a confused state of mind by means of movement. If the motives for the Transgressor's crime were as clear, the ballet would be an unqualified success.

The role of Polyhymnia would be improved by some revision as well as a new costume. The lady, dispensing altogether too much sweetness and light, is as boring as her counterpart in real life would be. If this part could be pulled together and shortened it would have more point. Her costume—a most unpleasant blue—is the only failure in the entire set.

The setting by Raymond Breinen, better known as an easel painter, might appear too grand and spacious for such a sordid scene if architectural fragments did not enclose the action. It cleverly conveys the idea of an underprivileged neighborhood in a great city. There is nothing definitely regional about the architecture although it strongly suggests a northern European locale. The cloudy background for the epilogue rolls up to disclose distant towers with winged horses advancing. Are they meant to be swift messengers of retribution or was Mr. Breinen unable to resist introducing his favorite motive into the scene? Whatever the answer, it is an extraordinarily impressive effect. The costumes manage to combine a suggestion of classical drapery with ordinary dress, the decorative and the sordid, in a brilliant manner.

Undertow is the first of the Tudor ballets to have a specially composed score, by William Schuman, one of America's outstanding composers. It has been said that the slow pace at the beginning of the work was due to the composer's unwillingness to make cuts. From the moment Polyhymnia enters to the strains of what sounds like a revival mission hymn the musical interest never flags. The same tune with intoxicated overtones serves the Bacchantes well. In the murder episode there is a hair-raising crescendo that adds immeasurably to the dramatic tension. This score is a distinguished addition to contemporary ballet music and will undoubtedly be heard as a concert suite.

In response to the demand for program notes, a glossary of mythological terms has been added to the program. These have not clarified the action to any remarkable degree. Providing the three divisions of the ballet with subjects (birth and infancy; adolescence and manhood; guilt) has proved more helpful.

Undertow is far from being as satisfying a work of art as *Jardin aux Lilas* or *Pillar of Fire*. No work by Antony Tudor, however, can be less than provocative. No doubt audiences will continue to be baffled by its obscurities for many seasons to come.

UNION PACIFIC

An American ballet in one act and four scenes; libretto by Archibald MacLeish; music by Nicolas Nabokoff, based on folk songs of the period 1860; choreography by Léonide Massine; scenery by Albert Johnson; costumes by Irene Sharaff.

UNION PACIFIC was first performed by Colonel W. de Basil's Ballet Russe on April 6, 1934 at the Forest Theater, Philadelphia, with the following cast:

THE SURVEYOR OF THE IRISH CREW *André Eglevsky*	HIS ASSISTANT *Sono Osato*
	THE MORMON MISSIONARY
THE LADY-GAY *Eugenia Delarova*	*Valentinoff*
THE SURVEYOR OF THE CHINESE CREW *David Lichine*	THE MEXICAN GIRL
	Tamara Toumanova
THE BARMAN *Léonide Massine*	THE CAMERA MAN *Roland Guerard*

Mexicans, Capitalists, Irish Workmen, Chinese Workmen, Gamblers, Girls, Indians

◇◇◇◇◇◇◇◇◇◇◇◇◇◇◇◇

There is an inner curtain representing a blueprint of the construction plans for the railroad.

Scene 1. The railroad right-of-way east of Promontory Point. The Irish Crew is seen at work, driving spikes. They are a rough-and-ready lot, hard-working but not grim about it.

Scene 2. The railroad right-of-way west of Promontory Point. The Chinese Crew are carrying in railroad ties and laying them in place. They scurry in and out like ants under the direction of the Surveyor. The Lady-Gay strolls out from the Big Tent. Her buxom charms make an immediate impression on the Surveyor.

Scene 3. The Big Tent. The Big Tent is the dance hall and gambling resort where surveyors and workmen spend their free time. A horde of gamblers, dance-hall girls, and camp-followers have assembled to get what they can out of this unaccustomed situation. A Mexican Girl performs the hat dance for their entertainment. The Lady-Gay and the Chinese Surveyor come in. The Irish Surveyor tries to lure her to his table. A Mormon Missionary, sedate in ministerial black, enters. He is easily distracted from his mission when the Barman offers him a quick drink. The Barman dances a mad *pas seul,* which at first bores and then amuses the customers.

The strained relations that the Lady-Gay has caused between the two surveyors spread to their crews. A general brawl breaks out. The dance-hall girls try to make peace, but their efforts merely add to the confusion which brings the scene to a close.

Scene 4. The railroad right-of-way at Promontory Point. The rival gangs work feverishly to be first at the meeting-point. As the last spike is driven, two engines arrive from opposite sides carrying groups of railroad officials and their families. There is general good feeling. The Barman and his Assistant circulate through the crowd pouring drinks, while rival gangs, officials, and dance-hall girls join in a hymn. Indians look on curiously and the Camera Man takes a picture of the historic occasion.

Union Pacific was the first and most successful excursion into the American scene by a Russian choreographer. It was not greeted with any particular acclaim by the critics, who seemed to think that the Russians were carrying their invasion of the United States too far. Probably if they had foreseen the dull ineptitudes of *The New Yorker* and *Saratoga,* they might have withheld their strictures. After all, *Union Pacific* was a sincere attempt at balletic comment on a dramatic event in American history, as well as a tribute to a country that provided eager audiences for the European repertoire. There was reason in the critical complaint about the mixture in styles—a mixture of the realistic and the abstract. However, there was some artistic justification for this: the abstract treatment was used only in the scene in which the Chinese were seen at work. Their automatic movements may have been meant to provide a social comment on the difference in status between free workmen and contract laborers. All other scenes, especially the episodes in the Big Tent, were treated with a realism that many found shocking.

Two memorable performances high-lighted *Union Pacific*: the Barman and the Lady-Gay. In the Barman, Léonide Massine created a portrait worthy to stand beside the Miller in *The Three-Cornered Hat* and the Cancan Dancer in *La Boutique Fantasque*. His solo in the Big Tent scene inevitably stopped the show when performed by its creator.[1] Later when another dancer assumed this role, it lost character. The steps—a fantastic mixture of ragtime, cakewalk, and heaven knows what—remained the same, but the strange stuffed-doll quality that gave it savor was gone. Eugenia Delarova created the role of the Lady-Gay, but it will be associated with Irina Baronova by anyone who saw her do it. With a hard make-up and a wonderfully vulgar costume, she was a balletic Mae West, a remarkable feat of characterization for so young a dancer.

The score of *Union Pacific,* specially composed by Nicolas Nabokoff, made clever use of the less sentimental songs of Stephen Foster, particularly *Oh! Susanna.* The décor by Albert Johnson provided a suitable if not exciting background for the action. The costumes by Irene Sharaff were a theatrical version of the dress of the period. The final scene was most effective pictorially, setting and costumes uniting to produce a Currier and Ives lithograph.

It was not until the advent of *Billy the Kid* and *Rodeo* that *Union Pacific* was outclassed as an example of Americana in ballet.

[1] When Massine danced this solo at a recent concert at the Lewisohn Stadium, it demonstrated that even when detached from its context, it is still capable of arousing enthusiasm.

VOICES OF SPRING

Book and choreography by Mikhail Mordkin; music by Johann Strauss, arranged by Mois Zlatin; scenery and costumes by Lee Simonson.

VOICES OF SPRING was performed for the first time at the Alvin Theater, New York, on November 10, 1938, with the following cast:

OLD MAN	*Noel Charise*	FLOWER VENDOR IN GREEN	
OLD LADY	*Ashby Acree*		*Nina Stroganova*
LAMPLIGHTER	*Savva Andreieff*	FLOWER VENDOR IN EMERALD	
THE FLIRT	*Karen Conrad*		*Patricia Bowman*
TWO CADETS	*Vladimir Dokoudovsky,*	LIEUTENANT	*Leon Varkas*
	Kari Karnakoski	CAPTAIN	*Edward Caton*
BOY IN GREY	*Dimitri Romanoff*	GENERAL	*Mikhail Mordkin*

Girls, Cavaliers, Street Cleaners, Citizens of Vienna

◆◆◆◆◆◆◆◆◆◆◆◆◆◆◆

The scene is the Belvedere Gardens in Vienna on a holiday morning in spring. An elderly couple seated on a park bench watch sympathetically as boys and girls stroll by. A Lamplighter on his morning rounds attracts the fancy of the Flirt. The arrival of two Cadets distracts her and she trips gaily off with them. The Flower Girl in Green, accompanied by the Boy in Grey, comes with her barrow to set up shop. There is a great deal of maneuvering, which is complicated by the entrance of the Flower Girl in Emerald, who not only wishes to appropriate the best location for her barrow, but is not averse to commandeering the Boy in Grey as well. Fortunately, the advent of a dashing Lieutenant provides her with a new quarry. The Flower Girl in Green removes herself, her barrow, and the Boy in Grey before her predatory rival can change her mind.

Now a little comedy of flirtation begins. The Lieutenant offers the Girl in Emerald his devotion. Finding that this is not enough, he adds the promise of a ring. This is better, but as it is contingent on the Lieutenant's being promoted—a distant prospect—she remains cold. A Captain, passing by, stops to buy a flower. A second look at the Flower Girl in Emerald causes him to send the Lieutenant on his way—an order that the Lieutenant is obliged to obey. Just as the Captain is summoning all his charm to make an impression, a General makes a grandiose entry on the scene. With a wave of his hand he dismisses the Captain, and takes up where his subordinate left off. Spring in the air has thrown him into a reminiscent mood. Remembering his youthful flirtations, he is inclined to experiment to see if his charm still works. The Flower Girl in Emerald plays up nicely, and in no time at all he is teaching her how to dance a mazurka, which obviously he considers no member of the younger generation capable of performing properly.

A moment or two after the departure of the General a sudden spring shower sends the rest of the characters of the comedy scurrying for shelter—the elderly couple, the Flirt and her Cadets, the Flower Girl in Green and the Boy in Grey; even the Captain has found feminine companionship. Only the Flower Girl in Emerald is left alone to pick her disconsolate way among the puddles, almost overbalanced by a hastily produced umbrella. While she is reflecting on the rewards of fickleness, the Lieutenant returns and claims her. Oblivious of the weather, they embrace and run away from the scene.

Voices of Spring belongs to that family of ballets of which the ancestor and best-known member is *Le Beau Danube*. This example of the genre is not unworthy of its forbear. The score is bright, tuneful, and composed of not too hackneyed examples of Johann Strauss's music. The costumes for the girls have an enchanting suggestion of the 1860's in sleeve and bodice. The setting, commonplace enough, has the virtue of not distracting attention from the dance patterns.

Choreographically the ballet has several good points. The pantomime is of unusual clarity, as might be expected from Mikhail Mordkin, who was trained in Russia in a period when mime was a living tradition. The *pas de trois* for the flirt and the two Cadets featured *double tours en l'air* and *entrechats six,* which sometimes became *entrechats huit* when Karen Conrad was in good form. As the Girl in Emerald, Patricia Bowman traveled a diagonal line in slow *fouettés*—one of the most spectacular feats of balance seen during the current revival of ballet. Later the role was performed by Irina Baronova, who, not sharing Miss Bowman's ability to dance in slow motion, substituted a series of double and triple *fouettés* at this point —a more ordinary, but still impressive achievement of virtuosity.

Actually, the most interesting feature of *Voices of Spring* was the performance of Mikhail Mordkin as the General. His superb stage presence and authoritative pantomime made a simple role the center of attention and carried intimations of the golden age of ballet.

Voices of Spring, revived by Ballet Theatre with the original décor and costumes, was included in its first program, given on January 11, 1940 at the Center Theater, New York. As the Mordkin Ballet had been more or less incorporated into Ballet Theatre, there were few changes in the cast. The most important of these were: Yurek Shabelevsky (Lieutenant), Peter Michael (Captain), and Edward Caton (General). Edward Caton's General retained some of the importance with which Mordkin had endowed the part. In the hands of Harold Haskin, and later Eugene Loring, it lost all distinction, and the gallant old General became a senile "wolf" taking advantage of an opportunity.

Voices of Spring has vanished from the current repertoire of Ballet Theatre. As far as may be ascertained, the last New York performance took place at the Lewisohn Stadium in June 1940. The designations of some of the characters had been changed on the program: the Flower Girl in Green became the Flower Vendor; the Flower Girl in Emerald, the Toast of Vienna. This production boasted the presence in the cast of Antony Tudor and Hugh Laing as the two Cadets—unusual roles for these dancers.

GLOSSARY

THERE are two manuals of ballet technique that may be profitably consulted by those readers who would really like to learn something about it. They are addressed to laymen rather than dancers, though there are dancers who would not be wasting time spent with them. They are: Lincoln Kirstein's *Ballet Alphabet, a Primer for Laymen,* with drawings by Paul Cadmus, and Kay Ambrose's *The Ballet-Lover's Pocket-Book, Technique without tears for the Ballet-lover,* illustrated by the author. The Cadmus illustrations are fine from an artistic point of view, as well as being clearly defined expositions of the various positions and poses. Kay Ambrose's drawings are an integral part of the text and depict the dancer in motion with spirit and accuracy. These books supplement each other nicely.

This glossary defines only those terms used in this text. There are many others that do not come within the scope of this work, as only the simplest sequences of steps have been described.

I am deeply indebted to Alpheus Koon of Ballet Theatre. Without him, I could not possibly have set down these explanations, all of which were worked out step by step by Mr. Koon while I endeavored to set down what I saw. I attempted to define each step or pose in terms of movement, rather than by reference to another ballet idiom, always excepting the positions which are indispensable. This has at times been impossible, but I have done my best. It all seemed clear enough at the time: I hope that readers will find it equally so. Alpheus Koon received his training at the School of American Ballet and the Vilzak-Shollar School of Ballet. The terminology is that in use by the teachers at those admirable institutions.

Positions: All steps in the classical ballet are based on the five positions.
> *1st Position*: Feet are placed with heels together, and the entire leg from the hip is turned out at an angle of 180 degrees.
> *2nd Position*: Duplicate of the first except that there is a space between the dancer's heels corresponding to one and one half times the length of the dancer's foot. This is an open position.

3rd Position (obsolete): Similar to first, except that ankles are placed together.

4th Position: Legs crossed, feet parallel to each other as in fifth position. Between the dancer's feet there is an open space one and one half times the length of the dancer's foot. This is an open position.

5th Position: Legs are crossed with feet parallel, the toe of one touching the heel of the other. This is a closed position. Try to remember this one, as almost all steps begin from a fifth position and many of them end the same way. There are several illustrations in this book showing dancers in fifth position.

Positions may be held *à terre,* on demi-point, and *sur les pointes.* At all times the turnout is from the hip, never from the knees. A dancer who gives the impression of being sway-backed is not properly turned out and is undoubtedly forcing the turnout from the knees.

Adage, adagio: The opening section of the classical *pas de deux,* in which the ballerina, supported by her partner, exhibits her command of the balances and poses that characterize the vocabulary of the *danse d'école.* Much of the effectiveness of *adage* depends on a feeling of rapport between ballerina and partner, necessary for the perfect timing that is the first requisite for the successful performance of a *pas de deux.* In fact, their relations should be identical with those existing between singer and accompanist. Many excellent male dancers fail as partners, just as a good pianist is not necessarily a good accompanist. Anton Dolin and Paul Petroff are outstanding in this difficult art.

Arabesque: A pose in which the leg is raised at hip level in the air straight behind the body. It is the longest line that can be achieved by the human body, and may be performed with the arms in various positions, with the supporting leg slightly bent (*plié*); with the supporting leg bent, the other held straight and touching the floor (*arabesque par terre*). The important thing to remember is that if the leg in the air is held straight, it is an *arabesque.* There are illustrations of several types of *arabesques,* including the spectacular *penché.*

Assemblé: A step of elevation (literally, bringing the feet together), in which the working leg brushes to the side. As it goes into the air, the dancer pushes off the floor with the supporting leg, finish-

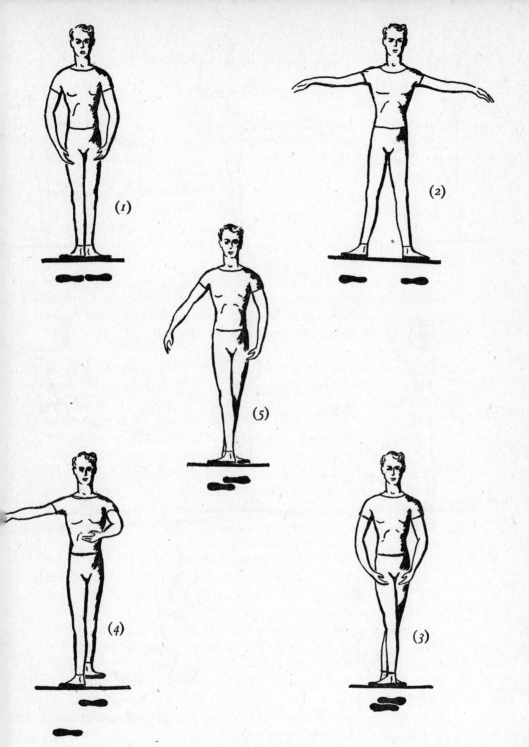

The five positions of the feet (the positions of the arms may vary)

A. *croisée devant*

B. *au quatrième devant*

C. *écartée*

D. *effacée*

E. *à la seconde*

F. *épaulée*

G. *au quatrième derrière*

H. *croisée derrière*

The eight positions of the body

ing with the feet together in fifth position on the ground. An *assemblé* may also be performed to the front or to the side; with varying degrees of elevation; with a beat, for greater brilliance; finally, with a *plié*, as in the Cecchetti *assemblé*, seen in *Pas de Quatre* and the Prelude in *Les Sylphides*.

Attitude: A pose in which the leg is extended behind the body with the knee bent at a ninety-degree angle, the leg turned out so that the knee is higher than the foot. The corresponding arm is raised in a half circle, the opposite arm extended straight out to the side. In an *attitude en avant*, the bent leg is extended to the front. There are illustrations of both types. The *attitude* is the photographer's despair: when a picture of this pose is taken from directly in front of the subject, the result looks as though part of the dancer's leg had completely disappeared. Our illustrations are taken from an angle that eliminates this phenomenon.

Au quatrième devant: One of the eight positions of the body, in which the leg is outstretched in fourth position in front of the body. *Au quatrième derrière* or *au quatrième en arrière* is the corresponding position with the leg outstretched behind the body.

Ballabile: A group number, often in waltz time, performed in classical ballets by the corps de ballet—the *"Valse de fleurs"* in *The Nutcracker* is an example.

Ballerina: Principal female soloists of a ballet company are by contemporary usage called ballerinas. By any standards of any age, Markova and Danilova are ballerinas. It is not correct to call any female dancer a ballerina, not even the leading dancer of a movie or a Broadway show.

Ballet d'action: A ballet with a definite plot. *La Fille Mal Gardée* and *Don Juan* are among the earliest examples of the *ballet d'action*.

Ballon: A quality in a dancer's movements that gives elasticity and lightness. A dancer with *ballon* never clumps heavily to earth. He appears to touch the ground only to rise again into the air. André Eglevsky and Ian Gibson have superb *ballon*.

Ballonné: A step of preparation: the dancer jumps, simultaneously executing a *battement* in air, followed by a bending of the leg at the knee.

Ballotté: This is a step that we found beyond our powers to describe intelligibly. On page 32 of *The Ballet-Lover's Pocket-Book*, there are seven drawings that follow the action of a *ballotté*. This step is performed repeatedly in Act I of *Giselle* by Giselle and Albrecht.

Battement: Literally, beating. There are two kinds:

(1) *Grand battement*: raising of the entire leg from the hip into a position in the air (*en l'air*). This may be executed in various directions—*quatrième en avant, quatrième en arrière, à la seconde*.

(2) *Petit battement*: a small beating by the foot against the ankle of the supporting leg. *Petits battements* are performed by the Swan Queen in the *adage* in Act II of *Swan Lake;* by the dying Mercutio as he is held by Romeo in *Romeo and Juliet*.

Batterie: A collective term meaning the entire vocabulary of beats—*brisé, cabriole, entrechat, royale*. Simple steps in which a beat may be included are: *assemblé, chassé, demi-fouetté, echappé, glissade, jeté, sissonne*.

Bourrée: A small traveling step in ordinary usage, in which the feet remain in fifth position, usually *sur les pointes*.

Bourrée au courant: Small running steps with feet in first position.

Brisé: A beaten step in which the working leg moves from a fifth position to side, strikes calf of opposite leg, returning to its original fifth position. It may be used with brilliant effect as a traveling step, as in *Coppélia,* when the ballerina makes a diagonal crossing of the stage performing *brisés*.

Brisé volé: Literally, flying *brisé,* in which each leg alternately becomes the working leg. This is a step of great brilliance, and is performed effectively in the Bluebird *pas de deux*.

Cabriole: Most frequently a step of elevation, which is performed by beating the entire leg against the other in the air. It may be performed directly in front (*en avant*) or behind (*en arrière*) the dancer's body. For greater brilliance it may be performed with a double beat. This step may be seen in the man's solo in *Les Sylphides*. It is also performed by the corps de ballet in Act I of *Giselle*.

Chaîné: A traveling step in which the feet are held in a firm first position, on point or demi-point, for a series of small regular turns. *Chaînés* are included in almost every classical variation.

Changement: A jump in fifth position in which the feet change position in the air. When done with a single beat in front or back, it becomes a *royale*.

Chassé: A traveling step, performed by jumping into the air in fifth position; on landing, the foot slides to an open position, fourth or second, according to direction. It may also be performed as a turning step. Literally, the feet chase each other.

Corps de ballet: Indispensable to any ballet company. They are called upon to display all the talents. In former times the corps de ballet was a dead end, and dancers began and ended their theatrical lives without advancing any further. Modern dancers and ballet companies take a different view. Nora Kaye, outstanding dramatic ballerina, began her career in Ballet Theatre in the corps de ballet—a group that in its first seasons could have given pointers in precision to the Rockettes.

Coryphée: Once used to designate a dancer who performed in a small group. The four little swans and the "friends" of Giselle and Swanilda used to be danced by coryphées.

Coupé jeté: See *Jeté*.

Danse d'école: Dancing based on the five positions; classical dancing. In this connection, it must be emphasized that classical dancing has nothing whatever to do with the aimless cavorting in more or less Greek draperies that used to be miscalled classical dancing. *Swan Lake* and *The Sleeping Beauty* are examples of the classic ballets of the nineteenth century; *Danses Concertantes* and *Ballet Imperial* represent a twentieth-century approach to classicism.

Degagé: Literally, disengaged; a step of preparation in which the non-working leg is extended at a low angle from the body. In *degagé* turns, the non-working leg is extended away from the supporting leg in the direction of the turn, and the movement is used as a preparation for the turn. Usually performed in series of single turns as in "finger" variation.

Demi-fouetté: See *Fouetté en tournant*.

Développé: An unfolding of the leg into a position in the air, *au quatrième devant, au quatrième en arrière, à la seconde*. In this movement the working leg always goes through the position known as *passé*.

Divertissement: A solo or ensemble dance that is complete in itself. There was a *divertissement* in almost all classical ballets. *Aurora's Wedding, Princess Aurora* (*Sleeping Beauty*), and *The Magic Swan* (*Swan Lake*) are *divertissement* acts. They may be rearranged or changed at discretion.

Échappé: A movement of opening, in the air or on the ground. A simple *échappé* is performed by opening the feet into a second position from a fifth position *en plié,* springing to the demi-point on opening. This may also be done by the dancer jumping straight into the air, the legs opening to front or back while in the air. In *Pas de Quatre* the four dancers join hands, forming a circle in which they face outward, and perform a series of *échappés* in unison.

Elevation: Ability to attain height in jumping. This depends on a good *plié* combined with the ability to push off the ground from the *plié*. Dancers with outstanding elevation who have been seen recently in New York include Karen Conrad, Rosella Hightower, Alicia Alonso, Tatiana Riabouchinska, David Lichine, Ian Gibson, Igor Youskevitch, and André Eglevsky. The elevation attained by Taglioni, and later by Nijinsky, is a legend of the dance world. It is probable that a good deal depends on proper breathing.

Emboîté: A small flicking movement done by alternately pointing the feet on the ground with the knee bent. May be seen in the Sugar Plum Fairy's variation (*The Nutcracker*) and Aurora's variation (*Princess Aurora*).

Grand emboîté: This is performed with straight knees, the feet passing in the air (known to vaudeville as the "hitch kick"). This is also performed in the Sugarplum Fairy's variation.

En balançoire: A seesaw step; the leg swings in an arc from the hip, forward and backward, passing through first position *par terre*. This may be seen in the second sailor's variation in *Fancy Free*.

En dedans: Literally, inside; a movement executed in a direction that leads toward the dancer's body. The role of Petrouchka is largely composed of steps *en dedans*.

En dehors: Literally, outside; a movement executed in a direction that leads or opens away from the dancer's body. The greater part of the classical vocabulary of the dance is *en dehors*.

En l'air: Steps and movements performed in the air, but it must be understood that preparatory steps must be performed *par terre,* at least until dancers grow wings.

Enchaînement: Any series of steps in a ballet.

Entrechat: A step of beating; a fifth-position jump with a crossing of the feet in the air. The number of crossings is limited by the dancer's ability and agility. Nijinsky is said to have achieved *en-*

trechat dix. Present-day dancers have not yet attained to this, at least in performance.

Épaulé: A position of the body in which the shoulder is twisted forward. Literally, shouldered.

Failli: A transitional step *par terre,* which passes sliding through first position into an open position (usually fourth in front).

Fouetté en tournant: A turn in which traction is obtained partly by a *relevé* of the supporting foot, partly by a whipping movement of the other leg. Thirty-two *fouettés en tournant* were performed for the first time in serious ballet by Pierina Legnani. Nicholas Legat claimed that the ballet was *Zolushka,* a revival by Petipa of a work by Perrot. Beaumont and other authorities ascribe this event to Act III of *Swan Lake* at the first Marinsky performance in 1895. Wherever it happened, the performance was considered too acrobatic for ballet by the purists, whose ideas did not disturb the enjoyment of those who found it thrilling. Balanchine, in *La Concurrence* and *Cotillon,* exploited Toumanova's ability to perform *fouettés* in unlimited numbers. In spite of propaganda to the contrary by writers who should know better, the correct performance of a series of *fouettés* (they should be done without the dancer traveling from her starting-point) is a difficult feat, and the dancer earns all the applause she gets.

Demi-fouetté: A derivative of the *fouetté en tournant.* The dancer changes with a half turn from a position *au quatrième devant* to an *arabesque,* achieving the turn by a twist of the torso. In the coda of *Swan Lake* the Queen makes her entrance performing a series of *demi-fouettés par terre* in a diagonal across the stage. Myrtha's solo in *Giselle* includes a spectacular series of *demi-fouettés en l'air.* These are real virtuoso steps, the abrupt change of position requiring a high degree of strength to achieve them with the necessary clean-cut precision.

Frappé: An exercise step performed most frequently in the classroom. It is executed by brushing the foot briskly away from the ankle of the supporting leg, alternately to front, side, and back. The coryphée seen on the stage at the rise of the curtain in *Gala Performance* is warming up by performing *frappés à la seconde.*

Gargouillade: A *pas de chat* executed with a *double rond de jambe en l'air, en dedans* in the direction of the step, *en dehors* by the leg that will close the step into fifth position. This step is almost as impossible to describe as it is to perform. Anyone who saw Rosella Hightower in the Sugarplum Fairy's variation, saw *gargouillades* performed with exquisite precision. Nora Kaye does them with satirical exaggeration in the coda of *Gala Performance*. Dancers performing the Sugarplum Fairy's variation usually substitute a less complicated but more showy step for the *gargouillades,* which, however, were always performed by Vera Trefilova, who set a standard for succeeding Sugarplum Fairies.

Glissade: A transitional and preparatory step executed by gliding from a fifth position to any open position.

Jeté: Literally, a throw; always a jumped step. There are a variety of *jetés*. The simplest form consists in a small jump to the side or in front, in which the dancer lands with the free foot at the knee of the supporting leg.

Grand jeté: A big leap executed by raising the leg off the ground in a *grand battement* traveling forward, pushing off the ground with the supporting leg. This is usually finished by an *arabesque*. While the dancer is in the air, both legs should be held straight. In Act II of *Giselle,* the Wilis, having disposed of Hilarion, leave the stage in groups, performing *glissade, jeté,* followed by two *grands jetés* —an *enchaînement* strongly suggestive of flight. Gibson, Youske- vitch, and Eglevsky among male dancers, and Rosella Hightower, Alicia Alonso, and Tatiana Riabouchinska among female dancers, achieve soaring flights in their *grands jetés*.

Coupé jeté: Similar to *grand jeté* except that the dancer crosses the pushing leg over the other leg as he leans forward. The leap is usually done from side to side. *Coupés jetés* are usually performed in series and form part of many classical variations for the male dancer—variation in *pas de trois* (*Swan Lake*) and *The Nut- cracker* are examples.

Jeté en tournant: Similar to *grand jeté* except that in mid-air the dancer's body turns and faces the direction from which the jump originated. *Jeté en tournant* may be seen in the Waltz in *Les Syl- phides,* the Bluebird *pas de deux,* etc.

Line: The outline presented by the dancer while executing steps and assuming poses. A good line depends on many things, some of them intangible, the fundamentals being acquired at birth. A dancer with less than perfect proportions can never hope to have the true classical line, although much has been made of a good turnout and a faultless kinetic memory by dancers who have the will and not the physique to be classical dancers.

Par terre: A step executed on the ground is said to be *par terre*. The Wilis in Act II of *Giselle* stand posed in *arabesque par terre*.

Pas d'action: A dance in which emotion or a definite action is expressed. When the Swan Queen makes her entrance and discovers the Prince, the *pas de deux* that follows, in which she expresses first terror, then a growing interest, is a *pas d'action*.

Pas de chat: A step of movement and elevation done to the side or in an oblique direction. The feet move from fifth position to fifth position through *passé* while in the air. This is a step that is difficult to define though easy to recognize. When the Swan Queen makes her entrance, she runs down the ramp, executes a *pas de chat,* and pauses dramatically.

Pas de cheval: Almost indistinguishable by the layman from a simple *emboîté*.

Pas de deux, trois, quatre, etc.: Dances executed by two, three, four, etc. The classical *pas de deux* had a definite structure. The Bluebird and other *pas de deux* follow this pattern.

Pas de papillon: A traveling step in which the legs are extended behind the body in the air, usually done in series. The French Ballerina and her partner perform *pas de papillon* in the coda of *Gala Performance*. It might be called a *grand emboîté* in reverse.

Passé: Frequently a transitional step. The dancer draws one leg up until the toes touch the back of the other knee. When this is held as a pose, it is known as a *retiré*. See illustration.

Piqué: Stepping directly on the point of the supporting foot in any desired position. In *piqué* turns, the dancer steps directly into the turn, the supporting foot being the one nearest the direction of the turn. If the turn is to the left, he steps into the turn with the left foot, and vice versa, the non-working leg being drawn up to the back of the knee. Usually executed in series of single or double turns, or alternately for greater brilliance. *Piqué* turns in a circle are a favorite tour de force in classical ballet. They may be seen in Aurora's variation (*Princess Aurora*). Dancers have substituted them for the thirty-two *fouettés* in the Act III *pas de deux* from *Swan Lake*.

Pirouette: A full turn on one foot, either on point or demi-point from any position. The motive power is obtained from a combination of *plié* and force-of-arm movement. *Pirouettes* may be performed in a variety of poses: *à la seconde, en attitude, en arabesque,* etc. They should finish with the dancer in the exact position from which he started. Eglevsky's fame is built largely on his ability to perform multiple *pirouettes* in any direction and in any tempo.

Plié: Literally, bent, or bending; a bending of the knees while the feet are on the ground. *Pliés* in four positions begin all ballet classes. The chief function of the *plié* is to stretch the tendons and muscles of the feet and legs. Almost every step in ballet begins and ends with a *plié*.

Pointes, sur les: When the female dancer rises to the tips of her toes, she is said to be *sur les pointes*. If she holds a pose arabesque or attitude, she is *sur la pointe*. There are many misconceptions about dancing *sur les pointes*. It has been regarded, with fantastic inaccuracy, as synonymous with ballet dancing, which was developing and extending its technique for more than two hundred years before Taglioni astonished western Europe by dancing *sur les pointes* in *La Sylphide*. Russians were less astonished because they were accustomed to male dancing *sur les pointes* by Cossack dancers. There is a fascinating article in *Dancing Times* (August 1945) by Joan Lawson: "Speculations about the Origin of 'Toe' Dancing," which should be read by anyone who is interested in the subject. Dancers are said to be on demi-point, or half-point, when they rise as far as possible on the ball of the foot without actually being *sur les pointes*.

Port de bras: In strict classical ballet, for each of the positions of the feet there is a corresponding position of the arms. The most important of these are the second, in which the arms are held in the form of a Latin cross, and the three fifth positions: *en bas* the arms curved toward each other and meeting a little below the waist; *en avant,* the arms held out at chest level; and *en haut,* the arms held curved over the head. It is important to hold the arms smoothly curved with no protruding elbows visible. While dancing, the arms change position. Dancers whose arms flail the air as they move present a fussy, restless outline. Unfortunately, it would appear to be easier to keep the feet under control than the arms. Alicia Markova has beautiful arm movements. Among the younger dancers, Margaret Banks has exceptionally fine arms. In Act II of

Glossary [361

Giselle, at the end of the ensemble for the Wilis, the entire group executes a *grand port de bras,* a free, noble movement that is one of the loveliest in ballet.

Relevé: A rising from the flat foot to point or demi-point, also from demi-point to point (very difficult). Almost always executed from a *plié.*

Retiré: See *Passé.*

Rond de jambe: The execution of a circle by the leg. In a *rond de jambe par terre,* the foot describes a circle on the floor (not a traveling step). The Prelude in *Les Sylphides* includes *rond de jambe par terre.* In a *rond de jambe en l'air,* the working leg is raised in a second position and the circle is made in the air by the leg moving from the knee. *Grand rond de jambe en l'air* is a large sweeping movement of the entire leg from the hip in a semicircle from front to back, or vice versa. This may be seen in the second variation in *Princess Aurora.*

Saut de basque: A traveling step; the dancer turns in the air with one foot drawn up in *passé* position. This used to be considered a man's step, but modern usage permits women to perform it. In Act II of *Giselle,* Giselle and Albrecht perform *sauts de basque* in opposite directions in the *pas de deux.* Hagar in the second half of *Pillar of Fire* travels from group to group in a *saut de basque.* In *Graduation Ball,* Rosella Hightower performed double *sauts de basque.*

Saut de chat: A jump forward from a fifth position (usually preceded by a *glissade*) in which the foot is drawn immediately into a *retiré* position while in the air. Both arms are outstretched in the direction of the jump. The final leap in *Spectre de la Rose* should be a *saut de chat.* When properly done it leaves an impression of soaring flight.

Sauté: A jump; used in connection with another term, it means that a jump is involved—*échappé sauté, sauté en arabesque,* etc.

Sissonne: A springing jump from fifth position in which the working leg acts as a lever, returning to fifth position. This step can be done in various directions and may be combined with beats in a male variation.

Soussus: A *relevé* in fifth position performed *sur les pointes* by women, on demi-point by men. Used by the latter as preparation for *entrechats* or double *tours en l'air.* It is a preparatory step that helps to pull the dancer on balance. Sometimes a male variation ends with a pose in this position.

Soutenu: A step of preparation; the dancer steps over one foot and turns at the same time. May be done from any position, and may end in fourth or fifth position. Distantly related to "right about face" in army drill.

Temps de poisson: A leap in the air in place in which the dancer's legs are extended together behind the body. The back must be arched as far as possible toward his feet. The position in the air resembles that of a fish leaping out of water. The second diagonal crossing in the Bluebird variation includes three *temps de poisson*.

Tour en l'air: A turn in the air in which the dancer rises straight into the air in a fifth position, executes a complete turn of the body, returning to the original position. Frequently performed with two complete turns.

Tutu: The distinctive costume worn by female dancers in classical ballet. It began as the costume that is worn in *Les Sylphides* (known as the tutu *à la* Taglioni, in honor of the first dancer to wear it). Later the skirt was shortened to the length of those worn by the corps de ballet in Act II of *Swan Lake,* still later to that worn by the Swan Queen. If modern costume-designers do not desist, the tutu will soon be a vestigial relict.

Variation: Ballet term for solo.

INDEX

NOTE: See also special Index of Ballets, page xx.

Index of Ballets

PRINTER'S NOTE

The text of this book is set in Granjon *a type named in compliment to Robert Granjon, type-cutter and printer—Antwerp, Lyons, Rome, Paris—active from 1523 to 1590. The boldest and most original designer of his time, he was one of the first to practise the trade of typefounder apart from that of printer.*

This type face was designed by George W. Jones, who based his drawings upon a type used by Claude Garamond (1510–61) in his beautiful French books, and more closely resembles Garamond's own than do any of the various modern types that bear his name.

The book was designed by James Hendrickson and was composed, printed, and bound by the Kingsport Press, Kingsport, Tennessee. The illustrations were printed by Parkway Printing Company, New York. The binding silhouette was drawn by Claire Bruce.